ALL HAIL THE LAMB!

Shalom!

S——

2 Cor. 4.7)

All hail the Lamb!

Sam Gordon

Revelation made simple

There's one storyline in this ultimate action thriller - Jesus!

Christian Year Publications

ISBN-13: 978 1 872734 50 7

Typeset by John Ritchie Ltd., Kilmarnock
Printed by Bell & Bain Ltd., Glasgow

DEDICATION
to
Lois
God's perfect gift for me,
who has faithfully stood beside me
and unfailingly encouraged me in my ministry

FIRST WORD

With the heart of a pastor and the skill of a seasoned expositor, Sam Gordon makes the book of Revelation not only understandable, but life changing. Sam isn't simply interested in correct exposition, but personal transformation in the life of every reader. This commentary is for all who want to grasp the truths of Revelation—all who truly long to see the coming glory of Jesus Christ.

Dr Stephen Davey
Senior Pastor, Colonial Baptist Church, Cary NC

All hail the Lamb!

SECOND THOUGHTS

Revelation is not like any other book in the Bible. When it comes to prophecy, Revelation has no equal. It is a page-turner!

It shows us God's programme for the ages as it projects us into the future and, along the way, gives us some breathtaking insights into the eternal purpose of God. It is a fast moving, upbeat account of God's agenda for today's world. When we read the signs of the times, it is clear that we are swiftly approaching the end of this age. The sand is running short in God's hourglass.

Revelation focuses our eyes on eternity. It reminds us of the utter folly of doing a tango in the dark with the devil as it thinks the unthinkable about life without a personal relationship with God. It draws back the curtain and gives us a fascinating glimpse into heaven itself; in actual fact, John had a wonderful taster and he was forever spoiled for life on Planet Earth!

I am reminded of the story of some parents who took their little boy to the pet shop for his birthday. They allowed him to pick any dog he wanted. The shop owner showed the boy every type of dog imaginable, but the boy picked the one who wagged its tail nonstop. 'Why did you pick that dog?' everyone asked. 'Because I want the one with the happy ending,' the boy replied.

Yes, when we read Revelation through at a single sitting, there is so much to excite us, so much for us to anticipate, so much to look forward to, it is the kind of book which leaves you sitting on the edge of your seat!

You may not understand all that you read in the Apocalypse, do not worry! Read on...it will do your heart good, it will encourage you in the Lord, it will stimulate your faith, it will motivate you to engage in ministry – and, the good news, you are guaranteed a blessing if you read the book through from cover to cover (Revelation 1:3).

Sam Gordon
Executive Director, Messianic Testimony
www.messianictestimony.com

Contents

Contents

CHAPTER 1
Jesus outshines them all

A dream or a nightmare?

'It's a dream!' 'An absolute nightmare!' 'You can't be serious. Not the book of *Revelation*!' Those are just three comments I heard recently from people who have been dipping their big toe into Revelation. It all depends on where you are coming from. And on where you are going to. It is hardly a book of fantasies and certainly not the kind of thing you want to read late at night before hopping into bed!

What we have here is a book that scratches where modern man is itching. It answers the questions men are asking, *Why are we here? What on earth is happening in today's world? Where is this out-of-control world heading?* All these, and many more!

Things are not as they seem and things are not the way they should be! The bottom line, God rules and reigns on high. That truth remains untarnished in a world badly bruised by one crippling crisis after another. It holds as true today in the third millennium as it did in the closing years of the first century. That is why Revelation is right up-to-date, never more relevant than now.

How are we to make sense of it? When you skim through its twenty-two chapters you quickly discover it is all about multi-headed beasts and cosmic upheaval, spectral battles and sky-splitting displays of supernatural power. A touch surreal. A tad spooky. At times, the scene is awesome and glorious; other times, it is baffling and frightening. Almost paradoxical!

Winston Churchill once described the former Soviet Union as

'a riddle wrapped in a mystery inside an enigma.' The plain fact is, many well-meaning, evangelical Christians view the book in much the same way. Richard Bewes makes a valid comment when he writes: 'Ordinary Christians have left it unread; turned off by the bizarre flights of fancy, by the mathematical labyrinths in which some of its readers appear to have become enmeshed.' That is a pity for they are the ones who are really missing out in so many ways.

There is no doubt in my mind that the picturesque images, mysterious symbols, and apocalyptic language combine to make Revelation one of the most challenging books to interpret in the entire Bible. Charles Swindoll reminds us: 'These visions of the future do not come from the pen of a crazed quack or wild-eyed fanatic.' In one sense that is probably an understatement, nevertheless it is true. There are four main interpretative approaches to unlocking the mysteries of the book.

Idealists

The idealist approach tends to view the images in a strictly non-literal manner. They see them as a collection of spiritualised symbols that represent timeless truths. From their perspective, Revelation is a profound illustration of the ultimate victory of good over evil, of triumph in face of adversity. Apart from anything else, the downside is that this view relegates the book to a place where it is neither a historical record nor a predictive prophecy.

Preterists

The preterist approach is inclined to limit the meaning of the book to its original readers. They say the images represent only first century subjects such as Caesar, Rome, and the persecution. They believe that all the events detailed by the Apostle John have already taken place and the prophecy is given to encourage the harassed church of that time. Such a view conveniently ignores the book's own claims to be a prophecy (cf. 1:3; 22:7). The proponents of this view have buried their head in the sand when it comes to the ripening of God's eternal purpose. One commentator said that the preterist builds a firm pedestal, but has no sculpture to place upon it when he is finished.

Historicists

The historicist approach sees the book as a timeline from the first century up to this present time. History written in advance! For them, the heptad of evangelical churches in chapters 2 and 3 depict seven distinct periods of church history. They resort to allegorising the text in order to find in it the various events they believe it depicts – that tends to be those events of history familiar to them, usually the history of western Europe; that subjective approach tends to open a Pandora's box of all things wild, weird, and wonderful, in relation to fanciful interpretation.

Futurists

The futurist approach tends to view the book, especially chapters 4 to 22, as an open window on the end of time. They say the various images represent the people allied to significant events that will play a key role in the final drama of global history. This approach, in contrast to the other three, does full justice to Revelation's inherent claim to be a prophecy.

That is a quick résumé of the four mainline views regarding the interpretation of Revelation. I imagine, you are probably wondering which approach I am going to adopt and follow! To me, when you compare Revelation with Daniel and other prophetic volumes, the best line of interpretation to take on board is that of the futurist. This view makes a lot of sense when it comes to understanding Bible prophecy, but it also maintains a consistent approach to biblical hermeneutics in relation to the rest of Scripture. The key to understanding the book of Revelation is not a PhD, but a sound knowledge of the Word of

God. John MacArthur sums it up: 'The futurist approach takes the book's meaning as God gave it.'

Having said that, I want to emphasise the hugely important fact that this manuscript was most relevant to the people living in John's day, people under intense pressure. It would give them the impetus they needed to hang in there and enormous encouragement to keep on going. It will certainly have provided them with an incentive when they realised that, at the end of the day, the Lord comes out on top!

The living Lord is the central figure, the main character, of the book. He is the one to whom all the symbols point. To miss seeing Christ in the book is like squinting into the sky at twelve noon and not seeing the sun. The presence of Christ is everywhere. Realistically, you cannot miss him!

When you come to Revelation for the first or second time, you may think the whole message is quite intimidating and you could be forgiven for feeling scared but, the more you get into it, the more you realise it is the most worshipful book in the Bible! From start to finish it radiates and reflects the glorious stateliness of Jesus our wonderful Lord! This book is a beautiful chronicle of God's mystery, majesty, and mercy, as he meticulously plans for the future of Planet Earth, and beyond!

Outlines are always helpful, like signposts on a journey. As far as I am aware, Revelation is the only book in the Bible that contains an inspired outline of its contents, as in 1:19. That makes it unique!

> **'the things that you have seen' (1)**
> **'those that are' (2-3)**
> **'those that are to take place after this' (4-22)**

John Phillips has an excellent outline of the book:

> **Visions of God (1)**
> **Visions of grace (2-3)**
> **Visions of government (4-20)**
> **Visions of glory (21-22)**

You can see what is happening. The focus of Revelation is on the person and majesty of Jesus Christ. The spotlight is on the Lord of all glory. He is the coming King of kings and centre stage is where he deserves to be.

We can look at it from another angle. An old pastor friend of mine, Willie Mullan, now with the Lord, gave me an outline many years ago, one I have never forgotten.

Jesus is the Lord in the midst of the churches (1-3)
Jesus is the Lamb in the midst of the throne (4-5)
Jesus is the Lion in the midst of the nations (6-18)
Jesus is the Lover in the midst of the wedding
    celebrations (19-20)
Jesus is the Light in the midst of eternal glory (21-22)

On a recent visit to England's famous Keswick Convention, I picked up a novel commentary by Anne Graham Lotz. Her outline warmed my heart ... based on what a vision of the glory of God can do for us, it gives us:

    Hope ... when depressed (1)
    Hope ... when deluded (2-3)
    Hope ... when discouraged (4-5)
    Hope ... when distressed (6-19)
    Hope ... when defeated (20-22:5)
    Hope that ignites our hearts (22:6-21)

A dear friend, Stephen Davey, who has written the foreword to this commentary, has one of the best outlines I have yet to read on Revelation with four main points:

The sovereignty of Christ in his church (1-5)
The severity of Christ in his chastisement (6-18)
The supremacy of Christ in his coming (19-20)
The satisfaction of Christ in his new creation (21-22)

1:1-3

'The revelation of Jesus Christ'

Those five words in the opening phrase of verse 1 say all that has to be said for they tell us straightaway what is on the heart and mind of God! He puts all his cards on the table and he leaves us in no doubt as to the thinking behind this particular book. It is not an imaginative piece of spiritual fiction. It is a revelation of his Son, the Lord Jesus Christ! This book is both *about* him and *by* him—his sovereignty, his severity, his superiority, and his supremacy.

An open book

The word *revelation* means an unveiling, a disclosure, an uncovering. Things that would be normally hidden from us are made known in apocalyptic writing. Such writing takes you behind the scenes and reveals the unseen principles that affect history, and the future.

It comes from the Greek word *apokalupsis* which appears eighteen times in the New Testament, always when used of a person, with the meaning 'to become visible' (cf. Luke 2:32; Romans 8:19; 1 Corinthians 1:7; 1 Peter 1:7). We get our English word 'apocalypse' from it. That explains why this final chapter in God's storybook of redemption is sometimes called, the Apocalypse.

To change the analogy, God is turning over the pages of his photograph album and showing us pictures of Christ. We have the Holy Spirit drawing back the curtain and giving us the rare privilege of seeing the glorified Christ in heaven. At the same time, almost in the same breath, he shows us the fulfilment of his sovereign purposes in the world.

It is thrilling to recognise that Revelation is like an open book as God reveals his agenda to his church. Remember Daniel, when he finished writing his monumental prophecy, he was told in 12:4 to 'shut up the words and seal the book.' John is told exactly the opposite! We read in 22:10, *Do not seal up the words of the prophecy of this book, for the time is near.*

Why the gaping difference? Because Calvary has come, the resurrection has happened, the Holy Spirit has descended, the church has been born, and a new age has been ushered in called the Last Days (cf. Hebrews 1:1-2). When it comes to the maturing of the purposes of God, God is not on a go-slow, he is not dilly-dallying nor dragging his heels, he is fast fulfilling his Word.

The key phrase is in 1:3 and, again, in 22:10, *the time is near.* The implication is that his advent is soon, it is imminent, the Lord is at hand! Each day is one day nearer and, with every passing hour, we are rapidly approaching the climax of the ages. We are looking forward with bated breath to the magic moment when the King returns.

A unique book

Because of the way it was given

How did it all come about? The answer is found in verses 1 and 2, where we read, *The revelation of Jesus Christ, which God gave him to show to his servants the things that must soon take place. He made it known by sending his angel to his servant John, who bore witness to the word of God and to the testimony of Jesus Christ, even to all that he saw.*

What apparently happened was this: God the Father gave the revelation to the Son as a reward for his faithfulness during his humiliation at Calvary – the book describes with a remarkable eye for detail his exaltation; then the Son shared it with the Apostle John by means of a third party, an angel, whom he used as an intermediary, a go-between; when the angel had given it to John, he then gave it to the church.

(As an aside, it is worth noting that the words 'angel' or 'angels' are used seventy-one times in the book, more than in any other book in the Bible. In fact, one out of every four uses in Scripture of those words is in Revelation.)

Sometimes the Lord himself gave the vital information to John, as in the second half of chapter 1. At other times, the message was conveyed to him by an elder, as in 7:13. There were occasions when it was communicated directly to him by an angel, as in 17:1 and 19:9-10. From time to time there was 'a voice from heaven' which told John what to say and what to do, as alluded to in 10:4. The lesson is: whatever the channel of communication, it was all inspired by the Holy Spirit and, for what it is worth, John was often taken into another realm in the Spirit.

No matter what angle you view it from, this book has the stamp of God written all over it. His thumbprint is on every page! The golden thread of eternity is woven right through it. That impression is echoed and substantiated in verse 2, where we read that he *bore witness to the word of God and to the testimony of Jesus Christ.*

Because of the worth of its message

Do you want to be blessed? Read the book of Revelation! You may not fully understand it ... join the club! You may not be able to unravel all its mysteries and the symbols may seem seriously irrelevant in today's hi-tech, consumer-oriented environment. You may not be able to crack the code to adequately decipher what John is saying ... do not worry! Just keep on reading!

You may be tempted to ask, Why persevere when the odds are stacked against me? Well, the answer is immediate, it is right there in verse 3, where we read, *Blessed is the one who reads aloud the words of this prophecy, and blessed are those who hear, and who keep what is written in it, for the time is near.*

Did you see that? If you read it, if you hear it read, you are guaranteed a blessing! This is the only book in the entire Bible which promises a blessing like this. That makes it a little bit special! Echoes of James 1:25, methinks. It is equally true to say that if someone comes along and tampers with the message, he is the loser for he will be cursed. You find that warning label in 22:18-19. The message is crystal clear: read it, hear it, take it to heart, obey it, then trust God for the blessing which is sure to follow! I cannot think of a better way to get a blessing.

Why study the book?

Some people feel it is best to leave it alone; they feel more at home with the soothing poetry of the Psalms, the romance of Ruth, the richness of Romans 8, and the simple promises of the Beatitudes. They much prefer to leave a tome like this to the theological heavyweights or the professional pundits! Their attitude is to avoid it because it is too difficult to understand, too controversial to discuss, too meaningless to be personally relevant. To put it mildly, that is a rather negative approach!

We do not study it because we have a one-track-mind fascination with the future; it is definitely not because we are in the risky business of setting dates. As Warren Wiersbe says: 'We do it not because we are on the planning committee for the Second Advent, we do it because we are on the welcoming committee!'

We study it because we passionately love the Lord and are numbered among those who genuinely 'long for his appearing' (2 Timothy 4:8). We approach a book like this with the adrenaline flowing through our veins, with our heart beating faster, and with our mind filled with the twin components of wonder and worship. We can do no better than come like John and fall down in humility before the nail-scarred feet of Jesus.

A moment with majesty leaves us overwhelmed, gasping for breath! 'We stand in awe of him.' We come because we want to get to know Jesus better. That has to be the supreme goal, the aspiration, the yearning in each of our hearts.

Because the time is near

What is the big deal? Because John tells us at the end of verse 3 that *the time is near.* The six million dollar question, How near is near? 2,000 years have flown by and with a lot of water having gone under the bridge we are certainly a lot closer now than they were then.

When John put quill to parchment, he was a relatively old man in the sunset years. He wrote the book about the year 95 AD. At that time he was living in exile on an island in the Greek Aegean Sea. Patmos is one of a cluster of small islands off the coast of modern-day Turkey which were ceded to Greece after the Second World War.

It goes without saying that a lot has happened in the intervening years so the thought encapsulated here is one of extreme suddenness. It has the strategically important element of surprise in it. The phrase conveys the idea not of immediacy, but of imminence. It is soon and could happen at any minute!

When we talk about the advent of Jesus, we need to be ready, watching, and waiting. We should be living with a sense of expectancy in our hearts, a keen sense of anticipation, for it may be today when Jesus breaks through the clouds! The panoply of events which are prophesied in this book can happen at any time and without any advance warning.

It is not clutching at straws to say that we are standing on the threshold of a whole new era. We are teetering on the brink of something big happening in the world in which we live. We are hovering on the edge of God doing something spectacularly special in relation to Israel and the nations. The more you stop and think about it, the more you realise, it is as close as that. We have long since passed the eleventh hour; in fact, it has never been so late before.

And that is the paramount message John wants to get across to each of us at this precise moment in time—Jesus is coming again! And when he does, a lot of what we have in the book will come to pass. Then, what is now 'his' story will rapidly become history! So this book is not only focusing attention on the coming King, it also informs us of the purpose of his kingdom.

Depending on where you live, you probably have national elections every four or five years; in the run-up to the polls the politicians tell us why we should elect them and what their programme will be if they win office. Revelation is the gripping account of Jesus' campaign to rule Planet Earth. We are told, without ambiguity, of his relationship to the church, his appointment by the Father to the throne, his crusade against the satanic forces of evil, and his final victory. There is no need to count the votes for he (and we) know the result already!

Because he made it known

Let us backtrack for a moment to verse 1 where we read, *He made it known.* This is a most interesting turn of phrase. Some Bible translations use the word 'signified' in this context and it, literally, means 'to give a sign or signal.' This is a book comprised of many signs and symbols with at least half explained in the book itself. For example, lamps represent assemblies of God's people, stars represent angels, and incense odours represent the prayers of saints (cf. 1:20; 8:3-4).

Where we need to exercise spiritual caution and resist the temptation to get carried away is when we try to define those symbols which are not explained. When that is the case, we need to look at other parts of the Bible in an attempt to unravel the mystery, for biblical symbols are consistent with the whole of biblical revelation. God does not say one thing in one place and then say something different in another place. It is a fundamental principle of hermeneutics that God is his own interpreter.

When we deviate from that axiom, we run into all kinds of problems and are at serious risk of coming up with all sorts of fanciful ideas. They may sound really amazing and look good on paper, they may be bright ideas and add a touch more gloss to what is there; after all, what is 20% more hype to something which is quite sensational already! Well, just because it tickles your fancy does not necessarily mean to say it is right! If we opt to go down that road, sure, we will come up with a smattering of mouth-watering ideas, but we will end up missing the message because we cannot see the wood for the trees. We must anchor our interpretation to what God has already revealed.

1:4-6

First, John introduces himself and tells us the people to whom he is writing. When he has done that, he then offers to them an unbelievable greeting: *John to the seven churches that are in Asia* (1:4). We have no problem identifying these seven churches as they are explicitly detailed for us in verse 11. They are then singled out for further special attention in chapters 2 and 3.

It is interesting to note that the Apostle Paul sent a number of different letters to seven churches. He wrote to the believers in Rome, Corinth, Galatia, Ephesus, Philippi, Colossae, and Thessalonica. Now we have John sending one book to seven different churches. There is no question about it, it was for them alright! In the sweet providence of God, it is also for us. Here is God's last word to man, his final message to churches scattered all around the world. What a tremendous way to start a book!

A benediction at the beginning

He offers to everyone *grace* and *peace*. This is a dual blessing. These are the twin towers of the gospel of Christ. We have grace and peace and what we need to underscore is the order in which they are mentioned. This is of mega importance for if we do not get it right here, we will end up putting the cart before the horse.

You can never know peace in your heart without first experiencing the grace of God. Peace is a wonderful spinoff from the grace of God. Grace is the fountain of which peace is the stream. You could not wish anything better for a person than to extend to him a measure of grace and peace.

Grace is something which comes to us that we do not deserve and which we cannot repay. Grace stoops to where we are and lifts us to where we ought to be. Peace is something which happens within us; it is a freedom from inner distraction which enables us to enjoy an internal rest. Peace is a tranquillity of soul that frees you from fear and takes the sharp edges off your anxiety and tension.

Grace and peace do not come from ourselves, no matter how positive our thoughts may be; they do not come from others, no matter how assuring their counsel and advice may be. They come directly from the open heart and open hand of our loving heavenly Father. God is the dispenser of both and he does it in a lavish manner.

Meet a God for whom time is of no consequence

John goes on to tell us in verse 4 that the one who has given this priceless blessing to us is someone *who is and who was and who is to come.* These extraordinary characteristics cannot be ascribed to anyone else but God the Father; quite honestly, no one else fits the bill. He is described here in anthropomorphic terms because that is the only way we can possibly hope to understand it—he views God through the lens of time dimensions (past, present, and future), although he is timeless.

Here is one who transcends time, the Eternal God, one with whom there was no beginning and with whom there is no end; one who has always existed and who cuts across all the ages of time. Here is one who reads the past, who rides the present, and who rules the future; one who dwells in all tenses of time for he is 'I Am' (Exodus 3:14). 'God is just as much in control of our unknown future and unnerving present as he is of our unpleasant past,' writes Charles Swindoll.

And what does he do? He gathers the ages into one hand and he holds the world in his other hand and, even though he is responsible for running the show, he takes quality time out and he whispers a word into each of our hearts, when he says, *grace to you and peace.*

Seven in relation to the Spirit

It is interesting that the final phrase of verse 4 makes reference to *the seven spirits who are before his throne.* This is a veiled reference appropriate to the Holy Spirit. It can be easily translated to read, 'the sevenfold Spirit' (cf. Zechariah 4:2-7). John is talking about one Holy Spirit with a sevenfold ministry as recorded in Isaiah 11:2, where we read, 'the Spirit of the Lord shall rest upon him, the Spirit of wisdom and understanding, the Spirit of counsel and might, the Spirit of knowledge and the fear of the Lord.'

The number seven gives the game away for it speaks of the perfection of his person and the plenitude of his power. He is perfect and complete in himself because he is God! He is taking up a position before the throne of God. The question is, Why?

His is a unique role in relation to the Godhead in that he is the executor of the purposes of God. Up until now the Holy Spirit has been the executor of God's purposes in grace; he will become the executor of God's purposes in government. The blessing mentioned earlier comes from God the Father and God the Holy Spirit, but right here in verse 5, it also comes from God the Son, even our Lord Jesus Christ.

A threefold description of the Lord Jesus

'The faithful witness'

That enables us to see him as a *prophet* and it underlines his credibility.

'The firstborn of the dead'

That enables us to see him as a *priest* and it highlights his superiority.

'The ruler of kings on earth'

That enables us to see him as a *king* and it makes much of his sovereignty.

Jesus Christ—Prophet, Priest, and King! Three splendid titles, three identifiable roles, three impeccable credentials, each of which can be narrowed down to find their focal point in one individual (cf. Psalm 89:27, 37).

A trio of titles in verse 5 that reveal the Lord's relationship to the present age

Faithful witness: the age begins

That is the reason Jesus came into a dark, degenerate world, fast spiralling out of control as it goes from bad to worse. He came to bear witness to the name of God, to the nature of sin, to the need for personal righteousness, and to the nearness of judgment. As a faithful witness, Jesus brought the exceedingly good tidings of a great salvation through faith in his finished work at Calvary.

Firstborn of the dead: the age continues

Here is one who has tasted death for every man, who has risen in triumph from the tomb, and who has ascended into Glory to implement God's programme for the ages. *Firstborn* actually implies priority and sovereignty for it is suggestive of a title of honour. He is the leader of all who will ultimately rise from the dead to everlasting life. In that sense, he is preeminent, the premier one.

Ruler of kings on earth: the age ends

Here is one who was born in a barn, who died on a wooden cross, who was buried in a borrowed tomb in a beautiful floral garden and, yes, he is the same one who is coming back to rule and reign! He is returning in pomp and power! Think of the regal nature of such a splendid occasion, it is a royal visit like no other; the sheer magnificence of the sight and the awesomeness of the moment blows the mind! It is something you will not want to miss!

Here is the Trinity in action. The book begins with a blessing from the triune God who offers to you and me the rich blessing of grace and peace!

From benediction to doxology

When we receive this blessing, the least we can do is offer him a benediction in return. And that is what we have in the last half of verse 5 and also in verse 6, *To him who loves us and has freed us from our sins by his blood, and made us a kingdom, priests to his God and Father, to him be glory and dominion forever and ever. Amen!* We have his plan of redemption in the first part and his purpose for the believer in the second part.

Back in John's day, the individual counted for nothing—men and women were disposable cargo. Kings counted. The state counted. Caesar counted. But, as Steven Lawson notes, 'the oppressed millions of the Roman Empire were mere chattel.' Yet, with Christ, they counted for everything! Each person mattered to him. Jesus Christ is the principal character of the book but, here, he is the one who gives us our own place in the not-yet finished story. He takes the lead part, we simply walk on and do our bit. Surely, that puts the amazing back into grace!

A God of love

This glowing doxology is directed initially *to him who loves us.* Here is a God who has loved us from eternity past, who continues to love us with an unbreakable love, and who will keep on loving us until we come to the end of the road; and, even when we reach heaven itself, it will only be to experience the extravagance of his love in a fuller measure. His is an expansive heart overflowing with love; you only have to look at the cross to see how great is his love. His is a love with no limits, a love that will not let us go, a love that keeps on loving, no matter what. The old song says:

O the love that sought me,
O the blood that bought me,
O the grace that brought me to the fold!

A God of grace

This paean of praise makes much of the wonderful grace of God in our lives as it reinforces the tremendous power of God to change lives for the better. He has freed us, because sin is a chain that binds us; he has washed us (as one translation has it), because sin is a stain that blots us. How has he done it? *By his blood!* 'There was no other way a God of love could find, but Calvary.' In a different generation, Charles Wesley got it right when he penned the words:

He breaks the power of cancelled sin,
He sets the prisoner free;
His blood can make the foulest clean,
His blood avails for me.

That is not all! For the God who loved us and loosed us is the same God who lifted us!

A God who elevates

We are a kingdom, and that means we have all the majesty of a prince; we are priests, and that means we now have a ministry to others and on behalf of others. We have power with men and God. Put them both together and you begin to understand what Peter meant when he called us 'a royal priesthood' (1 Peter 2:9). What we have here is best summed up in the words of a great old hymn:

Wonderful grace of Jesus, greater than all my sin!
How shall my tongue describe it, where shall its praise begin,
Taking away my burden, setting my spirit free,
For the wonderful grace of Jesus, reaches me!

All hail the Lamb!

Grace for us ... Glory for him!

And it does, for that is the meaning of the closing few words in the benediction. It is *to him be glory and dominion forever and ever.*

It is personal for it is directed exclusively to him. His is the glory that outshines the noonday sun; this is the glory he had with the Father before the world began.

It is positional for it is a glory which one day will be acknowledged by all mankind when he returns in splendour from the sky.

It is perpetual for it goes on forever and ever. There is no stopping it, it just keeps on rolling. And rightly so! For he alone deserves it!

It is no wonder John says a hearty *Amen* at the end of it. It is the right word at the right time. A word of affirmation, and agreement.

1:7-8

The coming of Christ ... a sneak preview

After the introduction and greetings, verse 7 begins the first great prophetic oracle in the book. It sets the tone for the rest of the volume with one prediction hard on the heels of another. This is a powerful reminder that history is not just drifting aimlessly along; rather, everything is moving purposefully and deliberately to the most momentous event to hit Planet Earth since its inception. The great juggernaut of history rumbles toward its final consummation.

The 'A' of anticipation

Behold. It is a simple six-letter word which is bandied about on a daily basis; nevertheless, it calls for rapt attention. It is used around twenty-five times in the book and it means, *look for yourself.* This exclamation is intended to arouse the mind and activate the heart to seriously contemplate what follows. We have a responsibility to be avidly watching for the second advent of Christ.

The 'A' of association

He is coming with the clouds. At his ascension from the Mount of Olives, Jesus was received into heaven by a cloud (cf. Acts 1:9-11). When he returns at the end of time, he is coming back with the clouds of heaven! The cloud is linked with the visible manifestation of the presence of God, as in the shekinah glory of the tabernacle and temple eras. It also symbolises the brilliant light that accompanies the divine presence; actually, it was a light so powerful that no one could see it and live (cf. Exodus 33:20). It is worth noting that the present tense of the phrase suggests that Christ is already en-route; that would indicate his coming is certain for nothing and no one will stand in his way.

The 'A' of attitude

Every eye will see him, even those who pierced him, and all tribes of the earth will wail on account of him. This is Philippians 2:9-10 coming alive. Make no mistake about it! Every eye will see him and, with the wonder of modern technology, that is possible right now. Such an event will be witnessed simultaneously by all people in both hemispheres. In a touch of irony, it also includes those who pierced him and, it has to be said, that is not just a passing reference to the Roman soldiers who nailed him to the cross.

A similar allusion to this is found in the Old Testament book of Zechariah where it applies specifically to the various groups within the house of Israel (cf. 12:10-14). What we have here envisaged is a stunning demonstration of the power of God, the awesome victory of a triumphant Christ! To make the occasion so much bigger and better, it will be out there in the public domain for all to see. People will quickly realise that he is the one they ignored, rejected, and spurned, the one to whom they gave the cold shoulder. In that moment, on bended knee, they will cry out that 'Jesus Christ is Lord!' Humanity has a date with Jesus.

Again, John follows with a second *Amen* but this time he prefaces it with the words, *Even so.* It is almost like a double amen for John's response uses the strongest words of affirmation in the Greek and Hebrew languages. It is like someone saying, 'Yes, Lord; yes, Lord!' There is undiluted passion and steely conviction in his voice.

The character of Christ

In verse 8 it would appear that the Lord is putting his signature on the prophecy recorded in the previous verse. It is a guarantee that it will happen for he is the divine underwriter! The mere mention of his name is sufficient warranty in and of itself. In a bold attempt to eliminate any nagging fears or suspicions that his people may have, his promise is set against the velvet backdrop of three of his attributes: he is an all-knowing, eternal, and all-powerful God.

He is 'the Alpha and the Omega'

These are the first and last letters in the Greek alphabet so the Lord reminds us that he is the beginning and the end; he is all the letters in between for he is God's alphabet. He is the first and final source of knowledge, wisdom, and understanding. He knows everything. He has never had a new thought! Our Lord is everything that can be said. He is God's first word, full word, and final word. He is omniscient.

This does not only apply to the Lord Jesus, the Living Word, for it can also be applied to the written Word. On one side of the shelf we have book number one, Genesis. On the other side, we have book number sixty-six, Revelation. These are the bookends of the canon of Scripture.

In Revelation, we see the completion and fulfilment of the work God began in Genesis. If Genesis is the seedbed of all theology, then Revelation offers the fruit of all theology; it is the golden clasp which binds the volume of the Bible together. The parallels to these two books are many:

GENESIS	REVELATION
The first man, Adam, reigns on Planet Earth.	The last man reigns in heaven in Glory.
The darkness and the seas are created.	There is no more darkness, nor any sea.
A bride, Eve, is presented to her husband.	The church, as a radiant bride, is presented to her husband, the Lord Jesus Christ.
We see the tree of life in the midst of the Garden of Eden.	We see the fruit-bearing tree of life in God's new creation.
The beginning of sin brings death and a curse.	Sin is done away with; there is no more curse and no more dying.
Satan appears to man for the first time.	He appears for the last time.
Man is driven from the Garden and the presence of God.	Man sees the face of God in Glory and he is brought into a place of intimate communion with the Lord.
Men look for a city by faith.	The holy city, the new Jerusalem, as the eternal home of the redeemed, is seen coming down out of heaven from God.
We see paradise lost.	We see paradise regained.

He is the one 'who is and who was and who is to come, the Almighty'

In three words, he is omnipotent. Here is the eternal God who spans the generations, who can do anything, and everything. There is power in his presence! It was Amy Carmichael who wrote: 'When we are facing the impossible, we can count upon the God of the impossible!' Ten times this appellation is used in the New Testament, with nine here in Revelation.

What an amazing title! Here is a God who is gloriously able; man will surely fail, the old devil is living on borrowed time, but God is able. He will prevail. He will succeed. He will be victorious at the end of the day. Fantastic! That has to be very good news for you and me at this point in time! A former Chancellor of Germany, Helmut Kohl, said: 'The wheel of history is turning faster now.' Right.

John was an old man on a remote island and he is the one who was to write the greatest story of all time. More often than not, that is how God chooses to work. He takes the most unlikely and most unpromising material and he shapes us into the kind of people he wants us to be. He longs that we might find our potential realised in him. I am thrilled that the God who is willing to take the time and invest so much energy into moulding your life and mine is the same God who is actively working behind the scenes in today's world. He knows what he is doing and he knows where he is going. He sees tomorrow, and the day beyond. Like John, we fall down before him and worship!

1:9-11

The recipient of the vision

The recipient of the vision is the Apostle John. He is the same man who singlehandedly wrote the Gospel of eternal life, who often leaned on the bosom of Jesus and, in later years, skilfully wrote three letters on the theme of love. He started out in life as a fisherman, then he heard the call of God. He responded positively to the claims of Christ on his life and, eventually, he became a close friend and trusted confidante to the Lord Jesus. He was there on snowcapped Hermon, the Mount of Transfiguration; he was there in the Garden of Gethsemane; he was there at the foot of the cross on Calvary. Some of the last words Christ spoke in this world were given to John when he encouraged him to look after his dear mother, Mary (cf. John 19:25-27). This is the man who now receives an awesome vision of the shimmering effulgence of the glory of God.

John would never be the same again. Here is the man who, on earth, looked into the face of Jesus. Here, in Revelation, he sees the lovely face of Jesus in heaven itself. Having sampled heaven, he would be forever spoiled for life on Planet Earth. One of the lessons we reflect on at this point is: who we are is not nearly as important as who he is—the fact that Jesus is coming overshadows the fact that we have arrived!

The reason for his exile

It is clear from verse 9 that John had been banished to Patmos. His only crimes were those related to his personal faith and trust in Jesus. He tells us he was there *on account of the word of God and the testimony of Jesus.* He witnessed bravely to his dynamic relationship with Christ. He unashamedly nailed his colours to the mast with a spirit of tenacity. And he paid the price for his faithful, unequivocal, uncompromising preaching of the gospel of Jesus Christ which now cost him his personal freedom.

The authorities had the option of silencing him by throwing him to the lions; if they had gone down that road, John would have been hailed a martyr. That was the last thing they wanted. So they did the next best thing when they shipped him off to the prison island of Patmos.

Tradition has it that before he was deported and sent off into exile, John was first plunged into boiling oil. That does not bear thinking about! Life was tough on this barren, rugged, craggy isle where vegetation was scarcely seen. It was an inhospitable place about fifteen miles off the coast from Ephesus. It was a volcanic island about ten miles long and six miles wide. It was the Alcatraz of the day. It was like being transported to Siberia for the winter.

John spent his days labouring in the mines and quarries, breaking rocks as a member of a chain gang. He was separated from other believers and cut off from his family. He suffered severe persecution and had meagre rations in terms of decent food. He was improperly dressed and slept on the bare ground in a dark cave. As you will appreciate, John experienced considerable deprivation. And remember, he is around ninety years of age! On a human level, this was the last thing he needed!

How true it is, sometimes it is out of the suffering of God's people that we have some of the greatest triumphs. At times, it is often when circumstances look darkest and in moments of loneliness and despair that God has the opportunity to shine brightest.

For John, this tiny prison island became the gateway to heaven. The Patmos of persecution enabled John to walk through a wide open door to a further period of service and an extended time of unscheduled ministry. John probably thought that his life and long fruitful ministry were all behind him but, in the good providence of God and unknown to him, his most significant ministry was still before him.

His reference to himself

John speaks of himself as *your brother and partner in the tribulation and the kingdom and the patient endurance that are in Jesus.* He was no stranger to trial and trouble, and neither were they so each could identify with the other. Sure, we have an apostle here, but he is not in the business of waving titles around for he sees himself as a *brother.* His was a household name in the early church and yet he is happy and feels privileged to share in their sufferings. What a man, one who knows how to empathise.

When the bad times come, so many of us cry, 'Why me?' Perhaps the question would be better rephrased, 'Why not me?' After all is said and done, why should we be exempt from life's trials? Why should we be immune from the hassles of daily living?

His reaction to adversity

John had every right to bemoan his fate. He had been a faithful follower of Jesus and now, in spite of his total dedication to Christ and his cause, he is a common prisoner, and on top of that, he is pension material as a geriatric! He could have buried his wrinkled brow in his calloused hands and said, 'What did I do to deserve all this?' But he did not! Have you ever wondered, Why did John not react that way? Why is he so incredibly different to the rest of us mortals? Why does he have such a sweet spirit? We have the answer in verse 10, for we read there that John was *in the Spirit.*

His remarkable experience

The real meaning of being 'in the Spirit'

John obviously lived his life in the fulness of the Holy Spirit from Monday to Saturday, and Sunday was no exception. John was 'out in the sticks' and, at the same time, he was in the Spirit. Two places at once! It was a double location: a human and a heavenly environment. He was fettered and shackled by Rome but he was also at the feet of Jesus.

John was not only witnessing for the Lord, he was an adoring worshipper of the Lord, and he discovered a priceless secret. It is one that Margaret Thatcher frequently referred to when she was Prime Minister of the UK. The baroness, as she was known because of her life peerage, animatedly spoke of 10 Downing Street as 'living above the shop.' That is the vital lesson John grasped. He worked down here but he lived up there!

The real meaning of 'the Lord's day'

When we read about the Lord's day in this context, it is best seen as a reference to Sunday, the first day of the week. Towards the end of Acts, as the church began to separate more and more from the synagogue, this became the normal and preferred day of meeting for the early believers—it was seen as a day of triumph, a day that celebrated the resurrection of Jesus.

Ignatius, writing just 15 years after John wrote the Revelation, said: 'The Christians ceased to keep the Jewish Sabbath and lived by the Lord's day, on which our life shines, thanks to him.' Pliny, the unbelieving Roman governor and no friend to the early church, wrote around the same time: 'The Christians gather on Sunday, the first day of the week, to sing praises to their Lord Jesus.' Justin Martyr, a church leader, wrote 45 years later: 'We all hold this common gathering on Sunday, since it is the day when Jesus Christ our Saviour rose from the dead.'

For John, to be *in the Spirit* means he was catapulted into the future and given a remarkable preview of things to come. And what he saw with his own two eyes is what he has written in this great book; it was all recorded on a scroll, as mentioned in verse 11. It was then promptly despatched to the seven churches in Asia Minor, specifically selected because they were strategically located in the key cities of the seven postal districts into which Asia was divided. They were, therefore, the central points for disseminating information.

John tells us that he *heard behind [him] a loud voice like a trumpet.* It was not only loud, it was clear and concise. And when he turned around in response to the voice, he could not believe his eyes for *he saw seven golden lampstands.* These represent the seven church fellowships to whom he is writing (briefly referred to in verse 11), the assemblies in Ephesus, Smyrna, Pergamum, Thyatira, Sardis, Philadelphia, and Laodicea.

1:12-16

There, centre stage among the lampstands, is the one who is the focal point of this breathtaking vision, he saw Jesus! Remember, he had not seen the Lord for the best part of six decades, until now. John sees him and is electrified! He collapsed. He froze in time and space. The pieces of the jigsaw all came together and John saw the Lord, as we will some day. Think of it! In that day, we will see the King in all his beauty!

In verses 12 and 13 he is standing among the lampstands; by the time you come to 2:1 he is walking among the seven golden lampstands. John MacArthur reminds us: 'These were like the common portable oil lamps placed on lampstands that were used to light rooms at night.' From John's perspective, they typify churches as lights of the world (cf. Philippians 2:15). They are *golden* because gold was the most exclusive precious metal. The implication is that the church is to God the most beautiful and valuable entity on earth, so costly that Jesus was willing to purchase it with his own blood (cf. Acts 20:28).

He is there! When two or three are met together in his name, he is among them. No matter how many or how few, the Lord is always there. That is his promise and he always honours his precious Word (cf. Matthew 18:20). He is seen to be central in authority. He is sovereign in his presence. He indwells his church to lead and empower it. How we need to feel and sense the reality of his presence and power in our churches today! The reality is, we do not matter, other people are not that important, our programmes and activities are not the be-all and end-all: the living Christ is at the centre!

John's ninefold vision of Jesus

I came across a lovely story the other day. It was about a father who was trying to get peace to read his copy of *The Telegraph*. The problem was, every time he settled down and was engrossed with his nose in the paper, his little girl kept asking him questions. And so he came up with the bright idea that he would give her something to do! A diversionary tactic, at least that was what he hoped!

He leafed through one of the missionary magazines lying on the coffee table and found a map of the world. He cut it out in small pieces, and said: 'Look, here's a map of the world, see if you can put the jigsaw puzzle together!' Feeling rather chuffed, he settled down for the nth time.

In a few minutes, she was back! He just could not believe it! Taken completely by surprise, he asked her: 'How did you do it so fast?' Like a flash of lightning, she replied: 'Well, Dad, it was easy, I found a picture of Jesus on the other side and I knew when I had him in the right place, the whole world would be all right!'

Simple, yet profound!

This portion is a brilliant masterpiece of Christology. Every single stroke of the Spirit's brush on the canvas of Scripture has a special meaning for John sees Jesus as he is! This is a brilliant showcase of the Son of Man. I believe there is wonderful truth in the familiar lines penned by Helen Lemmel:

> *Turn your eyes upon Jesus,*
> *Look full in his wonderful face;*
> *And the things of earth will grow strangely dim*
> *In the light of his glory and grace.*

As the Son of Man ... the Lord is risen!

Here is the one with whom John conversed in his Gospel; now, at the end of the journey, this same Jesus is still there. That is reassuring! He has not changed for 'yesterday and today and forever' Jesus is the same (Hebrews 13:8). He became a man for us so that he might know human life by personal experience. He knows what we are like. He knows what makes us tick. He has been touched with the feeling of our weakness and need. He is the one who experienced great problems of pain, persecution, and pressure; and, now, John was seeing Jesus in the midst of those who also had great problems!

The Son of Man was a favourite title which the Lord Jesus often used when speaking about himself. Although it seems to speak of his humanity, in reality, it is a pointer to his deity. As Richard Bewes says: 'It had both overtones of divinity and undertones of humanity.' It has special meaning to students of Bible prophecy. Away back in Daniel 7:26-27 we see the Son of Man being given a kingdom that shall never be destroyed. He is set before us on that auspicious occasion as the coming Messiah.

The Son of Man: God became a man – that is the heart of the gospel message. If he is not God, then he can do nothing to save us from our sin; if he is not man, then he could not have died and paid the price for our sin. At one and the same time, he is both God and man! Not half-God, half-man. But perfectly God, perfectly man.

There is a lovely thought envisaged here: the fact that Christ retains his humanity following his resurrection is a guarantee to all believers of our bodily resurrection, as well as a blessing that we will have an everlasting revelation of God in human form. He forever like us, and we forever like him. That is a tremendous aid to our understanding of the life which is to come.

As the great High Priest ... the Lord is reigning!

We read of him that he is *clothed with a long robe and with a golden sash around his chest.* This is not the short tunic garment of the average peasant of Middle Eastern culture. Rather, it is a garment of wealth which denotes high position and points in the direction of royalty. There is something similar alluded to in Isaiah 6:1 where we read that 'the train of his robe filled the temple.' What a sight for the human eye! It speaks of the greatness of Christ. In some ways, it is not unlike the garment of the high priest in Exodus 39.

The sash or girdle speaks of service. It is not on the loins, the place of strength; it is on the chest, the place of compassion! The fact that it is golden suggests that it is everlasting. We read in Hebrews 7:17 that Jesus is a priest, not after the order of Aaron, but after the order of Melchizedek. His is a priesthood which is unchanging, undertaking, and understanding.

Reflect for a moment on the majesty of the priestly ministry of Jesus Christ for the golden sash around the chest also speaks of his authority as King of kings. When Isaiah had his vision of the Lord, he saw the train of his robe filling the temple in a scene of unsurpassed royalty and dignity. That thought of our regal Lord is captured in the beautiful song:

Majesty! Worship his majesty!
Unto Jesus be glory, honour and praise;
Majesty, kingdom authority, flows from his throne unto his own.
His anthem raise!
So exalt, lift up on high the name of Jesus!
Magnify, come glorify Christ Jesus the King!
Majesty, worship his majesty, Jesus who died, now glorified,
King of all Kings!

As the Ancient of Days ... the Lord is righteous!

In his third thumbnail sketch, John describes him quite vividly when he says that *the hairs of his head were white, like white wool, like snow.* This is strangely similar to the picture found in Daniel 7:9 of the one who is from everlasting to everlasting.

Here is one who is all-wise; that means there are no accidents with him in control, he makes no mistakes, he knows exactly what he is doing, he never has to second-guess himself, his hindsight is never better than his foresight, his wisdom does not improve with age or experience, he does it exactly right first time!

It also speaks of one who is totally pure, one who is whiter than white as the Redeemer and Saviour of his people. It is not in his nature to be mean, or vindictive, or sadistic, or cruel, or petty, or selfish. He is just not like that! The fact remains that the sinfulness of man cannot exist in the presence of the blinding holiness of Jesus. A single look at him and we quickly realise, here is one who is unimpeachable!

As the Judge ... the Lord is revealing!

In the fourth vignette, we read that his *eyes were like a flame of fire.* He is the one who sees all things. He has X-ray vision. 20/20 vision. Absolutely nothing is hidden from him. He is the one who can penetrate the depths, he can see beyond the façade, he has eyes which can search the innermost being. Peter knew that to be true in the courtyard (cf. Luke 22:54-62). It was Matthew Henry who noted: 'God not only sees men, he sees through them!' You cannot run away from him or hide behind any mask, he sees through it all. He has no hidden agenda for, in that day when we see him, all will be brought out into the open.

Because his eyes are like fire, he is indignant and angry with so much of what he sees. He will judge for man is responsible for his actions and accountable for whatever he does. He will do that which is right and he will be seen to do that which is right.

As the Lamb of God ... the Lord is relentless!

In verse 15 we are told that *his feet were like burnished bronze, refined in a furnace.* In the Old Testament era the mention of brass or bronze always indicated judgment. In the tabernacle the first piece of furniture inside the gate was the brazen altar where the lamb was sacrificed as an atonement for the sin of the individual. The lamb was consumed because the bronze could stand the fire. Under the old economy the fire consumed the lamb; at Calvary it is the Lamb who consumed the fire. This also looks forward to the day when, as the Lion of the tribe of Judah, he will put all his enemies and every evil power beneath his feet. He will crush his foes!

As the Voice of our Beloved ... the Lord is regal!

We are then reminded that *his voice was like the roar of many waters* ... something similar is noted in Ezekiel 43:2 where the voice of the God of Israel is spoken of. Think of their incredible power as the waters roar and rush by; the Niagara syndrome, tens of millions of cascading gallons tumbling irretrievably over the edge. John probably has in mind the mighty ocean waves incessantly crashing against the jagged rocks of Patmos. It is the kind of thing that keeps him awake at night.

The fact is, when Jesus speaks all men will hear and know that he has spoken. David tells us that 'the voice of the Lord is over the waters; the God of glory thunders, the Lord, over many waters; the voice of the Lord is powerful, the voice of the Lord is full of majesty' (Psalm 29:3-4). The ear-splitting sound of his voice will shake the four corners of heaven and earth. One deafening word from him and puny men will jump! A single word from him drowns out all other voices!

As the Lord of the Harvest ... the Lord is the regulator!

In his right hand he held seven stars. These are the angels directly related to each of the seven churches, the messengers or the spiritual leaders linked to each congregation, and they are in his hand. That is a safe and secure place to be! But it is also a place where he can shape us! If I am not in his hand where he can use me and mould me, I am wasting my time. Because of the frailty of our flesh and the foibles of our human nature, we need to place ourselves under his control out of deference to him. After all is said and done, he is the one in charge. Unassailable.

He is in total control of all the forces in today's world, seen and unseen. They are in his right hand, the hand of power. Someone has said: 'The things that overtake us are not overlooked by him, they are overruled by him!' It is not that the Lord is careless, we know he is not, for the hand that holds the stars still bears the scars of Calvary's nails.

As the Captain of our Salvation ... the Lord is resourceful!

From his mouth came a sharp two-edged sword. That is the

potent Word of God for that is what will guide us along the journey of life and on into heaven itself. The Lord has gone on before us, and by his Word, and with his Word, and through his Word, he will ensure our safe arrival.

Allied to that truth is the fact that he will defend his church against external threats as in 19:15, 21. By the same token, he will exercise a ministry of judgment on those enemies from within the church for he will fell them with his Word (cf. 2:12, 16; Acts 20:30). John MacArthur reminds us: 'Those who attack Christ's church, those who would sow lies, create discord, or otherwise harm his people, will be personally dealt with by the Lord of the church.' The Word is invincible.

As the Altogether Lovely One ... the Lord is resplendent!

In the closing phrase of verse 16 (which John borrowed from Judges 5:31), we discover that *his face was like the sun shining in full strength.* What a radiant countenance! So bright and so warm, it is dazzling and blinding, resplendent in all its glory! This is the glow of God! The sun radiates four million tons of heat a second; the sun, as we know, can bless and burn. In such light, all else fades for he is preeminent. Incomparable. Unique! Unapproachable ... yet, by his grace and through faith, we draw near.

1:17-20

A vision ... too hot to handle!

Given a sensationally astonishing vision of the glorified Christ, John, bless him, just melted in the Lord's presence. There he was, viewing the majesty of the man he knew in Judea and he got the wobbles. He lost consciousness when his heart missed a beat and his legs turned to jelly. This was an instinctive human reaction of devastating fear. It paralysed him as he fell enervated to the ground! Speechless. Shook up. All because, at that moment, he saw what he was like and he saw what

God was like. Anne Graham Lotz points out: 'John's patience and preoccupation with Christ resulted in his prostration before Christ.'

There are many instances recorded in Scripture where ordinary men have had a similarly frightening encounter with the living God. There is one common denominator. To a man, the reaction of those who genuinely saw the Lord was one of fear. Those brought face-to-face with the incandescent glory of a thrice holy God are terrified, petrified, realising their sinful unworthiness to be in his company.

Many examples spring to mind, but the more obvious ones are: Abraham, he fell flat on his face when God talked with him; Moses, he hid his face for he was afraid; Isaiah, he saw the Lord seated on a throne in the temple and he cried out, 'Woe to me, I am ruined!'; the three disciples on the Mount of Transfiguration, they saw his face shining like the noonday sun and their immediate response was to fall to their knees; Saul of Tarsus, he dropped to the ground and was temporarily blinded.

It should not surprise us that John fainted. This man, made of exactly the same material as the rest of us, was overwhelmed by the loftiness and nobility of the glorified Son of Man. He shrivelled and shrank from such an awesome encounter. It was all too much for John, he was out of his depth.

A visit ... how the Lord handled him!

We read in verse 17, *When I saw him, I fell at his feet as though dead.* The sequel to this is quite astonishing for the Lord did not leave John lying there in limp mode. We read in verses 17 and 18, *But he laid his right hand on me, saying, 'Fear not, I am the first and the last, and the living one. I died, and behold I am alive forevermore, and I have the keys of Death and Hades.'* Here is Jesus, the man with a personal touch!

This is a tender pick-me-up kind of touch, a touch of reassurance that says 'all is well.' When Jesus placed his right hand on the trembling shoulder of John, he said to him, in effect, 'Don't be afraid, John! It's me!' John must have remembered those two words, *I am* ... it was he who recorded them seven times in his Gospel. Not 'I was' or even 'I will be', but *I am* – Jesus was saying, 'I am the God of the now.' Ah, just the mention of that name must have meant everything to a traumatised John.

I think it is wonderful to realise that Jesus was not afraid to touch ordinary people. When you read through the Gospel narrative, you find he touched all sorts of people: when he healed a leper, he touched him; when he restored sight to the blind, he put his hands upon their eyes; the touch of his hand brought healing to broken lives and strength to those who were crushed, it brought comfort and acceptance to those who were marginalised to the fringes of society.

How Jesus introduced himself

The express words of comfort and consolation that Jesus gave to John are based on his person – who he is, and on his authority – what he has.

'I am the First and the Last' ... the all-sufficient One!

There were none before Jesus and there will be none after him, nothing came before him and nothing will come after him. There never was a time when he did not exist and there never will be a time when he does not exist. He is from everlasting to everlasting, the eternal Word. This was a title used of God in the Old Testament (cf. Isaiah 44:6; 48:12). By virtue of the fact that Jesus took it to himself, it means he is asserting his deity.

'I am the Living One' ... the all-victorious One!

John would recall this designation with little or no difficulty. He had heard it many times before and he knew precisely what it meant. Like the previous one, this title is also used interchangeably within the Godhead (cf. Joshua 3:10; Psalm 84:2; Romans 9:16).

'I have the keys of Death and Hades' ... the all-powerful One!

He was more or less saying to John that he was sovereign in all matters relating to time and eternity. What tremendous encouragement that is for the children of God! We need not fear life for he is the Living One. We need not fear death because he died and is alive, having conquered death! We need not fear eternity for he has the keys in his hand. Our future is in his hands and it could not be in a safer pair of hands. He has the whole world there and we are there as well! Every time I read these wonderful verses, these luminous words, I cannot help but recall the words of the song:

> *God of glory, we exalt Your name;*
> *You who reign in majesty;*
> *we lift our hearts to You*
> *and we will worship,*
> *praise, and magnify*
> *Your holy name.*
> *In power resplendent*
> *You reign in glory;*
> *Eternal King,*
> *You reign for ever:*
> *Your word is mighty,*
> *releasing captives,*
> *Your love is gracious –*
> *You are my God!*

Jesus' commission to John

When you see what happened to John and read what follows in the rest of the book, you quickly realise that this vision was for real; this man was not suffering from hallucinations, he was not living his life in dream mode. He saw and recorded events that will shape the future of every one of earth's teeming millions. Revelation is one of those books that can knock us out of our complacency and our fear of the future, and into confident living.

The commission given to John in verse 19 gets to the heart of the matter when he is told to, *Write therefore the things that you have seen, those that are and those that are to take place after this.* Basically, this triple command encompasses the past, the present, and the future.

Jesus' explanation of the stars

In the next verse, verse 20, he then unravels the mystery surrounding the seven stars and the seven golden lampstands. He makes the connection between them and the letters to the seven churches in Asia Minor. This is a classic example of Scripture explaining itself! We have no problem identifying the seven churches. John talks about them further up the chapter in verse 11 and again you find them detailed in chapters 2 and 3 as being specific churches in specific locations. Actually, when you start with Ephesus and finish with Laodicea, you have gone on a circular tour of the region—a round trip of the seven postal districts—covering about 300 miles or just under 500 kilometres.

The problem is not with the churches, it is with the angels or the stars! There are many people who have genuine queries at this point. They ask, Why seven? That is the number of perfection, completeness, and fulness. It is as if the Lord is saying: 'Here is a picture of the church in its totality.' They say, Can we easily identify the seven stars? Who is John speaking about when he talks about them? Each of the seven letters is prefaced with the phrase, *To the angel of the church in Ephesus* or wherever.

The 'angel' refers to the pastor or leader of a church

This idea is based on the fact that the broad meaning of the word 'angel' is that of a messenger. When the Lord has a special message for his people in a given church, the best way to impart it is to go directly to the leadership of that church and share it with those whom the church has set apart for that specific role. When that happens, they then have the solemn responsibility of passing it on to the members of the congregation over which they have spiritual oversight.

No mileage would be gained if our Lord was to bypass the recognised leadership of a local assembly and appeal over their heads to the ordinary people sitting in the cushioned oak pews on a Sunday morning. You only get people's backs up if you go down that particular road and, in the final analysis, you do not achieve very much with such a heavy-handed approach. Whatever, before the Lord tells them what they are doing wrong, he tells them what they are doing right ... an important principle for us to take on board!

Some folk today are living their lives on a different wavelength to the Lord for they do not think churches are important. God does not look at it like that. He believes they are very important! So much so that he shared a vision with John, not of one church, but of seven, and in chapters 2 and 3, we see them through his looking glass with each one bearing his unique signature.

Most people have an opinion about their local church and they are not behind the door when it comes to telling you what they think! 'It's dead, it's too old-fashioned, it's over the top, they've gone charismatic, they're far too liberal, it's too right-wing, walk in there and you get caught in a time warp, they're up-to-date in that place, they're relevant!' Comments, you have heard them! Criticisms, you have maybe made them! You ask three people about their church and you will walk away with four or five different impressions!

When you look at the churches which John is talking about, people who were living near the end of the first century, you sit back, fold your arms, and say to yourself, 'Well, well. Time has not changed anything ... people are still people ... problems are still problems ... they are just like some of our modern churches two millennia down the road!'

They were real churches—people attended them, people sang in them, people worshipped in them, people prayed in them, people found the Lord as Saviour in them, people listened to the Word preached in them. Two thousand years later we come back and pay them a visit. We take a fresh look at these churches in the first century because there is a lot we can learn from them.

Obviously, every one has their own style when it comes to writing letters, and the Head of the church is no different! The seven letters outlined here follow a clear pattern: one, they all begin with an attribute of Christ being highlighted; two, there is normally a compliment or two; three, there is, in most instances, a note of criticism; and, four, there is a strong word of correction or a specific challenge. To each congregation, the message in electronic media-speak is, 'You've got mail.'

Three attributes of the seven churches

They are real

We need to realise that Christ had a direct message to seven actual churches at that particular time. There were many more which he could have chosen but he opted for these. So we have seven letters to seven real churches. They were contemporary. Each one was different. You cannot really compare churches and expect to do them justice. When we view them from a practical perspective, we note that each one gives a special promise to the overcomer!

They are relevant

The message to each church was relevant then and it is so relevant today! They are meant to be applied by all churches in all ages. When you see them as a composite, you soon realise that somewhere on that list, you will find a church that closely resembles yours and mine. These letters are as current as today's calendar. They are of perennial value!

They are representative

When you take them all together, they give us a preview, an

overview, of church history from Pentecost to the advent of Jesus. That means each church depicts a particular period of church history. In that sense, we can view them from a prophetic standpoint. They give us a panorama, a sweep, a vista of church history. The implication is, there are seven great periods of the Christian era, and when you look back into history, you can see that picture unfolding and evolving before your eyes. So we have here a chronological account of church history.

A potted history of the church from Day One

Period 1   The church at Ephesus: the primitive church from Pentecost to the end of the 1st century

The challenging comment for this era is found in 2:5 where we read, *Remember therefore from where you have fallen.* Even in the halcyon days of the apostles, there was a gradual cooling of their love for the Lord Jesus. The drive and dynamic that characterised the early years was replaced by a more staid, settled-down form of Christianity. The church rested on her oars and started to drift from her moorings. She began to tolerate trends and teachings that brought a razor-sharp response from the likes of Paul and Peter, John and Jude, in their letters.

Period 2   The church at Smyrna: the persecuted church from 100 to around 313

For ten days you will have tribulation (2:10). When you go back in the annals of church history, there were ten major outbreaks of persecution against the church of Jesus Christ. The last one, under Diocletian, was so concentrated it lasted for the best part of a decade; it was cruel in the extreme as Rome vented her spleen against the Lord's own people. Their only crime was that they were deeply devoted to Jesus, they worshipped and revered him as Lord. Whether to the lion or before a sword, so many of God's dear people faced death with a song of praise and a word of prayer and thanksgiving on their lips. These folk proved that the blood of the martyr was, indeed, the seed of the church.

Period 3   The church at Pergamum: the pampered church from 314 to 590

The telling phrase found in 2:14 that speaks of *the teaching of Balaam* underlines the serious problems which marked this day and generation. It was riddled with compromise and this was never more the case than in the days of Constantine when he popularised Christianity. This was, undoubtedly, a sea change for the worse.

The church became prosperous and worldly; it was chic to be a Christian at this point in time. It was during this time that there was a marriage of sorts, a kind of merger between church and state. We live even today with the legacy of that momentous, historic decision. Here is a church whose character is seriously blurred and whose testimony is radically diminished.

When you compare the second and third periods of church history, Campbell Morgan offers a rather perceptive comment when he says: 'It's a very remarkable thing that the church of Christ patronised has always been the church of Christ impure.'

Period 4   The church at Thyatira: the papal church from 590 to 1517

The period represented here is that of the Dark Ages and is highlighted best by the emergence and strategic influence of the papal church. Here is a millennium when the light was almost extinguished. It has often been called the devil's millennium for ordinary people were kept in a place of ignorance as regards spiritual truth.

The clue to this era is probably found in 2:20 where we read, *you tolerate that woman Jezebel.* She was a pagan woman married to one of Israel's worst and weakest kings. She became the secret power behind the throne and made a priest-ridden paganism the national religion.

The question is, What happened after the days of Constantine? Rome became the effective centre of ecclesiastical affairs. History confirms that days of corruption followed, days of evil and rampant wickedness were soon the norm, so much so that the church became the home of heathenism. We can trace many developments during those dark days such as the acceptance of pagan feast days as Christian festivals, pagan gods became Christian saints, pagan rituals received new life as Christian rites, pagan priests became the ordained servants of the church. These were dark days, there is no question about that.

Period 5   The church at Sardis: the prophetic church from 1517 to 1700

This period reveals a prophetic glimpse of the Protestant church. The essence of Protestant religion is summed up in the words of 3:1, *You have the reputation of being alive, but you are dead.* We sincerely thank the Lord for those who escaped from the clutches of pagan-organised religion and ushered in a brand new era. The Reformation was brought in by godly, gifted men of the calibre and ilk of Wycliffe, Hus, Luther, Melanchthon, Zwingli, Knox, and Calvin, all household names to those within evangelical circles. The sad fact is, it was not very long before its impetus died out. It is true, according to 3:2, that there are things that remain but what is left does not look good; it is on the way out, about to breathe its last!

Period 6   The church at Philadelphia: the partitioned church from 1700 to 1900

Most evangelical scholars are agreed on the fact that the Reformation did not go far enough. The downside of that fateful movement is that you have various groupings or denominations emerging with each one espousing its own pet doctrines.

Having said that, it was also a time when the phrase found in 3:8 is most relevant, we read of *an open door.* For many believers, there was a welcome return to a simplicity of faith as they sat under the plain teaching of the Word of God. It also suggests a season of great revival when God moved in powerful ways in the lives of individuals and communities.

Many missionary societies were born in this era because men had a burden to reach others with the life-changing message of the gospel. They had a vision which reached beyond these shores to the regions beyond. We are talking of such men as the Wesley brothers, Charles and John; D L Moody and Ira Sankey; Charles Finney, William Carey, David Livingstone, Hudson Taylor, Adoniram Judson, who mark this period as quite distinctive, and so many more!

God brought the church back from the brink. He drew her close to himself and then sent her forth with renewed passion and zeal to reach a lost world.

Period 7   The church at Laodicea: the present-day church from 1900 to ...

The character of our day and generation is best summed up in the descriptive word used in 3:16 where it talks about people being *lukewarm.* They are neither cold nor hot; they are neither one thing nor the other; they are sitting on the proverbial fence; they want the best of both worlds with one foot in the world and the other in the church. It is a nauseating pot pourri of anything and everything, an incredible mishmash of you-name-it-you-have-it! Not very encouraging, is it?

There you see the history of the church of Christ. We have leapt across the centuries. We have spanned these seven great periods of time from Day One up to the present. Our only hope is to get back to the Bible, back to God, back to Calvary, back to an empty tomb, back to a throne occupied in heaven itself! There is a great need for each of us to examine our own lives!

Are we like the Christians in the church at Ephesus, an evangelical centre of witness where they had everything but the greatest thing? Are we like the believers in Smyrna, a suffering church? Are we like the folk down in Pergamum who make up an inner city church? Perhaps we are found among those in Thyatira who are pretty much an urban fellowship? What about those in Sardis, are we part of a liberal community? Are some of us like the folk in Philadelphia, part of an active missionary-minded church? Are we up to our necks in a church like the one at Laodicea where Christianity is weak and tepid?

That is an enormous challenge to every one of us for, today, the church is at the crossroads. We are, at this precise moment, in the era portrayed by the lukewarm church; it is the time of the last church on Planet Earth prior to the Second Coming of Christ!

It reminds me of this scenario: the hour hand on God's time clock is wound up and spinning. We are being swept along the path of history by a swift wind at our back. Our individual ability to weather the storm will come from our understanding of the Word of God. We need only to give heed to an age-old message that has reverberated down through the centuries in the final verse in chapter 3 (remember, he fires the same parting shot to every church) where he says, *He who has an ear, let him hear what the Spirit says to the churches.*

It is true, each of these seven letters to seven ancient churches was written with history in mind. Their history. Future history. Your history. My history. We are links in that unbroken chain of church history! Our response to these studies in Revelation will determine the impact we make today, and tomorrow! Let us never forget, we are history makers!

CHAPTER 2

Things Jesus saw when he turned up at church

A dream or a nightmare?

'Do you love me?'

That was the simple, straightforward question a Russian peasant named Tevye asked his wife in the musical, *Fiddler on the Roof.*

Love him? The problem was Golde had never even met Tevye until the day of their arranged wedding! Now, after twenty-five years of marriage, he wants to talk of love? It just sounds so ridiculous, so alien to her that she thinks he has indigestion and should lie down.

Tevye repeats the question, in earnest.

Golde wonders at his thinking, is there a hidden agenda? Then she explains how hard she has worked as his wife – cooking his meals, washing his clothes, having his children, and so on, and so forth.

Still, it does not satisfy the inquisitive Tevye. So he asks the same question, one more time.

This time, with more than a hint of exasperation, Golde falls back on the obvious: she is his wife, after all!

Still not content with the answer, Tevye persists ... does she love him?

It took a wee while for the response to come, but come, it certainly did. Golde answers in the affirmative, she does indeed love him, realising that her life has not just been an endless cycle of meaningless chores. In all honesty, she has worked so hard *because* of her commitment and love for Tevye.

It is possible, though, as Tevye recognised and almost dreaded, for activity to replace love!

Therein lies the danger ...

2:1-7

Ephesus ... the city of 'first landing'

Ephesus was the chief city of the province of Asia. It was known as the vanity fair of Asia and was widely acclaimed as one of the top three cities of the eastern Mediterranean. It was a thriving centre for trade, business, and commerce, with its own harbour and a population approaching a quarter million inhabitants. It was a pagan city with all sorts of weird things taking place. You name it, they had it!

Ephesus could boast with considerable pride that within its boundary there stood one of the seven wonders of the world, the famous temple of Diana or Artemis. It featured a gross, multi-breasted, colossal statue-cum-monstrosity to the goddess of sex and fertility. This shrine actually served as the bank of Asia; it doubled as an art gallery and played host as a safe sanctuary for the criminal fraternity as they found political asylum from the long arm of Roman law. The temple grounds were a chaotic cacophony of priests, prostitutes, bankers, criminals, musicians, dancers, and frenzied, hysterical worshippers. It was a virtual cesspool of iniquity.

The city was also known for its great library which rivalled those of Rome, Athens, and Alexandria. It was a cultural centre, a place where you could find people from all over the world representing every occupation, language, and belief. It was called a 'free city.' Because of their loyalty to the Empire, the city was allowed to be self-governing. There was no Roman garrison present. A spirit of independence permeated the atmosphere and that is seen in the lifestyle that many chose to follow.

It is there, in the midst of that godless, hedonistic city, that God planted a thriving congregation. As one writer says: 'It is better to run a mission at the gates of hell than to preach to the choir. God often builds his church where the circumstances seem the least favourable. That's the grace of God.'

Ephesus ... the church

What is so incredibly special about the church at Ephesus? It is the only church in the New Testament which has letters addressed to it by two apostles, Paul and John. When Paul wrote his letter, the church was in its heyday, at its peak, at its very best. Paul revealed many wonderful truths to many different churches but none excel that which he shared with the folk in Ephesus, surely the Everest of his epistles. He prays for them twice: one, a request for more light (cf. 1:15-23) and, two, a request for more love (cf. 3:14-21).

But when John picked up his quill a few years later and wrote, it was the crisis church of the day! The tide was going out, they had lost their way and left their first love. The furnace was still there but the fire was almost extinct. There was a measure of warmth but the coals had lost their glow; a case of the dying embers syndrome. A coolness had crept into their relationship with the Lord. It is to this community of believers that the Lord now speaks.

We have here a company of people who were members of an evangelical fellowship. When Paul made Ephesus a centre for evangelism during the three years he spent there, the church apparently flourished (cf. Acts 18-19). After Paul's release from prison, he probably visited the church another time and established his young protégé, Timothy, as pastor (cf. 1 Timothy 1:3). It is well within the bounds of possibility that John may have succeeded Timothy. A fairly impressive group of ministers for any congregation! These were the big guns in the early church. It was stellar leadership, if you want to see them as *stars* as the Lord does in verse 1.

The all-important question, What is in the letter which has been delivered to the leadership of the church at Ephesus?

The Master's revelation

The Lord writes to *the angel of the church*. This reminds us that he has his own messenger, his servant, in every church. This is the person responsible for the spiritual welfare and pastoral care of the people of God.

Where is the messenger? He is held as a star in the *right hand* of Jesus, the place of power and authority. That is the only place where his servants can be strengthened and sustained. When we are there, we are under his control, for he is the manager of every messenger. As John MacArthur says: 'It indicates that they are his ministers, under his power, as he mediates his sovereign rule in the church through its human leaders.'

Where is the Master? He is walking *among the seven golden lampstands* surveying the churches under his control. He is walking up and down every aisle reminding us that the members are ruled by the divine overseer. He is the master of the members. They are reminded of a beautiful truth that he is in their midst. So long as he is in the central place, they can enjoy a real sense of his presence.

The Master's remarks

This was a very good church to belong to. They are extremely active and there is so much to commend it. It was a dynamic fellowship and a lot of dedicated people went along. It was a church where discipline was exercised and where the leadership had the rare gift of spiritual discernment. When you stand back and look inside, one is impressed.

They are serving for the Lord talks about their *works*. The place was buzzing, things were happening in Ephesus. They were not content to sit up in the bleachers on the terraces; they are down there where the action is, on the field of play! They are diligent. Nothing passive about them.

They are sacrificing for mention is made of their *toil.* A number of the members were extremely busy and probably a few were reaching the point of exhaustion. The word describes all-out effort; it demands all that a person can give physically, mentally, and emotionally. It was gutsy stuff! Holy sweat rolled down their brow as they ministered in his name.

They are stedfast for Jesus highlights their *patient endurance* as a rich quality. They kept on going even when the going was getting tougher and the hill steeper. They stuck with it. This was no grit-your-teeth-and-bear-it mentality for they showed triumphant fortitude. It was not fatalistic resignation but a courageous acceptance of hardship.

They are separated as they did not let any Tom, Dick, or Harry into the pulpit. Prospective preachers were vetted and they had to be seen to be genuine. Here we have men in key positions who were alert to false teaching and doctrinal error. They had their finger on the pulse and their ear to the ground. They could smell a heretic a mile off. These believers separated themselves from anything that smacked of false doctrine and they would have nothing to do with those who peddled their pseudo spiritual wares. When they heard a theological error, flares went up. 'False teachers were given an apple and a road map,' writes Steven Lawson.

This little church was a citadel of orthodoxy, a bastion to biblical truth, a fortress for the faith. This is of mega importance for the church that stands for nothing will generally fall for anything! A ministry can be only as strong as its doctrinal purity. Their faith was undiluted and unpolluted. No shades of grey with them.

They are a suffering fellowship for they bore massively heavy burdens. In spite of the cross they were carrying, they never called it quits. They did not give up or give in. These folk were bearing up under a stressful load but the thought of throwing the towel into the ring never entered their minds.

Looks like a good church? They are standing up to the task in hand, standing for the truth of Scripture, and standing firm in the hour of trial; sure, we take our hat off to them. We salute them for their faithful, rock solid, biblical ministry. This was no exclusive, spiritual country club; they did not look like saints on Sunday and act like aint's on Monday!

But ... a little word which packs a powerful punch ... the Lord sensed, and knew, something was not quite right! Something significant was missing!

The Master's rebuke

When I read verse 4 I discover that the penetrating, laser eyes of the Lord detected a fatal weakness in the fellowship. There was a potentially serious flaw, he has a bone to pick with them! They had everything but the main thing!

'You have abandoned the love you had at first'

Our greatest strengths can often become our greatest weaknesses. As Charles Swindoll says: 'The Ephesians were the pit bulls of orthodoxy – guarding truth, chasing away false teachers. But in their zeal, they substituted knowledge for knowing, hating for loving.' Someone has written: 'These believers had not only become professional and perfunctory in the expression of their faith, they had become deluded by the importance of service, placing it above their love for Jesus Christ.'

That is the solemn verdict of the Lord who was looking behind the brick exterior. The passion is gone, the fire is almost out, there are only smouldering remains left. They were going through the motions, it was all so mechanical. Full heads, busy feet, empty hearts. The days were full, the diary was crammed, the numbers attending were encouraging but, like a slow puncture, first love had evaporated, gone with the wind. There is the real tragedy of the church at Ephesus. (A quick glance at Jeremiah 2:2-13 and Ezekiel 16:8-15 illustrates what happens when the honeymoon ends for the people of God.)

What is 'the love you had at first'?

Can we define it? It is the love we had for Jesus when we first knew him; the kind of love which stops the heart or, if it does not stop the heart, it certainly makes it beat faster. It is the brand of love that will do anything for the person who is loved. It is love with no strings attached!

But, over the years, the thrill goes and we begin to take him for granted; spiritually, we go off the boil. Our blazing passion cools off to a flickering flame. The wonder of it all has more or less gone from our daily experience. We do not feel excited about him any more. We become comfortable in our lifestyle, cushioned with all the trappings of faith, and complicated in our outlook. We become sophisticated saints when, all of the time, he is looking only for our love. He wants a people who will be taken up with him and taken in with him. But even though all was not well, all was not lost!

The Master's request

His impassioned appeal is found in the final paragraph of the letter and it entails a threefold strategy, three Rs ...

> Remember what it was like!
> Repent and turn your life around!
> Repeat and do the things you used to do!

They had to remember back to when they first came to personal faith in Christ, they had to refocus on those times when they really loved the Saviour, and they had to replay that initial excitement. They had to swing a U-turn.

Remember! It was time to *remember* the freshness, fervency, and fire of their first love. To remember when it was springtime in their souls. To remember how they yearned to learn more of the Word. To remember how their hearts were overflowing with a love for Christ and his people. To remember when they had hearts filled with holy passion for the souls of sinful men. It is apparent from what the Lord says that memory is the handmaid of revival.

Repent! They were also to *repent* and get back to where they once were in their relationship with the Lord. He told them quite bluntly if they did not get their act together, he would come and the light would be extinguished. They needed to sort out their personal priorities and look again at the agenda of their lives. Failure on their part spelt removal and the Lord was deadly serious when he said it.

How do we know? Today you can walk around the ancient city of Ephesus, as I have often done, and what do you see? Ruins! O the grave danger of losing our first love for Jesus! Here is a church that was missing out and a people who were missing out. Yes, it is possible to be busy for God without being a blessing for God; it is possible to fly the flag of orthodoxy and not have a commitment and love for biblical truth in your heart. I wonder, can you say without blushing, 'I love Jesus!' 'It is not virtue that can save the world or anyone in it, but love,' wrote Archbishop Temple.

The promise is given in verse 7 that if they do what he wants them to do, he will give them the ability *to eat of the tree of life, which is in the paradise of God.* What a tremendous promise to claim! What does it mean?

The tree of life, a symbol of eternal life, was originally found in the Garden of Eden (cf. Genesis 2:9). Adam and Eve forfeited this blessing when they sinned against the Lord, but for you and me who are forgiven by the grace of God, the promise holds true. He offers us the assurance of eternal life, the prospect of being with the Lord forever in the paradise of God. Eden was a shadow of what our future holds as the people of God!

Repeat! It makes a lot of sense to put God first in our lives.

After all, this exciting promise is as relevant today as it was when it was first given so many years ago. Let us pull out all the stops and get back to a life of walking with the Lord! What is the point of having a saved soul and, at the same time, having a lost life? Let us put him first!

2:8-11

Smyrna ... where life was tough as a believer

You will be familiar with the saying that 'the blood of the martyr is the seed of the church.' That is exactly what happened to the good folk in Smyrna. Polycarp was a former bishop of the church in Smyrna. His name is etched on the granite of history. He was a student and disciple of the Apostle John.

In the year 155 AD Polycarp was in the eventide of life; for him, the sun was setting and the shadows lengthening on a long, fruitful life. He was in his mid-80s when one day the unthinkable happened, there was the dreaded knock on the front door! When he answered, he was met by the Roman authorities who promptly took him away. He was hauled before the courts and told to renounce Jesus Christ. He flatly refused. He never flinched or wavered. This is what he said: '86 years I have served the Lord Jesus. He never did me any harm. He has been faithful to me. How can I blaspheme my King, my Lord, and my Saviour?' The outcome? He was burned alive, and died rejoicing in the Lord Jesus.

Smyrna ... where life was a soft touch for the locals

Back in the days of John, the city was a thriving, bustling seaport, renowned as a centre of commerce and known as the gateway from the east into Europe. Picturesque in its setting, it was fronted by the coast of the Aegean Sea and flanked by a cypress-clad, circular hill called the Pagos. It had its very own 'street of gold.'

It was famous for its fabulous wealth, a beautiful city because of its architecture. It housed the largest public theatre in Asia as well as a famous stadium and library. Some historians say it was the most exquisite city the Greeks ever built, a designer's dream. The local Chamber of Commerce hailed it as the pride of Asia. Proudly, 'First in Asia in beauty and size' was inscribed on their coins.

Years earlier, Alexander the Great had determined to make Smyrna the model Greek city. To many, it was. Its one claim to international fame was that it was the birthplace of the Greek epic poet, Homer.

Today, under a new name, Izmir is the third largest city in Turkey with a population of around 200,000 people and is home to the prestigious Aegean University. It is a major international trade centre and base for the headquarters of NATOs southern command. A city of prominence has emerged from the ancient ruins of Smyrna.

It is hard to believe in these idyllic surroundings that there was a church under tremendous pressure, under fire, in the crucible of suffering. It was tough! It was a long uphill struggle. It is into this situation that our Lord comes when he pays them a surprise visit.

Smyrna actually means 'myrrh' which is a fragrant spice; it is a resinous substance used as a perfume for the living (cf. Matthew 2:11) and the dead (cf. John 19:39). It was obtained when the flowering myrrh tree was pierced or crushed. In an amazing way, the church lives up to that name. There was a rare scent, a beautiful aroma, emitted from the suffering saints within her walls.

Words of introduction

In his initial comment, the risen Lord revealed himself as *the first and the last, who died and came to life* (cf. Isaiah 44:6; 48:12). Basically, he wants to remind them of his unique position for he is the exalted, enthroned Lord. Charles Swindoll says: 'In the opening line of his letter to the Smyrnaean believers, Jesus immediately taps into the universal language of suffering and extends hope to a church near dead for thirst of encouragement.'

He talks about himself

As one who is the *first* it means he is director of his people; he goes before us. He is up front. He is ahead of us. As one who is the *last* he is protector of his people; he follows behind us. He is at the rear. As one who *died and came to life* he is victor of his people; we are on the winning team. We will not miss out, nor lose out. We are on the victory side. Ours is the team that, ultimately, will triumph.

Here is a church made up of boring, ordinary people living their lives on the ragged edge. There were two completely opposite extremes: there was the loving fellowship of the family of God and there was the hostile, cruel society in which they lived.

Jesus sees himself as one who effectively bridges the gap. He can encompass such extremes. He can span the divide. He was present at the beginning of creation, being there at its dawn. He will be there when it all grinds to a halt. As it were, he is top line, bottom line, and every line between.

Words of identification

The Lord then proceeds to identify what is happening in the church at Smyrna. This he does in verse 9 where he says, *I know.* Two words that communicated volumes to pained hearts. That says it all! That was all they needed to know. There is nothing he does not know, right down to the minutest detail. He is familiar with all the facts, aware of all their fears, sees and knows all their faces, up-to-date with all that is happening in their families, and au fait with all the comings and goings in the fellowship.

God knows! He could sit where they were sitting, that was no problem to him; he could stand alongside and give them a shoulder to lean on. He could offer loads of sympathy to them and, by the same token, he could empathise with them, for Jesus knows all about our struggles. He knows every pinpoint of pain and every little flicker of feeling we experience as his children. And what a titanic struggle! There was *tribulation and poverty*. In classical Greek, the term for tribulation paints a picture of a huge rock crushing whatever lies beneath it. This was symptomatic of their experience for their pressure was so intense, they felt as though they were caught in a vice and slowly squeezed. This was adversity in capital letters. There was nothing glamorous about their lifestyle as they had been reduced to beggars. They were destitute, having lost everything. They were, so to speak, out on the street. All of this, because they were in the will of God!

The lovely thing is that the Lord Jesus can identify with them. He left the ivory palaces of heaven and came down to earth. He who was rich became poor. He knows, sure he does! He has been there, done that! He could put his arm around them and say, *I know!* That would have meant everything to them. It was Corrie ten Boom who said: 'There is no pit so deep that Christ is not deeper still.'

Words of insight

It really is quite remarkable because, in the next breath, Jesus says to them, in spite of what you do not have, *you are rich.* They had something money could not buy. What they had in him was worth more than acres of diamonds. They had a priceless treasure in the presence of Jesus. They were rich in faith, love, and grace (cf. 2 Corinthians 8:9; James 2:5). There was a depth to their fellowship that is only born in the hour of great trial. There was nothing shallow or superficial about them. There was an added dimension to their walk with the Lord. They lived on the edge of eternity. Heaven was in their hearts.

Words of intrigue

He also informs them in verse 9 that he knows *the slander*

of those who say that they are Jews and are not, but are a synagogue of Satan. These folk were being slandered by many people in town. Locally, they were victims of a scurrilous smear campaign to discredit them. Their reputation was being ruined as they were grossly misrepresented with salvo after salvo of verbal bullets. Talk about character assassination and protracted intimidation, they knew all about it!

It begs the question, Who was doing it? The Lord points the finger and lays the blame fairly and squarely at the door of those who are paid-up members on the devil's payroll. Satan's undercover agents. And, yet again, he says to them, *I know.*

Words of information

The Lord drops a bombshell into their lap. The chances are it was something they did not want to hear. He told them: *Do not fear what you are about to suffer. Behold, the devil is about to throw some of you into prison, that you may be tested, and for ten days you will have tribulation.* He breaks the news that there would be more trials and troubles for them to pass through, more ups and downs to face on the journey of life. Suffering as a saint is still on the cards. *Ten days* seemed like ten lifetimes.

What they needed to realise was this: God was allowing it to happen. He permitted it. He knows how much they can take so he sets a time limit. And he never moves the goalposts. It would have a starting point, and a finishing point. *Ten days*, it would not last eleven! After all, had he not introduced himself to them as *the first and the last*?

Words of incentive

The penny would eventually drop and they would realise that this is all that really matters in this life. He says to them, and to us: *Be faithful unto death, and I will give you the crown of life.* In other words, do not buckle under! Our willingness to die for Christ is the ultimate proof of our loyalty to him. We are not ready to live until we are ready to die. Therefore, be loyal, be strong, be courageous. Do not shrink from the trials of this life and his grace will see you through.

In our day, a Christian pastor speaking in Nicaragua about persecution and the future once said: 'It is the strangest thing. But where the war has been the bloodiest, where the needs are the most desperate, this is where the church has grown the most. Yes, brethren, become martyrs. Yet remember that the heavier the cross, the more powerful the resurrection.'

He guarantees the future with the promise of a crown of life. At the end of the day,

> *It will be worth it all when we see Jesus;*
> *Life's trials will seem so small, when we see Christ.*
> *One glimpse of his dear face, all sorrow will erase,*
> *So bravely run the race, till we see Christ!*

He knows all about our circumstances. If things stay the same, the Lord will be our fortress. If things get worse, the Lord will see us through. Here were a handful of people on the verge of cracking up under the tremendous strain they were facing. The stress was unbearable but the glorified Lord says to them, *'take heart ... the cross is not greater than my grace!'*

2:12-17

Pergamum ... the culture capital of Asia

Can you imagine a capital city bristling with civil servants and military personnel? Add to that a university full of bookish, half-rim-spectacled intellectuals. Make sure it houses an eminent teaching hospital and quite a few rather strange alternative religions. When you put all that together and more, you could well be thinking about this place.

If Ephesus was like New York City, and if Smyrna was comparable to Atlanta, it is not hard to see the reason why Pergamum was touted as the Washington DC of Asia. The sheer beauty of the city would leave even the most cynical traveller breathless.

It was renowned as a centre of culture. It boasted one of the finest libraries in the world with over 200,000 handwritten volumes, second only to the world famous library in Alexandria, Egypt. It was the place where parchment—a new writing material made from animal skins—was first developed. Such a city attracted the best brains and boffins in academia.

It was also a focus of religion. You name it, they were sure to have it. It was a city infested with idolatry, a notorious place where religious groups mushroomed. Anybody with anything to say could find a soap box and pontificate. Every corner was a veritable Speakers Corner as in London's Hyde Park. As far back as 29 BC it became the first city of Asia to receive permission from Rome to build a temple dedicated to the worship of a living human ruler. That was only the thin edge of the wedge for, within a relatively brief period, Pergamum had three temples in which Roman emperors were worshipped as gods.

Sadly, the church in Pergamum was faltering as she had almost lost her way. We could describe it as an inner city church surrounded by concrete tower blocks. Here is a church guilty of compromise as they wanted the best of both worlds. They wanted to run with the foxes and hunt with the hounds. She was flirting with the world and, by so doing, was two-timing the Lord Jesus.

There are four chillingly accurate statements we can make about the church as we read her profile in 2:12-17.

There were Christians in the church

This letter is not penned to professors sitting in ivory towers. It is addressed to believers who were living on the edge of hell. These were everyday people struggling to keep their faith in what has been called, Satan's city. Verse 13 reminds us that Jesus knows they live in a highly dangerous environment, for he says, *I know where you dwell, where Satan's throne is.*

They were behind enemy lines, the devil's territory, the enemy's backyard. It is where Satan has his throne. He visited other towns, but he lived in Pergamum. He is seen in Scripture as 'the prince of this world' and, for a time, it would appear that his global activities were centred on Pergamum. A beachhead for evil. What a terrible place to live! I cannot think of anywhere worse to live than next door to Satan's bunker!

Many of the Christians were devoting their time to the cause of Christ. Much energy was expended in the service of God. He is most appreciative of all they were doing for him and in his name. He knows about their loyalty as they were true to his name. There was nothing wishy-washy about them.

The battle fought here was over the deity of Jesus Christ. His is a name above all other names and in Pergamum that did not go down very well. It was a war between Caesar and Christ – who is Lord? These folk were willing to stand up and be counted. Because of their intense loyalty, some paid the supreme sacrifice. They died because they would not deny the Lord Jesus. When pressed, they did not flinch; when threatened, they did not flee; when tested, they stayed true.

Antipas whose name means 'against all' lived up to his name. He is singled out for special mention in verse 13 as someone who refused to give an inch to the political correctness of the day. Commended by the Lord for his faithfulness, this brother (maybe he was the pastor) gave his life for the cause of right in a day of wrong. He is reputed to have been roasted slowly in a brass kettle during the persecution instigated by Emperor Domitian. Under enormous pressure, these folk did not bend or break. They were brave and bold.

There is confusion in the church

Verses 14 and 15 say as much. The Lord says, *I have a few things against you: you have some there who hold the teaching of Balaam, who taught Balak to put a stumbling block before the sons of Israel, so that they might eat food sacrificed to idols and practice sexual immorality. So also you have some who hold the teaching of the Nicolaitans.* There were some choice people, some fine young people, some key personnel, but there was something there that should not have been there. If the truth be told, he has a couple of things against them. Two doctrines: one, the teaching of Balaam and, two, the teaching of the Nicolaitans.

These twin doctrines infiltrated their fellowship. People swallowed them hook, line, and sinker. Usually sinker. As a result, their testimony was ruined and their effectiveness for God was eroded. They lost the razor sharp edge in their witness for Jesus. They were blunt! Sadly, the false teaching was openly tolerated rather than being confronted and removed. They were content to put up with it because the leaders did not want to rock the boat. It was the 'anything for a quiet life' syndrome. They were happy to sweep it under the carpet and hope it would go away.

The doctrine of Balaam would say, let us be more relaxed in our loyalties. You can read all about the well documented exploits of Balaam in Numbers 22-25. In a nutshell, he went softly, softly on sin and encouraged the people of God to compromise. He had one plank in his theology: if you cannot beat them, join them. It is fitting in with the prevailing mindset, it is the 'accommodation' principle put into practice; if you like, it is the 'all things to all men' philosophy!

The doctrine of the Nicolaitans would declare, let us be more restricted in our leadership. These guys were akin to the heavy shepherding movement seen in some of our evangelical churches. Here we have the emergence of a form of clericalism in which leaders would lord it over their people. It is a kind of dictatorship that crept in through the back door when people were not fully aware of the implications. It put a massive wedge between the clergy and the person sitting in the back seat.

There is a crisis in the church

They certainly had their problems in Pergamum! There was a sense of total bewilderment. The people sitting in the pews were feeling uncertain and unsure what they believed. Jesus pulled no punches as he lays it on the line to them in a few carefully chosen, scathing words found in verse 16 where he says, *Therefore repent. If not, I will come to you soon and war against them with the sword of my mouth.* Phew, rather them than me hearing words like that!

Put bluntly, the Lord says, either you sort out the problem among yourselves or I will come and do it for you. At the end of the day, it is a clarion call to repentance, a rousing call for them to get right with God. His intention is transparently clear as he has placed all his cards on the table. They know precisely where he stands; now the ball is fairly and squarely in their court.

When he introduced himself, he referred to the fact that he has a sharp double-edged sword at his disposal. Now you see the reason why, they have a double error in their assembly. He is the Living Word and with the sword of the Word, he would cut their feet from under them. This is a powerful reminder that the Word does the work. He calls his believing people to a life of separation, to a path of holiness; he longs for each of them to come to a point where they are sold out exclusively to him.

There is a challenge to the church

In verse 17, in modern speak, Jesus more or less says: you have two ears, do not only listen to what I am saying to you, be sure to hear what I am saying! If they did that, if they bit the bullet, if they lived a life of overcoming, then two things would be given to them.

They would receive a portion of *hidden manna* which means that Christ would nourish and sustain them. He would be to them as the bread of life. They could enjoy spiritual fellowship with him, even in their darkest hour. They could, by faith, feast upon him. Anne Graham Lotz writes: 'Jesus promises hidden manna to those who not only overcome doubt, denial, distortion, and dilution of his Word, but who also repent of tolerating those who do.'

He would also give them *a white stone with a new name written on the stone.* This probably refers to the Urim and Thummim we read about in the Old Testament (cf. Exodus 28:30; Numbers 27:21; Ezra 2:63). It means they could enjoy an intimacy of friendship with him. They would be justified and acquitted. They could sit freely at his table in his banqueting house.

This is an age when anything goes and is acceptable, when standards are falling by the hour. It is an age of compromise, tolerance, and political correctness! The old devil is having a field day for modern man has virtually abandoned God. Today's world has ditched God's laws and openly spurned his values. All around us the waters are muddied! Satan is a past master in the craft of seduction. It is the mix and match syndrome in religion. There is an Arabian proverb that says: 'He who lives all of his life trying to please and appease everyone will die in sadness.'

What we learn from the church in Pergamum is that God wants us to be different and distinctive. And, because of that, we need to be determined and daring. We need a fresh dose of Acts 4:12 which tells us that 'there is salvation in no one else, for there is no other name under heaven given among men by which we must be saved.'

We need to come to a point where we start to share with a watching world that Jesus Christ is unique, and because he is unique, it follows that Christianity is unique. There is always the danger of compromise in a situation of religious pluralism and Christ can never be merely one of many viable alternatives. Could it be that the Lord is saying to your church and mine, to the global church of this century, 'Look, now is the time to get your act together; it is high time to come clean; this is a defining moment, it is time to stand clear. I want your undivided attention and your total allegiance.'

2:18-29

Thyatira ... where trade unionism flourished

This letter, the longest of the seven, was sent to the church in the smallest city; it was delivered to a group of people in what amounted to a hillbilly place, in the back of beyond. Pliny the Elder, who lived in the first century and died in the volcanic eruption that destroyed Pompeii, made reference to 'Thyatira and other unimportant communities.' Truth be told, it was an insignificant dot on the map of the Roman Empire. That speaks for itself!

It was a blue-collar town known for its numerous trade guilds – a working man's community. In fact, it was near impossible to make a decent living in Thyatira without being a paid-up, card-carrying member of one of the many unions or fraternals. If a person refused to pay the weekly dues and toe the obligatory party line, they were turfed 'out of work.' Basically, the trade unions called the shots.

On top of that, each guild was under the patronage of a pagan deity which was wheeled out at various religious festivals and other functions. As you can imagine, such occasions saw the worst excesses of debauchery. It was party time at the club; an excuse, if one were needed, for fully grown men to engage in behaviour that would make animals blush with embarrassment.

Thyatira was a sentinel military town. It was originally settled to intercept any foreign armies approaching Pergamum. Before an invading foe could threaten the capital city, it had to first knock the stuffing out of the folks in Thyatira.

One writer summarises: 'This was Thyatira. A small town. Hard working. Country. Rough, tough, and coarse.'

Thyatira ... where one woman was a liability, not an asset

You will remember the thrilling story of Lydia in Acts 16. She was the 'seller of purple' who was gloriously converted when Paul was preaching in Philippi; home for her was not Philippi, as she was originally from Thyatira. In other words, Lydia worked as a sales rep for one of the Thyatiran trading-houses marketing its products in Europe. The chances are that she was instrumental in starting a church in her home city. She may have played a vital role in such a venture and she could well have been one of the foundation members.

It is ironic, but another woman had a major part to play in the downfall of the church at Thyatira. This fellowship was in grave danger of being swept out to sea on a tidal wave of heresy. It had broken anchor and was drifting from its moorings. Can we identify her? We certainly can! Her name, Jezebel. Even the mention of that name sends shivers down the spine as you recall her namesake in the Old Testament. A thumbnail sketch reveals her as a battle-axe who happened to be the wife of a weak-kneed Ahab. She spent all morning putting on her war paint and spent the rest of the day on the warpath! The devil in a blue dress! This woman in Thyatira is not much better for a woman to be called Jezebel is every bit as bad as calling a man Judas.

The bottom line for Thyatira and for us is, Who do I worship? Back in the 1960s the late A W Tozer observed that worship is the missing jewel in many of our lives. Real worship, heart worship, spiritual worship, is something God deserves and desires. But the acid test of our Christian experience comes when we ask ourselves the question, Who do I worship? That is the baseline in our relationship with God. We may worship a man or a church, but when we opt to go down that road, God is dethroned. That was the root problem in the church at Thyatira.

We can talk about the examination

Their hour of assessment has come. Their day of accountability has dawned. This is the moment when their ministry, methods, and message will be evaluated.

He is the Son of God. This is the only time this title is used in Revelation, yet John used it so often in the Gospel which bears his name. It speaks of the deity of the Lord, underscoring his supremacy, eternality, and authority. This title is in stark contrast to his portrayal as the Son of Man in the vision of chapter 1;

there, the emphasis was on his humiliation, here it is focused primarily on his status as one co-equal with the Father.

He is the Sovereign of the church. His eyes are *like a flame of fire.* In other words, the Lord misses absolutely nothing (if you have any doubts on that score, ask Hagar in Genesis 16:13). He sees what no one else can see. His penetrating gaze enables him to see everything that goes on, both in public and private. He sees through the disguises and pretensions of his people. He sees behind closed doors, he is conscious of all that happens in a closed mind, he is aware of what makes sinful man tick in a closed heart. Nothing can be hidden from the searching laser eye of God.

He is the Saviour of men because his *feet are like burnished bronze.* It reminds us of his severity when he moves in judgment against sin. He has an ability to trample sin and injustice underfoot. The brilliant glow from his feet depicts his purity and holiness as he stamps out impurity. His verdicts cannot be overturned.

We can look at the evidence

Their deeds. The Lord, in a wonderful piece of investigative journalism, says about them: *I know your works, your love and faith and service and patient endurance, and that your latter works exceed the first.* What we have here is a growing church and yet, at the same time, she is dabbling in sin. It is frighteningly possible! It is scary! The simple fact is, their rapid growth has nothing to do with them, it can all be attributed to the grace of God. God works in spite of us, not because of us!

It is an attractive church, at least on the outside. They had a proper motivation because their love is blossoming. Of the seven churches, this is the only one singled out for their *love.* They had a hugely effective ministry with a very full programme of activities for all ages and, apparently, meeting all types of need. They had the right message as they were orthodox in their basic beliefs. They had a tough mentality as they were bearing up well under an unbearably heavy load. This is the church at Thyatira ... well, not quite, there is more!

Their development. They were not standing still nor resting on their laurels. We read, they are now doing more than they did at first. The fellowship was moving forward, they are pulling out all the stops, it was a never-say-die spirit which they adopted. Nothing stagnant about them. Things were happening. Really happening! Impressed? Better believe it! These folk had so much going for them. But there was a big dark blotch on the landscape.

We can see the example

Sadly, their example is an appallingly bad one! This church had become a hotbed of heresy. The permissive society had gained an inroads into the church family. A spirit of sensual indulgence permeated the atmosphere. They had full hearts and empty heads. They were extremely tolerant and were willing to put up with anything and everything. What they conveniently turned a blind eye to, the Lord saw with two open eyes. What they brushed under the carpet, the Lord brought out into the open. What they did behind closed doors, the Lord made centre stage.

There was a cancer eating away at the lifeblood of the church and, even though the fellowship was haemorrhaging rather badly, they persistently refused to face up to the problem. It needed censorship and surgery, but they failed miserably when it came to dealing with the root cause. What was the issue? They tolerated a woman by the name of Jezebel. This is naming and shaming!

They are wrong in principle because they gave her an inch and she took a mile. They gave her a place of prominence in assembly affairs and she ended up putting the men in the shade for she was not willing to work under their guidance. She had her own agenda. She rode roughshod over their leadership and usurped their authority. To all intents and purposes, she ran the church, she pulled the strings. She was the power broker.

They are wrong in precept because she led them astray on a path of deception as she saw herself as *a prophetess* (20). She was a self-appointed mouthpiece for God. The fact is, not everyone who says they speak for God speaks for God!

They are wrong in practice because the sins we are talking about are those involving gross immorality and idolatry. It was a downward spiral. To add fuel to the fire, the Lord had given her ample opportunity to repent, to change her ways, but all to no avail. That is what we find in verse 21 where it says, *I gave her time to repent, but she refuses to repent of her sexual immorality.* It is a tragic situation that has snowballed. It has gone far beyond the point of no return and is totally out of hand. The chances are no one in their right mind ever thought it would end up like this!

We can hear the explanation

It is into this 'don't say anything that would hurt their feelings' situation that the Lord comes with a message based on a trio of *I wills,* for here is one who is unbelievably patient, even in the hour of judgment. He says in these verses, *I will throw her on to a sickbed, and those who commit adultery with her I will throw into great tribulation, unless they repent of her works, and I will strike her children dead.*

It is truly amazing but, even after she has said a defiant no, the Lord still leaves the door wide open. He still talks about the possibility of repentance. Should she continue to flout his laws and do her own thing, then he will act in a way which will not only be a salutary lesson to her but it will also serve as an example to others. That is what he means when he says, *And all the churches will know that I am he who searches mind and heart, and I will give to each of you according to your works.*

That reinforces the idea that judgment is not only intended to be something which is, first and foremost, disciplinary, it is also exemplary.

The one who is perfect in judgment is more than capable of getting the message across. He will drive home the inescapable truth that salvation is always according to faith but judgment is according to works. It does not matter what the sin is, it has a payday, someday. Every kick has a kickback! So far as a holy God is concerned, sin can never and will never go unchecked.

We can listen to the exhortation

My heart is stirred when I realise that even in a church like Thyatira, there are a handful of believers who have stayed loyal and true to the Lord Jesus. There may not be very many but the few that there are, are worth their weight in gold. Jesus assures them of his unfailing love and constant care. On a purely human level, they have plenty to worry about, they have more than they can handle and the upbeat news is, he knows all about it. He knows they have enough on their plate as it is so he commits himself to them by saying that he will not add to their load any more.

That is what is meant by the compact little phrase tucked away in verse 24, *I do not lay on you any other burden.* The Lord does not ask the impossible of his children. He does not want them to bend or buckle under the weight of excess baggage. He just reminds them that it will not be long until they see him face to face. And, between now and then, he wants them to stand firm, to hold their head high, and keep their light shining bright. And, should temptation come from someone like Ms. Jezebel, flee, and leave no forwarding address.

We can share in the encouragement

In verse 28 the Lord gives them a promise of *the morning star,* the star that appears just before the breaking of a new day (cf. Numbers 24:17-18). Astronomers identify the morning star as the planet Venus. It is the second planet from the sun and is the brightest object in the night sky. Depending on where it is in its orbital path, the morning star can be seen to rise as much as three hours before the sun. How wonderful it is to know, it is always darkest before the dawn! He says to them and, consequently, to us, *'I'm coming back, I'm coming soon!'* Hope is always present in the midst of the worst circumstances imaginable. And that is why we worship him, the glorified Lord, for our future is as bright and rosy as the promises of God.

That is why, like the few good folk remaining in Thyatira, we should not be taken by surprise and caught on the back foot when big problems occur in little, out of the way, obscure places. Big sin can happen in little churches and bad teaching can come from gifted people! The effect of one person's sin can destroy the effectiveness of an entire church. A salutary lesson for all, I think.

CHAPTER 3
The bad, the good, and the ugly

The story is told of a certain minister who had a reputation as an eccentric. One Sunday morning he told his congregation that he believed his church was dead. You can imagine the murmurous rumble from the oak pews when he said, 'Come back tonight, I'm going to preach the funeral service of the church.' The members were shocked, even horrified; they were speechless and couldn't believe their ears; needless to say, the attendance for the evening service was larger than it had been in years.

In front of the pews was a casket and, as the people sat in stunned silence, the pastor delivered the message. After the benediction, the pastor said, 'Some of you may not agree with me that this church is dead. So that you may be convinced, I'm going to ask you to view the remains. I want you to file by the casket, one by one, and see who is dead.'

In preparation for this unorthodox presentation, the minister had placed a mirror in the bottom of the casket. It is obvious who everyone saw when he came to view the deceased!

It is not a technique that I would be too enthusiastic to recommend or endorse; the fact is, he made a perfectly valid point and it was incredibly effective, the people would never forget it!

When you read the opening verses in chapter 3, you could be forgiven for feeling like the minister in the story! This portion reads more like the last rites than a letter. As Charles Swindoll says: 'What begins as a deathbed scene, however, suddenly shifts to an emergency room drama. Rather than officiating over a funeral, Christ makes a last ditch attempt to revive the hearts of the saints in Sardis.'

3:1-6

Sardis ... a church in a coffin

This church is found in a city described as one of the most famous cities in the world. Built on the summit of a hill, 1,500 feet above the Hermus valley floor, it was thought to be impregnable. It was, therefore, a relatively secure place to live. That is what the locals thought ... until, one day in 549 BC Cyrus, king of the Medo-Persians, captured Sardis by scaling a secret path up the cliff below. Once conquered, the city fell into a downward spiral from which they never recovered. Therein lies the danger of smug self-sufficiency; they were too complacent for their own good!

Sardis was also one of the oldest cities in Asia with a history dating back to the establishment of the Lydian kingdom, around 1200 BC. Names like King Midas of Phyrgia (yes, he of the famous golden-touch legend) and King Croesus, reputedly the wealthiest king of all time, were closely associated with the city.

Economically, Sardis was a boom town. It lay at the junction of five main roads, making it a centre for trade. It was fabulously wealthy and quickly became the playground for the rich and famous. If the city streets were not exactly paved with gold, they were the nearest thing to it. You could actually pan for gold in the streams within the city limits. Apparently, gold and silver coins were first minted here.

Sardinians were not afraid of hard manual work for over the years they built up a flourishing carpet manufacturing base. It was recognised as an important centre for wool production and the garment industry; in fact, Sardis claims to have discovered and developed the art of dyeing wool. Aesop, the famous writer of fables, may have been from Sardis. It was a picture postcard setting, quite ideal and most idyllic. The climate was excellent. The palaces and architecture were stunningly out of this world.

It had so much going for it! It had a name! One American

commentator notes: 'Cruising on past momentum, both the city and the church were alive in name only ... like Pittsburgh, where rampant unemployment has led many people into hard times.'

In this environment, the Lord met with his people. A church had been planted in the city. We are not told when it came into being. We have no idea who was used of the Lord to bring it to birth. What matters is this, the church was there. And just like the city, it had a name to live up to. Sure, it had a good name! It had a glowing reputation for miles around. It was the place to be seen to go to. It had a long line of worthies who exercised a ministry in its pulpit. The most prominent person from the church at Sardis known to history is Melito. He was an apologist who served as bishop of the area in the late second century.

It had a good heritage and a background to be proud of. It had a grand reputation, in the opinion of many, of being a live, vibrant church, a church with vitality but, from the Lord's perspective, and his is the only opinion that matters, it was dead. No life. No pulse. No heartbeat. They once lived on the cutting edge, now they have gone over the edge. It was a fruitless church! She was past her sell-by date, a has-been church. As someone has said: 'Theirs was a name without life, a form without power, a façade without reality.' They talked the talk and walked the walk, but it was all a hollow sham!

The lasting impression you get when you read this letter is that the church was dying through apathy and indifference. It had given up the struggle against the world around it. It had given up the fight and was not reaching its world for Jesus. A perennial problem! So many fine churches in our day are going down the same road. They talk about their glorious, illustrious past; they savour the immortal memory of great men who have laboured among them and have all the ingredients of former days. Sadly, they have misplaced their zeal and lost their enthusiasm for souls and the Lord.

If that alarming trend continues, the church will soon be a relic of the past. Surely that is a timely reminder to all of us of what can happen when apathy sets in. As Warren Wiersbe says: 'The church that does not reach out will eventually pass out!'

His assessment

Who is the one who surveys the dismal, depressing scene in Sardis? Who is the coroner who carries out a spiritual autopsy on the body of believers? Can we identify the person conducting a postmortem on the church? We certainly can! He is introduced in verse 1 as the one *who has the seven spirits of God and the seven stars.*

Seven spirits in one hand

This does not mean there are seven Holy Spirits operating at large in the world. It does mean there is one Holy Spirit with a sevenfold ministry. The phrase is probably an allusion to the comments found in Isaiah 11:2. Whatever, his is a ministry which is powerful, perfect, and plentiful in the hearts of men. The master key to revival in this—and any—dead church lies with the Spirit of God, this is his sole prerogative (cf. Zechariah 4:6).

Seven stars in the other hand

The seven stars are the messengers in each of the churches, those responsible for pastoral leadership in the local church. They are in the grip of the hand of God! They are controlled by him, held by him, directed and motivated by him. Christ is over all, but he delights to do his work through men.

These twin components are two sides of the same coin. The Spirit of God is actively working in the church and that automatically begs the question, Does the church match his holy character? Alongside his ministry and with his empowerment, the servants of God are working in the church and that poses another question, Does she measure up to her heavenly calling?

Your deeds

Over the years a great work has been done for the Lord in Sardis. Many people have been brought out of darkness into light, many evangelistic missions and special outreach events have been held, many missionaries have gone out to the regions beyond. There was something geared to all the family. These believers made a great show of being spiritual. As someone has said: 'They were Bible-toters and Bible-quoters!' You name it, they certainly did it. In the not too dim and distant past she had been the city's conscience. What a resounding reputation! They are alive! That is what we would be tempted to say; Jesus takes a look and says the exact opposite. Indeed, appearances can be deceptive.

You are dead!

To all intents and purposes, this church was a well-kept mausoleum, a morgue with a steeple. It was beautiful and dignified but inside were the bones of dead men. They were smug in their complacency, living down memory lane. The choir anthem was 'Embalmed in Gilead.' The catchwords of their earlier, better days were still remembered! They thought they had arrived, and were content. They had a superb sanctuary, a beautiful multipurpose building. They enjoyed each other's company. They were going through the motions. All was well outwardly: plenty of activity, packed to the doors, loads of money in the bank, progressive.

Yet, Jesus says, they are dead. They lacked reality. They were artificial. The church was a shrine to the good old days, to better times. There was nothing jubilant or buoyant about it; it was anaemic. It was a corpse wrapped in grave clothes, a church in a coffin. They were spiritually flat-lined. Stiff. What started off as a movement had, over the years, become a monument. Here was the church of the walking dead, full of spiritual zombies.

John MacArthur describes it as '... a museum in which stuffed animals are exhibited in their natural habitats. Everything appears to be normal, but nothing is alive.' She died because she relied on past success, because she allowed sin to creep into the membership, and because she was insensitive to her own spiritual condition.

The living Lord of the church now bares his heart. How it aches! How it pines! How it beats and bleeds!

His appeal

Wake up!

The divine correspondent says the obvious to them; when he opens his mouth, every word comes with a sharp, staccato ring to it, like a rat-a-tat-tat from a machine gun, *Wake up, and strengthen what remains and is about to die, for I have not found your works complete in the sight of my God. Remember, then, what you received and heard. Keep it, and repent.*

If it does anything, this tersely worded command pictures an individual shaking someone who is going into shock, possibly a coma from which there is no return. These words are like a slap in the face. They are like a splash of icy cold water thrown in your face. They are like a sniff of ammonia! The problem is, the people are sound asleep. Jesus says, 'Be alert! Open your eyes! Be vigilant! Come on, people, don't you see what's happening!'

Basically, the Lord wants them to take the first steps towards spiritual renewal and admit there is something wrong. They needed to pull themselves together and shake themselves out of their padded-pew mentality, their brick-walled lethargy, and their stained-glass complacency.

Wise up!

It appears as though they were not fully aware of the dreadful seriousness of their condition, for what little remained, and that was nothing much to write home about, was about to die off.

The candle light was flickering in the wind. To change the pun, they desperately needed to fan the flames. The dying embers can be brought together. Prayer can fan the smallest flame into a mighty blaze.

Work up!

The congregation had no alternative but to repent before the Lord and get back into top gear for God. If Jeremiah had been around in the first century, he would have called the people back to 'the ancient paths' (Jeremiah 6:16), a proven formula for revival and renewal. It is good to guard our spiritual heritage and we sincerely thank God for it, but it is fatal to embalm it! Faith must produce life and works in the here and now! Thank God, there is always a road to recovery. For the genuine believer, failure is never final!

His action

He reminds them at the end of verse 3 of his return when he would *come like a thief.* This was no idle threat he was making in an attempt to gee them up. Far from it! His comments are earthed to reality and etched in the granite of history.

William Ramsay in his commentary explains that the people had twice been conquered by stealth, because they were over confident of their security and unaware of their vulnerability. As I mentioned earlier, the first time they were taken had been seven hundred years earlier when Cyrus was eminently successful in his attempt to take the city. His victorious men entered through a cavity in the battlements of the fortress-like city. The second time this happened, 320 years later, Sardis fell to Antiochus the Great. History has an uncanny way of repeating itself and that was true on this occasion! It was the same again, third time around! Some people never learn!

The Lord speaks here of the hope of his second coming. The problem was the folk in Sardis had lost that keen sense of anticipation. The thought of expectancy had gone from their hearts. They had to learn again to live their lives in light of the soon return of Jesus Christ. They did not know when he would come, but come, he most certainly would. They would need to be ready lest they were caught napping unawares! They had to be sure there were no chinks in their armour!

His assurance

A handful were untainted. Jesus said, *Yet you have still a few names in Sardis, people who have not soiled their garments.* They were spiritually alive and seen as a godly remnant. There is never a day so dark that God does not have his stars to shine! In the days before the Flood, God had righteous Noah and godly Enoch. In the time of universal idolatry, there was saintly Abraham. Even in Sodom, there was Lot! He never leaves himself without a witness to his praise and glory (cf. 2 Kings 19:30-31; Isaiah 10:20-21; Romans 11:5).

They were virtuous but, under God, they would also be victorious. Jesus said, *they will walk with me in white, for they are worthy.* What a marvellous promise he gives them! The prospect of a heavenly investiture. They would enjoy the best of company as they shared sweet fellowship with their Lord. They have been cleansed and brought into a near place with their God. They will be clothed with his purity and stand justified in the sight of God. He says they are worthy but that is only because of the grace of God. At the end of the day, it is all because of him.

Like them, what a standing is ours! What security is ours for our names will remain in the book of life! We should be rejoicing as the happiest people on earth for we are on the winning side! The lesson is absolutely clear, dead bones can live, but only when the wind of God's Spirit breathes upon them.

3:7-13

Philadelphia ... where size counts for nothing

When compared to, say, Ephesus and Smyrna, Philadelphia

was a smaller city – 'smaller in prosperity, smaller in productivity, smaller in prestige.' That said, this city was strategically positioned for major impact. Because of its location, it was hugely significant in the lives that it touched for beyond this relatively small community lay the kingdoms of Lydia, Missia, and Phyrgia. The armies of Caesar were known to march through Philadelphia as they went to and from Rome. Merchants stopped by for refreshments and accommodation going to and from market. Without doubt, Philadelphia was a small cog in a big wheel, but it could not be done without!

No matter how wonderful a place is, there is always a downside. This city sat on a geological fault that made it vulnerable to volcanoes and earthquakes. And, in 17 AD, the world's most devastating earthquake rocked Philadelphia and eleven other cities, levelling the city and reducing it to ruin and rubble. Inevitably, in the years that followed, the foundations of the city were jolted by a series of violent aftershocks. That is when the locals concluded enough is enough, and they moved out to live in the surrounding fields for fear of being buried alive.

Philadelphia ... more than cheese!

The people in this church were lovely and loving. They were definitely not cheesed off! The name Philadelphia actually means, 'brotherly love.' That is what they had, and showed. It was a delightful fellowship, the ideal church. There were not very many of them, only a handful or two; it was a relatively small gathering as numbers go. Yet they were super and superb in their attitude to each other and to the work of the Lord. It may have been weak numerically, but it was truly wonderful.

There is not the slightest hint of rebuke from the Lord. There is nothing but fulsome praise and warm commendation given to it. In his eyes, they scored 10 marks out of a possible 10. Their entire life, inside and out, backward and forward, up and deep down, is pleasing to him. What a testimony this beautiful body of believers had!

It was, according to John Phillips, a revival church: they experienced an *evangelical* revival because they caught a world vision. They experienced an *ecclesiastical* revival because they dealt with those who would have brought a deadening, disruptive influence into the church. They had overcome those who tried to snare them with all sorts of tradition. They also experienced an *eschatological* revival because the truth of the second coming of Jesus was its beacon light.

Charles Finney once said: 'Revival begins when God points his finger at you.' And Gipsy Smyth said: 'If you want revival, go inside your room, close the door, lock it, get on the floor and draw a circle around yourself and pray that God would revive everything inside the circle—not outside.'

And so, the Lord stands before the congregation at Philadelphia, not to offer blame, but blessing. He offers them, not the threat of fearful vengeance, but the prospect of a fresh vision. Here is the gripping story of the little church which tried; a classic illustration of the 'small is beautiful' concept for here is the small church with a big God!

The power of Christ

The Lord is in total charge. He is in command, in the driving seat. He is on the throne, ruling and reigning. It is his authority that is behind the open door. His revelation of himself to them comes straight from his heart; this in contrast to most of the other letters where it is straight from the shoulder.

The righteousness of the King

We see him as one who is *holy* and *true*. He is holy in his character, words, actions, and purposes. He is utterly separate from sin, his character is absolutely unblemished and flawless. In this, Jesus Christ is staggeringly unique. In thought, word, and deed, he is holy. He is wholly holy.

He is also true and that is his intrinsic nature. In a world riddled with error and falsehood, in a society where men fabricate evidence, he is truth personified; he is totally reliable and completely dependable. He is original, he is not a cheap imitation. He is authentic, he is not manufactured. Jesus Christ is the real McCoy.

Because he is *holy*, he is right in his character. Because he is *true*, he is right in his conduct. He could not be different in his actions from what he is in his attributes. He does what he does because he is who he is!

The resources of the King

He also *has the key of David.* You can read about this in Isaiah 22:22, 'I will place on his shoulder the key to the house of David.' The mention of David's name in the equation is an attempt to focus attention on the messianic office as it relates to one who is great David's, greater Son. The one who has the key has authority with immediate access to the treasures of the king. What unsearchable riches are there! The riches of his goodness, grace, and glory!

The regality of the King

He is the one *who opens and no one will shut, who shuts and no one opens.* He opens and shuts doors. When he opens, no man can shut; and when he shuts, no man can open! He is the invincible sovereign. He is all-powerful, omnipotent. He opens the door of salvation. He opens the door to a life of fruitful service. He opens the door of Scripture as we come to him with expectant hearts. If he opens the door, then we must work; if he shuts the door, then we must wait. Thank God for open doors!

How stupid we are when we try to knock down barriers he has deliberately set up! How foolish we are when we fail to walk down paths he has painstakingly cleared! The open door is ever the symbol of a golden opportunity and we should grasp it with open hearts and seize the moment with open hands. A Christian leader used to make this his regular prayer: 'Lord, give me eyes to see, and grace to seize, every opportunity for thee!' That is what the believers did in Philadelphia.

The believers knew exactly what the Lord was talking about when he referred to open doors. The city was, literally, referred to as 'the city of the open door.' It was the doorway to the east. It had been built as a missionary city for the Greek culture and the Greek language to spread throughout the east into what is now modern Turkey. It would be a launch-pad to disseminate Greek philosophy further afield. And they were successful.

The Lord was aware of their weakness but he also knew their willingness! They are reaching out into the regions beyond, rising to the challenge of spreading the gospel. They are located in a most strategic area for they were a gateway to many areas of the ancient world. They are at the crossroads. Now, he says to them: 'There is the open door; there may not be very many of you, but go through it, go on, go forward.'

The Lord knows all about them that there is to know. They are not the strongest nor the most influential, they did not have any great numbers and very few outstanding leaders, there were no unusual talents, they were not in the premier league, they did not have much to offer; but God took them the way they were, he accepted them and used them (the same idea is found in 1 Corinthians 1:26-29). They live from hand to mouth—God's hand to their mouth. Strugglers, yes ... stragglers, no!

The lesson is one we all need to learn: We can be too big for God to use but we can never be too small! We should not be surprised by the potential of one local church, nor should we ever underestimate the power of one person's testimony.

They may have been little in power but they were big in potential. Their commitment to the things that really mattered is a challenge to all. They were so dedicated that they guarded the gospel by adhering to the Word of God. They were known for their biblical fidelity; they were small, but faithful! In many ways, the church at Philadelphia succeeded where the church at Sardis failed. No compromise, no departure, no apostasy.

Their faith was valid. Real. Genuine. Their devotion was

quite special too because here was a group of people with backbone. They were rock solid; men of iron, men of steel, men of conviction. Nothing moved them. They had not been blown off-course with every wind of doctrine. No, they were very much in love with their Saviour, the Lord Jesus Christ.

Charles Swindoll makes the valid comment: 'In a beautiful reflection, the Philadelphian believers mirrored the character of the one who wrote to them. When Jesus looked at them, he saw himself. The church could receive no greater compliment, project no greater image.'

The protection of Christ

He deals principally here with two great issues of major importance.

The hostility of a pagan secular world

He says in verse 9, *I will make those of the synagogue of Satan who say that they are Jews and are not, but lie – behold, I will make them come and bow down before your feet, and they will learn that I have loved you.* The Christians in Philadelphia were getting a rough ride from some of the local Jews. Because of their rejection of Jesus as Messiah, they are branded as those whose allegiance is to the other side, namely, to Satan. Though they claimed they were Jews, that claim was a downright lie. They were economical with the pure truth. Racially, culturally, and ceremonially, they were Jews; but spiritually, definitely not! They did not fit in with Paul's definition of a true Jew, as outlined in Romans 2:28-29.

The Lord reminds them that no matter what is happening around them, and no matter what lies before them, he will still be with them. They could count upon him to stay by their side and go through each harrowing experience with them. He would not, and could not, leave them alone. They have been loyal to him, in return he will not turn his back on them.

The coming hour of global trial

Because you have kept my word about patient endurance, I will keep you from the hour of trial that is coming on the whole world, to try those who dwell on the earth. This is truly wonderful for it indicates that the Lord has a special plan that will keep them (and us) from the worldwide Tribulation which is sure to come! The *hour of trial* is a reference to the Great Tribulation which I will describe in detail in later chapters (cf. Matthew 24:21). Notice, he does not say, 'I will keep you *through* the hour of trial' but *from* the hour of trial. This refers to the moment when millions will be missing, the event we know as the rapture of the saints of God, the believer's ultimate trip when Jesus will catch away his redeemed people for himself (cf. 1 Thessalonians 4:13-18). We clearly see therefore, in this promise, that the church will not go through the Tribulation.

These words, in verse 10, are a powerful encouragement and a motivational incentive to us, especially in such decadent times as we are living at present. They clearly show to us that all saints, sinners, and situations are under his sovereign control. God is still on the throne! Our God reigns! As someone has said: 'If we take care of God's work, he will take care of our battles.'

An old country preacher from the southern states of the USA expressed it like this: 'It is time for our church to wake up and sing up, preach up and pray up and never give up or let up or back up or shut up, until the church is filled up or we go up. Amen!'

The purpose of Christ

I am coming soon. According to verse 11 one day the clouds will part and Christ will return. The thought here is of imminence. What a day, glorious day, that will be! He could come back at any moment, at any time. Nothing else needs to happen. No signs need to be fulfilled. He is coming ... soon! And it may be today!

Hold fast what you have, so that no one may seize your crown. So, with the prospect of a better day just around the corner, the Lord encourages them to hold on. Do not be tempted to surrender! It is not worth it! For when we see him, there will be a crown given to us, that is our reward. We do not want to miss out or lose out, we do not want to be empty handed. One of those great crowns is the crown of life, the symbol of final victory.

The promise of Christ

The one who conquers, I will make him a pillar in the temple of my God. We shall overcome, some day, and when we do, he says, he will make us a pillar in the temple of the Lord! The thought here is of that which is strong and stable. It also incorporates the twin ideas of permanence and immovability. Pillars can also represent honour; in pagan temples they were often carved in such a way as to honour a particular deity. The marvellous promise afforded to us is that we will have an eternal place of honour in the house of God. We will be secure in glory and be there forever. He will take a piece of clay and make it into a pillar!

He will also mark us for we will be identified in three ways. Here we see something of the Lord's infinite greatness in that we bear his name. It depicts ownership, signifying that all true believers belong to God. It suggests something of the intimate, personal relationship we will enjoy with him forever. The Lord's invincible government is reflected in the phrase, *the name of the city of my God.* We will be recognised as a member of the aristocracy of heaven. We belong to no mean city, even the *new Jerusalem.* We have eternal citizenship in heaven's capital city.

He will also write on us his *own new name.* Here is an echo of his inherent glory. When you think about him, he is truly incomparable! The half has not been told. Then, his name was Jehovah ... today, his name is Jesus ... tomorrow, in God's future, his name is something 'no eye has seen, nor ear heard, nor the heart of man imagined, what God has prepared for those who love him' (1 Corinthians 2:9). We must be content with that! Charles Swindoll offers the following upbeat, encouraging words: 'A new name, not just a facelift or a cosmetic alteration but a whole new identity. And Jesus promises that this one will last forever.'

What a church! What a Christ!

3:14-22

Laodicea ... a church that makes God sick

We have eavesdropped on our Lord's assessment of each of the six other churches. Some of them were good, some were bad, some were quite indifferent. There was praise for some and rebuke for others. There was a mixture of commendation and constructive criticism. Churches are not bricks and mortar, they are people, and where you have people, you have problems. Problems should not be seen as a threat but viewed as an opportunity to exercise our faith, to flex our spiritual muscle, and to discover a new dimension in God.

To react like that, we need to have hearts in tune with his great purpose and plan. We need to have ears open to hear what he says. That is the prime reason why the supreme challenge is there as a postscript to every letter. It is not just tagged on at the end for the purpose of effect or because he was unsure of what to say. He says, *He who has an ear, let him hear what the Spirit says to the churches.* The message 2,000 years ago was personal to that church in that generation, but surely, it is relevant to today's church in today's world!

That means the church at Laodicea speaks loud and clear with a stirring challenge in the third millennium. It is epitomised as a lukewarm fellowship. In a city better known for its high finance, high fashion, and high life, the church in Laodicea was at an all-time low. She was on a real downer. She was a fashionable, elitist, rich man's church, yet something significant was tragically missing.

The church, then and now, is called to live in a highly secular society. We are in a world where materialism is god, this is a consumer-oriented age. Here is a church which needed to get its act together and establish some priorities. It needed to sort out its agenda and fix clear goals. In short, here was a church that needed a profound sense of God.

How does the Lord handle this particularly errant fellowship? Well, he does what he has done so often before! He introduces himself in verse 14 to the lackadaisical church of Laodicea in a variety of ways; the contrast is patently obvious as he identifies himself using three divine titles.

He is 'the Amen'

That is a phrase we use every time we pray, it is a Hebrew term of assent. It is a term Jesus used frequently to introduce some important statements. The AV would say, 'verily, verily,' and the NIV would say, 'I tell you the truth.' He could just as easily have said, 'amen, amen.' We say 'amen' at the end of our prayers, or we say 'amen' when someone else is praying. It means we agree with what has been prayed. Jesus is God's affirmation (cf. Isaiah 65:16). He is God's amen! He is God's yes-man. Because Christ is *the Amen* it implies that he will always have the last word.

He is 'the faithful and true witness'

This would indicate that he sees through the sham of the Laodicean church. He sees through their show and shallowness. He tells it like it really is. Why? Because of who he is. He will not dilute the truth because he is the faithful one. He will not distort the truth because he is the one who is true. He communicates the truth, the whole truth, and nothing but the truth. He is not a spin doctor who puts a gloss or a shine on a particular story; what he sees, he says!

As the faithful one, he is faithful to the purposes of God and the people of God.
As the true one, he is true to the Lord's own children.

In our hour of need, he is always there; he is true to his word, for his word is his bond.

He is 'the beginning of God's creation'

This could be translated to read that all creation has its origin in him. Paul was on a similar wavelength when he said in Colossians 1:16, 'For by him all things were created.' In other words, he is the source and origin of creation. Michael Wilcock explains the significance of this title when he writes: 'For the sake of this disastrous church, he presents himself as the beginning, or (less misleadingly) the origin, of God's creation, the one who is able to go right down into the chaotic abyss of Laodicea's failure and make her anew, as he once made the world.'

As the 'Amen' he is the all-conquering one.
As the 'faithful and true witness' he is the all-convicting one.
As the 'beginning of God's creation' he is the all-controlling one.

He analyses their problem

Having introduced himself to the congregation at Laodicea, he now focuses his attention on the many areas of concern which he perceives to be at the root of their diverse problems. He is not impressed, or well pleased, or enamoured with what he sees! No praise. No warm words of commendation. No affirmation. Nothing positive. Only rebuke.

No vitality!

When he looks behind the façade of a healthy exterior, he puts his finger on the problem straightaway. He is aware of all that is happening. He knows all about their appalling compromise and their abject complacency. They did not care! They did not take Christ seriously, they did not take the Bible seriously, they did not take the cross seriously, they did not take sin seriously, they did not take the lost world seriously. As one writer says: 'Being a Christian was like a holy hobby to them!'

He tells them the truth about their spiritual state with remarkable precision. His diagnosis is spot-on. They are sitting on the fence; they lost their vigour because they were neither hot nor cold, they were lukewarm and tepid. G Campbell Morgan wrote: 'Lukewarmness is the worst form of all blasphemy.' He says they are just like the local drinking water, and that was nothing to write home about; it was flat, the sparkle had disappeared, and the fizz was gone!

Jesus is not over the moon with them at all. Theirs is a nominal experience; sitting in a lukewarm bath of religion, their Christianity is flabby and effete. He takes one look at them and, quite honestly, he feels sick. They give him a terrible feeling of nausea. He wants to vomit, to throw up! When God looks at apostasy, he gets angry, and when he looks at indifference, he becomes ill!

No values!

They said they were rich, but he thought differently. They were full of spiritual pride. They had up-to-date statistics to prove the point, the church's annual report was a good read! They reckoned they were streets ahead of the church at the bottom of the next road. The trouble was they measured what they had by human standards, not by God's rule of thumb. As John MacArthur notes: 'They were rich in spiritual pride but bankrupt in saving grace. Believing they were to be envied, they were in fact to be pitied.'

No vision!

There was a blur in their perception of their true condition.

They could not see reality. They could not see the wood for the trees. They were living in a fool's false paradise. They were living in cloud-cuckoo land. They were oozing with seriously inflated egos over a church about to be rejected and they did not seem to see it! They did not see themselves as they really were, they could not see the Lord standing outside the front door, they failed to see the open doors of opportunity to spread the Word. Basically, they were empire builders, immersed in a world of their own making, building their own kingdom.

No vesture!

In the eyes of God, they were naked, wretched, and pitiful. Someone has said about them that 'they sat, they soaked, and they soured!' Jesus saw them in their true colours for he saw them as they really were. What a church! They had their problems!

Let us not jump the gun too quickly, though. It is easy to write them off, but what about our zeal for Jesus? What about our personal sense of values? Where is our treasure? What about our degree of commitment? What about our vision, our goals?

They had seemingly insurmountable problems, and lots of them; how wonderful to realise that God is oozing with grace! He wants the very best for each of us. The chances are they would be stung and angered by his criticisms. When we feel hurt or angry we want to settle the score. Thank God, that Jesus' nature is to offer grace.

He advocates a prescription

He pleads with them in verses 18 and 19 to get their lives sorted out before it is too late when he says, *I counsel you to buy from me gold refined by fire, so that you may be rich, and white garments so that you may clothe yourself and the shame of your nakedness may not be seen, and salve to anoint your eyes, so that you may see.*

They needed a reality to their faith which would come about only when the gold is tried in the fire. It would take trials to bring them into a deeper appreciation of the glories of Christ. He longs for them to be clothed in white garments, suggestive of a life of holiness. The lukewarm lifestyle of the Laodicean church needed to be transformed into a lifestyle of red-hot zeal for the Lord. They needed the cataracts removed from their eyes so that their vision of Christ could be unblurred and undimmed.

It is interesting that in the city of Laodicea there was a renowned medical school. One of the medicinal products, manufactured and exported from that medical centre, was a tablet that sold all over the Roman empire. It was used to heal a wide range of eye ailments; the instructions said to crush the tablet, mix it with a small amount of water, rub it on the eyes, and wait for the healing.

Jesus took a piece of local knowledge and reminded the blind Laodiceans that they needed more than their precious eye salve to see: they needed the truth of God which only Christ could bring to them. They needed a new perspective on life and a new perception of those things of eternal worth and value. We are left in no doubt that the blessings of God are not for sale, neither are they up for grabs; if they want the rich blessings of God, there is a price to pay to have them.

He asserts a priority

This verse is a text we have all known from childhood and it is one that is often used as the basis for a good evangelistic sermon but, in this context, it is definitely not a text for evangelism. It is a stirring appeal to the child of God to realise the possibilities open to him when Christ is at the centre of his life. It is an open letter to the congregation and in it the Lord distinctly says: 'Look, I'm here, the problem is, I'm standing outside the door, and I desperately want to come in!'

We read, *Behold, I stand at the door and knock. If anyone hears my voice and opens the door, I will come in to him and eat with him, and he with me* (verse 20). The thought here is not one of union with Christ, but communion with Christ. The best remedy for backsliding is to be fully occupied with the Lord Jesus. He is thinking about fellowship with a capital F.

He starts knocking on the door of our lives through changing circumstances and he starts calling for a positive response through his Word. He will not force his way into our lives; he will not kick down the door into our hearts; he will not come in all guns blazing; he will never use a sledgehammer to crack a nut. He will wait until he is invited. The reality is, he just wanted to spend time sharing with them. He wanted them to get to know him a little better and, when that happened, both would reap handsome dividends.

He adds a promise

Supper room to throne room! Jesus Christ adds a promise in his final comments in verse 21 by showing us how we can move from one room to another that is bigger and better! We read: *The one who conquers, I will grant him to sit with me on my throne, as I also conquered and sat down with my Father on his throne.*

On the great occasions of state, eastern kings did not occupy a single-seat throne but a broad-based dais. Honoured guests would be invited to sit alongside the monarch and share his glory. Amazing, for that is what Christ promises those who are faithful to him. We will share with him the 'throne of his glory' (Matthew 25:31).

It is through communion with Christ that we find victory and live a life of overcoming. What a noble incentive! One day, we will rule and reign with him! To enjoy rich fellowship with Christ in the kingdom and throughout the countless ages of eternity is sufficient blessing beyond all comprehension. And when we arrive over there, it will surpass our wildest dreams. I cannot think of a better way to end my life and I cannot think of a more challenging way to end a letter.

A higher throne

We are moving into one of the most exciting portions you will come across anywhere in the Word of God. There are many high points in Scripture, many significant peaks in terms of Christian teaching, many key passages which embrace the great doctrines of the Faith, none surpass this duo of chapters, Revelation 4 and 5. Here we are touching the throne! And you cannot get much closer to the Lord than that!

The tremendous theme of exultation woven into the fabric of chapter 4 is: 'Let's worship the Lord—he is the Creator, the giver of life!' On a similar vein, the keynote of chapter 5 is also one of spontaneous worship but this time the difference is one of distinction for the inspired composition is: 'Let's worship the Lord—he is our Redeemer, the giver of new life!' The lyrics of the old gospel song say it succinctly when they capture the wonder of that special moment when 'the great Creator became my Saviour.'

4:1

The incredible experience of John on the Isle of Patmos was that he was given a triple vision of the grace of God, the government of God, and the glory of God. The prophet Micaiah had a similar encounter when he saw the Lord sitting on his glorious throne 'and all the host of heaven standing beside him on his right and on his left' (1 Kings 22:19). 'God reigns over the nations,' declared the Psalmist, 'God sits on his holy throne' (Psalm 47:8). Isaiah was humbled, after the death of King Uzziah, when he saw an earthly throne vacant and a heavenly throne occupied (cf. Isaiah 6:1). An unbelievable moment for Daniel was when he realised that the God of heaven was in total control of events on Planet Earth for that is when he knew in his heart of hearts that God rules and reigns (cf. Daniel 7:9-10).

This illustrious quintet have one factor in common: in one way or another, all touched a higher throne! But John's experience was unique for he was summoned into heaven itself.

After this I looked, John writes, *and behold, a door standing open in heaven. And the first voice, which I heard speaking to me like a trumpet, said, 'Come up here, and I will show you what must take place after this.'*

Even though John was still a prisoner on Patmos and well into his golden years, he is given a preview of coming attractions, a prelaunch disclosure of things to come. He saw a sweeping panorama of God's prophetic programme in advance, a vista of God's agenda for the nations of the world. The message from the throne is: God is not idle—he is active; God is not unseated—he is not up for re-election; God is not absent or distant or forgetful or uncaring—he is unveiling and orchestrating the events of human history. The plot is not lost!

A breathtaking moment! Indeed. What we read in the remaining chapters of Revelation is a record of what John saw with his own two eyes.

The hinge of the book

It is helpful to note that verse 1 begins and ends with the same two words: *after this.* These words actually form the hinge of Revelation. This is a transition as we progress from point number two on to point number three in the index of the book as detailed in 1:19.

Now you see it, now you don't

We discovered in the previous chapter that the Lord has finished his engaging correspondence with the church at Laodicea, the last of the seven letters to the seven churches in Asia Minor. After this, the church is never mentioned again in Revelation. There is a fullstop so far as the church, the body of Christ, is concerned at the end of chapter 3. Seven times in chapters 2 and 3 we read, *He who has an ear, let him hear what the Spirit says to the churches.* Then in 13:9 we read, *if anyone has an ear, let him hear.* Did you detect the double difference there? Number one, the Spirit is missing. Number two, the church is missing!

Why is that the case? The people of God who comprise the church are in heaven while those people, left behind on earth, are suffering in the Tribulation (that is the technical term given to the period of seven years between the two phases of the advent of Christ).

What's in a name?

Another intriguing fact: the church's favourite name for God is Father, but from chapter 4 until the end of chapter 19, he is not once addressed as Father; in actual fact, he is called God, the Lord, the Almighty, and a few other names by which he was commonly known in the Old Testament era.

A heartbeat from heaven

The inclusion of the word *trumpet* in verse 1 is highly suggestive. It bears comparison with 1 Thessalonians 4:13-18 and 1 Corinthians 15:52. When Jesus returns to the air for his redeemed people, the world will not hear the dulcet tones of his voice, nor will they hear the trumpet sound. The ears of the sinner will be deaf and his eyes will be blind. If the truth be told, the rapture of the church will take place so fast that, literally, millions from all around the world will be missing in a fleeting moment. Those who love the Lord will be here on earth one minute and, before you have finished saying their name, they will be with Christ in the Glory before the minute is up! In the 'twinkling of an eye' we will be in eternity ... it is as near as that, only a heartbeat away! Verse 1 is a beautiful illustration of what will happen to God's people when the church age has run its course.

Heaven's open door policy

In chapter 3 we saw a door closed with Christ seeking entrance into a local fellowship of believers; now, in chapter 4, a door is wide open and we behold the regal splendour of our God for the open door leads us through into a throne room where the King is sitting! An open door implies a welcome when you walk through it. John is ushered into the oval office of heaven where the Father, Son, and Holy Spirit sit and confer with one another over important matters of state. Jeremiah was on the ball when he wrote of it in 17:12 as, 'a glorious throne set on high from the beginning.'

Two times in the Apocalypse do we read of an open door. The first one is here in 4:1 and the second is further on in 19:11. The first, someone is going up in response to an invitation to come and see; the second dictates that somebody comes down for there we see the coming King returning to earth on a white stallion!

4:2-3a

The mystery of the throne

For John to get from earth to heaven something miraculous had to happen. There is no way he could get there under his own steam, that was a stark impossibility, a total non-starter; he had to be transported there, courtesy of another. His trip into the heavenly world is best explained by the choice of phrase in verse 2 where it informs us that he *was in the Spirit.* God would take him there. John was not transported into some mystical fantasyland nor was he taken into a daydream world of Disneyesque make-believe for this was no mind expanding hallucinatory vision; for John, this was real, he was taken where he had never been before, he was transported spiritually into the reality of heaven.

When he arrived, John could not believe his eyes! Sensational! Spectacular! Amazing! It defied description for human language fails to convey what is seen; it is awesome, strange, and unexpected. Like dear old John, we feel out of our depth for what we have here is something outside the realm of normal human experience. Most modern-day people who claim to have visions of heaven tend to emphasise the trivial and bizarre. But John's vision focused on the glorious throne of God and the ineffable majesty of the one who sits on it.

The Bible records, *and behold, a throne stood in heaven, with one seated on the throne.* It is interesting to note that in verses 5, 6 and 9 there are four prepositions or phrases which all specifically relate to the throne: *on* the throne, *around* the throne, *from* the throne, and *before* the throne. The mere mention of a throne in heaven is enough to convince us that the Lord is sovereign and in charge of global affairs; his throne is immovable and permanent—when all else has come and gone, his throne will still be there! John MacArthur reminds us: 'That is a comforting realisation in light of the horror and trauma of the endtime events about to be revealed in chapters 6-19.'

On the throne

John sees someone sitting on the throne in a posture of someone ruling and reigning! The thought is not one of resting because the work of redemption has been accomplished, but reigning because judgment is about to take place. Do you see how he describes him in verse 3? He says, *And he who sat there had the appearance of jasper and carnelian.*

The one who occupies the throne is described as a stone. That is hard to imagine. How can any man even begin to describe God? But, the more you stop and think about it, the more you realise how wonderful a description it really is. Like Moses before him, John did not see the actual face of God. No man can do that and live to tell the rest of the story. John simply records that God revealed himself in a dazzling nimbus of coloured lights. It was a scintillating display of colour brilliantly refracting all the colours of the spectrum.

A jasper is a clear gem, as clear as crystal (21:11), a bit like a diamond. It is true to say that the glory of God is more perfect than any gem displayed in an upmarket jewellers on the High Street. The carnelian is a stone comparable to the ruby.

The jasper speaks of the rigid nature of the government of God. His laws are fixed, firm, unyielding, unbending, and unrelenting. That is what today's world badly needs, a firm hand. The jasper is, therefore, symbolic of his government and the way he runs it. No ground is given with the divine 'not an inch' policy.

The carnelian is suggestive of the righteous nature of the government of God. It is a deep fiery, flashing, blood-red stone, and it powerfully reminds us that God is 'a consuming fire' (Hebrews 12:29). You will remember that the fire on Israel's altars was to burn on and on, it was never to go out (cf. Leviticus 6:8-13). So long as sin exists, God's attitude toward sin is one of burning holiness and blazing wrath. His anger against sin burns and flashes like the radiant glow of the carnelian.

When you put the jasper and carnelian together, they underline the humanity connected with the government of God. The high priest in Israel wore on his multicoloured outer garment, the ephod, a breastplate of twelve precious stones; on each stone was engraved a name of one of the twelve tribes of Israel. They were always on his heart when he went into the presence of God on their behalf, and we all know the heart is the place of love and affection. The first stone (representing Reuben) and the last stone (representing Benjamin) of the twelve sons of Jacob was a jasper and a carnelian. As an aside, it is also possible that the names of Reuben ('behold, a son') and Benjamin ('son of my right hand') pictures God the Son, the Lord Jesus Christ, sitting at his Father's right hand in Glory.

4:3b-6

The majesty of the throne

When we look at the second part of verse 3 we discover there that *around the throne was a rainbow that had the appearance of an emerald.* This reminds us ...

His judgment is independent

To mention that the rainbow went around the throne like a circle underlines the truth that perfection is symbolised. It also represents eternity for a circle has no beginning or end. Because it was not merely an arc, but a complete circle, it indicates that in heaven all things are completed. The fact it was emerald in colour intimates that the anticipated judgment is directly related to Planet Earth.

His judgment has integrity

The whole scenario is a reminder that, in the final analysis, judgment when it comes will be in keeping with the covenant of God. It speaks of a God who keeps his promises and who honours every commitment he has made. That is detailed for us as far back as Genesis 9:12-17 when God entered into a covenant with Noah which, he said, would continue 'for all generations to come.'

Even though the judgment anticipated here is imminent, the presence of the rainbow is a tangible token that God will be merciful when he strikes the earth. A similar truth is echoed in the impassioned prayer of Habakkuk where he pleads with the Lord, 'in wrath remember mercy' (Habakkuk 3:2). As John MacArthur has said: 'God's attributes always operate in perfect harmony. His wrath never operates at the expense of his faithfulness; his judgments never abrogate his promises. God's power and holiness would cause us to live in abject terror were it not for his faithfulness and mercy.'

A rainbow generally appears after the storm has passed. It normally appears in the sky when the storm has subsided, and abated. But, here in chapter 4, we see the rainbow before the storm! We infer from this that, so far as the Christian is concerned, the storm is something we do not have to worry about. It will not affect the church at all for the emerald can also be taken to signify the colour of life. If that is the case, then the rainbow is a cameo of eternal life which guarantees that the future of the people of God is something to look forward to with bated breath, rather than a feeling of dread and apprehension.

The royal court

The next major item is found in verse 4, where we read that, *around the throne were twenty-four thrones, and seated on the thrones were twenty-four elders, clothed in white garments, with golden crowns of gold on their heads.*

This is the first time we come across these noble individuals where their relationship to the throne is of more than passing interest. They are around the throne of God in heaven and that is what needs to be emphasised. It is apparent that the rainbow was around the throne vertically while these persons are sitting around the throne horizontally. They are, as it were, the king's court. They function as a kind of jury and they underline the formal nature of the proceedings which John is privileged to watch. Their role is not to determine whether man is guilty or innocent, their primary role is to approve the righteous acts of the judge of all the earth.

The royal courtiers

Can we identify these twenty-four elders? Who are they?

Are they angels? I do not think they are angels for a couple of reasons. Number one, angels are not numbered and you find that alluded to in Hebrews 12:22 where the writer is talking about the 'the city of the living God, the heavenly Jerusalem.' He goes on to tell us, 'You have come to...innumerable angels in festal gathering.' We have here a great gathering of celebrating angels whom we join in praising God.

The second reason is that angels are not crowned or enthroned. When you look at 7:11 and compare it with 5:8-11, you find that the elders are clearly distinguished from the angels and the crown which they wear is the victor's crown (the Greek word *stephanos*) and we have no evidence in Scripture that angels receive rewards.

Are they the redeemed? The elders here probably represent the people of God in heaven, a people enthroned and rewarded. There were twenty-four courses of priests who came from the line of Aaron in the Old Testament temple system (cf. 1 Chronicles 24:3-5, 18). When Daniel saw the thrones set up in 7:9 they were empty but, when John saw them, they had been filled. Could it be since there were twelve tribes of Israel and twelve apostles that the number twenty-four symbolises the completion of the people of God? These elders, therefore, comprise the leaders of our heavenly delegation.

Respected Bible teacher Harry Ironside put the case concisely, when he wrote: 'When the twenty-four elders met in the temple precincts in Jerusalem, the whole priestly house was represented. The elders in heaven represent the whole heavenly priesthood. In vision they are seen—not as a multitudinous host of millions of saved worshippers, but just twenty-four elders, symbolising the entire company.'

'The entire picture,' one writer notes, 'is one of dignified seriousness, instant availability, and deep, genuine sincerity in service. There was no confusion, no casualness, no resistance, and no procrastination in the Lord's court.'

The golden crown

The crowns they wear are available to each of us. There are five crowns mentioned in Scripture which are given as rewards to the Lord's own people.

The *crown of incorruption* (cf. 1 Corinthians 9:25) is given specially to those who live a disciplined life. It is for all those who run the race of life with a clear goal in view and a definite sense of purpose. The *crown of life* (cf. James 1:12) is for those who, with patience, endure the hardest of trials. It is for those who hang in there when the going is incredibly tough. The *crown of rejoicing* (cf. 1 Thessalonians 2:19-20) is designed for those who joyously express their faith. It is for those who are happy to share their faith with others and who take seriously the Great Commission in that they pull out all the stops as they seek to win men and women to Jesus Christ. The *crown of glory* (cf. 1 Peter 5:1-4) is given particularly to those who show faithfulness to the truth of Scripture in all their ministry of the Word of God. The *crown of righteousness* (cf. 2 Timothy 4:8) is designated for those who love his appearing. It is for those keen believers who scan the horizon as they eagerly await the return of Jesus Christ.

There is the potential for us to win something in that final day when we cross the finish line in a blaze of glory! Having said that, the downside is the New Testament also makes it very clear that there will be those in heaven who have nothing to show for it. Men and women who have nothing but leaves for the Master, who are there by the skin of their teeth. Because of the amazing grace of God, 'they are,' as Paul advises us in 1 Corinthians 3:15, 'saved, but only as through fire.' They are the ones who have wasted their lives on God's second best and who, as John says in his epistle, have lost their reward (cf. 1 John 2:28; 2 John 8). The possibility of securing a crown has been taken away from them.

The white robes

The group of elders whom we read of in verse 4 are said to be clothed in white robes and have crowns of gold on their heads. That, in itself, is most instructive for we read in the letters to the seven churches that these are the promises given to those who overcome (2:10; 3:5, 21). Again, the white garments symbolise Christ's righteousness imputed to believers at salvation. That is another pointer in favour of these men being identified with the church of Jesus Christ.

Their awesome environment

I was captivated when I read the words of Psalm 89:7 to find that, no matter how wonderful and glorious it is for these men to be in the immediate presence of the Lord, to be so near to him, to be within a hair's breadth of him, their elevation to such unthinkable heights fades into oblivion when we realise that the Lord 'is awesome above all who are around him.' It does not matter one iota who you are or how close you are, the eternal God is still centre stage. The spotlight is shining on him! He is transcendent, unequalled, and unrivalled. Our God is truly magnificent!

'Worthy, O worthy are You, Lord!
Worthy to be thanked and praised and worshipped and adored!'

A sound and light show

We discover from verse 5 that *from the throne came flashes of lightning, and rumblings and peals of thunder.* It was not only what John saw with his eyes which was of considerable magnitude, it was also what he heard with his ears. John was treated to a sound and light show which was out of this world in terms of its impact on him as a spectator. The fast moving proceedings going on before him are accompanied by terrifying sights and sounds: thunder and lightning! The atmosphere was electric, highly charged with activity and energy. It is more than enough to make any grown man quake in his boots; it is a vivid reminder to all of us that it is 'a dreadful thing to fall into the hands of the living God' (Hebrews 10:31 NIV).

The simplest way to explain it is that this sensational display announces a coming storm which will manifest God's presence, God's power, and God's wrath in a mighty way. The combined forces of nature are harnessed and used by him to illustrate the power which he has at his disposal. This is not a one-off. It is something which is repeated several times in the book as a kind of reference point. On every occasion they are mentioned, they are indicative of the judgment of God against rampant evil. You find these audio visual symbols spoken of in 8:5, 11:19 and 16:18.

These phenomena are closely associated with the monumental moment when God gave the Law on Mount Sinai. Moses records in Exodus 19:16 that the mountain was covered by dark clouds, lit by flashes of lightning, and the earth shook constantly with great thundering rumbles. In fact, the sight was so awesome and impressive that the people of Israel were so stunned with fear that they were numb. I think we can safely assume that these symbols represent the comprehensive judgment of God.

Seven lamps

The same verse informs us that *before the throne were burning seven torches of fire, which are the seven spirits of God.* The reference here is to the presence of the Holy Spirit on the morning of judgment. He is there in all his fulness and acting in the role of prosecutor of the human race.

His work today in relation to the sinner is to reprove the world of 'sin, righteousness, and judgment to come' (John 16:8-11). In that final day, when the age of grace has come to an end, as the omniscient one, he will have all the available facts at his disposal. No stone will be left unturned. All documentation will be laid bare before him and he will be seen to do what is right before God as the judge of all the earth.

In this sighting of the Spirit, he is pictured not as the inspiring tongue of fire, or the warmth of an illuminating candle, or the soft flutter of a dove, but as a divine war torch as in Judges 7:16-20 and Nahum 2:3-4. James Allen concludes: 'This new symbol reflects this new ministry in the Tribulation days.' The implication is that the comforter of those who love Christ will be the consumer of those who wilfully reject him!

It is fascinating to compare the seven lamps with the seven-branched lampstand or *menorah* located in the holy place of the tabernacle and temple. Its main function was to cast light on the ark of the covenant and the mercy seat in the holy of holies. In a similar vein, the chief ministry of the Holy Spirit is to throw light on Jesus Christ in our lives so that we can see him and understand him better.

A sea of glass

Verse 6 provides us with a most unusual piece of data for we read, *and before the throne there was as it were a sea of glass, like crystal.* Something similar is mentioned in 15:2 where we read, *And I saw what appeared to be a sea of glass mingled with fire.* While the latter one is mingled with fire, this one is definitely not.

When you backtrack to Exodus 24:10 you find that Moses and a number of eminent leaders among the people received a similar manifestation of the presence of the Lord. We read that 'under his feet as it were a pavement of sapphire stone, like the very heaven for clearness.'

In John's day, ordinary glass would have been anything but clear; it was more like a cloudy brown bottle-glass. Steve Wilmshurst makes that point that 'glass that was clear as crystal would have been staggeringly expensive, so again this is an image of infinite value as well as stunning beauty.'

It is a well established fact that ancient monarchs created something similar in front of their thrones. Such a no go, don't come too near area, indicated the separation between the king and his subjects. It emphasised their sense of royalty, gave them a seriously inflated ego, and made them feel distinctly superior. They were aloof and much preferred it that way; to all intents and purposes, they were unapproachable!

Perhaps the primary point of the sea of glass before the throne of God is to picture the unsullied holiness, transcendent majesty, and purity of God himself. This simply underscores the fact that he is wholly separate from his creation; it underlines the fact that he is God. The transparency of that sea of glass could reasonably draw attention to God's penetrating gaze into all things that take place on earth. He misses absolutely nothing, seeing all things!

Cheer leaders in heaven

Around the throne, on each side of the throne, are four living creatures. These creatures resemble the cherubim that the prophet Ezekiel saw in his visions in the early chapters of his prophecy and they are mentioned no fewer than twelve times in the first ten chapters of his book. When we listen to their praise in verse 8 they remind us of the seraphim of Isaiah 6. It seems, therefore, that this group of four angels has a distinctive role to play in the unfolding drama of God's plan.

Their proximity to God. These angels are closer to God than the other spirit messengers, as well as the elders, in that they have a unique position in relation to the throne.

Their role. It is well within the bounds of possibility to describe this quartet of angels as the worship leaders of heaven when you see the response to their actions. They certainly inspire everyone else in heaven to pour out their worship toward the one who sits upon the throne. They celebrate the government of God in their capacity as cheer leaders. They are intimately involved for they are at the heart of divine government.

Their significance. I was intrigued to read that *they are full of eyes in front and behind.* This statement is highly suggestive of the omniscience of the one who sits on the throne. These angelic beings do his bidding with a deep awareness of his desire and plan. The eyes are often used to represent the wisdom of God. They enable us to think about his incredible powers of discernment, they focus on the remarkable insight which he has into every event of life, they home in on the fact that he is all-knowing.

Their mystery. We discover in verse 8 that *each of them with six wings, are full of eyes all around and within.* It is obviously difficult to visualise such a heavenly being, we have never seen one nor met one! At times, it can seem a little bizarre, there is almost an air of mystery surrounding them. It is surreal. It is the kind of scene you expect to see in a Steven Spielberg movie! Nevertheless, no matter how weird they may appear, they are intrinsically wonderful because of the brilliant job assigned to them. What a tremendous privilege is theirs!

4:7

Talking angels

In this verse, we are provided with an identikit picture of the four living creatures: *The first living creature like a lion, the second living creature like an ox, the third living creature with the face of a man, and the fourth living creature like an eagle in flight.* There are a couple of ways in which we can look at these four living creatures:

As symbols of God's creation and covenant. The faces of the living creatures parallel God's definitive statement in Genesis 9:9-10 where we read of the covenant he made with Noah, 'I establish my covenant with you and your offspring after you, and with every living creature that is with you, the birds, the livestock, and every beast of the earth with you, as many as came out of the ark; it is for every beast of the earth.'

The divine covenant is with Noah and you see that reflected in the face of the man; the birds are depicted by the flying eagle; the livestock are represented by the face of an ox; and all the other beasts correspond with the face of the lion. This view is given street cred because of the presence of the emerald rainbow around the throne which again is a sign of the creation covenant. God has a covenant with his creation and he rules his creation from his throne. The implication is that irrespective of what happens down here, his works will continue to praise him and all nature will join hands in worshipping him.

As an illustration of Christ. Matthew is the royal Gospel of the King and is well illustrated by the lion. Mark emphasises the servant aspect of the Lord's ministry and is best seen in the ox. Luke presents Christ as the compassionate Son of Man and is obviously portrayed in the face of the man. The last Gospel correspondent, John, conveys the idea that Christ is the Son of God, magnifying his deity and is, therefore, best likened to the flying eagle.

No matter which of the two views is your preferred option, two facts are beyond dispute. Fact one: That each of the four faces reflect one particular aspect of the likeness of the Lord. John Phillips has commented in a rather succinct manner: 'They are so much like him because they are so much with him!' Fact two: That they appear in this vision to enhance further the significance and glory of the throne of God.

It seems what they are doing is even more important. These living creatures are saturated with a sense of the felt reality of the presence of God all around them. They are strangely aware of the closeness of God. The whole atmosphere is permeated with the undiluted wonder of their worship and praise.

4:8

Singing angels

The four living creatures cannot contain themselves, they are bursting at the seams! *Day and night they never cease to say, 'Holy, holy, holy, is the Lord God Almighty, who was and is and is to come.'*

And so, all day, every day, all night, every night, they joyfully extol the wonders of his holiness, they magnify his power and ability, they declare the truth that God is eternal. It is a continuous oratorio of praise and worship. It is unstoppable!

Angels celebrate and recognise the holiness of God. Three times over they acknowledge it. It is a triple affirmation of who he is in person and nature. The Puritan preacher, Jonathan Edwards, has written: 'Holiness is more than a mere attribute of God, it is the sum of all his attributes, the outshining of all that God is.'

That they repeat the word *holy* three times may be for added emphasis; they really believe it, they have no doubts as to its veracity, they are totally committed to it and know it is true. It may be a coded reference to the Trinity, God in three persons, and in that sense, each usage of the word refers to one member of the Godhead.

When they address him as *Lord God Almighty* they appreciate something of his power, his omnipotence. Here is the God who can do anything, but fail! This was how the Lord revealed himself to Abraham so long ago, as one who is the strongest, most powerful being, utterly devoid of any weakness, one whose conquering power and overpowering strength none can oppose. He is the God who can do it!

The name *Almighty* is used nine times in Revelation. The only other time it is mentioned in the New Testament is in 2 Corinthians 6:18. Having said that, it is found at least 31 times in Job and that is a book which puts the spotlight on the power of God in the world of nature. The picture emerging is fairly clear. Here is a God who acts, moves, and performs and, every time he does something at a personal level, on a national scale, or even on a global front, it never contradicts his holiness. His attributes and actions are working in perfect harmony.

The final phrase in the verse which encompasses three tenses is one we came across in the first chapter. It speaks of a God who is everlasting in his nature: he is above time, beyond time, and outside of time. By the same token, he is ever present in current affairs. He is the God of today, the God of now!

4:9-10

Praise is contagious!

Did you see what happened when the four living creatures sang their praises to the Lord? Their praise triggers off an immediate impromptu response from the elders; it is contagious, infectious! *And whenever the living creatures give glory and honour and thanks to him who is seated on the throne, who lives forever and ever, the twenty-four elders fall down before him who is seated on the throne and worship him who lives forever and ever. They cast their crowns before the throne.*

The net result is that heaven reverberates with generous thanksgiving and praise unto the Lord. The whole place resonates with an unfinished symphony of joyful worship. When they fall down before the exalted Lord, they give him his proper place, they recognise his sole authority and peerless position, they take the place of abject humility before the throne of God. When they cast their crowns at the feet of the Sovereign Lord, they realise that before him no one else is worthy to wear a crown. His is the singular right to rule and reign. He alone deserves the adoration, adulation, and acclaim of his people.

The thought behind the word *worship* in verse 10 is the telling forth of the worth of God. What you think of God will be reflected in how you worship him, in the worth you ascribe to him. Someone has coined the phrase that worship is a royal acclamation of his worth. Like the elders and the four living creatures, we do well to follow their example and become active members of the Lord's appreciation society!

4:11

Praise is God-centred!

The stanza which the elders sing to him says, *Worthy are you, our Lord and God, to receive glory and honour and power, for you created all things, and by your will they existed and were created.* The theme of their song is on God's glory manifested in creation. Basically, they are acknowledging that he has the right to redeem and judge his creation. Their song anticipates paradise lost becoming paradise regained!

> *It tells me what he deserves:*
> God deserves glory, honour, and power.
> *It tells me why he deserves it:*
> He is the great creator and sustainer of all things.
> He is the one who brought something out of nothing.
> He is the one who keeps it all together.

It was John Calvin who said that 'creation is the theatre of his glory.' The psalmist David says as much in the opening verses of Psalm 19. When that truth grips your heart and mind, you cannot do anything else but praise him.

Our response. The best response is to borrow the words that we have here in verse 11 and make them a personal tribute to the one who is our God of grace and glory. When you sing a song like that down here and when you hear a song like this emanating from over there, you realise there is nothing boring about heaven, nothing dull about the home of the redeemed! It is a land of eternal song, where praise is the norm!

These few words are a stirring melody of pure theology, biblical doctrine set to music. God is seen as the centre of everything, in the driving seat, and on the throne. Heaven rules ... it is as simple as that! For John, the throne of God, the real throne, is not in Rome, just as today it is not in London, Paris, Moscow, Beijing, or Washington. If the world's story is a great drama, here is the wonderful truth: the Director's chair is still occupied. Our God is on his throne!

Revelation 4 holds far more than just a casual glimpse into the world of heaven and the world of tomorrow. It is a vivid collage of images which focus our eyes on what true worship should be, at all times, and in all places.

CHAPTER 5

Ode to Jesus!

Unforgettable! That is one way to describe John's experience when ushered into the throne room of heaven. It took his breath away. He is lost for words, even spellbound. The indescribable thrill for John is to see the Lamb become the centre of everything—he sees him in a place of preeminence; and, slowly but surely, John is occupied with the Lamb, captivated by the one in the midst of the throne. The Lamb is the theme of their song, the centre of their thoughts, and the object of their adoration. Why? Well, over there, 'the Lamb is all the glory in Immanuel's land!'

Now, for John, the Lamb steps from the shadows into the spotlight and every eye is focused on him. His every move is watched. That is what the poet had in mind when he wrote: *Lamb of God, our souls adore thee, While upon thy face we gaze.*

5:1

The scroll

Then I saw in the right hand of him who was seated on the throne a scroll written within and on the back, sealed with seven seals.

What is it? The scroll is an official document that determines the outcome of life on Planet Earth. It contains the secrets of our world's affairs and its history. It unveils the destiny of the nations and shows the crisis and climax of global history. It is the title deeds of earth and represents all that the Father promised to the Son because of his sacrifice at Calvary.

Why was it sealed? Roman law required that a will be sealed seven times. History confirms that the wills of both Caesar Augustus and the Emperor Vespasian were sealed in this way. The book nestling in the outstretched hand of God is a binding document relevant to the redemption of the world. It belongs to one who has paid the price, therefore, he has the legal right to open it and reveal what is written on it.

We need to remember that many of the symbols in Revelation are best interpreted in light of the Old Testament. This one goes back to Jeremiah 32, a chapter which explains the thinking behind Jewish law as regards the redemption of a piece of land. Its primary purpose was to help those in Israel who fell behind with the repayment of their debts, who, as a result, automatically lost their land. The land was forfeited, but they were not without hope, because they had the right to buy back the land at some point in the future.

Even if they did not take advantage of this facility, even if they could not, the law made it absolutely clear that, after a prescribed period of time, their heir or next of kin could buy it. In this way, the land remained in the family and could be handed down from generation to generation.

In Jeremiah 32 God told his servant, the prophet, that his cousin Hanamel would ask him to redeem a field at Anathoth in the territory of Benjamin. Jeremiah did all he was meant to do and he bought it for a sum of seventeen shekels of silver. But there is more! When his cousin lost the plot of land, two scrolls or contracts containing the terms of reference for redeeming the land were drafted. One unsealed scroll became a public record and was there for all to see. The second scroll was rolled up, sealed with seven seals, and placed for safe storage in a clay jar in the temple. It was brought out only when someone showed proof of his right to redeem the land. After this happened, the temple priest would retrieve the scroll, unseal it, and read it. If everything was in order, the redeemer would receive it and be recognised as the rightful owner of the land.

Why writing on both sides? This is quite amazing for the ancients hardly ever wrote on both sides of a scroll. Generally, only one side was formed smooth for writing, while the reverse was rough and uneven. A scroll with writing on both sides is symbolic of a full and important message. It suggests that it contains the full story, the complete script of God's plan.

Why was it written? The fact that God's plan was written in the form of a scroll rather than simply being revealed by a voice is of huge significance. A written scroll is symbolic of that which is permanent. It is about truth which is indelible. What God has written, no one can amend! It is truth unchanged, and unchanging!

5:2

The challenge

And I saw a mighty angel proclaiming with a loud voice, 'Who is worthy to open the scroll and break its seals?' He is enquiring, Who is worthy to rule the world? Who is fit to rule the world? Who can unravel the plot?

Who is the angel?

The word *mighty* in relation to the angel could emphasise the importance of the angel and his message but it could also be a clue as to which angel is involved. Some Bible teachers hold that it refers to the angel Gabriel whose name means 'strength of God.' You will recall, it was Gabriel who communicated to Daniel about future events (cf. Daniel 8:16).

The Greek word for *proclaiming* speaks of a herald passing on the precise message which he has been given. He would make no comments on it, he would add no commentary to it, he would not attempt to explain it in any way; he would, simply, tell it like it is!

The fact that he conveyed the message with *a loud voice* implies that his message is one of great concern and of greater urgency. It underlines the gravity of the message and the sheer importance of what is being said. It is God's Word and cannot be taken lightly. God has spoken and that is it!

Who is worthy?

The question posed by the angel is a probing one, for he asked, *Who is worthy?* He did not ask, Who is willing? Down through the years many have been willing, keen, and enthusiastic to rule the world; it has been the dream of world leaders and the aspiration of dictators. The prospect of world domination has appealed to quite a few across the decades. For many religions this has been their avowed intention—their goal and ambition—to rule the world! There are people today who are devotees of one cult or another who are fanatical in their pursuit of global supremacy, and woe betides anyone who stands in their way!

This has been the driving force behind many individuals over the centuries; it remains the ultimate thing to play for in the hands of some of those who are major players on the stage of world politics. Some of the key movers and shakers in today's generation will tell you as much. They have no inhibitions. This is what fires them. They eat it, drink it, sleep it ... it is a passion! Yes, they are willing! There is no question about that!

Maybe you are thinking, 'Ah, that's a bit far-fetched, you're pushing it too far, Sam.' Not really! When you look back through the annals of history, it has all happened before and, we all know, history has an uncanny way of repeating itself!

You only have to go as far back as Nebuchadnezzar to see what I mean. He was Number One in the pecking order so far as Babylon was concerned, but his empire soon fell. Alexander the Great thought he achieved a Utopian empire. He wept when there were no more worlds to conquer! In the space of a year, he was a dead man, and within a handful of years, his empire disintegrated. Julius Caesar led his legions across the face of Europe to impose the Pax Romana upon the world by force of arms. History tells us that Rome ultimately fell; there was moral corruption on the inside and there were assaults from the outside by northern barbarians. Charlemagne and Napoleon, each in his own way and own time, sought to place the world under the banner of France; Adolf Hitler in the last great war envisioned a worldwide Reich that would last for a millennium.

The graveyards of history are littered with fallen conquerors and their shattered dreams. They are yesterday's men. The best of men and worst of men have all gone down this road. They have one common denominator, *they all failed because not one was worthy!*

5:3

The response

And no one in heaven or on earth or under the earth was able to open the scroll or look into it. The question which echoed around the world was met with stony silence! The response is nil. Nothing stirred, not a single person moved. Heaven is searched in a vain attempt to find someone who can open the scroll, not even the angels who are before the throne of God can do anything about it. Not a single individual on earth has the ability to do anything about it: no man or woman, no politician, no prime minister or president, no world banker or industrialist, no pope or archbishop, no philosopher or leading thinker, no revolutionary. No one! And with an incredible stroke of the quill on the papyrus, we are told that no one under the earth has the power to do anything about it either: no fallen angels, no spirits of departed men, not even the prince of darkness himself!

It is an eerie silence. There is a hush all around and you can feel the tension in the air. You can sense the impotence of man when faced with such a rousing challenge. This is a verse which beyond all others puts creation firmly in its place!

5:4

The impact

The fruitless search tears John apart. He is emotionally distraught for we read that he *began to weep loudly because no one was found worthy to open the scroll or to look into it.* Poor John! He is broken hearted. Devastated, he breaks down and floods into tears. He just cannot control his feelings any longer. He is a fully grown man, yet he cries here like a young child who has lost its favourite toy.

John knows this world needs redemption, he knows it needs a leader. He knows the scroll must be opened and the seals broken for the purposes of God to be fulfilled. The fact that there was no one worthy to do it spelt gloom into the mind of John. Horror gripped his soul, hopelessness gripped his heart, helplessness gripped his mind! Anne Graham Lotz says: 'He must have sobbed and sobbed with shame for the failure of the entire human race to be what God had originally intended it to be!'

If this was the way it was going to be, he felt his life was in vain; it meant he had been exiled for no apparent reason. His many friends had been martyred for a lost cause. He weeps because he feels the plan of God will not come to pass nor come to fruition, it will all grind to a premature halt, the brakes will be applied to the unfolding drama of redemption. This is what really bothers him, this is the big problem, hence his display of raw emotion.

This is the first time any man ever shed a tear in heaven! The good news is, it will be the last for, as the old song tells us, 'Tears will never stain the streets of heaven.' Before you and I reach that far better land, we are told at the end of the book that *he will wipe away every tear from their eyes.*

5:5

The solution

The silence is broken as one of the elders says to John, *Weep no more; behold, the Lion of the tribe of Judah, the Root of David, has conquered, so that he can open the scroll and its seven seals.* It is a moment of high drama. God has solved the problem! The twenty-four elders of the heavenly council who meet in session around the throne know the answer. One of them moves across to where John is standing and divulges the secret to him. He informs him that someone has been found who is worthy and tells him exactly who that someone is.

In coded language, the elder introduces him as the *Lion of the tribe of Judah, the root of David.* John knows exactly who the elder is referring to, he knows well his Old Testament theology: it is the Lord Jesus Christ! It can be no other! He matches the description like no one else. We know that to be true. John knew that to be the case. It seems he just needed to be reminded of it another time.

The Messiah: The two names given to Christ in verse 5 are significant Jewish titles. The average Jew would be familiar with them because they are steeped in the ancient traditions of Judaism. They refer to a couple of old prophecies which predict that there would come one from the tribe of Judah and from the family of David who would ultimately rule the world. The first is mentioned away back in Genesis 49 where we find Jacob on his deathbed. He has his twelve sons standing around and he has a special word for each one. In verses 8-12 he pronounces a blessing on his son, Judah. The second reference is mentioned in Isaiah 11:1-2.

These twin titles find their fulfilment when they converge in one person. Like two great rivers they come together from different angles and form one which then flows on throughout eternity. They merge in the Messiah, the Christ, the Redeemer, the Saviour of the world. He is the focal point of world history and Bible prophecy.

The references here to the *Lion of Judah* and the *Root of David* are clear signs that Israel is coming back to centre stage as the end of human history approaches. As the scroll begins to unroll, God is calling Israel to the ultimate fulfilment of promises made to her so long ago. All of earth's history is moving toward a climax and the key to it all is the nation of Israel. The key to understanding history, the only way to make sense of history, is to see where Israel fits in the picture. The earth cannot be blessed until the nation of Israel is blessed (cf. Psalm 67)!

Even though the Messiah came to Israel and Israel rejected its Messiah, and even though God has chosen the church as his instrument of ministry to the world from the time of Christ until now, the time of Israel's full restoration is just around the corner. It is coming and it is not too far distant! The Old Testament prophets foretold it and John describes it here in Revelation; the Messiah, the promised Lion of Judah, the Root of David, is coming to tie up the loose ends and bring to a glorious finale the consummation of the purposes of God.

Jesus alone has triumphed!

There is no human solution to the big problems facing the world today, there is no earthly panacea for the evils of the human race, there is no human answer to the important questions man is asking right now. In the words of the song, our Lord is 'the Christ of every crisis.' He is the only one who can undo the tangles of life. He is the only one who can unravel the mysteries of this world. He is the one the Apostle John was told to look at, to fix his eyes on.

His titles: *The Lion of the tribe of Judah, the Root of David.* Each word in the title is worth pondering over, each word in the name has something special to say. It plugs the gaps in our thinking as to who Jesus really is. Here we are given a marvellous opportunity to dig a little deeper and, when we do that, we unearth some priceless treasures.

> *The lion tells me of his majesty.*
> *The tribe suggests to me his humanity.*
> *The thought of Judah conveys to me his nationality.*
> *The root speaks of his deity.*

We need to understand so far as his humanity was concerned, he had his roots *in* David; but, so far as his deity is concerned, he is the Root *of* David. At one and the same time, he is both David's Lord and great David's, greater Son. He is the Eternal One, the Ancient of Days, the God who is from everlasting to everlasting.

The mention of the name David reminds me of his royalty.

Did you see what he has done? He has conquered! He has triumphed! He has prevailed! And that speaks of his victory. We know this to be absolutely true. It is watertight.

John goes on to advise us that *he can open the scroll and its seven seals.* Here is one who, in response to the question from the angel, can step forward into the limelight and take the scroll and do what needs to be done in relation to it. Here is one who is worthy! The elder said to John, *Behold.* When John turned around, what do you think he saw? Did he see a lion?

5:6

What John saw: a lamb!

And between the throne and the four living creatures and among the elders I saw a Lamb standing, as though it had been slain. What a moment it must have been for John! He was expecting a lion and he saw a lamb! I wonder what his initial reaction was? Scripture is silent, it does not tell us.

Seems strange, yet the more you stop and think about it the more it all makes good sense. What we have here are two themes which are right at the heart of the Old Testament. The lion speaks of majesty and power, rule and authority, whilst the lamb is a symbol of meekness, innocence, and sacrifice. Lions conquer, lambs submit. Lions roar, lambs go to slaughter. Here, bound together in a powerful overlapping image is the Lion-Lamb, the one who is the fulfilment of God's earthly promises to Israel and his heavenly calling of the church.

Leon Morris makes the observation that most nations, looking for a symbol of strength, choose powerful animals or birds of prey—the Russian bear, the British lion, the American spread eagle, and so on. 'It is only the kingdom of heaven that would dare to use as its symbol of might, not the Lion for which John was looking but the helpless Lamb, and at that, a slain Lamb.'

Jesus is spoken of as *the Lamb* at least twenty-eight times in Revelation. God's anger is depicted as *the wrath of the Lamb* in 6:16; cleansing is by *the blood of the Lamb* in 7:14; the church is seen as *his Bride* in 19:7; the massed choirs of heaven praise him with a song titled, *Worthy is the Lamb* in 5:12.

What is even more remarkable is this for the Greek word for *lamb* is a most unusual word. It means, 'a little pet lamb.' This is fantastic! Satan is described as a great red dragon, world power is in the hands of a fearful Beast, the forces of hell are everywhere, and against all this, God sets a Lamb! At first glance, it seems a disastrous mismatch to pit a lamb against such colossal opposition, but God knows exactly what he is doing. He has the last laugh!

Did you see where the Lamb is? He is in heaven, in the midst, at the throne! No longer do we see him in a manger in a cattle shed and no more is he found wandering through the cobbled streets of the golden city of Jerusalem. You will not see him hanging on a cross of shame nor even buried in a borrowed tomb in a beautiful floral garden. He is in the Glory! He is at the Father's right hand, exalted far above all! He has defeated every enemy, he controls events on earth from his operations room in heaven, he knows precisely what is happening anywhere, at any time. He has his finger on the pulse. Here is one whose suffering has been turned into glory! That is good news for the people of God for he has promised to do the same for us!

How John saw the Lamb

He saw him as a Lamb *as though it had been slain.* This is incredible! The Greek verb is in the perfect tense indicating a past event which is effective today! There is the power of the blood of Calvary, the wonder-working power of the death of Christ! It was effective then and, two millennia down the road, it is no less effective now! As John Phillips says: 'Eternity in the past knew no other future than Calvary, eternity in the future knows no other past than Calvary.' Calvary is the hinge on which the door of redemption turns. The cross makes a difference!

John also saw him ready to proceed with his mission. When you flick back in your Bible to Hebrews 1 you find the Lamb seated at the Father's right hand, his work of redemption finished. The job he came to do at Calvary is complete so far as purchasing our salvation is concerned. But here in verse 6 we see him *standing*. It suggests that he is about to pick up the pieces and get on with the work the Father has given him to do.

He is omni ...

He saw him *with seven horns and with seven eyes, which are the seven spirits of God sent out into all the earth*. The seven horns speak of one who is omnipotent, one who is all-powerful, one who can do anything, one who is all-strong. The seven eyes remind us he is omniscient for here is one who knows everything; one who is all-seeing, intelligent, and discerning. He has total understanding of the events and dynamics of human history. He is a God who is aware! Putting both traits together, we are reminded of the words of the Apostle Paul who told us that in Christ we have 'the power of God and wisdom of God' combined (1 Corinthians 1:24). We are informed that he is omnipresent for he is everywhere; he is the Lamb in all situations. Here are the attributes of deity, qualities you will not find in anyone else, apart from our Redeemer.

We have perfection in the Lamb without spot or blemish.
We have power in the Lion of the tribe of Judah.
We have perception in the Lord of all knowledge and wisdom.

This is no ordinary Lamb ... this is God in the person of his Son, the Lord Jesus Christ!

5:7

The Lamb takes the scroll

And he went and took the scroll from the right hand of him who was seated on the throne. John is so matter of fact, yet it is no less thrilling for that! Here is one who can do it, the only one who can do it! The big question is, Why can Christ step forward to claim the title deeds? Because he can honestly say:

The world is mine by right of creation, I made it!
The world is mine by right of Calvary, I redeemed it!
The world is mine by right of conquest, I am coming back
    again to claim it!

Jesus Christ is heir of all things! He is undisputed in his power in the universe. The reins of the government of the world passed into his nail scarred palm! The motto of the Moravian church is an excellent one in this context for it says, 'The Lamb has conquered!'

5:8

The response of the elders and four living creatures

And when he had taken the scroll, the four living creatures and the twenty four elders fell down before the Lamb. They fall down and worship! They could not do anything better than that! They bow their knees before him to acknowledge his supremacy and recognise his sovereignty.

Each holding a harp. The harp was the traditional instrument of worship from the Old Testament, mentioned especially in the Psalms (see Psalms 33, 98, 147). I love to hear the music of the harp. It does something for me, deep inside. It is special.

When we get to heaven we will hear it over there, that is the icing on the cake. The harp symbolises the music of inanimate creation. Not only will all human beings glorify God but all of creation will give praise and worship to him. Just as the strings of the harp vibrate in harmony, so one day will the whole of creation vibrate in harmonious worship of God.

And golden bowls full of incense, which are the prayers of the saints. These elders have a priestly role in the presence of the Lord as they present the prayers of the saints to God. We first come across the altar of incense in the tabernacle and later in the temple. It was located in the holy place along with two other pieces of furniture: the table of shewbread and the seven-branched lampstand. It stood directly in front of the veil which separated the holy place from the holy of holies.

When the priest stood at the golden altar, he was representing the people of Israel before the Lord. The incense rising from the altar typifies the people's prayers ascending to the courts of heaven. Prayer is seen as a fragrant offering to the Lord. It emits a beautiful perfume, an aroma which God breathes in. It brings immense joy to the heart of God when his people spend time in intercession.

There are a couple of interesting thoughts which spring to mind when thinking about prayer in this context. One, the church in heaven will be praying for those who become believers in the dark days of the Tribulation period as well as for the nation of Israel. It would seem that those who are with the Lord will be conscious of what is happening down here on earth. Two, these prayers represent the long standing prayer of God's people which our Lord instructed us in Matthew 6:10 to pray, 'Your kingdom come.'

5:9-10

And they sang a new song. Their immediate reaction is one of positive praise for they recognise his so great salvation! They cannot contain themselves any longer so they break forth into song. It is a benediction of praise, a great doxology. The Greek word for *song* gives us our English word 'ode', which is a lyrical poem intended to be sung. We recognise this word in the classical world of music, the most obvious being Beethoven's 9th Symphony which includes his famous Ode to Joy.

It is a brand *new* song! The Greek word for *new* does not mean 'new' from the standpoint of time, but 'new' in terms of quality. It is fresh, unique, original; it has never been heard before! (This is fascinating for when we turn back to the Psalms we find they speak often of singing 'a new song' to the Lord. We find it in Psalms 33:3; 40:3; 96:1; 98:1, to name but a few. The prophet Isaiah jumps on the bandwagon and tells us in 42:10 to 'sing to the Lord a new song, his praise from the ends of the earth.' We read in Revelation 14:3 that the 144,000 Jewish believers from the Tribulation do something similar; the only difference is theirs is a song unique to them for no one else could learn it!)

The words of this new song are recorded for us: *Worthy are you to take the scroll and to open its seals, for you were slain, and by your blood you ransomed people for God from every tribe and language and people and nation, and you have made them a kingdom and priests to our God, and they shall reign on the earth.*

We can learn some wonderful truths from this song expressly dedicated to the Lamb. One, it is a **worship** song for it tells us that he is worthy! It puts the main beam on Jesus. Two, it is a song with an **evangelistic** thrust for it reminds us that he paid the price for our salvation. Heaven sings about the cross and makes much of his precious blood. Three, it is a song with a **missionary** emphasis for it reaches to the ends of the earth; it embraces all men everywhere. God's love is for the world; it does not matter what one's ethnic origin may be nor the colour of one's skin, God has a big heart for ordinary people and his compassion reaches to the farthest outposts on earth. It is multinational, multicultural, and multiracial. Four, it is a **devotional** song for it reminds us of our unique position in that we are a kingdom of priests. We have power with God and men; we have the majesty of a prince as we exercise the ministry of a priest. And, five, it is a song with a **prophetic** slant for it tells of a coming day when we will reign with him down here in this world. The focus is on the coming millennial kingdom, a thousand years of Jesus rule, an era when Jesus will reign and the glory of the Lord will cover the earth as the waters cover the sea.

5:11-13

The song of the angels

John is captivated with all that is happening around him. He looked a second time and he *heard around the throne and the living creatures and the elders the voice of many angels, numbering myriads of myriads and thousands of thousands, saying with a loud voice, 'Worthy is the Lamb who was slain, to receive power and wealth and wisdom and might and honour and glory and blessing!'* A multitude of angels, an innumerable company! There are so many, there are too many to count! But that is not the end of the story. There is more!

The song of all creation

John continues, *And I heard every creature in heaven and on earth and under the earth and in the sea, and all that is in them, saying, 'To him who sits on the throne and to the Lamb be blessing and honour and glory and might forever and ever!'* This vast congregation offering praise to the Lord is not confined to heaven, it is universal, global, everywhere! It is above the earth, on the earth, and under the earth. It is from every conceivable corner. The entire universe rocked in praise and roared in acclamation to the Lamb upon the throne. There is tumultuous praise ringing out! It is a massed choir in a celebration of the greatness of God! Ah, the one unequalled in position and undisputed in power also receives universal praise.

The praise item contains seven characteristics thereby indicating the fulness of worship that he deserves. Everything you can think of in terms of adoration should be given to him. Four of these seven features are repeated in the final song which is ascribed to the one who sits on the throne as well as to the Lamb. And it is not just for a year or two, it lasts for eternity, forever and ever!

5:14

The inevitable response

It all comes to a glorious climax when the four living creatures say *amen* and we also read in verse 14 that *the elders fell down and worshipped.* To quote Adrian Rogers: 'Jesus Christ is exclusively worthy. There is none other. He is exceedingly worthy because of Calvary, because of creation, because of conquest. He is eternally worthy forever and ever.' There is no option or alternative, there is nothing else we can do but follow their noble example and fall down before him and worship! Josiah Conder wrote:

> *In thee most perfectly expressed,*
> *The Father's glories shine;*
> *Of the full deity possessed,*
> *Eternally divine:*
> *Worthy, O Lamb of God, art thou,*
> *That every knee to thee should bow.*

Well may we say along with them, 'Amen!'

CHAPTER 6
An equine quartet

In the previous two chapters we found ourselves in heaven, close to the throne of God; we were aware of the dazzling majesty of the Lamb upon the throne and conscious of the glowing, blazing reflection of God's glory emanating from the throne. Now the picture changes dramatically to a heart-stopping scene on earth. Before, there was nothing but spontaneous praise and worship; now, there is one terrifying judgment hard on the hoof-beats of another.

When the trumpet sounds ...

> *The church will be gone.*
> *The Holy Spirit will be removed.*
> *The salt and light will be absent!*

Big trouble begins ...

These are days of unprecedented tribulation when Satan will initiate and implement an orchestrated campaign of terror throughout the world. You can read all about it in Joel and in quite a few of the other Minor Prophets, and in Matthew 24 in the Olivet discourse. It makes the hair stand on the back of your neck. It is a period of seven years when man will be under the domination of the devil to such an extent that he has never known before in a time of unparalleled trouble.

The storm clouds are gathering. The spiritual barometer is dropping. There is tension in the air. When you talk to Joe Public on the Main Street or in the shopping mall, he is not exactly oozing with confidence either; there is an air of pessimism, a

138

sense of ominous foreboding hangs over his head like a dark cloud. The average person is uneasy and apprehensive. That is the mood we sense in our day and generation.

It is a well documented fact, the globe bristles with all sorts of sophisticated weaponry. There is barely a day goes by when we do not hear some passing reference to nuclear weapons, chemical weapons, the arsenals of a worldwide Armageddon. The world still shudders at the very real possibility of economic, ecological, and energy crises. Poverty, hunger, terrorism, AIDS and crime, are just a handful of the problems that tear at the fabric of our society.

The timescale

When is it all going to take place? Where do these pieces slot into God's prophetic timeline? If we answer that, we will make life a lot easier for ourselves when we get into the thick of Revelation. One of the easiest ways to satisfactorily explain it is to turn back to Daniel 9:24-27. That chapter has been variously described, but prophetic pundits generally feel it is the backbone of Bible prophecy and the spinal cord of prophetic truth. Daniel describes a great calendar of events spanning not just centuries, but millennia. They reach from his own day right on into our own future.

The seventy weeks: 490 years

This unique calendar is marked out as a timespan of what Daniel calls 'seventy weeks.' These 'weeks' are not seven-day weeks as in Sunday through to Saturday; they make a lot more sense when they are interpreted as 'weeks' of years, each week corresponding to a seven-year period. From Daniel's perspective, therefore, his vision encompassed a period of 490 years [for a fuller explanation, see my commentary on Daniel, *Heaven Rules*].

445 BC: the start of the prophecy

We are left in no doubt as to the starting point of this operation.

It was the year 445 BC when the go-ahead was given for the rebuilding of the walls of Jerusalem in the days of Artaxerxes. It was then, unknown to him, that the prophetic time clock started ticking. Read all about that exciting building project in the early chapters of Nehemiah.

31 AD: the presentation of the Messiah

The finishing point of this 69 weeks, or 483 years, is when Messiah was presented as the Prince or the Anointed One. This is a reference to his triumphal entry on Palm Sunday into Jerusalem on the back of a donkey. That was when the milling crowds gave him the green carpet treatment and hailed him with the words, 'Behold your king!' Sir Robert Anderson, of Scotland Yard fame, has calculated that from the first day to the last day there is a total of 173,880 days. We need to realise that figure is derived from the Hebrew calendar which is based on a 360-day lunar year. It is remarkable, but not in the least surprising, that this is equivalent to 483 years, just as the prophet said it would be.

500 years before the event, God drew an 'X' on the exact date Jesus would appear as the long-awaited Son of David. That implies, if Jews living in the time of Jesus had studied Daniel they would have realised that before their very eyes prophecy was being fulfilled! In the bright spotlight of Daniel's prophecy, Jesus could hardly be missed. This was Jerusalem's golden day!

All this is water under the bridge. The 483 years have been consigned to the annals of history. You can read all about them in detail in any decent encyclopaedia. They are gathering dust in the mists of antiquity.

The remaining 7 years

So far so good, but we have accounted for only 483 years; we are still left with an instalment of seven years to match the total 490 years. What happened to them? Where have they gone?

Where do they fit in God's prophetic agenda? The events Daniel was told about concerning this period of time have not happened, as yet. So far as God's schedule is concerned, they are still future and when they do occur they will be closely associated with the nation of Israel.

Jesus himself refers to these occurrences in the final week of Daniel's prophecy in his great prophetic sermon, recorded in Matthew 24. Before his death, as he talked with his disciples on the Mount of Olives, he told them what must come to pass by sketching for them a panorama of endtime happenings. He filled them in on the vital details as he gave them a rundown on his prophetic programme of the ages. As you sift your way through this comprehensive outline, you quickly realise these men were privy to an enormous amount of information.

Jesus, in the course of his comments, referred several times to what he calls 'the end of the age' and other times he just spoke about 'the end.' That little phrase he borrowed from Daniel who used it over and over again. The final seven-year period in Daniel 9 is exactly the same circumstance to which Jesus is referring. The two concepts dovetail together, fitting perfectly like two pieces made for each other in a jigsaw puzzle. It has nothing to do with coincidence, and everything to do with inspiration. It is during these significant years that Israel will once again be running on the mainline track in relation to world events.

This seven-year period which Daniel and the Lord Jesus talk about actually comprises the fascinating and sometimes frightening series of episodes which we read about in Revelation. There is a considerable overlap between what they say and what you have here in chapters 6-19, one throws a lot of light on the other.

Three action packed sections:

Chapters 6-9	The first 3½ years
Chapters 10-14	The events which transpire in the middle of the Tribulation
Chapters 15-19	The final 3½ years

Three phases of God's judgment:

Phase 1 occurs as each of the seven seals is opened one at a time. This is a time when the Lamb is prominent.

Phase 2 is ushered in with the sounding of the first of seven trumpets and, when each one is heard, some further catastrophe happens in the world. Angels are hyperactive on the frontline. During this period Satan rules the world.

Phase 3 takes place when seven bowls of God's wrath are systematically poured out on Planet Earth. It is clear that God himself is directing events.

Under this heptad of severe judgments, the world is ultimately rescued by God at the second coming of Jesus Christ in power and glory. It appears that what we have in chapters 6 and 7 is a preview of what will happen in the early days of this awful term of Tribulation. It is a horrendous era characterised by three R's: the R of retribution, response, and redemption.

6:1-2

The chapter opens with John sitting in the grandstand as a spectator watching all that is happening on the field of play. God does not rush into anything, he bides his time for each seal is opened one at a time! There is almost a sense of reluctance on his part. If he wanted he could judge all at once, getting it over and done with in milliseconds. As someone said: 'He could just blink his eye and send Planet Earth spinning out of control, flinging the human race off into the oblivion of the universe.'

The Lamb opens the first seal

John *watched when the Lamb opened one of the seven seals.* Obviously, the Lord has the scroll in his hand as he opens seal number one. He goes through the same procedure four times and, on each occasion, it is followed by an invitation from one of the four living creatures.

John informs us, *And I heard one of the four living creatures say with a voice like thunder, 'Come!'* The message from them is fairly clear to John. He cannot mistake it. It is a single word, *come!* The sound of their voice is compared to a roll of thunder. It portends coming judgment; it is an omen that a storm is about to break, a signal that no matter how bad it is today, there is worse to come. It is the tone of majesty and might!

The first mention of thunder in the Bible is in connection with God's judgment upon Egypt in Exodus 9:23. This voice as a clap of thunder sounds at the beginning of the Tribulation, the time of 'Jacob's trouble' (Jeremiah 30:7). It appears that the volume is turned higher as the thunder rolls with increasing crescendo for seven years until the lightning of Christ's second coming to earth strikes (cf. Matthew 24:27).

The first scene: a white stallion bearing a dark prince

Then John writes, *I looked, and behold, a white horse! And its rider had a bow, and a crown was given to him, and he came out conquering, and to conquer.* This must have been quite a spectacle for the aged John.

We have here a dark rider on a white horse. He enters the world scene with a flashing smile exuding an air of total confidence. He chooses for his grand entrance a white horse, the symbol of a conqueror in oriental imagery. At the beginning of the Tribulation this shady individual enters as a victorious leader. The person we are dealing with in verse 2 is none other than the Antichrist, the great counterfeit, the imitation Christ; he is the devil's Messiah, Satan's superman. He may have a crown on his head but it is only a victor's crown, he has been crowned by Satan! The crown that adorns the brow of our Saviour is a kingly crown, a royal diadem. There is no comparison between the two.

A bow with no arrows!

Did you see what this rider has in his hand? A bow with no arrows! This future world dictator begins his career as a peacemaker lulling people into a false sense of security. Here is one who successfully unites the nations of the world, who effectively solves many of the problems currently experienced in the Middle East; one whose help will not only be welcomed, it will be sought; one who leads a bloodless coup in the corridors of power for he promotes peace in the midst of global turmoil; one who is the greatest conman of all time, the cleverest mimic ever to walk on the face of the earth ... he will conquer without war.

The world of today is actively looking for someone who fits the bill, a charismatic Mr Fixit. So, when this hero arrives on the stage, his PR team will not have much work to do. The man on the street will welcome him with wide open arms; ordinary, decent people will worship him for they see him as a kind of divine superstar.

One commentator said the Antichrist will have '... the oratorical skill of a John Kennedy, the inspirational power of a Winston Churchill, the determination of a Joseph Stalin, and the vision of a Karl Marx. He will have the respectability of a Gandhi, the military prowess of a Douglas MacArthur, the charm of a Will Rogers, and the genius of a King Solomon.'

Delusion!

This is the moment the Apostle Paul talks about in 2 Thessalonians 2:11-12 where he writes about 'a strong delusion.' He tells us, in that day, men who refused to believe the truth as it is in Jesus Christ will be so blinded that they will believe the lie, they will swallow all that this man tells them. We read in John 5:43 that the nations which turned their back on Jesus Christ will be ready to receive the devil's christ. People will heave an enormous sigh of relief believing their future will be a million times better than they could ever have imagined.

This man will breathe hope into hearts, promise prosperity, make them feel good about themselves, and he will present himself as one who is the answer to their prayers. That spells delusion, with a capital D!

The worrying reality is, this deceiving horseman is no stranger in today's world. It is fairly obvious to any clear headed person that we live in an age of runaway deception. In fact, the more outrageous the lie, the more people seem to believe it!

6:3-4

The Lamb opens the second seal

The second living creature instructs John to *'Come!'* And, as before, John responds.

The second scene: a red horse bearing a sinister warrior

This time John says, *And out came another horse, bright red. Its rider was permitted to take peace from the earth, so that people should slay one another, and he was given a great sword.*

A sword in his hand!

First of all, you see him with a bow in his hand; this time around, it is all so different. It is all change. The bow has gone; it is a sword he is wielding now! And he is not afraid to use it! What began as a peace mission ends in hostility and bloodshed. The world's euphoric mood of peace and harmony will be rudely shattered, it will be shortlived as the second horse and rider appear on the scene. When people say, 'Peace, peace,' the chilling reality is, 'there is no peace' (cf. 1 Thessalonians 5:3).

Three things happen when this man appears: one, world peace is ended; two, many people are killed; and, three, military power is placed in the hands of one man.

The red horseman represents not only nation rising against

nation and kingdom against kingdom, but man fighting against individual man. This is class war, race war, and religious war. It is civil unrest and anarchy. It is the kind of thing that takes place when social order breaks down, when mobs of people take to the streets and begin killing with abandon. He ushers in a time of murder, assassination, bloodshed, and revolution; he presides over a maelstrom of rebellion and revolt!

The 1989 massacre of Tiananmen Square in China is a microcosm of what will take place when the rider on the red horse brings his war machine into full force; we have all watched the news flashes from Sudan, Chechnya, the Balkans, Baghdad, and 9/11 on our television screens ... live pictures beamed direct into our homes from around the world of such alarming, blood-curdling events.

The *great sword* which the rider has been given was in John's day seen as a weapon of mass destruction. It was a powerful tool in the wrong pair of hands. It is even worse for this tyrant is empowered and energised by the devil himself.

The question needs to be asked, Does the Bible envisage a day when a battle will be fought with weapons of mass destruction which are now stockpiled around the world? I am not looking for an answer but it is something to seriously think about.

Destruction!

Down through history we have become increasingly aware that red is a colour associated with terror and terrorist organisations. It is ironic that in Revelation the devil is described as the great *red* dragon and the Antichrist is portrayed in chapter 17 as a *scarlet Beast*. The message is loud and clear, destruction follows in the wake of delusion. It is a proven fact of history that when a devil-inspired leader comes upon the world stage with big ideas of conquest in his evil mind, there always follows war, havoc, and destruction. General Omar Bradley once said about our generation: 'We know more about war than about peace. We know more about killing than about living. We are a world of nuclear giants and ethical infants.' Sober words, indeed.

6:5-6

The Lamb opens the third seal

In the same pattern as before, the third living creature instructs John to *'Come!'* John is startled and shocked by what he sees, it leaves him dismayed and taken aback.

The third scene: a black horse bearing a cunning merchandiser

John describes the scene: *I looked, and, behold, a black horse! And its rider had a pair of scales in his hand. And I heard what seemed to be a voice in the midst of the four living creatures, saying, 'A quart of wheat for a denarius, and three quarts of barley for a denarius, and do not harm the oil and wine!'* No matter where you look in the world, you usually find hard times come to a country when it is caught up in some kind of internal conflict. When war comes, food is often in short supply. The black horse of famine rides behind the red horse of war during the Tribulation bringing worldwide starvation to the citizens of Planet Earth.

To get some idea of how severe this famine will be, consider that it took from the beginning of history until 1850 for the world population to reach one billion people. From 1850 to 1930 the figure rose to two billion. From 1930 to 1960 the population grew to three billion. Then it took only fifteen more years to reach four billion. Today, according to the United States Census Bureau (USCB), that figure is over seven billion. And it is rising every day! So you can imagine the effect a worldwide famine would have.

A pair of scales

One of the inevitable outcomes of such a state of affairs is seen in the market place where prices change dramatically. The economic balance is altered because the world economy will be bankrupt. With the modern stock markets in New York, Tokyo, Frankfurt, Paris, and London now tied together, it is easy to see how the crash of one would lead to the crash of others in a domino effect. Inflation is a foregone conclusion and, in spite of all the efforts of governments and banking moguls, it will spiral out of control.

It is the old story: when strong men go off to war and a country's resources are poured into armaments, the availability of food drops, while prices soar. John informs us that a day's pay, a sort of first century minimum wage, will not buy very much in the supermarket—a quart of wheat or three quarts of barley. Not much of a choice!

The problem is, inflation will cause prices to rise so high that a man will have to work all day to make enough money to buy enough wheat for one meal for his family. That is basic. It is almost as if the breadwinner will take his hard earned pittance to the central market and be measured out his ration.

The mention of barley adds a new dimension to the whole scenario for barley is the food they fed to their animals. Families will turn to this kind of food in order to survive. It may be a panic measure but when you are faced with crying children who have hunger pangs clawing away at their tummies, what is the alternative? It is the mindset which articulates: 'I can have three meals a day of barley whilst I can have only one meal a day of wheat.'

The note regarding the oil and wine is the final nail in the coffin for all those who are eking out an existence. At the close of the first century the Roman empire was struggling with a desperate shortage of wheat and other staple foods; the delay of one grain ship from Egypt bound for Rome could spark riots in the capital, but there was no shortage of wine. James Allen makes the point that 'it is a mistake to regard the oil and the wine as luxuries; they were absolutely essential to normal living.'

The oil was used for cooking, lighting, washing (equivalent to soap), and healing (ointment), and the wine, in the absence of safe drinkable water, was the normal drink with meals. Allen continues: 'The blow for men is that, while still available, they had to be sacrificed to maintain life; there was no money to buy them!' Inflation had taken its toll. The picture emerging here is one of economic collapse.

It is interesting to compare this situation with the one we come across in chapter 13. It seems that inflation may well be the justification the Antichrist will use to impose rigid controls over buying and selling. It is no wonder he will be able to control the economy for the ball is at his feet. He will do so by introducing a strict monetary policy and, at the same time, promise to feed the starving masses so long as they are willing to toe the party line! The triple 6, the so-called 'mark of the Beast,' comes into vogue, but more of that later.

Drought!

The scarcity of food will automatically lead to all sorts of health and community problems on a colossal scale. Such a harrowing experience which reduces people to scraping the bottom of a barrel for something to live on inevitably wears them down, it destroys their will and saps their strength. Family life disintegrates. Law and order disappear.

An incredibly vivid picture of people enveloped in such a tragedy is presented for us in the book of Lamentations. We read in 4:8-9 that '... their face is blacker than soot; they are not recognised in the streets; their skin has shrivelled on their bones; it has become as dry as wood. Happier were the victims of the sword than the victims of hunger, who wasted away, pierced by lack of the fruits of the field.'

That is grim. It is a recurring scene we have all witnessed far too frequently on our television screens in recent days. It is real, devastating, and alarming; it is human misery at its worst, an appallingly senseless, stupid tragedy. It is bad today but at least it is localised. In that day, it will be infinitely worse for it will be global. In all honesty, it does not bear thinking about.

6:7-8

The Lamb opens the fourth seal

And, yet again, the fourth living creature summons John to *'Come!'* And, yet again, John looks at the macabre vision unfolding before his eyes.

The fourth scene: an ashen-coloured horse bearing Death and Hades

The word *pale* is actually a root word for 'green.' It means, a sickly green; the thought is one of decay, rottenness, and gangrene. It is a ghastly yellow-green, the colour of a corpse that is decomposing. John describes in verse 8 what he saw, *I looked, and behold, a pale horse! And its rider's name was Death, and Hades followed him. And they were given authority over a fourth of the earth, to kill with sword and with famine and with pestilence and by wild beasts of the earth.*

This picture is slightly different to the previous three in that this rider is identified for us as *Death.* We are also told he has an unsavoury accomplice following close by, a figure called *Hades.* Death takes the body and Hades takes the soul! The statistics are disconcerting for John advises us that 25% of the world's population will die as a direct result of the opening of the fourth seal. No matter how hard you try to paint a rosy picture, you simply cannot! The chilling fact remains that it is 1 in 4 people. If it were to happen today, that would be a minimum 1.8 billion people!

There are four methods by which this mass extermination will occur: **the sword**. This is a reference primarily to murder. It is the deadly assault of one individual human being upon another. Because society will be in such an atrocious mess, people will take the law into their own hands, they will settle old scores, they will mete out instant justice in a manner that suits them. It is internecine conflict, bloodletting at its worst!

Famine and widespread starvation. We mentioned that earlier when we looked at the third horseman; this serves to emphasise the seriousness of the prevailing situation. We have all seen distressing pictures of lands and lives ravaged by drought. We have seen the cracked ground, the swollen, distended bellies of little children with spindly legs and hollow eyes. Any relief worker will tell you that the death which accompanies starvation is one of the most horrible deaths imaginable.

Pestilence. A pestilence or plague can be defined as an epidemic, a rapidly spreading disease. When people think of such an occurrence, they often mention AIDS as a distinct possibility. It may be, it may not be; what it does is to bring this passage into sharp focus. We are told that more people died of the epidemics of influenza and typhoid after World War I than died in the war itself. In fourteenth-century Europe, one third of the population died because of the bubonic plague spread by rats. When civilisation crumbles, mankind's defences against disease break down as well. When there is no decent sanitation system, no safe drinking water and not enough nutritious food, diseases like cholera, typhoid, and dysentery spread like wildfire. Who knows, but the plague outlined here may even be linked with the modern horror of biological warfare; it could refer to the killing of masses of people by unleashing clouds of deadly viruses.

Wild beasts. Many fall victim to the ferocious attacks of predatory creatures. The fact is, they are closely linked with the plague. The most harmful and pernicious creature on earth, so far as man is concerned, is not the lion or bear, it is the rat! It is clever, adaptable, and destructive. I understand that if 95% of the rat population is exterminated in a given area, it will replace itself within one year. I am also told that rats have killed more people than all the wars in history. It makes its home wherever man is found and it carries as many as thirty-five known diseases. Their fleas carry bubonic plague and history verifies the impact that had throughout Europe six hundred years ago. Their fleas also carry typhus; in four centuries that has killed an estimated 200 million people. The beasts in verse 8 are not only linked with the plague, they are also intertwined with the future. Rats menace human food supplies by devouring and contaminating them. That happens especially in underdeveloped nations which can least afford to suffer such incalculable loss.

Death ... Damnation!

With the opening of each successive seal there is a chain of events that can easily be traced: delusion, destruction, drought, death, damnation. And there is worse to come! It makes me shudder for those who do not know Jesus as Lord and Saviour! I would not want to be standing in their shoes in these early days of the Tribulation! If I were a curiosity seeker, a prophecy buff without a personal relationship with Jesus Christ, I think I would hit the floor on both knees, right now!

Before we put the spotlight on seal number five, let me backtrack for a moment. The utter devastation of what is about to happen has gripped my heart. There are rough times ahead for this world, days of terror and chaos, days when man will reel from one crisis to another. The period spoken of here is the same as Jesus talked about in Matthew 24:21 where we read, 'For then there will be great tribulation, such as has not been from the beginning of the world until now, no, and never will be.' That is what Jesus said about it!

When we turn back to the words of the royal prophet Zephaniah, we have an opportunity to mull over his comments in 1:14-16, 'The great day of the Lord is near, near and hastening fast; the sound of the day of the Lord is bitter; the mighty man cries aloud there. A day of wrath is that day, a day of distress and anguish, a day of ruin and devastation, a day of darkness and gloom, a day of clouds and thick darkness, a day of trumpet blast and battle cry against the fortified cities and against the lofty battlements.' The words in chapter 6 are not much better. In verse 17 this time is described as *the great day of their wrath.* A lot of people are going to die. One quarter of all humanity perishes during this nightmare era in world history. It is estimated that during the Second World War, one out of forty people lost their lives (over 50 million), that was bad enough; here, it is one in four who are plunged into the abyss of death.

Every time I think about this I want to tell more people about Jesus, the one who is mighty to save! That is what Bible prophecy is all about; it should motivate us to communicate to others our faith in a living God.

6:9-11

The Lamb opens the fifth seal

There is an immediate response on two fronts: in heaven, where we read of the martyrs and their cry is heart-rending when they say, *'Avenge us!'* Alongside that, there is an instant response on earth for we hear a cry falling from the lips of sinful men, an unbelievably solemn one, when they say, *'Hide us!'* In one, we become aware of the brutal persecution of the last days; in the other, we are confronted with the blind panic of the last days.

In this section, we are brought face to face with the wrath of an angry God. Now we know why Jesus said for men to 'flee from the wrath to come' (cf. Matthew 3:7). It all fits neatly into place. It all makes a lot of sense when you read chapter 6, and beyond. It is scary, hair-raising, and unnerving. According to Hebrews 10:31, 'It is a dreadful thing to fall into the hands of the living God.'

The cry of the martyr

We read, *I saw under the altar the souls of those who had been slain for the word of God and for the witness they had borne.* John is writing about those who have been martyred, who paid the supreme sacrifice. Their love for the Lord Jesus and their loyalty to God has cost them everything, even their lives. These are the ones who will die during the dark, dreary days of Satan's rule and reign of terror. These new believers, people who are only days and weeks, or maybe at most a few months old in the Lord, will be victimised in ways we cannot begin to imagine.

When the restraint of the Holy Spirit has been removed and all hell is let loose, the world rulers of that day will vent their hatred upon anyone who does not bow the knee to the Antichrist. These good folk will die because they are men and women of steely conviction who are not ashamed to confess the lovely name of their Lord in a word of testimony to their contemporaries.

The wording in verse 9 lends a fair bit of credibility to the thought that the martyrs seen here are also those who have died in past history. One writes says: 'Most of them are not famous and never make it on to the television news. They are unknowns, like the woman evangelist killed in Nigeria one day, the group beheaded in Indonesia the next, the pastor murdered in Karnataka State in India the day after that, or the nameless prisoners being beaten to death in the prison camps of North Korea, and many thousands of others, tortured, shot, beheaded, starved, bombed, in Iran, Sudan, Indonesia, China, Mexico and too many other countries to name.'

The Institute of Religion and Democracy in Washington DC says there were more martyrs produced in the twentieth century than in every other century combined since the time of Christ. The Manila Conference on World Evangelism estimated that, since 1950, at least ten million believers have been put to death for their faith.

These brave folk have a very special place in the heart of God and are honoured in a most exceptional way. On earth, they are helpless victims on the losing side, hated and despised by their killers. Down here, they are unknown. But how different it looks in heaven! Their place is nearest the throne. They are the heroes of heaven.

The significance of the altar

The martyrs are *under the altar.* That is a pointed reference to the brazen altar that was mentioned in the furnishings for the tabernacle in the wilderness. What happened was this: when the Old Testament priest presented an animal sacrifice, the blood was poured out at the base of the altar (cf. Leviticus 4:7-8). From an Old Testament perspective, blood represented life (cf. Leviticus 17:11). These martyrs, through their sacrifice, poured out their lives as a drink offering to the glory of God. The Apostle Paul says something similar when he uses the same figure of speech in Philippians 2:17 and 2 Timothy 4:6.

The anger of the martyrs

In verse 10 we read, *They called out with a loud voice, 'O Sovereign Lord, holy and true, how long before you will judge and avenge our blood on those who dwell on the earth?'* It is a cry for God to act speedily, swiftly, and decisively. It is an earnest plea for God to step into the situation and exercise a ministry of judgment (cf. Psalm 94:1-5). They say, 'Avenge us!'

You may be saying, 'That's not a very Christian thing to pray!' You say, 'Look at Jesus, he prayed for those who were doing unthinkable things to him; Stephen did the same when he lifted his eyes to heaven and prayed for his murderers on earth.' Yes, you are absolutely right! I am quite sure these folk also prayed for those who butchered them; it is the proper thing to do, according to Matthew 5.

The question here is not *whether* God will act, but *when* he will act! They cry out in a loud voice, *How long?* Basically, they are appealing to God's character. They recognise that he is sovereign; he calls the tune, he writes the score. They know he is Lord. They appreciate the fact that the authority is his alone for he has all power at his disposal. It is just a question of when it will happen. For them, as for the rest of us, the waiting is always the hardest!

I want to emphasise again that if these believing martyrs had been living in our time, their cry for vengeance would be wrong. In this present age, God is showing grace and mercy to the worst of men and we are told to pray for those who treat us like door mats. However, in the dark era of the Tribulation, God will be handing down judgment. It is a different era, a different mindset, and so this cry is not only understandable, it is perfectly justified.

God answers prayer!

In verse 11 we read, *Then they were each given a white robe and told to rest a little longer, until the number of their fellow servants and their brothers should be complete, who were to be killed as they themselves had been.* What an amazing verse! It gives us a peep behind the scenes. God heard their cry and responded by pulling back the curtain and sharing with them a little of what happens on the other side. Here we have some incredible insights into the providence of God in his dealings with his children. There are five points which I have found quite helpful in coming to a clearer understanding of this verse:

The dead are conscious. This knocks on the head the erroneous teaching of 'soul sleep.' These martyrs are aware of the promises of God. That is the only possible explanation for their cry in verse 10.

It is possible that those who have died have an intermediate body until they receive their final resurrection body. That is the new body Paul talked about in Philippians 3 and 1 Corinthians 15. The other one is temporary in nature. The white robe indicates their salvation, their righteousness before God. 'Clothed in his righteousness alone, Faultless to stand before the throne' sings out the hymnwriter, Edward Mote. You cannot hang a robe on a spirit! It needs a body.

Dead believers are said to be resting. What a lovely phrase! We read later in 14:13 that the dead are blessed because *they rest from their labours.* The struggles, trials, and heartaches of this life are over for those who have died in the Lord.

God's plan is right on schedule. It might appear the opposite when you look around and see all that is happening in a crazy world. It may seem as if things are careering recklessly out of control, they are not! God has a plan, an agenda, a timetable. The key words here are *until* and *complete.* God is on track! He is not running late!

Many believers will be killed during the Tribulation period. This is something which our God allows to happen. The encouraging truth is that nothing can touch the believer unless it passes through the grid of the will of God. He has a plan for every one of us. He has a special plan for every one of them. He has a purpose that explains each apparent delay in his plan when we view it from a human perspective.

These good folk are referred to as *fellow servants* and *brothers.* This is a possible reference to both Gentiles and Jews who will lay down their lives during this horrendous time. We have in this verse a preview of things to come.

6:12-17

The Lamb opens the sixth seal

Worldwide convulsions and catastrophes

The language is quite clinical in the terse statement which follows. It says in five matter-of-fact words, *there was a great earthquake.* This is the first of three major earthquakes which vigorously shake the nations; they rock the world for the consequences are global (read about the other two in chapters 11 and 16). All of nature will be affected to an alarming degree: the sun, the moon, the stars, the heavens, the mountains, and the islands of the sea. This is no endtime hype, this is no hallucination. It is real! It is devastating!

A graphic description

In verses 12-14 John records the details of the vision, *The sun became black as sackcloth, the full moon became like blood, and the stars of the sky fell to the earth as the fig tree sheds its winter fruit when shaken by a gale. The sky vanished like a scroll that is being rolled up, and every mountain and island was removed from its place.*

We read of a similar occurrence in the prophecy of Joel. He says in 2:30-31 that God will 'show wonders in the heavens and on the earth, blood and fire and columns of smoke. The sun shall be turned to darkness, and the moon to blood, before the great and awesome day of the Lord comes.' He reaffirms this by adding in 3:15 that 'the sun and the moon are darkened, and the stars withdraw their shining.'

When you read the insights of the great evangelical prophet Isaiah, you quickly realise that something big is going to happen, soon! He says, in language reminiscent of John, that 'the stars of the heavens and their constellations will not give their light; the sun will be dark at its rising, and the moon will not shed its light' (Isaiah 13:10). He says as much again in 34:4, only this time the idiom is more colourful and vivid: 'All the host of heaven shall rot away, and the skies roll up like a scroll. All their host shall fall, as leaves fall from the vine, like leaves falling from the fig tree.' Strong stuff!

Amos, the country-cousin prophet, refers to it as well. He says in 8:9 that the Sovereign Lord 'will make the sun go down at noon and darken the earth in broad daylight.'

Its impact on the people

Do you see the impact this will have on the inhabitants of Planet Earth? There is a lot of chaos and confusion out there as men are plunged into the dark depths of despair. We read in verses 15-17 that *the kings of the earth and the great ones and the generals and the rich and the powerful, and everyone, slave and free, hid themselves in the caves and among the rocks of the mountains, calling to the mountains and rocks, 'Fall on us and hide us from the face of him who is seated on the throne, and from the wrath of the Lamb, for the great day of their wrath has come, and who can stand?'*

Sobering words! Solemn words! The shuddering impact of this colossal upheaval in world affairs does not only affect the underclass, it covers every strata of society. The entire population are in a state of blind panic. It does not matter where you find yourself on the social ladder, everybody is running around like a headless chicken. Royal lineage or humble origin makes no difference, whether a five-star military commander or a captain of industry, all are conscious that there is a God dealing with earth. The bottom has fallen out of their tiny world. God has brought man to his knees!

When a man gets down on his knees, it is not always to repent and pray the sinner's prayer! There are times he can turn the other way and vent his spleen on those around him and on the unseen God above him and that is exactly what happens here. In that day, those who refuse to believe will have reached a stage where they simply cannot believe. They have gone beyond the point of no return.

Their consternation is there for all to see. World leaders have no answers to all that is happening. They are in the same boat as ordinary Joe or Sadie standing at the bar with a pint in their hand in the local working men's club. They are filled with fear, gripped in the tentacles of terror. They run and hide for that is their first instinct. It is the natural thing to do. They want to hide; the reality is, it is an attempt to get away from the Lord.

These are the days we read of in Luke 21:25-26 where it talks about men's hearts failing them for fear. These folk are shaking like a leaf, stunned, and crying! It is quite pathetic in one sense, they do not know what has hit them. On the other hand, they are very much aware that God has intervened. They are reeling under the force of the wrath of God. It is severe, intense, and an unusual phenomenon. It is what the insurance brokers call 'an act of God.' That is a fairly accurate appraisal of this world-shattering event which has engulfed mankind. In a word, there is pandemonium.

The plea of the people

This is the greatest earthquake in history, the greatest cosmic disturbance in history, and the greatest prayer meeting in history! The problem is, they are praying for the wrong thing. They are crying to the mountains, *'hide us!'* and to the rocks, *'fall on us!'* because they see death as an appealing escape route to oblivion. So much for atheism, and agnosticism, and every other ism as men face up to the reality of facing God! The day of the wrath of God and the Lamb has finally come!

'... who can stand?'

The scene closes with a rhetorical question which remains unanswered. It is an echo of the stomach-curdling words you find in Nahum 1:6 and Malachi 3:2. Paul says something similar in 1 Thessalonians 5:3. The fact is you know and I know, *none can stand!*

CHAPTER 7

Numbered and numberless

Sherlock Holmes. I can see him, puffing on his pipe, magnifying glass in hand, examining all the clues. I can hear him say, 'Elementary, my dear Watson!' Our friend Sherlock solved many baffling crimes by, first, having a clear mind and, second, by deductive reasoning. A lot of people when they come to Revelation wish they were a twenty-first century version of Sherlock Holmes. The whole book is shrouded in a cloak of mystery that needs to be unravelled and they think you have to be an expert to crack it.

Just like Mr Holmes, there are times when you have to sit back and review all the facts in a case. There are times when it is best to put on the brakes, stop, and think. We need to sift through all the information at our disposal and seek to learn important lessons from it. Maybe we need to ask the question, What have we seen in our study so far?

The seven-sealed scroll has continued to unroll. In chapter 6, we watched as six seals were opened, bringing one judgment after another crashing down on earth. Seeds of devastation were spread with increasing, frightening intensity. We looked at a time of unprecedented disaster, unrelieved terror, and unimaginable slaughter that lies ahead for the world.

The white horse gallops on to the world scene carrying the man of deception, the coming world dictator. Then the red horse appears, he claws the air and any semblance of peace is abolished. Then the black horse with its rider causes consternation, creating hunger and economic disaster. Then the pale horse with its deadly duo in the saddle makes life unbearable for the population as he spreads a dangerous life-threatening plague in his path. Seal number five reveals the brave, courageous martyrs of the Tribulation. When the sixth seal is opened, it unleashes one of the most devastating earthquakes the world has ever seen. It will make the Richter scale look tame as it tries to record all the details.

One astronomer has dubbed the whole scenario, 'a nuclear winter.' Is it any wonder the question is left hanging at the end of chapter 6, *'Who can stand?'* Who can put up with these heart-stopping catastrophes without losing his mind? Who can survive these seismic events?

7:1-3

The purpose of the angels

John informs us, *After this I saw four angels standing at the four corners of the earth, holding back the four winds of the earth, that no wind might blow on the earth or sea or against any tree.* God despatches his special messengers in times of trouble, so he sends four angels to hold back the destruction to come on the earth, sea, and trees. At each point of the compass—north, south, east, and west—they are holding back the four winds of the earth which, in the Bible, are often linked to the judgment of God (cf. Jeremiah 49:36; Daniel 7:2; Hosea 13:15).

The global storm is brewing and the tempest is raging. It is worldwide and, believe it or not, they actually stop it happening for a while. During this time of cessation, there will be no wind, no mountain breezes, no waves breaking on the shore, no rustling of leaves in the forests, no movement of clouds in the sky; everything will be deathly still. In itself, that is an unimaginable display of power!

The reason is actually given in verse 2 where we are privy to a conversation between the angels, *Then I saw another angel ascending from the rising of the sun, with the seal of the living God, and he called with a loud voice to the four angels who had been given power to harm earth and sea, saying, 'Do not harm the earth or the sea or the trees ...'*

Angel number five is the one with the seal. The final disaster comes from the east when Armageddon is ripe (cf. 16:12-16). The Lord Jesus also comes from the east when he returns in power and glory (cf. Matthew 24:27), an allusion to a prophecy in Malachi 4:1-3. From John's perspective on the Isle of Patmos, the east is toward the land of Israel, where God's promised salvation came through Jesus the Messiah and from where the twelve tribes of Israel came – members of which are about to be sealed.

Then, in an unmistakably loud voice that reaches the four corners of the earth, the angel declares that judgment is on hold until the servants of God are sealed. The scene now shifts from judgment on the ungodly to special protection for the godly. What a treasured moment that promises to be!

The divine rationale

God has something tremendously important that he wants to do and it shows us in a powerful way that he is a God of grace and tender mercy. God is on the throne! There is a banner floating across the sky that is plain for all to see. It says in bold, capital letters, HEAVEN RULES! God is in control. He reigns on high. He calls the tune. The cameo John gives serves to underline the truth of the sovereignty of God and his providential care for his own people. There is no promise too hard for God to keep for, as Adrian Rogers reminds us, 'Every Jew you see and every headline you read are sermons about the faithfulness of God.'

He wants to put a seal on a certain group of people. We see that at the end of verse 3, where it says, *Do not harm the earth or the sea or the trees, until we have sealed the servants of our God on their foreheads.* The picture flashing on our screen is the selection of a special group of people. These good folk will be allocated a specific mission to be carried out when the darkness is deepening in the early part of the Tribulation. (More later about their unique role.)

The divine imprint

When we talk about a seal, what do we really mean? A seal indicates ownership. It speaks of protection (cf. Genesis

41:42; Esther 3:10; 8:2, 8; Daniel 6:17; Matthew 27:66). This is not the first time God has sealed off some of his people from judgment. When he sent the Flood, he sealed Noah and his family from the rest of the human race. When he destroyed Jericho, he sealed Rahab and her household by means of a scarlet cord. He did the same for Lot and his family when they escaped from Sodom, just before the fire fell. He sealed the firstborn in Egypt when they applied the blood to the lintel and doorposts of their homes. Back in John's day, it was a common custom for masters to seal or brand slaves.

We, as believers, are sealed today by the Holy Spirit of God (cf. Ephesians 1:13; 4:30). This is God's guarantee to us that we are saved, a divine confirmation that we are safe and one day he will take us home to heaven. This is because we belong to him and he has undertaken to look after us this side of Glory.

7:4-8

The people sealed

In verse 4 we are told a little more about this specially selected group of people, *And I heard the number of the sealed, 144,000, sealed from every tribe of the sons of Israel.* In a day to come, God will seal 144,000 Jewish people! They are the firstfruits of Israel which, as a nation, will be redeemed before Christ returns (cf. Romans 11:26). In every age, God has his faithful remnant. We read in 14:1 that they receive the Father's name as their seal (in marked contrast to the mark of the Beast which the Antichrist will give those who follow him).

Israelites identified

This impressive number is comprised of 12,000 from each of the twelve tribes of Israel and, when you cast your eye down to verses 5-8, you will notice that a dozen tribes are detailed for us. There are some aspects of this list which pose problems.

There are three questions which immediately spring to mind: One, why is the tribe of Levi included when it had no inheritance with the other tribes? Two, why is Joseph named but not his son Ephraim who is usually connected with his brother Manasseh? Three, why is the tribe of Dan omitted and yet it is included in the list in Ezekiel 48 when the land is divided out? The answers are not as easy as you may think! God knows and that is sufficient for me. In moments like these, I am just so glad that 'the secret things belong to the Lord.'

We are talking about the tribes of Judah, Reuben, Gad, Asher, Naphtali, Manasseh, Simeon, Levi, Issachar, Zebulun, Joseph, and Benjamin. This is priceless information for it means we have no problem identifying these endtime evangelists. John MacArthur notes: 'While the tribal records were lost when the Romans sacked Jerusalem in 70 AD, God knows who belongs to each tribe.' From the Jewish people, therefore, will come the greatest missionary force the world has ever known! They are Jews! They are only Jews!

There are some well-known religious groups who have taken this definitive number on board and have woven it into their doctrinal position; it forms an integral part of their statement of faith as an organisation and we all know from doorstep encounters that many of their committed members are enthusiastic exponents of it.

On the other hand, those of whom John is speaking are sons of father Abraham—redeemed Jews—who owe their total allegiance to Jesus Christ. The hand of God has been placed on their lives for an extra special reason in an extra special season for to them is given the awesome responsibility of sharing the good news of Jesus to a people living their lives as if there were no tomorrow. Saved, sealed, and sent!

To the ends of the earth

They have a specific work to do for the Lord. The 144,000 itinerant preachers will be Spirit-filled, Spirit-led, and Spirit-anointed. They will go here and there proclaiming the gospel of the kingdom; they are bold and fearless in their witness to Jesus Christ. They will go into all the world, yea, to the uttermost ends of the earth. The power and dynamic of their preaching will inspire others with tremendous courage. They will finish the unfinished task of world evangelisation and, take note, it is all going to happen during these dark days of terror.

Sometimes we are inclined to forget that it was twelve Jews who turned the world upside down in the first century! Just imagine what 12,000 times twelve will do in the not too distant future!

When you see what happens during this era, you begin to realise it moves rapidly from bad to worse, and beyond. We catch fleeting glimpses of the inbred hatred of the Antichrist. We see the passionately fanatical commitment of his devotees and it is during these terrible times that the hand of God will be on the lives of these courageous witnesses to Jehovah. The Lord will protect them until their ministry is finished. He will look after them until their mission is accomplished. Anne Graham Lotz has written: 'God's sealed protection ensures that armies cannot touch them, floods cannot drown them, fires cannot burn them, famines cannot starve them, torture chambers and concentration camps cannot hold them, and the secret police cannot hinder them!'

The God who protected three young men in a fiery furnace in Daniel's day has not changed (cf. Daniel 3). He is just the same and he can do it again! These servants are sealed because of the promise of God. They will enter the kingdom at the end of the seven years Tribulation to reign with Christ and his glorified church. They are kept from harm during the Tribulation so that they might be alive when the millennium begins; God's covenant promises to his people will be honoured.

7:9-10

The people described

We come across a very familiar phrase in verse 9 when John says, *After this I looked.* This implies a connection between the two groups mentioned – the Jewish preachers were the instruments God used to bring these people to a personal faith in Jesus Christ. There is a clear link between the 144,000 who can be numbered and the *great multitude that no one could number.* There is the amazing ability of Christ to save men and women, to rescue them from the grip of the enemy, to pluck them as brands from the burning. There is no person too hard for God to save. There is a mighty display of the grace of God in the lives of ordinary people. It is an innumerable company, so great they are uncountable! There is the dynamism of the gospel of God's dear Son.

The day of Pentecost was a wonderful day when 3,000 were saved on that day alone! That was a great victory but it is nothing compared to this! Nineveh repented at the preaching of Jonah – a conservative estimate tells us around one million people were saved but that is nothing compared to this! Some three million people followed Moses out of Egypt because they sheltered under the blood – that was absolutely great but this surpasses that by a long shot!

Here we have a vast congregation of redeemed people and it is impossible to calculate with any degree of accuracy how many there are. The way John puts it disappoints the statisticians among us. The number is not that important, it is the people that count! And there they are, *standing before the throne and before the Lamb.* What a fantastic locale! They are in the grandstand of Glory, the front row of heaven. They see the King in all his exquisite beauty!

Their nationality

John says they are from all around the world. They are *from every nation, from all tribes and peoples and languages.* That means what it says. Not one is missing; every people group, every ethnic group, none are passed by! There are no more unreached peoples now as John sees this international community before the throne. In Acts 2 there was a roll call of the nations at Pentecost but it was nothing like this! One commentator makes the point: 'The more the Antichrist fans the flames of repression during the Tribulation, the more the Holy Spirit fans the flames of revival!'

Today, we face a task unfinished in terms of global evangelism. The church has not finished the job handed down to her in the Great Commission (cf. Matthew 28:19-20; Mark 16:15). So much has happened in the last few years as missionary organisations have pushed back the barriers. Enormous strides forward have been taken as the darkness in some regions of the world has been penetrated for the first time. In our lifetime, modern technology is being harnessed as never before as the gospel is beamed into hearts and homes in areas where it is impossible for man to take it.

And yet, in spite of all that is being achieved and accomplished, the stark reality is there are just under 3 billion people—almost 6,900 people groups and over 40% of the world's population—who, at this moment in time, have not heard the precious name of Jesus in their own language (figures gleaned from the Joshua Project 2014). The exciting news is in that day in the Tribulation, saints will bring the whole project to a grand finale!

Something similar is echoed in Matthew 24:14 where we read, 'and this gospel of the kingdom will be proclaimed throughout the whole world as a testimony to all nations, and then the end will come.' In the darkest hour of human history yet to come, the greatest harvest of souls the world has ever seen will take place. Millions who have never heard the gospel will one day be swept into the kingdom of God.

This multitude will consist entirely of those who never heard the gospel before the Lord's return for the church and the beginning of the Day of the Lord. Those who already had an opportunity to hear the gospel and who deliberately rejected it, prior to the moment when Christ returns to the air for his people, will have hardened their hearts against the Lord Jesus. For them, there is no second chance!

One writer puts it like this: 'During those terrible days of judgment, when the witches of war ride their nuclear brooms across the darkening skies of the world's last night, thousands who have never heard before will hear the gospel of the coming kingdom of God, and they will believe.'

Their nature

We discover in verse 9 they were *clothed in white robes, with palm branches in their hands.* They are virtuous and victorious! Overcomers! The white robes clearly point to their righteousness and salvation. The palm branches are a picture of triumph and rejoicing. These folk have every reason to be glad in their God, they have so much to sing about.

It is a celebration of the grace of God for they are first to recognise that salvation belongs to the Lord. We read in verse 10, *And crying out with a loud voice, 'Salvation belongs to our God who sits on the throne, and to the Lamb.'* Yes, they paid the supreme sacrifice (they are the ones we read about in 6:11). It cost them everything yet that does not dampen their desire to thank God for so great a salvation as they exult in worshipping him with a loud voice (cf. Psalm 66:1; 100:1). They are not over the top in their praise, even though it sounds as though they are over the moon! They are saved even though their exit from the world has been one of horror and pain.

It is a celebration of the government of God for they acknowledge the one who sits on the throne. Their days on earth were dark and dreadful, times were harsh and cruel. No doubt they cried out many times, 'Why, O Lord, why?' and, 'How long, O Lord, how long?' In moments when all was sinking around them and they were in grave danger of going under themselves, they maybe felt as if God was silent, the heavens were like brass, evil appeared to triumph on every street corner, and the heathen raged. The thoughts must have filtered through their mind on more than one occasion, has God abdicated, has God stepped down, has God been toppled from power? But now, they see him on the throne; now they know, he is still actively in control as sovereign!

It is a celebration of the gift of God. The focus is on the Lamb. They are in heaven not because they were willing to be martyred for their new-found faith in Jesus, or gave their bodies to be burned, or were counted as sheep for the slaughter, or rendered destitute and subjected to a torrent of vulgar abuse from everyone in the community, or endured to the end and came through the Great Tribulation ... no, a thousand times no! They are there only because of the Lamb, and well they know it! It is a humble recognition that they owe everything to the one who is seated on a higher throne. Their song is a vocal tribute to their God whose grace is amazing and to the Lamb whose death is atoning.

7:11-12

The stimulus of praise

There is no shortage of real worship in heaven. Verse 11 is an outburst of spontaneous praise that does not die away. Heaven is full of people who do not deserve to be there! That is why they get so excited and enthused about the grace and mercy of God; that is why they fall down in loving submission before the King of glory.

It is contagious!

The angels cannot resist joining in. John informs us, *All the angels were standing around the throne and around the elders and the four living creatures, and they fell on their faces before the throne and worshipped God.* It is the ripple in the pool syndrome. When the rest of heaven see these victorious martyrs standing before the throne, dressed in their magnificent white robes, waving their green palm branches high above their heads, and when they hear them lift up their voices in an anthem of praise, they cannot contain themselves! They cannot stand on the sidelines and resist the opportunity to join in ... so the numbers are swelled considerably and the volume is turned up so much higher as this great, massed choir praises the God of glory! It is natural and unrehearsed, it had to happen! And, thank God, it did!

It is harmonious!

They are all singing from the same song sheet and the lyrics are recorded for us in verse 12, *Amen! Blessing and glory and wisdom and thanksgiving and honour and power and might be to our God forever and ever. Amen!*

That is the kind of song you could sing at the Last Night of the Proms! The chances are this kind of rousing worship would make some Christians nervous. You could hear them for miles around! Most of us have been conditioned not to make any noise in our churches or, if we do, it tends to be fairly muffled.

What about waving palm branches? Well, that is an activity most folk associate with some kind of religious ritual which takes place in some churches of a certain ilk on Palm Sunday. It is not the done thing! As far as falling on your face goes, that would happen only if you fell asleep in a prayer meeting!

When you look at worship in heaven, God intends it to be a stimulating, invigorating, bracing experience. When the fire of God is kindled in our hearts, there is no point in chafing at the bit; we are animated in the presence of our God.

An expression of victory and gratitude

They worship God because out of the fire and fury of the Great Tribulation has come such a multitude of martyrs. His strength has been made perfect in human weakness. From our limited perspective, we are prone to weep because of our trials and troubles, but on the other side of death, we shall worship God for it. These victorious saints are a tremendous challenge to us. We should see to it that we act in such a way that God is praised by those who surround his throne. The words of Fanny Crosby's much-loved song complement it beautifully:

> *Blessed assurance, Jesus is mine;*
> *O, what a foretaste of glory divine!*
> *Heir of salvation, purchase of God,*
> *Born of his Spirit, washed in his blood.*
> *This is my story, this is my song,*
> *Praising my Saviour, all the day long!*

And it goes right back to the words of the psalmist, 'Let everything that has breath, praise the Lord' (Psalm 150:6 NIV). In one gigantic leap into the future, John has given us a glimpse of believers dancing in the aisles of glory. Heaven will reverberate with the sound of music! For them, the misery of earth will be over, they are in a glorious new world! Home, at last! So far as the angels are concerned we are told in Luke 15:1-10 that they rejoice over one sinner saved, imagine what they will do when all these saints come marching in!

The amen sandwich!

The ascription of praise begins and ends with a hearty *Amen!* It is a word of affirmation, a word to get you going on the right note. It rounds off their praise and reminds us, 'this is true, we're all agreed.' It is the 'and so say all of us' syndrome. It is real, it is right! It sharpens our focus and puts the main beam on Jesus. It is the kind of word they could repeat after every phrase in the song.

When you look at the jam in the amen sandwich you find there are seven characteristics outlined, we have *blessing and glory, wisdom and thanksgiving, honour and power and might.* This indicates the fulness of worship that the Lord deserves and that is where the number seven, the perfect number, comes into the equation. Everything you can think of in terms of adoration should be given freely to him. This is very similar to what we read being ascribed to him in the doxology of chapter 5. It is pure praise directed to a God who is eternal with the inference that this paean of praise will continue throughout the everlasting ages of eternity. There is no stopping it for such worship will never cease through an endless eternity.

7:13-17

A conversation about the martyrs

We read in verse 13 that one of the elders comes across to John and pointing a finger at the crowd assembled before the throne asked him a twofold question. He said, *Who are these, clothed in white robes, and from where have they come?* John's response is brief and honest, a straightforward, *Sir, you know!* The implication, John did not know! The elder knew all along who they were but God wanted John to know and, in a strange kind of way, he wants us to know as well. He continues in verse 14 to describe them by saying, *These are the ones coming out of the great tribulation. They have washed their robes and made them white in the blood of the Lamb.*

The abiding lesson is this: these glorious martyrs have not died as yet; in fact, they may not even have been born yet! But the Lord wants the saints of all the ages to know all about them.

God wants them to be properly recognised, they really do deserve it! He also wants them to be properly rewarded, according to his promises. They will have a special place, complete protection, and eternal peace. He wants them to be given the acclaim which is rightfully theirs. He is happy for them to receive the commendation of their peers.

The martyrs are a special group of people, unique to the Tribulation period. And yet, their salvation, like ours, is all because of the power of the blood of Jesus to cleanse from sin. Today, and in all our tomorrows, the message of the gospel remains the same as Paul himself said, 'We preach Christ crucified' (1 Corinthians 1:23).

Their role in heaven

John tells us, *They are before the throne of God, and serve him day and night in his temple.* The matchless blessing afforded these martyred believers is that they find themselves in the proximate presence of the Lord. They cannot get much nearer! As close as that! To be before the throne, the centrepiece of heaven, is always seen as a position of prominence and honour. It is the focal point and their lives will be lived in relation to it and the one who sits upon it. The preposition *before* is significant for it speaks of intimate fellowship with no sense of being at a distance from God even in that innumerable company.

A life of indefatigable service

Another special privilege is extended to them in that they will not only see the Lord, they will also serve him, day and night. Heaven is not only a place of rest from earthly labour and struggling with the many hassles and problems of this life, it is a place where a varied ministry can be effectively carried on. We will not be whiling the hours away twiddling our thumbs in heaven. We will not be sitting all day on fluffy clouds strumming a harp. We are going to be busy!

Some Bible teachers have had problems with the phrase, *day and night,* bearing in mind that there is no night in heaven (22:5). That dilemma can be resolved easily when we see it as an expression which means we will continuously serve the Lord; we will not need sleep or restoration as is so essential to life down here on earth. It is really nothing more than a figure of speech which underlines the truth that over there these folk are free from every limitation of this life.

Their service is said to occur in the *temple of God* and, again, this is a clear reference to the immediate presence of the Lord, not to anything else. You find this clarified later in chapter 21. When we get home to heaven we will walk constantly and unbrokenly in the Lord's presence. There will be uninterrupted communion. We will serve him without any signs of weariness, staleness, or weakness. No feelings of tiredness! We will never before have been so deliriously happy in any employment! It will be service with a smile on our lips and a song in our hearts!

A life of infinite security

We read at the end of verse 15 that *he who sits on the throne will shelter them with his presence.* What a beautiful analogy, covered by God's tent! This is God's broadest protection! The words are quoted from the promise God gave his people in Isaiah 49:10 and Psalm 121:5-6. He provides a canopy for them in heaven. What a stunning picture of the enjoyment of the warmth of God's love and the sheer delights of his near presence! We are enveloped in a place close to his heart; we are wrapped around with an overwhelming sense of his presence. That means, there is nothing to fear or dread.

Down here, in this world, there is so much tension, stress, and strain, so much aggro! When you put it all into the melting pot it breeds a high level of insecurity in the heart and mind; the unassailable fact is that over there nothing and no one can harm the people of God. Thank God, just like them, we are untouchable! Praise God, we are unreachable, as well!

There is another contrast with life down here. We read in verse 16, *They shall hunger no more, neither thirst anymore.* Bearing in mind these martyrs came through the Tribulation, these words take on an entirely new meaning. In those awful days they knew considerable deprivation and were prevented from partaking of the essentials of life. They were harassed to such an extent that the basics of life were denied them. Many days they were forced to go without a decent meal and many a night they went to bed with an empty stomach, all because they were marching to the beat of a different drum. It was tough. It was not easy. But, in heaven, it is all a thing of the past. There is no lack in God's provision. There will never be a sense of something missing. We will have everything we desire and desire everything we have.

At the end of verse 16 we read, *the sun shall not strike them, nor any scorching heat.* In heaven the forces of nature will not mitigate against us. The sun is a wonderful bonus to many and it is something we can really enjoy and derive much benefit from; but, you can get too much of a good thing and that is when the problems start! Down here, these folk were subject to the elements of nature; they had been exposed to the extremes of heat and cold, light and dark. We will not face that complication in heaven for over there the environment is user-friendly. We will not need the sun for the glory of the exalted Lord will shine upon us, yet even that will not consume us in its heat or blind us in its dazzling power!

A life of intimate satisfaction

We come to the climax in verse 17 where we read, *For the Lamb in the midst of the throne will be their shepherd.* We will be shepherded by the Lamb! We have a dual picture here for the Lord Jesus Christ is both the Lamb and the Shepherd! As the Lamb of God who gave his life for us at Calvary, he bought us with his precious blood. As the Shepherd, who supplies our every need, he will look after us in every way imaginable.

Our happiness and welfare are his major concern. This is highlighted in the next phrase which tells us that *he will guide them to springs of living water.* Water in the Bible is often a symbol of salvation and eternal life. That truth is echoed in the words of Jesus when he spoke to the woman at Jacob's well in John 4:13-14. He leads us to the fountainhead, the source and focus of spiritual life and blessing. Here is life in abundant fulness!

The last sentence in chapter 7 is one that God's people have valued and appreciated so much down the years. It is one you often hear read at a funeral or in a situation where people are passing through some kind of devastatingly traumatic experience. John says, *And God will wipe away every tear from their eyes.* Great news! In this life our joys and our fun times are often tempered by our many sorrows for we are no stranger to the vale of tears.

Did you see what he does with our tears? He wipes them away! They are gone! His is a ministry of tenderness and comfort (cf. Isaiah 25:8). So far as he is concerned, the past is put behind us and when we arrive in heaven, it is to a brand new future where burdens are no more! The saints in Glory will be occupied with the beauty and wonder of heaven and the worship of their Saviour. Because the tears are gone, the vision we have of Christ is unblurred!

What an exhilarating prospect awaits those we read about in this amazing chapter. For you and me, our future is as good as it could possibly be; it is brighter than we could possibly imagine. Many voices. Only one Saviour. On that note, Carrie Breck captured the emotion of the moment well when she penned:

> *Face to face with Christ my Saviour,*
> *Face to face, what will it be?*
> *When with rapture I behold him,*
> *Jesus Christ, who died for me!*

CHAPTER 8

The lull before the storm

8:1-2

The prelude

We read when the Lamb opened the seventh seal that *there was silence in heaven for about half an hour.* This is really difficult to imagine and hard to visualise. It is such a contrast to all that has been happening; moments before there was rousing praise, spontaneous worship, wonderful music, and bright singing. We have just been participating in a lively celebration where the focus was on the government and grace of God. We have just been to a praise party in heaven and now all goes strangely quiet.

It is a dramatic pause, a hugely effective pause. It is the silence of mystery, intrigue, and suspense. It is probably the longest silence heaven has ever known, a time when all heaven holds its breath. As one writer says: 'Heaven will be silent! Awesomely, fearsomely, pregnantly silent!'

Most of us realise that thirty minutes is a fair wee while especially when you are waiting for something big to happen. It may be compared to the silence in a courtroom before the foreman of a jury returns a verdict. It is like waiting at the end of a telephone line for some important news to arrive. It is the kind of silence you can almost feel, as though you were able to touch it.

His pause in judgment is like the eye of a hurricane, a lull that gives the world time to reflect on its rebellion, blasphemy, sin, and evil actions. God gives the human race time to think things over. It is the calm prior to the storm, the lull before the tempest rages, a brief moment of peace in advance of the hour when the turbulence begins. It is the silence of foreboding, of intense expectation, of awe at what God is about to do.

John MacArthur says: 'The greatest event since the Fall is about to take place and all heaven is seen waiting in suspenseful expectancy.' Basically, we are waiting for God to take the initiative and make the next move. The plain fact is, number seven seal is so awesome and so terrifying that no one in heaven dares breathe a word.

We can walk down three paths to discover some rich lessons from this silence for our own lives, it speaks of a sense of:

Awe before the Lord. You find this truth echoed in Habakkuk 2:20 where we read of the divine summons, 'The Lord is in his holy temple; let all the earth keep silence before him.' Zephaniah 1:7 warns, 'Be silent before the Lord God! For the day of the Lord is near.' The same challenging outlook is found in Psalm 76:8-9 and, again, in Zechariah 2:13.

Peace before the Lord. No one had any grounds for complaint as the Lord silenced all opposition. It has become clear at last that the judge of all the earth has done right!

Expectation before the Lord. Such a silence prepares us for the awfulness of the judgments that will soon follow. We read all about these in graphic detail in the remaining verses of the chapter. They make the hair stand on the back of your neck!

The period of silence is punctuated at the front end with the opening sentiments of Psalm 46:10 where the Lord is saying, 'Be still, and know that I am God!' As the thirty minutes draws to a close, the silence is broken with the declaration of intent from the same verse where it tells us, 'I will be exalted among the nations, I will be exalted in the earth!'

Seven trumpets!

John informs us in verse 2, *Then I saw the seven angels who*

stand before God, and seven trumpets were given to them.
Again, we find the number seven is very much to the fore; it
is in harmony with the seven seals and seven bowls, phases
one and three of God's judgment programme. The fact that
these angels stand before the living God indicates a place of
prominence, such as is given to the angel Gabriel in Luke 1:19.
They have a special nearness to the throne of God and are,
therefore, higher up the pecking order in angelic rank and status
(cf. Colossians 1:16; 1 Peter 3:22). In Jewish tradition this
heptad of angels is often called 'the angels of the Presence.'

Trumpets have always had a special place in Jewish national
life (cf. Numbers 10). They had at least three important functions:
one, to call the people together as an entire community, verses
1-8; two, to announce the outbreak of war, verse 9; and, three,
to advise the people of special times, such as feasts and
festivals, verse 10. (The trumpets sounded at Mt Sinai when
the Law was given to Moses, as in Exodus 19. The trumpets
were blown when Solomon was anointed and enthroned king,
as in 1 Kings 1. The trumpets were heard at the conquest of
the city of Jericho, as in Joshua 6.)

When we place these three incidents together, there is a
clear picture emerging on the canvas: to sound seven trumpets
would certainly announce a declaration of war as well as the
fact that God's king was enthroned in Glory and was about
to judge his enemies, as detailed in Psalm 2. As trumpets
declared defeat to Jericho, so they will ultimately bring defeat
to Babylon. Joel says in 2:1, 'Blow a trumpet in Zion; sound an
alarm on my holy mountain! Let all the inhabitants of the land
tremble, for the day of the Lord is coming; it is near.'

8:3-5

The prayers

John writes, *And another angel came and stood at the altar
with a golden censer, and he was given much incense to offer
with the prayers of all the saints on the golden altar before the*

throne, and the smoke of the incense, with the prayers of the saints, rose before God from the hand of the angel. We now see a lovely picture that finds its roots away back in the pages of the Old Testament. It is a profound illustration of what the priests did every day of their lives, every morning and evening they put incense on the golden altar that stood before the veil of the holy place using a golden censer.

On one day of the year, the Day of Atonement, the feast of Yom Kippur, the high priest went behind and beyond the veil (cf. Leviticus 16). It was then the people remembered the words of God to Moses when he said, 'There ... I will meet with you' (Exodus 25:22). The role of the priest is to offer the prayers of the people to God. The smoke of the burning incense on the altar represents prayers rising to God and, in this scene, these are the prayers of all the saints!

There are three important lessons we can learn from this about prayer:

Prayer is a privilege

These are *the prayers of all the saints*. Not just some of them, or even most of them, but all of them! Yours and mine, included! Saints are not specially selected dead people who have been canonised and emblazoned on stained glass windows, far from it! They are very much alive! If you are a Christian, you are a saint! Prayer should occupy a place at the heart of the Christian life. It is a Calvary-bought privilege. We have access into the presence of God through the merits of the death of Jesus. We come as creatures before the great Creator, as sinners before a holy and just God, and as children before a loving, heavenly Father.

God helps us when we pray

That is precisely what is happening in these verses. The prayers of the saints rise up before the Lord, are made acceptable to God, are well-pleasing in his sight, and are agreeable to his perfect will. When you look at the symbol, it is the application of incense that makes the prayers suitable to God. Go further back behind the symbol and you will discover we have two great means of assistance promised to every believer so that we may pray aright. Both of them are mentioned in Romans 8: we have the intercession of the Holy Spirit in verses 26-27 and the intercession of the Lord Jesus in verse 34. It is marvellous news that we have such enormous help in prayer!

God answers prayer

That is what happens in verse 5 where we read, *Then the angel took the censer and filled it with fire from the altar and threw it on the earth.* Their prayers were heard and made an impact on the heart and mind of God! They asked in 6:10, *How long?* Well, here is the answer: *NOW!* It is maybe not the answer they expected, but it is the one they got! God will always vindicate his name. He will avenge himself against his enemies, he will glorify his people, he will bring in his kingdom and when you pray 'how long?' such an answer is inevitable. The storm is about to begin; and, whether we realise it or not, prayer has played a vital part.

There is a direct relationship between prayer and the judgment of God, a vital link between the throne and the altar! The veiled message coming out of these verses is that the throne and the altar are related. The real purpose of prayer is not to get man's will done in heaven, but to get God's will done on earth! Sometimes that spells j-u-d-g-m-e-n-t. True prayer is extremely serious business, so we had better not move the altar too far from the throne!

Following the offering of the prayers of God's people, the silence is abruptly shattered by an electric storm with far-reaching consequences; a divine firestorm bursts upon this planet for we read in verse 5 that *there were peals of thunder, rumblings, flashes of lightning, and an earthquake.* Prayer which can precipitate such things must be potent! The prayers of God's people have been flung into the scales and have tipped the balance heavily in favour of an immediate resumption of hostilities by heaven. The results are catastrophic as God's judgment falls upon the earth like a massive fireball out of the sky. The storm is all the more shocking in its suddenness, contrasted with the silence and stillness that preceded it. The striking characteristic of these judgments is the precise way in which they are carried out.

8:6-12

The punishments

Now the seven angels who had the seven trumpets prepared to blow them. One by one the angels will sound their trumpets, and as they do, something happens immediately after each blast. It is as though each catastrophe is given a kickstart. What you see taking place here is not unlike the ten plagues in Egypt which we read about in Exodus 7-11. There is an uncanny, spine-chilling resemblance between them.

The first four trumpet judgments are natural in that they affect nature to a greater or lesser degree. They are directed towards the land, the salt water, the fresh water, and the heavenly bodies. They cause massive environmental damage and spell desolation in bold capital letters! It is an ecological nightmare.

Trumpets five and six involve the release of hordes of demonic forces. They first torment people and, not content with that, proceed to kill them. A harrowing account of the terrible misery they inflict is recorded in chapter 9. The caption we write over this particular sequence of events is liberation; however, it is like the proverbial scorpion, there is a sting in the tail.

The seventh trumpet is recorded in chapter 11 and involves a serious crisis among all the nations of the world. The reason why is fairly obvious. The stirring message resounding from heaven to earth is summed up in the sentence, *The kingdom of the world has become the kingdom of our Lord and of his Christ, and he shall reign forever and ever* (11:15).

The first angel sounds his trumpet

The first angel blew his trumpet, and there followed hail and fire, mixed with blood, and these were thrown upon the earth. And a third of the earth was burned up, and a third of the trees were burned up, and all green grass was burned up (8:7).

This judgment is reminiscent of the seventh plague that befell Egypt back in the days when Moses was having big problems with Pharaoh. Then it was restricted to hail and lightning and that was severe enough. The Bible records in a diary-like entry in Exodus 9:24 that it was the worst storm 'in all the land of Egypt since it became a nation.' That is one for the history books. It is a minute that has been registered for posterity in the meteorological records of that day. This time, it is hail and lightning, mingled with blood!

This is not a new phenomenon for scientists and historians have recorded other times when red rain fell from the sky. *The Atmosphere* is the title of a book published in the 19th century and it documents a number of such occurrences in Europe and elsewhere. It refers specifically to the red rain which fell near the Italian city of Genoa in 1744. It appears that similar events have been tabled in the 20th century as well.

We all know that hail storms can do colossal damage, their impact is terrible but when it is mixed with fire (which may refer to some kind of severe electrical storm) the possibilities of desolation are staggering. It is a global legacy of disaster. We need to let the truth of this sink in. This is not confined to some isolated region populated by a few nomads in the middle of nowhere, this scene is multiplied many times over on every continent on the face of the earth.

One third of the earth is burned up ... it is blackened land, charred and smouldering. To all intents and purposes, it will be rendered unusable.

One third of the trees are burned up in one huge forest fire. That puts a new slant on the meaning of the word 'deforestation' and it also means the door is left wide open for communities to be wiped out by rising flood water and such like.

One third of the grass is set on fire. This will affect animal life which depends upon grass for food. The food supply chain will be seriously disrupted and that is especially true in relation to meat and dairy products.

The appearance of the planet will be drastically altered. Life will never be the same again. The earth will experience an immense ecological upheaval that will make our toxic dumps seem like a children's playground. Devastation on this scale affects the delicate balance of nature. Even before the dust has settled, this has an immediate impact on the quality of life which can be enjoyed by the inhabitants of the earth. It also spells doom and gloom when you think about the availability of food on the supermarket shelves. Earth Day that year will be a dismal affair; in a scorched and ravaged world there will be little of the environment left to celebrate!

The second angel sounds his trumpet

Something like a great mountain, burning with fire, was thrown into the sea, and a third of the sea became blood. A third of the living creatures in the sea died, and a third of the ships were destroyed (8:8-9).

The first plague of Egypt turned the water of the Nile into blood, that fact is established in Exodus 7. Something similar occurs when the second trumpet sounds. The cause behind this disaster is described by John in symbolic language when he says it was like a huge burning mountain tossed into the sea. Some Bible commentators see all sorts of wild things happening here! Some believe it could be the direct result of a violent volcanic eruption like a Mount Etna Mark 2. The greatest devastation that John had probably heard of during his lifetime was the eruption of Mount Vesuvius in 79 AD which, literally, buried Pompeii and destroyed ships anchored offshore in the Bay of Naples.

Or it could be something akin to a giant meteorite or asteroid surrounded by flaming gases set ablaze by the friction of the earth's atmosphere falling out of space and landing in the sea.

John MacArthur makes the point: 'It will hit, striking somewhere in the world's oceans with an explosive power far greater than that of an atomic bomb.' We really do not know!

One third of the sea is turned into blood. Two-thirds of the earth's surface is ocean and, when we grasp that, we are only scratching the surface. So we can only begin to visualise the extent of this awful judgment.

One third of the living creatures in the sea died. It is a foregone conclusion that the pollution of the water combined with the death of so much marine life will greatly influence the precarious balance of life in the oceans. That leads to other serious problems that cannot be easily rectified or solved. Think of the long-term impact on the depleted shipping industry, the loss of confidence in the mind of Joe Public, and the tragic, needless loss of human life and so many homes left without a breadwinner (cf. Hosea 4:3; Zephaniah 1:3).

It is hard to imagine but *one in every three ships will sink* causing untold congestion at sea. Think of the voluminous quantity of cargoes jettisoned; try to envision the utter chaos on the waterways and major shipping lanes of the world. The naval fleets of every major country will be crippled beyond help. And to make matters infinitely worse, seafood will be severely rationed, restaurants will go out of business, people will lose their source of income for their livelihood will be lost and the source of heart healthy food will radically dwindle.

So far as seafaring nations are concerned, this will be an economic disaster from which very few will ever recover. This is a financial collapse of unprecedented proportions. The boom years are a thing of the past; this cataclysmic downturn in their fortunes spells nothing but bust!

The third angel sounds his trumpet

When the third trumpet sounds, John tells us that *a great star fell from heaven, blazing like a torch, and it fell on a third of the rivers and on the springs of water. The name of the star is Wormwood. A third of the waters became wormwood, and many people died from the water, because it had been made bitter* (8:10-11).

A torchlike star falls from the sky and disintegrates when it enters the atmosphere and scatters itself throughout the earth. The fallout from such a body is what causes the problem. It may be a comet-like object or a meteorite.

One third of the rivers and springs are irreversibly polluted. Some folk are of the opinion that the type of poisoning envisaged here is a form of radiation. Water is basic to human survival. It is fundamental. We just cannot do without it. It is absolutely essential for mankind. This judgment impinges on the world's water supply to such an extent that one third of the waters are rendered unusable.

The grim statistic is recorded for us when we recognise that any who drink from this so-called bitter water will be signing their own death warrant. People will turn on their taps gasping for a drink of fresh water but, before another day has dawned, they will be just another name on the computer printout of fatalities arising from this dreadful epidemic. In our day, we are already grappling with the problem of increased pollution in our drinking water supplies but, in that future day, the fresh water supply will become as putrid as a Calcutta gutter. That is what life will be like during these awful times of Tribulation. This is not an attempt to sensationalise the story; it is simply telling it like it is! The facts are bad enough; they do not need to be embellished in any shape or form.

It is interesting to note that the name of this star is *Wormwood* which is a plant right out of the killing fields, similar to the sagebrush. The word translated 'wormwood' gives us our English word 'absinthe', a popular liqueur in some regions of the world. Because of its high toxicity, its manufacture is also banned in many countries. The Oxford dictionary advises that it is a green aniseed-flavoured potent liqueur based on wormwood which turns milky when water is added. In the Old Testament, it was synonymous with sorrow and great calamity.

Moses warned that idolatry would bring sorrow to Israel like a root producing wormwood (cf. Deuteronomy 29:18); Solomon warned that immorality might seem pleasant at the time but in the end it produces bitterness like wormwood (cf. Proverbs 5:4). It is a phrase that Jeremiah, the weeping prophet, used on more than one occasion. For example, he says in Lamentations 3:15, 'He has filled me with bitterness; he has sated me with wormwood.' The word translated wormwood is translated 'gall' in the NIV. Amos also uses it in his prophecy where he is talking about those who 'turn justice to wormwood and cast down righteousness to the earth' (Amos 5:7).

National Geographic Society lists about one hundred principal rivers in the world which range in length from the Amazon at 4,000 miles long to the Rio de la Plata, a mere 150 miles long. When you think about it like that, it is only then that the scale of this whole sad affair hits you between the eyes. It is a catastrophe of unbelievable magnitude!

The fourth angel sounds his trumpet

The fourth judgment is in contrast to the previous three for they had to do with the world of nature and it was the earth which was directly influenced. The fourth one is different in that it affects the heavens. Having said that, the inevitable repercussions will be felt on earth for many a long day!

We read in verse 12 that when the fourth angel sounded his trumpet, *A third of the sun was struck, and a third of the moon, and a third of the stars, so that a third of their light might be darkened, and a third of the day might be kept from shining, and likewise a third of the night.*

Each of these bodies has been worshipped by pagans all around the world for centuries, now God touches them to remind us that he alone must be worshipped. This judgment also reminds us of the ninth plague which lasted for three days which was visited on the land of Egypt, as recorded in Exodus 10:21-23. Remember what happened in early 2010 when a single volcano in Iceland began erupting, sending ash into the upper atmosphere and severely curtailing air travel throughout Europe?

It is obvious that the earth will become considerably darker. That will affect growth for there will be 33% less energy available to support the life systems required by man and nature. The vast changes in temperature will have a detrimental influence on human health and food production. It does not only affect nature, it also affects human nature, for the more darkness there is, the more crime there will be, and so it goes on and on!

The event outlined here by John is the same one anticipated by Jesus when he said in Luke 21:25-26 that 'there will be signs in sun and moon and stars, and on the earth distress of nations in perplexity because of the roaring of the sea and the waves, people fainting with fear and with foreboding of what is coming on the world. For the powers of the heavens will be shaken.' In addition to this prophecy, several Old Testament prophets say much the same thing (cf. Isaiah 13:10; Jeremiah 4:23; Ezekiel 32:7-8; Joel 2:31; 3:15; Amos 5:20).

It is quite startling when we analyse each of these four judgments for we quickly realise they all fall on creation. It is as though the Lord is saying, 'You've taken the natural world for granted, you've abused it, you've plundered it. You've depleted and destroyed many of its natural resources. You want a devastated world? Very well then, if that's what you want, that's what you'll have!' The worst judgment God can mete out to sinful man is to give man what he demands.

We are very conscious of the progress man has made in the fields of science, medicine, and technology, it is hard to keep abreast of all that is happening around us; at the same time, man is systematically destroying God's earth. After all is said and done, man has no one else to blame but himself. He has brought it all on himself; in one sense, it was self inflicted! So far as God is concerned, man always gets his comeuppance. One writer concludes: 'The greatest threat to our environment is not fluorocarbons or carbon monoxide or chemical plants or nuclear reactors or bulldozers or arsonists. The greatest threat to our environment is sin!'

8:13

The proclamation

Even with all the horrors that man has faced so far in the Tribulation, when will he begin to take God seriously? That is what John is driving home to our hearts in this closing verse of chapter 8.

The triple woe!

The celestial lights are dimmed to set the stage for a startling announcement. John tells us precisely what happened. He says, *Then I looked, and I heard an eagle crying with a loud voice as it flew directly overhead, 'Woe, woe, woe to those who dwell on the earth, at the blasts of the other trumpets that the three angels are about to blow!'*

I have never heard an eagle speak but John did, and the message he heard was not particularly cheerful! (There again, I've never heard a donkey speak, but Balaam did!) The message is a treble woe! It is a triple warning that says to people, 'Look, if you think this is bad, just wait; there is more to come and it is a million times worse!' There is a rising crescendo of judgments! The word *woe* is one of those unique expressions said to be onomatopoeic, that is, a word formed from a sound which conveys its meaning. It is a bit like the words 'cuckoo' or 'sizzle.' You can hear the sound and that gives you a clue to the meaning.

The targets

It should be noted that these judgments are directed to those whom John calls the 'inhabitants of the earth' (NIV). That is a little phrase which pops up no fewer than twelve times in Revelation and it has an interesting application. It is not only referring to those who live 'on' the earth; it is directed primarily to those who live 'for' the earth, those whose lives absorb the things of the earth. They are earthbound for they are immersed only in the things of time, and that is the root of all their problems. What a contrast to the people of God who are said to be heaven-bound!

The purposes of judgment

To get our lives sorted out. How do you feel about the judgment of God in your life? It frightens us. It chills our blood. It scares the living daylights out of us. It is supposed to! At the same time, it arrests our attention and arouses our fear. It should also sober us for it forces us to reassess the way we have been living our lives. As C S Lewis so memorably put it: 'God whispers to us in our pleasures, speaks in our conscience, but shouts in our pains: it is his megaphone to rouse a deaf world.'

To get us back on the right track. Judgment should also correct us for it forces us to face the unpleasant truth about ourselves. We do not like that, we recoil and shrink from it. It is like a mirror for it strips away our illusion and restores us to a realistic view of ourselves.

To remind me that there is someone bigger than me around. Judgment is meant to humble us for it underlines the truth that we are not autonomous, we are not in control of events and circumstances in this life, we are not masters of our own fate nor the captains of our own destiny.

To boost our morale. Last of all, judgment should quietly reassure us for it reminds us that God works in our lives in such a way that he wants to bring out the best in us. It is not something that God enjoys for the prophet informs us that it is 'his strange work' (cf. Isaiah 28:21). Perhaps, from our own experience, we can testify with the words of the hymn, *'With mercy and with judgment, my web of time he wove!'*

A tale of two armies

In every sense of the word Revelation 9 follows on from Revelation 8, a scary chapter which climaxed with a treble woe. It was God's way of saying to the world: 'Watch out, the worst is yet to come!' Come it did, in chapter 9! Here we have angel number five blowing the trumpet and an army comes from the pit in verses 1-12, then you have angel number six sounding the trumpet and an army comes from the east in verses 13-21. It is a sordid, sensational tale of two armies.

I think it might be helpful if we considered verses 1 and 2 and attempted to identify the leader of these locusts. He is spoken of as their king in verse 11, but the question is, Who is he? Can we pinpoint him with any reasonable degree of accuracy?

9:1-2

His position

He is described as *a star fallen from heaven to earth.* Here is the star that bit the dust! You will also find in verse 2 that this star is identified by the personal pronoun *he* which suggests we are talking about a real person.

When is a star an angel?

When you backtrack to 1:20 we are told that stars in the book of Revelation represent angels. That deduction seems fairly reasonable even in this particular setting. In fact, in 9:11 he is referred to as *the angel of the bottomless pit.*

A fallen star!

It had fallen from heaven to earth and when you read that your personal antenna begins to receive all kinds of signals. The general opinion is that this would imply some kind of moral failure on his part. In Jude 6-7 we learn about angels who experienced such ruin. The Bible also speaks of 'unclean spirits' and equates them with 'demons.'

When you meet a demon in the Gospel narrative, it is clear that they are extremely capable of controlling a person's mind and actions so much so that human beings can be demon possessed. The best example is the story in Luke 8 involving the man from Gadara. Remember the incredible transformation Jesus brought to this man's life; it is summed up in verse 35 where we read the man was 'clothed and in his right mind.'

Think about the devil for a moment. Satan is nothing more than an angel, a fallen angel! He fell from the sublime heights of heaven. He was an anointed cherub and was as near to the throne of God as it was possible to be. He was heaven's worship leader, God's masterpiece, a showpiece of what God could do, but he blew it and fell! He was limited in what he could achieve, he underestimated God and overestimated himself. He was limited in what he could foresee, there was a price to pay but he had no idea what this would be. He was limited in damage control, there was no turning back when he made an irrevocable choice. He was limited in his understanding of God, there was so much he obviously did not know!

It is quite incredible that even in this most ideal situation, a perfect environment, this angel made his choice, he exercised his right, and it proved to be one which was seriously flawed. It would appear he miscalculated the consequence of his decision and God's reaction to it.

Pride and arrogance got the better of him! His ambition was to be one up on the Lord of all glory. His passion was to be Number One. His aspiration was to be better than God. It was a high risk gamble which backfired badly. Jesus does not pay him any compliments when he labels him in John 8:44, 'a murderer from the beginning...a liar and the father of lies.' (You can read more about him and the events surrounding him being unceremoniously thrown out of heaven in Isaiah 14:12-15 and Ezekiel 28:12-16.) The Bible often refers to the 'devil and his angels.' It informs us that these are deceiving spirits. It tells us that Satan is the prince of the power of the air, the prince of darkness, and the prince of this world.

He loses access to heaven

When you read the book of Job you find that Satan has access to God in heaven, and when he pops in from time to time, it is with an armful of accusations against the people of God; one day that will end! Even today, one of the strings to his bow is that he accuses us as believers before the throne of God (cf. Romans 8:33-34). Satan will be removed from the heavens during the period of Tribulation. His final destiny is the lake of fire and there he will be tormented day and night forever and ever (20:10). The devil is always under the feet of Jesus!

His power

He has a key!

We read at the end of verse 1 that *the star...was given the key to the shaft of the bottomless pit.* It is a key to a subterranean abode. This means his power and authority are seriously limited. He can go so far and no further. He can do so much and no more. He has limits imposed by God. He has to operate within certain parameters which God has set down. In 1:18 we are told that *the keys of Death and Hades* are in the hands of Jesus Christ. Satan is not the king of hell, he is the chief prisoner!

The key that unlocks the chains of those demons in hell was given to Satan; he obviously did not have it in his control. God now allows him to unleash his fury against a world that has rejected Jesus. The day of God's wrath has come and, as always, God will use even the devil to accomplish his divine purposes.

The key in his hand is specifically for the shaft of the Abyss, the bottomless pit. It is described in Luke 16 as a place of torment. It is the place where the demons in pigskin swimsuits in Luke 8 did not want the Lord to send them! 2 Peter 2:4 reminds us that 'God did not spare angels when they sinned, but cast them into hell and committed them to chains of gloomy darkness to be kept until the judgment.' Later in the book, we discover that Satan himself will be penned up here for a thousand years when Jesus is reigning on earth.

He is the king!

The picture here is of a vast depth approached by a shaft whose top is covered. This is where the plague of locusts comes from; the Beast comes out of the same place (11:7). When you put them both together, it suggests that the Antichrist will be a demon-possessed human being who will then go on to deceive the world. We also note that he is described as the king of the locusts.

The power of the devil is clearly revealed in the simple statement we have in 9:11, for there we read, *They had as king over them the angel of the bottomless pit. His name in Hebrew is Abaddon, and in Greek he is called Apollyon.* One of the reasons for believing that this plague is not actual locusts is that it has a king. Proverbs 30:27 informs us that natural locusts do not have a king ruling over them!

The devil is the king of demons controlling a vast empire of evil spirits and through them he can influence the lives of countless millions of people. Unlike God, the devil is not omnipresent. He cannot be everywhere at the same time. Having said that, through his teeming minions, he can attack many people at any given moment. So he has a fair bit of mobility and a fair bit of clout to go along with it.

His purpose

We note in verse 11 that his name is *Abaddon* in the Hebrew and *Apollyon* in the Greek. The name means 'the destroyer.' That sums him up in a nutshell; he is out to wreck people's lives, to ruin ordinary men and women. We see him here as he really is, the mask is removed, the precariously thin veneer of respectability is stripped away, he is no angel of light, he is evil personified.

Having said that, he is on the warpath even today. He is on the prowl (cf. 1 Peter 5:8). He is doing everything in his power to trip up the people of God. He is doing all that he can to frustrate the efforts of those seeking to advance the cause of the gospel of Christ to the ends of the earth. It will be true then, even as it is today, that Satan to Jesus must bow. No matter what the devil does, God holds the trump card!

9:3-6

The locusts ... their authority

John says in verse 3, *Then from the smoke came locusts on the earth.* They are demons straight from the caverns of hell itself. Someone said that '... smoke billows from the prison house of evil unleashing the soot of hell.' John MacArthur suggests: 'The smoke polluting the sky symbolises the corruption of hell belched forth from the abyss to pollute the world.' A spiritual plague of demonic proportions breaks out upon the whole earth. They are swarming all over the place; in fact, there are so many we read that *the sun and the air were darkened* by them. The inevitable outcome where mankind is terrorised is fuelled by the work of millions of these fiendish beings.

John continues by pointing out that they *were given power like the power of scorpions of the earth.* One writer says: 'There is no more repulsive member of the spider family than the scorpion; the irritability of its nature, its implacability as it approaches its victim and the swiftness of its striking tail causes it to be greatly feared.' This statement of intent leaves no doubt in our minds that demons only operate under divine permission. Their power or authority comes ultimately from the Lord. We need to remember this for it means, even in the worst of times, that God is in total control. No matter what happens to any of us, the Lord remains firmly in charge.

The extent of it

We glean from verse 5 that *they were allowed to torment them for five months, but not to kill them.* The limit is set by God at five months, not a day more, not a day less. Yes, the Bible is that exact! It is Swiss precision. The boundary is established and it will not, it cannot, be breached.

Mention is made of the targets which are affected by this cutback in their strike capability in verse 4. We read, *They were told not to harm the grass of the earth or any green plant or any tree, but only those people who do not have the seal of God on their foreheads.* God's people—the 144,000—are wonderfully immune from the sting of the locusts as this concerted attack is specifically directed to those who are unsealed. They cause a lot of pain and leave a lot of unbelieving people writhing in severe agony with all sorts of medical complications. Their attacks on human beings will not be fatal for they are instructed not to kill. Men and women, on every continent, are like sitting ducks.

When a plague of locusts hits an area, they eat everything in sight (cf. 2 Chronicles 7:13). Every blade of grass, every leaf on a tree, every flower and stalk of grain is consumed. They have even been known to strip the bark from the trees. Joel has described such a swarm: 'The land is like the garden of Eden before them, but behind them is a desolate wilderness' (2:3). One swarm over the Red Sea in 1889 was reported to have covered 2,000 square miles. They have a voracious appetite which cannot be satisfied. That is how these demons will be! They have an insatiable lust to wreak havoc in the lives of people. This underlines the truth that God is sovereign for even the demons of hell are under divine management!

The effects of it

The raging torment of unbelievers is graphically described in verse 5 where John compares *their torment* to *the torment of a scorpion when it stings someone.* Here we have the crippling effect of their authority when the entire human race becomes dysfunctional. From what I understand, a scorpion sting is not life-threatening except in the case of small children. Apparently, the venom attacks the veins and the body's nervous system to such an extent that the intense pain and discomfort will last for several days. When the poison enters the system it sets the nerve centre on fire. That helps explain why people feel the way they do for their anguish is indescribable.

I read in a medical journal that there is nothing you can take to relieve the pain; in fact, a pain killer would only exacerbate the effect of the venom making the pain infinitely worse! The pain is often accompanied by temporary paralysis and a high fever and there is nothing you can do but grin and bear it. It has to be endured.

John drops a bombshell when he tells us this demonic invasion will persist for almost half a year! Five months—the normal lifespan of locusts, usually from May to September—is not that long if you are waiting for something exciting to happen in your life, but it is a terribly long time if you are waiting for something awful to end. Life will be intolerable. In fact, it is so debilitating that people actually want to die; the suffering is so severe that men will be driven to suicide. But God will frustrate their efforts. Their attempts to 'run away from it all' will come to nothing. The gun does not fire; the overdose is ineffective; the leap from a tall building is interrupted by some kind of invisible net!

Yes, they will try but they will not be successful. People will seek relief in death only to find that death has taken a holiday! That is what we read in verse 6, *And in those days people will seek death and will not find it. They will long to die, but death will flee from them.*

9:7-10

The locusts ... their appearance

The next paragraph is unbelievably colourful in its language. The description is so unlike ordinary locusts that we have to recognise John is using them to represent something entirely different; they are symbolic of demons and John is attempting to depict them in this way so that the people of his day will understand what he is talking about.

Overall, they are seen in verse 7 as *horses prepared for battle.* John sees a possible tie-up here with the prophecy in Joel 2:4-5 where the prophet says, 'Their appearance is like the appearance of horses, and like war horses they run. As with the rumbling of chariots, they leap on the tops of the mountains, like the crackling of a flame of fire devouring the stubble, like a powerful army drawn up for battle.' There is a fascinating consistency between them that is more than coincidental. They are both addressing the subject of the Day of the Lord.

The apostle then provides us with a specific description of them in the remaining verses in this section. He says, *On their heads were what looked like crowns of gold; their faces were like human faces, their hair like women's hair, and their teeth like lions' teeth; they had breastplates like breastplates of iron, and the noise of their wings was like the noise of many chariots rushing into battle. They have tails and stings like scorpions, and their power to hurt people for five months is in their tails.* Each comparison is introduced with the word *like* for what we have here is a brilliant portrayal of a powerful enemy armed for battle.

With bodies like horses they progress rapidly and stop at nothing. They have faces like men which suggests their cunning and craft; like their boss, they are as subtle as they come. Their heads are crowned and that is an allusion to their temporary rule over the world; they feel good when they think they are running the show! That they are covered with long hair is a hint at their tactics for they will entrap both men and women. They appear very alluring and they will use their stunning appearance to seduce unwitting individuals. They are hideously beautiful and brilliantly deceptive. They have teeth like those of lions for they are ready to shred and tear to pieces those they pounce upon. Their skin is like a coat of mail which implies they are callous and heartless; no matter how people shriek and groan, the demons are pitiless. When they fly, the noise is like an army of chariots rushing by; their victims will not be able to escape the terror of their arrival.

In that day all restraints will be removed, the gloves are off and man will reel from every blow the enemy inflicts on him. The horror of that day does not bear thinking about. It will be so much worse than we can possibly imagine, a nightmare for those who experience it. These demons may be hideous looking creatures but they are powerful, invincible, indestructible, and intelligent. It is typical of the old devil; it does not matter what he does, it is the nature of the beast; like the scorpion, there is always a sting in the tail!

9:12-13

By the time you come down to verse 12, John says all that needs to be said, *The first woe has passed; behold, two woes are still to come.*

A voice ... its sound and its source

With the sound of the trumpet ringing in his ear, John tells us that he *heard a voice from the four horns of the golden altar before God.* There is nothing strange or startling about this for John often informs us that he hears a voice coming from near the throne of God. It may be the voice of a special angel which John hears, or one of the cherubim who guard the glory of God or it may be one of the four living creatures who function as the worship leaders of heaven. All of these are well within the bounds of possibility.

On the other hand, it is not naïve to think that it could be the voice of God himself. Why should he not communicate personally and directly with the sixth angel? The voice is of supreme importance because of the grave message which is conveyed.

It came from the horns of the altar! That is what we came across in chapter 8. It is the altar of incense on which was offered before God the prayers of the saints who were then living on earth. In that passage, the angel took fire from the altar and threw it down upon the earth and horrific judgment followed.

It would appear that the impassioned prayers of the saints in 6:10 are finally answered in what happens next. Do you remember their prayer? *O Sovereign Lord, holy and true, how long before you will judge and avenge our blood on those who dwell on the earth?* This second woe, the sixth trumpet judgment, is God's specific answer to their heartfelt cry. It may not be what they had in mind or even anticipated but their plea is answered nonetheless. That is what really counts for, if it does nothing else, it underlines the signal truth that God is sovereign.

9:14-15

The control of this army

The message which filtered through to the sixth angel was clear and concise, there was no mistaking it. We read about it in verse 14 where the eavesdropping John spills the beans: It said *to the sixth angel who had the trumpet, 'Release the four angels who are bound at the great river Euphrates.'* That was some message! God's answer takes the form of releasing four powerful fallen angels who have been bound for centuries at this great river. They are set free in God's time; again, this underpins the truth I have tried to emphasise throughout our study that the Lord rules and reigns. He is in total control!

The use of the definite article *the* suggests that these four angels form a specific group. John MacArthur notes: 'Their precise identity is not revealed, but they may be the demons that controlled the four major world empires of Babylon, Medo-Persia, Greece, and Rome.' You read all about them in Daniel 10:12-14 where their ability to influence governments and nations is in the spotlight. They are an integral part of Satan's network of evil. That said, James Allen is right when he says, '... they are but pawns in a far wider divine purpose.'

Four leaders

This quartet of angels are the leaders of a huge army which John refers to in verse 16. He records the mind-boggling statistic by saying, *The number of mounted troops was twice ten thousand times ten thousand; I heard their number.* This staggering figure of 200 million troops made a significant impact on him. I imagine John was quite taken aback by the massive scale of this entire operation. For him, back in the first century, it must have blown his mind; for you and me living in the third millennium, it is not as far-fetched as some punters have made it appear. It is believable!

The cradle of civilisation

Did you notice where these angels were bound? The Euphrates, one of four rivers which came out of the garden paradise of Eden. It was here Satan first alighted on earth and made a successful attack upon the human race! It was here all of earth's miseries were introduced! It was here the first sin was committed and the first lie told. It was here the first murder was committed and the first martyr slain! It was here the Jews dragged out their bitter exile! It was here Babylon arose! It was here we have the prototype of the kingdom of the Antichrist! It is right here where four special emissaries of Satan are chafing at the bit!

Archaeologists consider the Euphrates as the birthplace of civilisation. God will use it as a graveyard at the end of time; in a mysterious way, he will wrap up the history of the world in this place.

It was with Abraham that God entered into a covenant regarding his people and the promised land. We read in Genesis 15:18 that the border would extend as far as the 'great river Euphrates.' The river serves as a natural frontier between the lands of the East and the Middle Eastern, European, and Western nations. It flows out of the mountains of Armenia, down through the present-day lands of Turkey, Syria, and Iraq, to the Persian Gulf. It is about 1,780 miles long and, just like the Nile, it floods in the months of March to May because of melting snows. In the ancient world, it formed the eastern fringe of the vast Roman Empire. History tells us the Romans lived in constant fear of the warlike Parthians who lived on the other side of the river. The same could be said of Israel for the great warrior nations of Assyria and Babylonia had previously come down from the north across the river into the Holy Land.

In recent times, the Euphrates River was strategically important during the 1991 Gulf War which liberated Kuwait. 'Stormin' Norman,' as they called him, was the top dog, the man in charge of Operation Desert Storm. During the one-hundred-hour ground campaign of that conflict, the US Army's 24th Mechanised and 101st Airborne Divisions trapped the elite Republican Guard of Iraq with its back against the Euphrates River. They were unable to escape, they had nowhere to hide and so were decimated in one of the most lopsided military victories of all time. And the rest is history!

The killing fields revisited

It is right here at this location that 9:15 will become a reality. John says, *So the four angels, who had been prepared for the hour, the day, the month, and the year, were released to kill a third of mankind.* There is nothing airy-fairy about God's timetable. We are not talking about just the year when this great event will take place; we are not narrowing it down to only a particular month in a particular year; we are not pinpointing only a specific day in a given month in a given year! No! We are more focused than that! We are down to the very hour when it will happen. God has this special moment circled in red on heaven's calendar! The date is set. And, be encouraged, God is never ahead of time and he is never late. He is always on time! His time.

When that predetermined hour arrives, all will go according to God's plan. Nothing can happen, nothing will happen, which will cause him to abort his mission. Again it stresses that everything is under his control and that includes all the demons of darkness. Not a speck of dust moves, not a blade of grass stirs, not an army can move, not a shot can be fired, without his knowing all about it.

The unthinkable repercussions of their release is the wholesale slaughter of one third of mankind. Earlier in the Tribulation 25% of the world's population was eliminated; that happened when seal judgment number four transpired. Still others have perished from drinking polluted water as recorded in 8:10-11 and, no doubt, there will have been many other casualties for one reason or another.

But now, what we have our attention focused on is that a further one third of the population is to be killed. Death, which had taken a brief holiday under the fifth trumpet, now returns with a vengeance. When you add all the numbers together, it means that a minimum 50% of the world's peoples have died before the middle of the Tribulation. That sends shivers down my spine! It is an alarming figure which causes me enormous concern. It is the size of the figure which is hard to comprehend; it is so big that it is hard to envisage, I cringe every time I think about it. That is why, today, we must pull out all the stops in order to share the good news of Jesus Christ with those who are still outside his global family. We owe it to them to warn them to flee from the coming day of God's wrath!

9:16-17

The characteristics of this army

John moves on in verse 16 to leave us in no doubt as to the incredible size of this army. He informs us that *the number of mounted troops was twice ten thousand times ten thousand.* Then, as if to reinforce his utter amazement at the staggering size of this military contingent, he says, *I heard their number.* It is almost as if the figure left him speechless and dumbfounded, he could not believe what he had just been told! It is a number which is so large it is difficult to comprehend. In his day there were not even two hundred million people living on the earth! We have seen news footage in recent days of mass demonstrations in a variety of global hotspots and some of these have added up to one million people; but, when you multiply that by two hundred, it blows the mind! I understand from military records that this number is almost twice as many troops as the Allied and Axis powers combined when they were at peak strength in World War II.

It is fairly realistic to assume that the army we are talking about here is one which comes from the lands of the rising sun. It has often been referred to as the 'yellow peril' for these vast nations of the Orient are the only ones able to fit the bill. China, for example, has a population hovering around 1.4 billion people. For them, to muster an army of this size is no big deal. (A few decades ago, Mao Tse-tung said that in the battle for the world, China could field an army of 200 million soldiers.) Logistically, there may be all sorts of problems, it would not be that easy. Numerically, they are home and dry.

One of the keys to understanding this second phase in God's judgment programme is to compare this portion with a similar event unfolding in phase three. You find it in 16:12-16 where we read about the Euphrates drying up as a curtain raiser to the campaign of Armageddon. In that scenario, the way is opened up for an incursion into the land of Israel from what John describes as *the kings from the east.* We will come back to that in more detail later; suffice to say, what we have here in chapter 9 is the world's greatest army causing absolute mayhem among the peoples of the world.

Aggressive and awesome!

John gives a powerful description of the horses and riders he saw in his vision. He says in verse 17 that *they wore breastplates the colour of fire and of sapphire and of sulphur, and the heads of the horses were like lions' heads, and fire and smoke and sulphur came out of their mouths.* Red, blue and yellow ... and when combined, they are an effective portrayal of what we can expect from these assailants in the field of battle. No matter how you interpret this verse, these combatants are an aggressive force and, when you see them in full flight, they are an awesome force as well. Someone said that 'the Allied landing on the Normandy beaches in 1944 will appear as a minor skirmish when measured against this attack.'

It seems clear what John envisions for us is the machinery of modern military capability translated into the terminology of his day. Breastplates of various colours suggest armoured chariots and could refer to tanks, troop carriers, missile launchers, rocket batteries, artillery pieces, and aircraft of various countries bearing the identifying colours of their nations of origin. This army is Satan's great attempt to deny to Christ the sovereignty of earth.

The lions mouths which spouted fire and smoke suggest cannons, mortars, rocket launchers, and even missiles killing great masses of people with fire, radiation, and poison gases. The fact that one third of the human race is destroyed in this conflict strongly implies that weapons of mass destruction are deployed. Some leaders are trigger happy and even in our day there are those who, it would appear, can hardly wait to flick the switch. In some countries, we have already witnessed the devastating results of germ warfare. The statistics are frightening and alarming but there is nothing unusual about them when you bear in mind the nature of this particular engagement.

9:18-21

The consequences of this army

This is echoed in verse 18 where it is confirmed that *a third of mankind was killed, by the fire and smoke and sulphur coming out of their mouths.* And there is another intriguing insight given to us by John in verse 19 where he says, *The power of the horses is in their mouths and in their tails, for their tails are like serpents with heads, and by means of them they wound.* What an amazing picture! These words could apply to various kinds of modern armaments such as helicopter gunships or even missiles which leave a snake-like trail in their wake and inflict injury with their warheads. They are lethal, fatal, and terminal. It is hard to say for we cannot be sure or dogmatic. At the end of the day, no matter how you look at it, it paints a picture of untold destruction on an unbelievable scale. It is monstrous slaughter, a wipeout.

Zero repentance

You would think by this time that men would be driven to their knees. You would imagine that men would be turning to God in their droves. Nothing could be further from the truth. That is the last thing on their mind. The truth is spelled out very clearly in the next verse and I think this is one of the most astounding verses in the entire book. John concludes in verse 20 that *the rest of mankind, who were not killed by these plagues, did not repent of the works of their hands.* Man is defiant! He shakes his fist in God's face!

In all honesty, would you not think that by this time the remaining earth survivors would fall down before God and beg for mercy? The 'God, get me out of this mess and I'll believe in you' form of prayer is not even uttered! There is not even the slightest hint of that happening, no record of anyone repenting. The statistics for people trusting in Jesus for the first time remain at zero. The stark reality is summed up in the words of one commentator when he writes: 'Nuclear war, earthquakes, plagues, deadly insects, people dying faster than babies being born, these disasters will not break the pagans.' It can be summed up in a few words, their hearts are harder than granite. They are like stone. These folk are highly religious; the problem is, the god they worship is the god of materialism.

They are living in a secular society which has relegated the true God to the bottom rung of the ladder. They are totally wrapped up in themselves and their own pursuits; they have no time for, nor interest in, the God of the Bible. They are happy to follow the Antichrist and give him loyal devotion. They fulfil their spiritual aspirations in demon worship and, at the same time, are enthusiastically committed to all kinds of religious experience through worshipping Satan.

John tells us they did not *give up worshipping demons and idols of gold and silver and bronze and stone and wood.* And then he adds with a hint of sarcasm in his voice, [idols] *which cannot see or hear or walk* (cf. Isaiah 44:9-20). A classic case of dead sinners worshipping dead gods! Henry Morris said that 'God will allow them to experience a little direct fellowship with their future cohabitants in the lake of fire.'

The final verse in the chapter catalogues four serious sins which are rampant during these depressingly familiar days of Tribulation. John says in verse 21, *Nor did they repent of their murders or their sorceries or their sexual immorality or their thefts.*

Murder. The first one on the list is murder; it speaks of violent crime and is the inevitable outcome in a crazed society where life is cheap. Killings will be so common that they will not be reported in the national media. This may even include the killing of the very young through infanticide and abortion and the killing of the elderly through involuntary euthanasia.

Sorcery. This speaks of the occult, spiritualism, witchcraft, and a strange fascination with the future which includes horoscopes and astrology. It is linked inextricably with drug culture. The Greek word is *pharmakeia* and it probably refers, in this instance, to mind-bending, mood-altering drugs. When these are taken and people are addicted to them, they switch between the worlds of fantasy and reality. It means they are immune to the disasters surrounding them.

Sexual immorality. The thought here is one of free love for all. It is the mindset which says, 'everybody's doing it, so why shouldn't I?' In such a libertine environment, people generally tend to revert back to their baser instincts where lust reigns supreme and many end up acting like animals.

Theft. This last item on the list highlights the crimes of fraud, burglary, and embezzlement. Such things happen when greed is the motivator.

This is what will happen during the Tribulation but, as you and I know from experience, we see it happening all around us in today's world. We have lost our moral bearings as a nation and we are drifting aimlessly out to sea. These four sins are part and parcel of our present culture. It is no wonder then that they will be centre stage in the not too distant future.

CHAPTER 10

The world at his feet

Sometimes life does not make sense. People often wrestle with hard questions:

Lord, where were you when my child died?
Lord, where were you when the missionaries were massacred?
Lord, where were you when the guerrillas abducted your servants?
Lord, why do bad guys seem to sail through life so easily?
Lord, where were you when life was so unfair?
Lord, why do bad things happen to good people?

As World War 11 loomed on the horizon, the Nazis deported Elie Wiesel, a Jew, and his whole family to the Auschwitz death camp. Later they transferred Wiesel to Buchenwald, another notorious concentration camp, where he spent part of his teenage years. While in the camps, both of his parents and his younger sister died.

The biographer, Francois Mauriac, wrote that for Wiesel: 'Nietzsche's cry was expressed in almost physical reality—God is dead. The God of love, the God of gentleness, the God of comfort, has vanished forevermore. And how many pious Jews have experienced this death? On that day, horrible even among those days of horror, when a child watched the hanging of another child who, he tells us, had the face of a sad angel, he heard someone behind him groan, "Where is God? Where can God be now?"'

Where is God when heaven seems silent? Revelation 10 shows us there is coming a day when the answers will be given. God does not leave us hanging by our finger tips; he does not keep us in suspense. We read in verse 7 that *the mystery of*

God would be fulfilled. That is a statement of fact. It tells me in a day soon to come that we will see the puzzle of the ages solved. Then all of life's enigmas will be adequately explained. We must await God's time!

With that in mind, I recall a story I heard many years ago about a farmer who worked hard in his field, which was bordered by his neighbour's field. Out of respect and reverence for the Lord's day, the old farmer never worked on a Sunday, while his neighbour always did. Although he worked hard to make up for it, the loss of time cost the farmer. His soil was not ploughed on time, his crops were not planted on time, and in the end, his autumn harvest was not as full and profitable as his neighbour's. When the neighbour pointed out the difference and told the farmer God seemed to have blessed him more even though he had not honoured the Lord's day, the old farmer replied, 'God doesn't settle all of his accounts in October!'

In chapter 10 we have another interlude, a longer intermission than previously which gives us a wonderful chance to catch our breath. So much has been happening. Events have been moving so fast that we can hardly keep pace. They are accelerating at breakneck speed. It has been so intense. Satan is having his heyday. The earth is going haywire. The heavy storm clouds have gathered and the anger of God has been felt across the world.

By this time, in the middle of the Tribulation, the statistics tell us that 50% of the population has died. The grim reaper has been actively at work. But what we have here is a preview of the triumph of Jesus. We see that the moment will come when Jesus is hailed as the mighty conqueror. The main reason we have it here is to enable us to take heart; at the end of the day, God is the winner, the Lamb wins!

We are right in the middle of the seven-year period of Tribulation. The events that take place now can be sorely depressing because the Antichrist shows himself in his true colours. The mask comes off when he breaks his agreement with the nation of Israel and, instead of assuring them of the peace which he initially promised, he begins to persecute them.

Israel as a people and nation face the tortuously harrowing prospect of another holocaust experience. Times will be seriously bad but, even in such an awful era of trial and trouble, God is not without a witness to the world.

10:1-4

The angel's description

John says in verse 1 that he *saw another mighty angel coming down from heaven*. This strong angel is distinct from the seven angels who sound the seven trumpets. John's use of the word *saw* indicates the beginning of a new vision; indeed, a vision of someone new. Actually, our God has plenty more of those at his beck and call. That begs the question, If this is the messenger boy, what must the one who sent him be like?

Over the years there has been a lot of speculation as to the identity of this particular angel with many believing that it is none other than the Lord Jesus Christ, simply because of the similarities in his description and that of the glorified Christ in 1:12-17.

Basically, there are five reasons why I think it does not refer to Jesus Christ. One, the Greek word for *another* indicates another of the same kind, that is, one like the trumpet angels mentioned earlier. Two, whenever Jesus Christ appears in Revelation John gives him an unmistakable title. Three, other *mighty* angels appear in the book, as in Revelation 5:2 and 18:21. Four, it would be impossible for Christ to take the action described in verses 5 and 6, raising *his right hand to heaven and [swearing] by him who lives forever and ever, who created heaven and what is in it, the earth and what is in it, and the sea and what is in it.* Since he is God, the risen Jesus Christ would swear by himself (cf. Hebrews 6:13). Five, this angel came down out of heaven to earth and if we identify him as Christ that would add another coming of Christ to the earth.

He was robed!

Science can explain the clouds but I like to see them as the special clothing of this heavenly messenger. He is wearing the drapery of the sky over his mighty shoulders. That symbolises his power, majesty, and glory, and the fact that he comes bringing judgment.

He has a rainbow!

We first came across the rainbow when it encircled the throne of God in chapter 4. Now it sits like a crown upon the head of this mighty angel. The rainbow was God's sign that he would never again destroy the world with a flood (cf. Genesis 9:12-16). Here it reminds us that even in the day of his wrath, God remembers mercy (cf. Habakkuk 3:2).

God is a God of faithfulness and all his promises will be fulfilled. The English poet, William Wordsworth, said: 'My heart leaps up when I behold a rainbow in the sky.' John must have felt the same way when he saw this special messenger. Revelation takes us on a rollercoaster ride of emotions. We go from heartache and depression to scenes of triumph and joyous celebration. It is the seesaw syndrome so far as the ripening of God's eternal purposes are concerned.

His face was like the sun. His brilliant, radiant glory lit up the earth like the blazing noonday sun. Not unlike the angels at the empty tomb on resurrection morning (cf. Luke 24:4). *His legs were like pillars of fire.* This is a stunning symbol of God's strength and the firmness, stability, and holiness of all his ways and purposes. Two more features strike me as most unusual.

A book in his hand!

In verse 2 we read that *he had a little scroll open in his hand. And he set his right foot on the sea, and his left foot on the land.* The book in his hand is a comparatively small scroll and it is open! We read Job's impassioned plea in 31:35 where he says, 'O, that I had one to hear me! O, that I had the indictment written by my adversary!' In that verse Job is referring to a 'charge sheet' produced by his legal opponent in a lawsuit. This 'indictment' contained a list of the charges to be put to the judge in the presence of the accused. A similar thought is found in Ezekiel 2:9.

The meaning of the Greek word used here for *scroll* is 'a small book, a document, especially a petition.' In legal-speak, it would be the indictment or the charge sheet against the accused. One commentator notes: 'It is the presentation of this charge which demands the lion-like voice of the angelic accuser ... this *little scroll* [is] God's indictment of the nations as he lays claim to the possession of earth.'

The world at his feet!

His posture is most captivating. It is the picture of a conqueror taking possession of his territory! He is claiming the whole world with his right foot on the sea and his left foot on the land, we see him standing there astride the earth like a giant colossus making a declaration that, as the agent of the throne, his is the right to rule and reign. James Allen notes: 'He is acting as a bailiff on behalf of the legal owner.' The world is his! The earth is the Lord's; he claims dominion over every land, from pole to pole, from sea to sea, from the rivers to the ends of the earth.

He shouts his message. We read in verse 3, *and [he] called out with a loud voice, like a lion roaring.* The devil roars like a lion to frighten his prey (cf. 1 Peter 5:8), but this declaration—the reading of the charge sheet—reflects the power and authority of God! This tremendous truth is expanded on in Psalm 95:3-5 and Isaiah 40:12-17. Many Old Testament prophets see a link between a lion-like roar and the thought of judgment (cf. Jeremiah 25:30; Hosea 11:10; Joel 3:16).

What a stirring announcement! It was so loud that Satan's roar seems like a soft whisper by comparison. It drowns out the devil in a way which he deserves, it muffles all that the enemy says. We read in verse 3, *When he called out, the seven thunders sounded.* It is just like a seven-gun salute in the skies. It is a booming reply; it sounds like something the movie moguls in Hollywood would orchestrate. Recall the words of Job 37:5 where we read, 'God thunders wondrously with his voice; he does great things that we cannot comprehend.' On a similar note, we read in Psalm 29:3 that 'the God of glory thunders!'

What follows next is quite unusual. John was about to write down what had been spoken, but he heard another message saying, *Seal up what the seven thunders have said, and do not write it down.* This is the first and only time in the book when John is forbidden to reveal the contents of the message shared with him. What was this message? We just do not know and there is no point in speculating. No amount of guessing will get us anywhere! Since God has chosen to veil the truth in this instance, it is best to leave it that way. The God who makes himself known is the same God who keeps his secrets. As J I Packer observed: 'We must be content not to know what the Scripture does not tell us.'

10:5-7

The angel's declaration

It is based on God's authority

This declaration is one which is carried out under oath. We read, *And the angel whom I saw standing on the sea and on the land raised his right hand to heaven and swore by him who lives forever and ever, who created heaven and what is in it, the earth and what is in it, and the sea and what is in it.* He swears in the name of one who is eternal and who is the great Creator. The words employed in this comprehensive statement reveal that the scope of God's creative power is all-encompassing. John MacArthur reminds us that 'his purpose for his creation will be fulfilled through judgment, renovation, destruction, and re-creation.'

It is rooted in God's timetable

He seems to be saying, 'Look, all the weight of deity is behind it, all heaven is behind it.' *There would be no more delay!* is the message given in verse 6. As sure as night follows day, and Tuesday comes after Monday, it is going to happen. If it does not take place, he would fail to be God! In essence, God is staking his very existence on his message.

The startling implication is that from this day forward, God's foot will be on the accelerator. Every stop is pulled out, all systems are up and running. There is no turning back! That is the message. God is on time. All is according to his schedule. Everything is going according to his plan. He has it all marked out on his calendar and when the hour comes, that is it! *There would be no more delay!*

For decades, centuries, all of time, man has been frustrated asking, Why the apparent delay? Why doesn't God step into the situation? Why doesn't God do something about it? No matter where we look, Satan is on the rampage. It appears that wrong is on the throne and right is on the scaffold. It seems that sin has run unchecked and evil has been unbridled.

Remember the souls under the altar? They asked about God's timetable in chapter 6. Remember the disciples? They came to Jesus privately and asked him in Matthew 24:3, 'What will be the sign of your coming and of the end of the age?' Yes, scoffers have taunted, saints have pleaded, the cry has ascended, *'How long, O Lord, how long?'*

It is grounded in God's promise

Well, the waiting is just about over! It is down the home straight! The end is in sight! Full steam ahead! We read in verse 7 that *the mystery of God would be fulfilled.* There is no stopping the Lord now as he moves into overdrive 'to unite all things in him, things in heaven and things on earth' (Ephesians 1:10). This is the consummation of God's plan in bringing his glorious kingdom in Christ to fulfilment. The groan of creation (cf. Romans 8:22) is about to be hushed.

10:8-11

The angel's directions

Up to this point John has been a virtual spectator in the grandstand of heaven. He is gobsmacked as he has watched each event unfold before his eyes. Now he becomes an actor in the drama of the Apocalypse. He hears a voice from heaven which tells him in verse 8 to *'Go, take the scroll that is open in the hand of the angel who is standing on the sea and on the land.'* And that is precisely what John does.

Sweet and sour!

No sooner has John done it than he hears the angel's voice a second time saying in verse 9, *'Take and eat it; it will make your stomach bitter, but in your mouth it will be sweet as honey.'* Sound strange? Yes and no! Tasting and eating in the Bible often refers to hearing and believing. Jeremiah and Ezekiel had a similar experience; both of them had to eat the Word before they could pass it on to others (cf. Jeremiah 15:16; Ezekiel 3:1-3).

Absorb and assimilate!

We need to absorb and assimilate the Word in our daily lives; it must become an integral part of us for only then can we share it. It is all about digesting the truth of God's Word and allowing it to permeate every part of our life. John was to immerse himself in the things of God and saturate himself with Scripture. What an experience this must have been for John! It was sweet to his taste but it was bitter in his belly. It was a bitter sweet experience!

Many of us can readily identify with John and how he feels at this point. When I study a book like this, I get so excited when I realise the countdown to the coming of Christ is getting nearer every day. It is great news. It is exhilarating. There is a new world waiting for us! At other times it can be so disturbing and depressing when I think of the awful fate of those who hear the truth and then reject it. They say 'no' to Jesus, even though the clock is ticking away.

The same gospel that makes it possible for me to go to heaven, puts someone else in hell. 'To one,' says Paul, '[it is] a fragrance from death to death, to the other a fragrance from life to life' (2 Corinthians 2:16). That is what prophetic truth is all about: it is a sweet and sour experience.

John hears the voice a third time in verse 11 when the angel says, *'You must again prophesy about many peoples and nations and languages and kings.'* John is reminded of his unique task for his mission is not yet complete, his work is not yet finished. Even though he is not exactly in the first flush of youth, there is still more for John to do! The same is true in your life and mine!

CHAPTER 11
Christmas Day in Jerusalem

Charles Dickens was a prolific writer. In his *Tale of Two Cities* he describes in vivid language what life was like immediately prior to the French revolution. At the very beginning of the story, he tells us with a cluster of pithy, colourful sayings:

It was the best of times, it was the worst of times;
it was the age of wisdom, it was the age of foolishness;
it was the epoch of belief, it was the epoch of incredulity;
it was the season of light, it was the season of darkness;
it was the spring of hope, it was the winter of despair;
we had everything before us, we had nothing before us;
we were all going direct to heaven, we were all going direct the other way.

Each statement is either a paradox or contradiction. The chilling reality is that people did not know whether they were coming or going. When I read through the opening verses of chapter 11 the same superlatives which Dickens used are most appropriate for the age which John is describing.

It is the worst of times, an age of foolishness, an epoch of incredulity, a season of darkness, a winter of despair, with nothing except judgment facing those who are conned and deluded by the Antichrist. On the other hand, when you look at it from a different angle, it is the best of times, an age of wisdom, a season of light, the spring of hope, with everything before those who are bound for heaven and home! The bottom line, for the unbeliever, the worst is yet to come; for the believer, the best is yet to be!

This is a most fascinating chapter. There are parts which are fairly easy to follow and there are other portions which are most difficult to grasp; that does not really matter too much for the golden thread woven into the fabric of this section is that God never leaves himself without a witness. As one Bible commentator said with remarkable insight: 'The more degenerate the times, the more definite the testimony.' Before the Flood, the Lord raised up Enoch and Noah and in the days of Israel's darkest apostasy, he raised up Elijah and Elisha. God will do the same again!

11:1-2

The temple measured

We are told that John *was given a measuring rod like a staff and was told, 'Rise and measure the temple of God and the altar and those who worship there, but do not measure the court outside the temple; leave that out, for it is given over to the nations, and they will trample the holy city for forty-two months.'* You are probably thinking 'that seems a rather strange thing to do!'

The reed which John is given is compared to a rod, one which is commonly grown in the Jordan Valley and, because of its light weight, is fairly versatile. They grow to an average height of fifteen to twenty feet. It has a hollow stalk, yet it is rigid enough to be used as a walking staff (cf. Ezekiel 29:6), it could even be shaved down into a pen (cf. 3 John 13). The stalks, when cut to twelve feet lengths, were excellent as a measuring device.

John is instructed by the divine director to act out the prophecy of the rebuilt temple that the regathered Jews will build in Jerusalem. The Old Testament prophet Ezekiel said the Jews will go back to Jerusalem in unbelief. We read as much in 36:24 and the verses which follow where he tells us, 'I will take you from the nations and gather you from all the countries and bring you into your own land.' The Jews will build a temple in the name of Jehovah God but they will not know him at all. (There is a vast amount of information on this in Ezekiel 40-41.)

The measurement is a symbolic action. We have come across it before in the prophecies of Ezekiel (40:3) and Zechariah (1:16) and we will come across it one more time in Revelation (21:14-17). These measurements represent God's ownership (cf. Zechariah 2:1-15; Psalm 16:6). He is staking his claim on them! The Lord was saying to John, 'I own this city and this temple and I claim both for myself!'

It is interesting to note that John was to measure a specific area known as *the temple of God and the altar.* This refers to the inner sanctuary which is made up of the holy place and the holy of holies. He was not to measure the entire temple complex. The command of God for John not to measure the outer court simply marks this area as being excluded from God's favour and blessing. It was, literally, abandoned to the unbeliever.

I have been to Jerusalem many times, I have spent hours walking all over the place, I have seen many sites of biblical, historical significance but I have never found the temple. The fact is, it is not there! Maybe I should qualify that statement and say, it is not there *yet!*

The history of the temple

The temple mount

Standing on the temple site today is the Dome of the Rock or the Mosque of Omar, as it is sometimes called. It is the third holiest Muslim shrine, built between 685 and 691 AD by the Arab caliph, Abdel Malik. Its brilliant blue Persian tiles of marble and mosaic and its soaring golden dome dominate one of the most fiercely contested pieces of real estate in the world! You can see it for miles around; it is truly resplendent and spectacular, especially when the sun is going down.

Islam regards the site of the Dome to be the place where the prophet Muhammad ascended into heaven. Standing alongside it is the silver Al Aqsa mosque. For the better part of two millennia, Jews, Muslims, and Christians have been slaughtered in their attempts to control this plot of land.

Solomon's temple

Away back in the halcyon days of King Solomon, in the first millennium BC, it was his stunningly magnificent temple which caught the eye. Taking seven years to build, it rose above the Jerusalem skyline until the invasion by Babylon in 586 BC when Nebuchadnezzar wasted no time in destroying it.

Zerubbabel's temple

Reconstruction began in 536 BC when the Lord sent Zerubbabel, the governor of Judah, to rebuild it after King Darius of Persia allowed some of the people to go back home to Jerusalem. It was finished in 516 BC, seventy years after its destruction (cf. Haggai 1:6-7; 2:9). When compared to the first, the second was but a shadow of its former glory.

Herod's temple

It was then lavishly rebuilt by King Herod over a period spanning 46 years. He made it one of the wonders of the world. According to the Jewish historian Josephus, the rabbis often said: 'He who has not seen Herod's temple has never seen a beautiful building.' If you had the time and found yourself in the city of Jerusalem, you could spend a fruitful couple of hours visiting a scale model of this.

A number of key events in the life of Jesus revolve around this particular temple, mentioned many times in the gospel narrative. The day came when Jesus prophesied to his disciples that not one stone of those great buildings would be left standing (cf. Mark 13:1-2).

The destruction of the temple

That is precisely what happened in 70 AD when Titus tightened his grip on Jerusalem (he was the son of the Roman Emperor Vespasian). He led the campaign to quell the Jewish uprising which began in 66 AD against Roman rule. It engulfed the entire region of Judea and it ended only after his troops laid siege to the city. In the process, he massacred the population; it is conservatively estimated that over one million Jews died by Roman swords. History confirms that the siege led to such cruel privation and starvation that the people of the city had no option but to eat their own children in order to survive! It was the first century equivalent of ethnic cleansing.

When the Romans finally breached the defences of Jerusalem, they levelled the city and razed the temple to the ground. Tradition tells us that the flames were so intense that the gold and silver adorning the temple buildings melted and ran between the cracks. The words of Jesus in Mark 13 were fulfilled and from that day to this there has been no Jewish temple on that sacred site.

The only remnant of the temple to be seen today is the western wall (Wailing Wall). Religious Jews come here day after day and, especially on the Sabbath, pour out their hearts in grief and anguish and plead for the Messiah to come. Three times a day, Orthodox Jews recite the words, 'May it be thy will that the temple be speedily rebuilt in our own time.'

There has been a lot of aggro, tension, and passion in recent days about rights of access to the temple site. The situation has been inflamed because of the actions of a few fanatical zealots trying to blow the whole site to pieces. Their goal is to clear the site and build the temple we are talking about here in chapter 11, but God has his own way of working and he does not need you, me, or them to speed up the process!

The Tribulation temple

When you turn back in your Bible to Daniel 9:24-27 the prophet foretold that a covenant would be signed between the Antichrist and the leader of the Jewish people and that after three and a half years the Antichrist would break the treaty and desecrate the temple. By then we will have gone full circle. It is almost a repeat performance of what Antiochus Epiphanes did in 168 BC which is a prototype of what will happen when Israel rebuilds the temple in the Tribulation.

We also read in 2 Thessalonians 2:3-4 that the Antichrist will set himself up as God in that temple. In other words, this temple will not be defiled by a statue of a pagan deity; it will be polluted by a man proclaiming himself to be God. This clash would usher in the second half of the Tribulation. That means the temple must be rebuilt for this to take place! The big question is, Where?

In order to answer the question surrounding the rebuilding of the temple, the exact location of the former temples must be correctly identified. One reason for this is that it is argued that the original site for the temple was divinely appointed (cf. Genesis 22:2; Exodus 15:17; 2 Samuel 24:18; 1 Chronicles 21:18).

Another reason is that there also appears to be a continuity between the temples. Each one was built with its holy of holies enclosing the same protrusion of Mount Moriah known as 'the foundation stone' (*Even ha-Shetiyah*). Because it was upon this stone that the ark of the covenant had been set and the divine presence in the shekinah glory had been manifest in 1 Kings 8, it is thought that no other place can be substituted. The problem has been in locating this place! Can we pinpoint with a reasonable degree of accuracy where it is?

Well, we can and we cannot! Ever since the Six Day War of 1967, when Jerusalem became a united city under Israeli control, there has been a tremendous amount of archaeological work done in and around the temple mount. One man, who stands out among many others, is Dr Asher Kaufman, a physics professor at the Hebrew University. He is an orthodox Jewish immigrant from Scotland who has long been interested in the topography of the temple mount.

After many years of probing and painstaking research, he

arrived at a startling conclusion. He said the ancient temple was actually about one hundred yards north of the traditionally held location in relation to the Dome of the Rock. His ideas first appeared in the local broadsheet, *The Jerusalem Post,* in the early 1980s. They then found their way into the pages of the highly acclaimed scholarly journal, *Biblical Archaeology Review,* in Spring 1983. And when you sit down and think them through, they make a lot of sense. They do not solve all the problems but they are certainly worthy of serious consideration. Let me give you a résumé of his main arguments:

The only gate that entered into the temple area from the east is appropriately called the Eastern Gate. This gate has been sealed since the Middle Ages. Most scholars believe it is built over the original eastern gate that led directly into the temple courtyard. I came across an interesting story in the *Mishnah* which illustrates the importance of this. It reveals that during the ceremony of the slaying of the red heifer (cf. Numbers 19) the high priest could look from the top of the Mount of Olives, directly over the eastern gate, into the temple sanctuary. This implies that the temple building was located directly behind the gate. This would not be the case if the temple were situated on the present site of the Dome of the Rock. If you were able to enter the bricked up Eastern Gate today, you would have to make a left turn going south to reach the Dome of the Rock.

Also, if you drew a straight line from the centre of the Eastern Gate, through the temple mount area, what do you think you would encounter? That line would go directly through a small domed structure that covers a round, flat piece of bedrock of Mount Moriah itself. This is known in Arabic by either of two names, the Dome of the Spirits or the Dome of the Tablets. It is intriguing, for when you read Josephus and compare his notes with a number of rabbinic sources, you discover that from the Second Temple period onward, the holy of holies was actually empty. The ark of the covenant had been removed before the destruction of the temple. In the temples of Zerubbabel and Herod, the only thing in the holy of holies was the flat bare rock of the mountain.

Could it be that this simple Muslim structure preserves an ancient idea that on the rock was the original ark containing the tablets of the Law engraved by the finger of God on Sinai? And could it be that the Dome of the Spirits is the site of the holy of holies where the glory of God dwelt in visible form? Maybe. Maybe not. If Dr Kaufman is correct, if his conclusions are valid, it means another temple could be built without even disturbing the Dome of the Rock!

This raises an interesting possibility relative to the task John has been given to measure the earthly temple. The scenario is: if the new temple is constructed to the north and slightly to the west of the Dome of the Rock, it means the outer court of the temple would encompass the complex we know as the Dome of the Rock. Some Bible commentators see a connecting link between this and the words of 11:2 where John is specifically told *not to measure the court outside the temple; leave that out, for it is given over to the nations.*

At the end of the day whatever happens, we know with certainty that the temple will be rebuilt and there will be some non-Jewish control of a portion of the temple mount for three and a half years. There is a line of demarcation clearly drawn. Because John is told not to measure the outer court, it implies that God is making a difference between those who know him and those who do not. There is a division between those who truly worship him and those who do not. This all transpires during the first half of the Tribulation.

If we can believe all that we hear and read, the preparations for the fulfilment of this prophecy are well underway. They have begun already, in our lifetime! I understand from other sources that detailed blueprints for the third temple have existed since the middle of the 1990s. I was equally amazed to discover that since 1987 a group of rabbinical researchers, designers, and craftsmen, under the direction of a prominent rabbi have been creating in the Jewish quarter of Jerusalem what they call a 'temple-in-waiting.' They are known collectively as the Temple Institute and much of their research is well-documented in various academic and religious publications. Some Yeshiva students are being trained in the order of priestly service. Many of these activists have been buying up Arab properties in the Muslim Quarter, next to the temple mount. So far as they are concerned, the closer they are to the temple, the better!

So many pieces are coming together in God's prophetic jigsaw that we can hardly believe it. Prophecy is being fulfilled before our eyes. The stage is set for so much is already in place; however, when it comes to the nitty-gritty of rebuilding the temple, like everything else, it is down to God's time.

In verse 2 we discover that Jerusalem is overrun by the Gentiles for a period of time that refers to the second half of the Tribulation. We read that *they will trample the holy city for forty-two months.* At the end of this era, the Lord will return in power and great glory to set up his millennial kingdom and bring to a finale the period known as 'the times of the Gentiles.' Jesus himself said as much in his prophecy of Luke 21:24 which began in 606 BC when Babylon began to devastate Judah and Jerusalem, and it will continue until the second advent of Jesus Christ as King of kings and Lord of lords (cf. Zechariah 14:9).

11:3-14

The two messengers

This is the story of two men who made their mark for God, who impacted the world in the end times, who appear on the stage with no fanfare and no advance publicity, who have no PR people to boost their ratings, and no spin doctors to put a gloss on their message; two men whose importance and influence dare not be underestimated; two men who remain anonymous in Scripture but whose fame is universal; two men whose real identity is concealed in the Bible but who end up as household names; two men in the business of performing miracles; two men who are immortal until their work for God is complete; two men who left people with their mouths gaping as they made a dramatic exit from Planet Earth; two men who found their niche in the purpose of God and, because of that, made a huge difference!

In an era when Satan has his two men, the Antichrist and False Prophet, so the Lord has his two men, and what a pair they are! The little phrase *my two witnesses* pays eloquent tribute to that fact! It is not hard to tell whose they are and whom they serve! They are automatically linked with the God of heaven as his representatives on earth. We have a most remarkable insight concerning them in 11:3 where the Lord says, *And I will grant authority to my two witnesses, and they will prophesy for 1,260 days, clothed in sackcloth.*

This is the first time we have come across the number 1,260 in our studies in Revelation. The previous verse spoke about 42 months and this was particularly relevant to the second half of the seven years of Tribulation. The key question is, What does the figure 1,260 refer to? It is a timespan and points to an era which lasts for three and a half years, using the biblical 360-day calendar as the basis for calculation.

The God who numbers the hairs on our head, who knows the name of every star in space, who sees a sparrow fall to the ground, is the God who is much more specific in recording the ministry of his two envoys than he is in mentioning the duration of the Antichrist's ranting. Did you notice that? He describes the vital ministry of his two spokesmen as a day by day ministry and counts it up to an exact figure. So far as Satan's superman is concerned, he talks about 42 months, that is all!

Does this refer to the first half or the second half of the Tribulation? There is some mileage to be gained in the fact that the two three-and-a-half-year periods are described in different ways, that is, as 42 months versus 1,260 days. A simple explanation is that John did it in order to show that they are not talking about the same time slot. In other words, they are two different halves of one seven-year epoch. This applies to the first half of the Tribulation because the Antichrist does all the shouting in the second half! The end of the first half is marked by the martyrdom of these two witnesses; the end of the second half is marked by the return of Christ to set up his millennial kingdom on earth.

The purpose of their calling

These two rugged individuals are empowered by the Lord for their special ministry in the last days; they are uniquely equipped by the Lord for the job he has for them to do; they are enabled by the Lord to fulfil the role for which he has chosen them. They face a daunting task, an uphill struggle. It is a lot for any man to handle. It is an enormous challenge but, with the help of God, they will be able to do it. Their confidence is rooted in God and there is no way he will let them down!

They have a message of prophecy. The ministry they exercise has a distinctive prophetic flavour. They are there to proclaim the good news of the kingdom; in the midst of chaos and crisis they point men to Jesus the King. That is what gives a sharp edge to all they have to say. They have a measure of success in the early days for it would seem that the 144,000 Jewish evangelists will respond to their preaching and, in turn, they will go to the ends of the earth proclaiming kingdom truth.

They have a message of repentance. We read that they are clothed in sackcloth (cf. Genesis 37:34; 2 Samuel 3:31; 1 Chronicles 21:16). None of your designer label, flashy, tailor-made expensive suits! This is the kind of cloth you pick up in the local flea market, not Savile Row. Burlap, a type of coarse canvas often made from jute, was the traditional garb of the Old Testament prophet when he was sent to warn of impending judgment; this is most appropriate for these latter-day prophets are preaching the need to mourn and lament over sin and get right with God!

They have a message of truth. They are also there as a kind of check and balance; they are there to tell the truth, to strip away the delusions, the lies, and satanic propaganda which the Antichrist is promoting. There was nothing attractive or glamorous about them. The men did not matter. It is the message that deserved top billing. Joe Public was not meant to look at them, he was supposed to listen to what they had to say.

The significance of their symbols

In verse 4, John describes these two agents in a rather unusual way. He says, *These are the two olive trees and the two lampstands that stand before the Lord of the earth.* If you know anything about the prophet Zechariah, you will recognise these twin symbols straightaway. You find them in chapter 4:1-14 of his book where he writes of two olive trees that drip their oil into a golden lampstand, as a witness to Israel in his day. John's reference here is an allusion to Joshua and Zerubbabel in the vision of Zechariah.

They were dual leaders of the local community; one had civic responsibilities and the other specialised in religious affairs. They are the ones who would take the people back to Israel from exile and inspire them to rebuild the fallen ruins of the temple. Zerubbabel would lay the foundation of the temple and finish it (cf. Zechariah 4:9). When the final stone was set in place, we read there would be shouts of 'God bless it, God bless it!' as if to emphasise that God's Spirit enabled them to achieve this tremendous goal.

This historical incident points to a future day when the temple will be rebuilt. Just as Joshua and Zerubbabel were used by the Lord to challenge the people to rebuild the house of the Lord, the two delegates from heaven will have a similar impact on the hearts of the Jewish people in the Tribulation. We can take it a step further when we realise that the olive oil is a beautiful symbol of the Holy Spirit. The light of their testimony is shining brightly because they have the Spirit of God flowing through them. They are full of life and light! They have the anointing of God upon their lives and ministry!

The identity of the witnesses

Can we identify them? Can we put a name to a face? Not

really, but we can have a go! These two proxies are real people, real men, flesh and blood. They are so real you can hear their voices, shake their hands, and show your feelings towards them. Over the years, these two witnesses have been equated with the two testaments of Scripture, one as the Old and one as the New. Others have said they represent the law and the gospel. Others say they depict Israel and the church, or Israel and the Word of God, as the two principal instruments of witness in the world. I do not think these views hold too much water. A fairly strong case can be made for Moses and Elijah, with one representing the law and the other, the prophets. Why?

Malachi predicted that Elijah would come to prepare the way for the Messiah (cf. Malachi 3:1-3; 4:5-6). Elijah never experienced death, therefore, he could return and die, just as the witnesses do. The witnesses have the same sign that was given to Elijah in regard to rain (verse 6). Elijah was one of two who appeared at the transfiguration of Jesus in Matthew 17:3 when the death of Jesus was the topic under debate.

Moses also appeared at the transfiguration of Jesus on snow-capped Mount Hermon (cf. Luke 9:28-36). Peter was also there as an eyewitness of the majesty of Christ and, when he writes about this event, he links it in with the second advent of Jesus; he sees it as a shadow of things to come (cf. 2 Peter 1:16-18). Moses also turned the waters into blood just as the two witnesses will do (cf. Exodus 7:19-20). Another contributory factor is that the body of Moses was preserved by God and only he is aware of its exact location. There is no grave for Moses anywhere in today's world. It is strange but in Jude 9 we see that the devil wanted to know where it was.

Another name has often been thrown into the ring and it is the name of Enoch. He is the man who walked closely with God in a pagan, secular society. He is on a similar footing to Elijah for, like him, he never died. For both, it was instant glory without ever tasting death. One minute they were here and the next they were gone to Glory! For them, there was no dark tunnel of death, it was the golden bridge of translation.

Actually, in some of the earliest Christian writings, there are references where Enoch and Elijah are named as the two witnesses. Having said that, the balance of probability weighs heavily in favour of Moses and Elijah. As someone said: 'Moses and Elijah, mighty men of old and mighty men of the future!'

The provision for their witness

They know the Lord's protection. We see in verse 5 that the two witnesses are not the least bit concerned about their personal security. They are immune and invincible until their work for God is finished. No one can touch them, no one can harm them, no one can lay a finger on them! John says, *If anyone would harm them, fire pours from their mouth and consumes their foes. If anyone would harm them, this is how he is doomed to be killed.* God looks after them! God watches over them! They have supernatural protection. If anyone gets too close and attempts to rough them up, they will wish they had not bothered for their end will be swift. Justice will be meted out instantly.

They know the Lord's power. A closer analysis of verse 6 reveals they have three supernatural weapons at their disposal. They are armed with **drought** for we read, *They have the power to shut the sky, that no rain may fall during the days of their prophesying.* It is back to the days of Elijah when the absence of rain lasted for three and a half years (cf. 1 Kings 17-18). If they wish, it could happen again. At least the weather forecasters cannot get it wrong for every day it will be dry and hot with not a cloud in the sky.

They are armed with **death** for we read, *and they have power over the waters to turn them into blood.* This has to be Moses Mark II. It happened the first time in Exodus 7 as one of the ten plagues visited on Egypt and there is nothing to say it cannot be repeated. Even though the magicians of Egypt were able to mimic that particular miracle, they were not able to reverse it.

The two witnesses are also armed with **disease** for they have power *to strike the earth with every kind of plague, as* *often as they desire.* In his day, Moses called for an infectious disease to spread among the cattle and he also called for man to experience all sorts of weird medical conditions brought about by one virus or another. When you think of what is happening in our world, it is not too far-fetched to believe that this kind of thing cannot happen again.

By any stretch of the imagination, these men are powerful individuals. They have the Lord on their side and they have a triple assault capability stashed away in their kit bag! For three and a half years, these men are untouchable, unbeatable, and unstoppable.

The ending of their witness

John underlines this fact with his opening comment in verse 7 when he says, *And when they have finished their testimony.* A man of God living in the centre of the will of God is immortal until his work for God is finished. Nothing can happen to these men, unless God gives the word. Satan could not silence them or slay them! When God is done, it is over. And not until then! Moses did not die until the tabernacle was finished building. Jesus did not die on the cross of Calvary until he cried with a loud voice, 'It is finished' (John 19:30). Paul did not die until he penned the words to young Timothy, 'I have finished the race' (2 Timothy 4:7).

Now their time has come. Their mission complete, their job done, their task finished! And so we read, *the beast that rises from the bottomless pit will make war on them and conquer them and kill them.* This is the first of 36 references to the Beast in Revelation. It is a clear reference to the coming world ruler, the Antichrist. He is Satan's puppet on a string, the devil incarnate. At his first real opportunity, the Antichrist goes for the jugular and kills them. They have been an irritant in his side. This is the first great act he will use to gain a wider following. The frenzied mob baying for blood will cheer the public executions. We need to remember that these two men are still in the centre of the purpose of God for their lives and, on this occasion, it spells martyrdom, just as it has for many of God's dear people down through the years.

The sin of the great city

John provides us with a few more details concerning their death when he writes in verse 8, *Their dead bodies will lie in the street of the great city that symbolically is called Sodom and Egypt, where their Lord was crucified.* They are not even given the dignity of a decent burial; they are left lying in the same spot where they fell to the ground. They are there for all to see! A macabre sight! A grotesque spectacle! The *great city* is a reference to Jerusalem. We know that because of the connection John makes with the death of the Lord Jesus. It is obviously a place of incredible violence. He also says it is like Sodom and Egypt. He is not handing out bouquets here! There is no prize for guessing what those places represented!

Sodom is a picture of unbelievable wickedness and immorality and would focus on the vice of the city of Jerusalem. Egypt is a symbol of oppression and slavery as well as being the capital of materialism. It depicts Jerusalem as a city renowned for its vanity. It is a sad fact, by the middle of the Tribulation, Jerusalem has become a centre of corruption and persecution. It is no longer the holy city, more like a city from hell. John is razor sharp in his honesty for he tells it like it is!

A public exhibition

Verse 9 really throws the cat among the pigeons for we read, *For three and a half days some from the peoples and tribes and languages and nations will gaze at their dead bodies and refuse to let them be placed in a tomb.* A staggering prediction for any man to make! In John's day this was an impossible feat, it just could not happen, but it can happen today with no problem. We have live TV pictures beamed into our homes from every continent and every time zone as major news stories are breaking. We can sit in the comfort and privacy of our lounge and watch events and dramas unfolding on the other side of the world.

Cameras will be despatched from every major news organisation for a special assignment in Jerusalem, and in homes and hotel rooms and on cinema screens in all the major centres of population and to the farthest corners of the earth, this event will be the top item of every news bulletin. This is the day when God will use mass media, the television, the satellite networks, the internet, to further his own ends. In that day, he will use modern technology to ultimately prove a point to a gloating population.

For years the critics have laughed at this prophecy, but now with the advances in science and technology from which we have all benefited, no one can scoff any longer! At the end of the day, God will have the last laugh. He knew about it all along, he was not taken by surprise nor caught napping! For him, the future is now!

When you realise that the bodies were left on display for eighty-four hours, it defies logic. Customary practice is for people to be buried within twenty-four hours in that part of the world! The attitude of people from the top down to this torrid affair smacks of sheer contempt. It shows how far man's moral decency has spun recklessly out of control. It is serious when man has degenerated to such an extent that his sense of respect for his fellow man is virtually nil. He is on a downward spiral.

A public celebration

What is even more incredible is that the people reckon it is time to have a party! And they do. We read in verse 10 that *those who dwell on the earth will rejoice over them and make merry and exchange presents, because these two prophets had been a torment to those who dwell on the earth.* Can you believe it, Christmas has come early! It is a satanic Christmas, an Antichrist-mas! It is a sham, a mockery, a counterfeit. It is geared to a pagan mindset for they turn these deaths into a public holiday, a time for fun and festivity. I am reminded of a saying that was common among ancient Roman generals: 'The corpse of an enemy always smells sweet.' They are glad to see the end of them! The Lord calls their witness a *testimony* but the world sees it as a *torment*.

It underlines the point that God has his agenda and it runs contrary to the ideas of the devil and his henchmen; heaven and hell are on a collision course. You can see this right here in this global carnival. The world is no friend to God, to the servants of God, and to the gospel of redeeming love and grace.

A public demonstration

The greatest party on earth grinds to an unscheduled halt! The jubilation ceases, the drink stops flowing, the singing is interrupted, the laughter dies down, there is nothing happening on the dance floor, a fun-loving party community is at a standstill! There is an eerie, stunned silence all around the world. People are frozen with fear. They are riveted to the spot! Their dream turns into a nightmare for we read in verse 11 that, *After the three and a half days a breath of life from God entered them, and they stood up on their feet, and great fear fell on those who saw them.*

Sometimes truth is stranger than fiction. The fact is, this is real. This is no joke. This is no figment of their fertile imagination run riot. Dead men live! Sure, for eighty-four hours you have two dead men lying on the concrete; one second later and the same two men are standing on their own two feet! Two decaying corpses have been renewed! The bits and pieces are put back together again, the vital organs are reactivated, and they are alive and kicking! This is nothing short of a miracle, something only God can do.

A triumphant resurrection

But that is not all for we read in verse 12, *Then they heard a loud voice from heaven saying to them, 'Come up here.'* And *they went up to heaven in a cloud, and their enemies watched them.* The vast crowds milling around the cordoned-off scene downtown Jerusalem did not only see what was happening to these two men, they also heard a loud voice from heaven saying, *'Come up here!'* These fellas have a triumphant rapture! They are here one minute and gone the next. They are bound for Glory!

The people are struck with panic for they have never seen anything quite like this before. Their man, the Antichrist, can do many signs and wonders but he cannot duplicate this! You can visualise the scene: as these two men are ascending into heaven, the people are left standing, shell-shocked and confused, the most they can do is watch and wonder. They certainly cannot explain what they have just seen and they cannot explain it away!

When our Lord ascended into heaven, he was watched by a handful of close friends (cf. Acts 1:9-11). When these men are translated into Glory, they are watched by their enemies. In that sense, God has the last laugh; he leaves them standing with their eyes gawking and mouths open wide! It is a classic case of divine retribution. Not even death can destroy the servants of God! No matter how we die, or where we die, there is a new day coming when we will be ushered into the immediate presence of Jesus. One day, we shall rise also!

A terrifying conclusion

The story is gathering pace with every event that takes place; the momentum is picking up as the seconds tick by on the prophetic clock. We read the grim news in verse 13 of yet another disaster when John informs us, *At that hour there was a great earthquake, and a tenth of the city fell. Seven thousand people were killed in the earthquake, and the rest were terrified and gave glory to the God of heaven.*

We have been down this road before but this time the impact of the earthquake, in terms of casualties and devastation, is much more localised. The earthmoving tremors and aftershock are focused on Jerusalem and its environs. This convulsion was no minor landslide; it was rated fairly high on the Richter scale for John classified it as *great* or 'severe' (NIV).

7,000 deaths and 10% of the infrastructure destroyed may not seem that significant, but in a city like Jerusalem, it is quite considerable. When you add this tragedy on top of the spine-chilling horror they have just seen with the ascension of the two witnesses, these poor folk do not know whether they are coming or going, they are reeling from one blow after another, staggering around like drunken men, and living on their nerves. Emotionally distraught and terrified, they are gripped with an unbelievable fever of fear.

The little phrase at the end of the verse which says [they] *gave glory to the God of heaven* would appear to indicate that this event drove some of them to their knees to call on the Lord and seek his face in repentance. Here is a remnant of Jewish people in Jerusalem who believe in the Lord and worship him. They recognise that he is the God of heaven and that he has the whole world in his hands. They realise that he is the one running the show and that it is better to be on his side!

This is another splendid example of a God of glory and grace giving man an opportunity to find forgiveness in his Son. There is no depth to which he will not stoop, no height to which he will not ascend, no length to which he will not go to save the lost from his own wrath for their sin. Because our God who is just is also merciful!

So far as the rest of them go, their hearts are pounding with fear and they cry to God to get them out of the mess they find themselves in; but there is a world of difference between calling on the Lord in terror and calling on the Lord in faith and repentance. It is one thing to be backed into a corner where you feel a sense of desperate hopelessness; it is quite a different matter for your heart to be breaking under conviction of sin. Then, in matter-of-fact language, John brings this act in the drama to a finale when he says in verse 14, *The second woe has passed; behold, the third woe is soon to come.* Two down, one to go!

11:15-19

The seventh angel sounds his trumpet

The extent of the Lord's majesty

The final few verses of chapter 11 introduce us to angel number seven and the momentous role he plays in the unfolding drama. This is a significant milestone in Revelation for we read in verse 15 that when he blew his trumpet *there were loud voices in heaven, saying, 'The kingdom of the world has become the kingdom of our Lord and of his Christ, and he shall reign forever and ever.'*

What a fantastic message! It is a timely reminder that God rules on high! The Lord reigns! Our God is Sovereign! Jesus is King! We are bowled over when we focus on the majesty of God and his plan for the world. What a breathtaking statement to usher in the second half of the Tribulation. This is the remaining three and a half years of Daniel's seventieth week. It is a statement of intent that God is taking over!

The *loud voices* which John refers to were probably the massed choirs of heaven; the whole place was resonating with the news that recognised and rejoiced that the Lord is King! It is a message that resounds from pole to pole and reverberates to the ends of the earth.

It is true to say that Christ does not claim his royal rights until he returns but the victory has been won already! This is the inheritance the Father promised the Son in the second Psalm. It is one he earned the exclusive right to claim because of his conquest over sin at the place called Calvary. Paul gives an interesting slant on this transaction when he focuses attention in 1 Corinthians 15:24 on a time 'when [Christ] delivers the kingdom to God the Father.' Paul says it will happen at that climactic moment when Jesus has destroyed 'every rule and every authority and power.'

It is equally correct to say that today he rules over a spiritual kingdom and that your redeemed heart and mine is his royal throne. We often sing the worship song, 'Reign in me, sovereign Lord, reign in me.' We need to give him his proper place and understand the implication of his rule in our lives for his kingdom is within us. In that day, it will be global and literal, it will be one thousand years of Jesus' rule. Is it any wonder the cry goes out from the hearts of those who follow great David's, greater Son, 'Bring back the King!' (cf. 2 Samuel 19).

The exaltation of the Lord's majesty

When the tremendous news is heard that Christ will reign forever and ever, there is an immediate response from the twenty-four elders in heaven. One minute they are sitting on their thrones before God and, the next, they are down on their faces worshipping the God of glory. The response was ecstatic, it was spontaneous, it was the right thing to do and there was no better time to do it. It was an acclamation of pure praise. Never devalue the currency of praise!

The fact that they got up from their thrones and fell down before him is a powerful example to us that this is what real worship is all about. It is a recognition of the greatness of God and, at the same time, that is reflected best in our humility before him. They knew their place before the Lord was one of obedience, worship, and submission. It is also a thrill for us to realise that the throne of God in heaven is occupied!

The initial thoughts of the prostrate elders are conveyed in words of sincere gratitude and thanks for who God is. John fills in the details in the opening phrase in verse 17 when he says, *We give thanks to you, Lord God Almighty, who is and who was.* This God marshals the angelic host of heaven; he was present in all our yesterdays for he is timeless in that he is eternal. He is with us today for he is God of the here and now!

They praise him because God's power is being proclaimed. In the closing sentence of verse 17 we read, *For you have taken your great power and begun to reign.*

They praise him because God's plan is being accomplished. This is inferred from verse 18, where we read, *The nations raged, but your wrath came.* The veiled reference here is to the rebellion of the nations of earth during the days of Tribulation. Did you notice their remarkable change in attitude? Their arrogance and joy, which we read about further up the chapter, has subsided; it did not last very long. Now the people are consumed with anger; there is an attitude of belligerence creeping into the minds of those who are living in these dreadful times. In fact, they are so volcanic in their outlook, the situation could erupt at any moment. One thing always leads to another and this is the final straw that breaks the camel's back as they prepare for Armageddon. They want to go their own way and do their own thing and that is why they are angry!

This verse also draws attention to the wrath of God for the Lamb is also the Lion. There are two Greek words for anger: *thumos* which means 'rage, passionate anger' and *orge,* the word used here, which means 'indignation, a settled attitude of wrath.' Warren Wiersbe makes the valid point that 'God's anger is not an outburst of temper; it is holy indignation against sin. God's anger is not dispassionate for he hates sin and loves righteousness and justice; but neither is it temperamental and unpredictable.'

They praise him because God's promise is being fulfilled. In the same verse we are told that the time has come *for the dead to be judged, and for rewarding your servants, the prophets and saints, and those who fear your name, both small and great.* John anticipates a day when the people of God will be rewarded.

They praise him because God's punishment is being declared. In the closing phrase of verse 18 John hits a much more sombre note when he talks about the Lord *destroying the destroyers of the earth.* Here God's punishment is being declared in unequivocal language. The wicked do not get off scot-free, no one gets away with anything; sooner or later, God will catch up with them and they will get their just desserts. One day they will find themselves in the dock when they stand before the great white throne (cf. Revelation 20:11-15). These people who live for earth and its pleasures are at the same time destroying the very earth that they profess to worship. Man exploits what God has entrusted to him. Man is a steward of creation, not the owner!

The expression of the Lord's majesty

John has another breathtaking vision for he writes, *Then God's temple in heaven was opened, and the ark of his covenant was seen within his temple. There were flashes of lightning, rumblings, peals of thunder, an earthquake, and heavy hail.* This chapter opened with a temple on earth and it ends with the temple of God in heaven! Here we have a visual reminder of God's sovereignty and faithfulness. The ark of God was the symbol of God's presence with his people. It stood behind the veil in the holy of holies. God's glory rested on the ark and God's Law was inside the ark in a beautiful illustration that the two must never be separated.

God is a holy God who must deal righteously with sin, he is also a faithful God who keeps his many promises to his people. The vision of the ark would greatly encourage God's suffering people. It would be a spiritual tonic and an uplift to them. It would remind them that God will fulfil his promises. John was saying to them: 'Look, God will reveal his glory ... give him time and trust him until he does!'

No sooner has John given them words of assurance when he reminds the rebels on earth that worse is to follow. But God's people need not fear the storms for their God is in total control. The ark reminds them of his continued presence and loyalty to them. At this juncture of the story, it is fairly obvious that the stage is being set for the dramatic appearance of the Beast, Satan's masterpiece, the false Christ who will control the world for a short time. (More about him further along!) Revelation 11 is a crucial chapter. We are now halfway through the book and midway through the period of Tribulation.

An invisible war: Michael versus the dragon

Act 4.Scene 14.

The setting is William Shakespeare's *Antony and Cleopatra*. The comment made is insightful for it is the moment when Antony says, 'Sometimes we see a cloud that's dragonish.'

That rings true when I flick through the pages of Revelation and zoom in on chapter 12. Here we have a dark cloud which looms over human history. It is an ominous thunder cloud that anticipates war on a scale beyond human comprehension. It is not merely a war fought on some remote battlefield on earth between two opposing armies! It is a war in heaven itself. It is an unseen conflict waged in the heavenlies. It is Dragon against Angel.

In the war of the universe, it is where good and evil vie for supremacy, the age-old struggle between the forces of darkness and light. Shining brightly against the black backcloth like a lone star in a night sky is a poignant symbol of virtue and vulnerability, a mother and her newborn child. Everything John sees in this vision is massive – the Greek word used is the term *mega*: a mega-woman (verse 1), a mega-dragon (verse 3), mega-wrath (verse 12), and a mega-eagle (verse 14).

And so, in chapter 12, we are spectators who watch the war between God and Satan and their heavenly armies. We also meet some leading characters in this great global conflict. At the end of the day, this really is a tremendous chapter rich in symbolism and, if we can crack the code, we are well on our way to putting the pieces of the jigsaw together. Some of them are reasonably straightforward, others are not so easy to ascertain.

12:1-2, 4b-6

Wonder woman

We read in verse 1 that *a great sign appeared in heaven.* That is quite an introduction to what comes next! The sign is a woman, described as *clothed with the sun, with the moon under her feet, and on her head a crown of twelve stars. She was pregnant and was crying out in birth pains and the agony of giving birth.* Further down the chapter in verse 5 we read, *She gave birth to a male child, one who is to rule all the nations with a rod of iron, but her child was caught up to God and to his throne.* You are probably well on your way to unravelling the identity of this wonder woman, but some folk see her as being someone other than who she really is.

Who she isn't!

Mary Baker Eddy had no hesitation in equating this person with herself. The male child she bore was seen as the Christian Science Movement which came into being in the year 1879. She goes on to describe the dragon as the mortal mind which is ready to devour the teaching set forth in their publication, *Science and Health.* This particular view is a bit like the proverbial sieve, it holds no water so far as biblical truth is concerned.

Mary, the mother of Jesus. This is a very popular view, especially within the framework of Roman Catholicism where Mary is seen as the Queen of Heaven. A Spanish artist named Murillo painted some famous pictures to prove that Mary was this woman. One of the paintings showed her great with child and portrayed her assumption into heaven. I can see where they are coming from and what they base their thinking on, but there is a trio of major hiccups with this interpretation. Number one, Mary did not have an assumption into heaven. Number two, why would she be shown pregnant in heaven after Jesus had already been born, resurrected, and himself ascended into heaven? Number three, try as hard as you will but you cannot fit Mary into verse 6, which we will look at later.

The Church. It seems fairly obvious that the woman in chapter 12 does not represent a single individual but rather a community of people. Other bright-eyed, well-intentioned folk come along and jump on the bandwagon and see the woman representing the church. That is an intriguing view but when you analyse it you quickly realise it is a nonstarter. It has an insurmountable hurdle to overcome. I think it is preposterous for the woman to represent the church because she is depicted as giving birth to Jesus. The historical fact is that Christ was never the child of the church, he is the founder of the church. The church did not produce the Lord Jesus, he is the one who produced the church! The church was born, as it were, out of the wounded side of Jesus.

Who she is!

The bulk of the evidence points in the direction that she represents the nation of Israel in her standing in the counsels of God (cf. Jeremiah 31:32; Ezekiel 16:32-35; Hosea 2:2; Isaiah 54:5). It is overwhelming. The clues are significant. We read about the sun, moon, and twelve stars in verse 1. There is only one other place in the Bible where you find all these symbols joined together in one place and that is in the well-known story of Joseph the dreamer in Genesis 37:9-11. In his famous dream, Joseph saw the sun, moon, and eleven stars bowing down before him in an act of submission. The sun represented his father, Jacob. The moon represented his mother, Rachel. The 11 stars represented his brothers.

We all know that Joseph's dream came true and from this graphic representation we can deduce that the woman was Israel and the twelve stars the founding fathers of her race. Joseph's dream was a token from God that Israel would be preserved through him. When you carry this forward into chapter 12 you catch a glimpse of the glorious dignity and exalted status which clothes the nation of Israel so far as God is concerned.

Down through the years she has failed repeatedly and miserably, but that does not diminish the fact that she belongs to God. He has not written off the nation nor has he eliminated her from his prophetic agenda. Her unique glory is the supreme glory of the heavens and that explains why Abraham's seed is likened to the stars in Genesis 15:5. It is no wonder the devil hates this nation for she is a powerful reminder to him of all that once was his and of the dizzy heights from which he fell.

She gives birth!

We also read in verse 5 that this woman gave birth to a son, *a male child*. Her cries of agony are an accurate portrayal of life in Israel around the time of the birth of Jesus. The nation was under the iron heel of Rome and the people had suffered intensely under the cruel oppression of Roman rule. The reference to pain in verse 2 is an indicator of the unthinkable and unbearable travail of the nation. They were going through an incredibly tough time.

In this context, the Messiah is the child of the nation of Israel as well as the child of Mary. The use of the word *man* is a pointer to his humanity. The use of the word *child* is a pointer to his humility.

The identification of this male child could not be clearer. Paul informs us in Romans 1:3 and Romans 9:5 that it was through Israel that Jesus Christ came into the world. We have an allusion to this event in Isaiah 66:7 and even further back in Genesis 3:15 he is spoken of there as well. Away back in the book of beginnings, this was the first promise and prophecy of Scripture that one day the seed of the woman would crush the serpent's head.

Jesus was born, he died at Calvary, he rose from the dead, he ascended on high, he sat down at the Father's right hand, today he is exalted far above all. He is hailed as a Prince and Saviour and when he comes again he will rule the nations with a rod of iron. John is talking here about the proposed millennial reign of Christ. It is a golden age, spanning one thousand years of rule with Jesus as King; it is a time of unprecedented prosperity on a global scale and an era of unparalleled blessing reaching out to the ends of the earth.

We will momentarily skip over verse 3 and the opening part of verse 4; we will come back to them for they are of considerable importance!

The menace of her enemy

Let us look at the gripping comment at the end of verse 4 where it says, *And the dragon stood before the woman who was about to give birth, so that when she bore her child he might devour it.* It is a kind of tableau, like a scene from Madame Tussaud's. You walk into a wax museum where you have all these lifesize, three-dimensional figures frozen in place at the climactic moment of some dramatic event. It is a playback on God's tape of global affairs, a slow motion action replay.

Satan, the great red dragon, is crouched with his fangs bared and eyes smouldering. He is watching Israel as she prepares to give birth to her long promised Son. She is pregnant and crying out in her labour pains. The dragon's avowed intention is absolutely clear; he seeks to devour Jesus as soon as he emerges from the womb of Israel and makes his appearance on the earth. He is determined to sideline the Redeemer. It is a road he has been down many times before. From Day One, when he heard God in the Garden of Eden spell out his ultimate fate, Satan has been bent on destroying the promised Seed.

He motivated Cain to kill Abel, but he had not bargained on the fact that God would raise up Seth to carry the royal seed; he caused such evil in the world that God destroyed the earth by means of a flood, but God saved righteous Noah and his immediate family, and once again the godly line was secured; he influenced Esau in a bold, brazen attempt to kill Jacob, but

God preserved Jacob; it looked like his big break was going to come with the slaying of Isaac, Abraham's son, through whom the covenant promises were to be fulfilled, but we know the happy outcome of that episode; he moved Pharaoh to destroy all the male Hebrew children, but God saved Moses; then, instead of being wiped out in Egypt, the people of God were delivered by God's mighty hand and outstretched arm; at other times in Israel's history, he tried to short-circuit the purpose of God by killing all the Jews so the Messiah could not be born— at one critical point, the royal line was limited to one little boy (cf. 2 Kings 11:1-3). Needless to say, Satan did not succeed!

The message from history

The key question emanating from chapter 12 is, What is the historical reality represented by this grim symbol-laden tableau? It is relatively easy to see the events of that time woven into the tapestry of 12:1-4. It takes us back to the birth of Jesus Christ, to that special moment in the history of the world when God became man; it takes us back to the Roman Empire and its crushing subjugation of the nation of Israel, to the time of King Herod the Great when he was the puppet king of Rome and it shows us the malice and enmity that filled his heart when he learned of the birth of the Saviour of the world.

Herod, in his early days, was a reasonable kind of bloke; that does not lessen the fact that he was a despot, but at least he was a forward-looking, progressive, benevolent one! By the time Jesus was born, he was renowned for his notoriously cruel streak. You did not argue with Herod! You did not step out of line or look at him the wrong way. His murderous paranoia was there for all to see. One day, in a fit of pique, he murdered his favourite among his eight wives as well as several of her family members. Later on, he brutally killed his own firstborn son, Antipas.

Tacitus, a cynical Roman historian, wrote of Herod: 'I had rather been Herod's pig than Herod's son; so dark and gruesome is the history of this man who murdered all his own family members.'

So his attempt to flush out the newborn Son of God by slaughtering the infants of Bethlehem was par for the course and the kind of action you would expect from such a man. Like a dragon, he lay in wait for the child to be born, then he pounced. So far as he was concerned, these children were surplus to requirements. They were no better than disposable items. He had no scruples about ordering their liquidation. Thank God, we know the sequel to the story for the Lord Jesus was spared, taken by Joseph and Mary to the land of Egypt, to a place of comparative safety.

One more time, one more incident, to add to a very long list; one more occasion when Satan was defeated and the purpose of God had not been thwarted! That is the glorious message of Revelation: God is victorious! From cover to cover, it is all about the triumph of Jesus. God always wins! He never loses! The devil can do so much and no more. He can go so far and no further.

Satan could not harm Jesus, for he is the one who came, verse 4.
Satan could not halt Jesus, for he is the one who conquered, verse 5.
Satan could not hinder Jesus, for he is the one who controls, verse 6.

Protection in Petra?

The spotlight reverts back to the woman and the main beam is shining on her as we read in verse 6, *And the woman fled into the wilderness, where she has a place prepared by God, in which she is to be nourished for 1,260 days.* The fleeing woman represents not the Jewish people as a whole for many Jews will be deceived and deluded by Antichrist, but she refers to a believing remnant among the nation of Israel.

This specific time allocation of 1,260 days is the period we often refer to as the Great Tribulation. It lasts for three and a half years, it is the second half of Daniel's seventieth week which we read about at the end of Daniel 9. The first half of this awful period is generally spoken of as 'the beginning of birth pains.' You find that colourful description in the Olivet Discourse of Matthew 24:8. By the time you come to the second half, the tempo has moved up quite a few beats. It is a time when Satan will do his worst. He is not in the mood or frame of mind to drag his heels. He is on the warpath, pulling out all the stops in overdrive. But all his plans will be foiled. The old fool never learns. He still has not grasped the fact that he is no match for the Lord. God has prepared a place already where the fleeing Jews will be safe and secure (cf. Matthew 24:16; Isaiah 16:3; 26:20-21).

A lot of Bible commentators feel the place referred to here is the ancient city of Petra which is just across the Israeli border in the land of Jordan, between the Dead Sea and the Gulf of Aqaba. The main gorge by which this rock-hewn city is approached looks down on a rivulet that threads its way along its entire length. Its rocky steeps are red and brown, purple and yellow. Its valley with its branching tributaries is about 4,500 feet long and is flanked on all sides by beetling sandstone cliffs. It is an awesome sight! An invading army would have to creep down that narrow, precipitous canyon, twisting and turning through the mountains, before ever the main citadel itself could be seen. Petra is a possibility, I suppose ... maybe, maybe not. God knows what he has in mind and, wherever it is, it is a place divinely chosen and appointed.

The delightful phrase, *prepared by God,* appears only one other time in the Bible. You find it in John 14:3 when Jesus turned and said to his forlorn disciples in the upper room, 'I go and prepare a place for you.' In that instance, it is a reference to the rooms in our Father's house, mansions in the sky. It is all about heaven and the eternal home of the redeemed.

The abiding truth is that God's loving care for the nation of Israel is unmistakable. To this day they continue as 'the apple of his eye' (Zechariah 2:8). They have an intrinsic role to play in the fulfilment of his prophetic schedule. They remain an integral part of his eternal purpose. The great news is, he has a location pinpointed on the map exclusively for them that will prove to be a place of gracious protection and generous provision (cf. Exodus 16:12ff). In the dark days of Tribulation, the Lord will look after them!

12:3-4a, 7-12

An enormous red dragon

It is because of the dark, dreadful days which are just around the corner that we need to preach the gospel with a real sense of urgency and passion to our contemporaries. Our ministry needs to have a sharp cutting evangelistic edge. The fact of the matter is: the death of sinners before the rapture of the church propels them into the unthinkable torment of hell. The survival of sinners after the church is translated to Glory propels them into the unrelenting torment of the Tribulation. Either way they do not win, they cannot win. Sooner or later, they come face to face with the devil. And that does not take into account what will happen when they meet their Maker! The picture is not a pleasant one!

The dragon's disposition

That is what John is referring to when he says in verse 3, *And another sign appeared in heaven: behold, a great red dragon, with seven heads and ten horns, and on his heads seven diadems.* Ah, now we know where people get the idea that Satan dresses in red and sports a long tail and horns! Folklore and fiction have given us all sorts of ideas about dragons, it even appears on the Welsh flag! Walk into any bookstore and dragons, in all shapes and sizes, are found in the pages of children's books, including the best-selling *Harry Potter*. The ancient prince of hell in verse 3 is not like any of those.

Steve Wilmshurst makes the point: 'If anything, he is more like the dragons in the works of Tolkien, who knew better than most how to portray terrifying monsters, such as Smaug in

The Hobbit. This dragon is greedy, voracious ... and utterly cynical.'

What we have depicted here is not a photograph of how the devil looks; rather, it is a symbolic representation of his cruel, vile nature. His colour is red for his path has always been covered with blood and death. From Day One he has been vehemently opposed to anything which even smacks of the name of Jesus. We know from the insightful comments of Jesus in John 8:44 that Satan is a murderer! History confirms that!

I read recently: 'When Satan saw the resurrection of Jesus, he didn't have an Easter celebration!' We all know how he reacted for he turned his fury on the church of Jesus Christ. He had those who preached the gospel crucified; some of them had the ultimate ignominy heaped on them for they were left hanging upside down. He had others sawn in pieces and hacked to bits. He had an uncountable number thrown to wild beasts in the arena. The devil saw it all as one big joke and, at the same time, it was a bit of fun and entertainment for the Roman generals and politicians. You can read the documented evidence of this in the closing verses of Hebrews 11.

In the early days of church history, no time was wasted until edicts were sent from Rome to destroy the Christians from the face of the earth. That is what occupied young Saul of Tarsus. It kept him extremely busy. He was on a mission to kill when he was miraculously converted on the Damascus Road. So far as the devil was concerned, the only good Christian was a dead one! As the years rolled by, it is conservatively estimated that upwards of 50 million Christians have paid the supreme sacrifice in fire and blood. Whether we realise it or not, this is the wrath of the dragon against the people of God!

That he is called a dragon does not do him any favours. It is a word which appears a number of times in the second half of Revelation. It shows him up for what he really is, in his true colours. He is a cruel and ruthless persecutor of the people of God.

The dragon's description

This dragon is a seven-headed monster; the number seven in Bible arithmetic signifies totality and the 'head' conveys the idea of intelligence. The implication is, he has an IQ that goes off the chart. He is a star, not a rising star, but a fallen star! He is a shrewd operator. He can effectively pull the wool over people's eyes and blind them to the truth. He lulls them into a false sense of security. That is what Paul tells us in 2 Corinthians 4:4 where we read, 'In their case the god of this world has blinded the minds of the unbelievers, to keep them from seeing the light of the gospel of the glory of Christ, who is the image of God.'

The devil has a plan for your life; it is to keep you in the dark and keep you from trusting Jesus Christ as your Lord and Saviour. It suits him perfectly to have you on his side! The statistics make grim reading for they clearly indicate he is winning with a lot of people. At this moment they are happy and content to dance in the dark with the devil, they prefer that to walking in the light with the Lord!

The fact that *he has seven heads and ten horns* links him with the Antichrist whom we read about in verse 1 of the next chapter. It shows his implicit involvement in the nations and governments of this world. These *heads* represent seven consecutive world empires running their course under Satan's dominion. For example, during the reign of the first six—Egypt to Rome—there was a deliberate attempt to wipe out Israel and thus rule out any possibility of Jesus Christ coming through the line of promise: one, Egypt represented in Pharaoh (cf. Ezekiel 29:3; Exodus 1:22); two, Assyria represented in Sennacherib (cf. Isaiah 7:13-14; Psalm 127:1); three, Babylon represented in Nebuchadnezzar (cf. Jeremiah 51:34); four, Medo-Persia represented in the activity of Haman under Ahasuerus (cf. Esther 3); five, Greece represented in Antiochus Epiphanes (cf. Daniel 11:21-32); six, Rome represented in Caesar (cf. Matthew 2:16-18); and, seven, Antichrist's future empire (cf. 13:1; 17:9-10).

There is a similar allusion to this in Daniel 10 where we read about the conflict raging between the prince of the kingdom of Persia and the heavenly angel. It is an invisible war between the unseen forces of good and evil. A territorial spirit is maybe not the best way to describe it but Daniel certainly gives the clear impression that there are localised angels who have a special interest in a given situation.

The seven diadems signify his power and authority over the major empires of the world. Again, we will go into this in a fuller way when we come to it later.

The dragon's downfall

In verse 4 we have a breathtaking statement when John takes us away back in time to the dim and distant past when it says of the devil that *his tail swept down a third of the stars of heaven and cast them to the earth.* The theologians generally refer to this as the fall of Satan and, obviously, when he was removed and expelled from heaven, he did not go quietly! He caused a bit of a stir! He took one in three of the angelic host with him and today they are referred to as fallen angels, demons, or evil spirits. Basically, they are emissaries of hell, the devil's secret agents who help him run the show. Satan's mafia is extremely well organised.

They are competent, superbly skilled in administration, highly intelligent, unusually gifted, fired with enthusiasm and dedicated. They passionately believe in what they are doing and are totally committed to the cause; they have the innate ability to orchestrate events for their own ends and have the know-how to pull strings and influence decisions among the movers and shakers in this world; they have enough clout to operate successfully in the big time and have what it takes to control the world behind the scenes!

Influence in heaven. The fact that the devil was able to successfully prejudice so many angels to join forces with him is indicative of the power and influence which he wields. We have no idea how many angels this involved in terms of actual numbers, no figures are revealed; we are given only a percentage in verse 4. Suffice to say, it was highly significant and it left a big gaping hole in the ranks of the holy, elect angels. It is true to say, he made his mark and he left his mark!

I came across an interesting story involving the British preacher Leonard Ravenhill, the author of the excellent best-selling book, *Why Revival Tarries*. Apparently he was in a prayer meeting on one occasion and he prayed something like this: 'Lord, we read where one third of the angels fell from heaven and, praise God, that means two thirds didn't fall! It means there are two angels for every demon. Thank you, Lord, for helping us look on the bright side!'

War in heaven. Let us jump over verses 5 and 6 (we looked at them earlier) and go to verse 7. Here we are confronted with some foreboding sounding words in the opening sentence, it is a matter-of-fact kind of statement, *Now war arose in heaven.* John then proceeds to fill in some of the missing details when he advises that, *Michael and his angels fighting against the dragon. And the dragon and his angels fought back, but he was defeated, and there was no longer any place for them in heaven. And the great dragon was thrown down, that ancient serpent, who is called the devil and Satan, the deceiver of the whole world—he was thrown down to the earth, and his angels were thrown down with him.* Strong words! The fact that there is war in heaven is nothing new; having said that, it is not the kind of thing you expect to find there.

The conflict we are talking about here has been raging from time immemorial for the devil has never given up thinking that his was the sole right to rule and reign. From the first day until now, he has been much too big for his boots and he has always had his beady green eyes on the throne of God. Even when he was unceremoniously thrown out of the presence of God the first time, he has never given up hope that one day his dream might just be realised. He finds it impossibly hard to give up and give in. There is not even a remote chance that he will throw the towel into the ring, there is no way he will wave the white flag and surrender; on the face of it, he does not know when he is beaten (cf. Isaiah 14; Ezekiel 28).

Kicked out of heaven. Up until now the devil has been

recognised as the prince of the power of the air. He has had reasonable, albeit limited, access into the presence of God to accuse the people of God, but here in this section, we see him falling even further for he is confined to earth, restricted to this world! God has had enough of his antics. He has put up with him long enough so the devil and his angels are banished forever from access into his presence. It is a highly efficient operation for the devil and his henchmen are flung from the sky in one clean sweep. To borrow a famous statement from Israel's persecuted past, not a hoof will be left behind!

The role of the warrior angel Michael

In this scene we bump into Michael for the first time in Revelation. An interesting character, his name means, 'One who is like unto God.' He is number one in the angelic pecking order with a special ministry in relation to the nation of Israel. We read about him elsewhere in Scripture on a few occasions.

In Jude he is embroiled in a raging controversy with the devil over the precise location of the body of Moses. Needless to say, he gives the devil short shrift. We also come across him in the book of the historian-cum-prophet, Daniel. In chapter 10 he is involved in the realm of conflict for he deals with the problem of unanswered prayer for Daniel where the abiding lesson is that God's delays are not God's denials. There was a battle raging in outer space between the forces of God and the powers of darkness. The crisis was solved only when Michael stepped down and personally intervened in the situation. In the last chapter of Daniel, we meet him again where he is seen as the 'great prince who protects' the people of Israel during some of the most frightening days of the Tribulation (Daniel 12:1).

When does all this happen? We touched on it briefly in chapter 9, but let me recap: Satan's ouster from heaven takes place at the halfway stage of the Tribulation. The devil takes it on the chin but he does not walk away subdued into retirement and oblivion. Far from it! He is no gentleman! He never has been and never will be. He does not accept defeat graciously. He is not cowering in a dark corner sulking, licking his unhealable wounds.

So far as the devil is concerned, events now move fairly rapidly. The next development for him is the bottomless pit and the final move is confinement to the lake of fire. He is on the way down and, in the providence of God, it will not be long until he is down and out!

The dragon's designation

The archenemy of the people of God is identified in verse 9 by four different names. *The dragon* which speaks of his abject cruelty. *The ancient serpent* reminds us of his cunning and crafty ways dating back as far as Adam and Eve in the beautifully idyllic Garden of Eden. He is the great deceiver. *The devil* portrays him as the accuser and slanderer of the Lord's people. He is only happy when he is pointing the finger at God's children. *Satan* describes him in his proactive role as the adversary and opposer of all that is right. He is a highly motivated activist. John's parting shot about him is succinct, *the deceiver of the whole world.* The devil deserves no credit for doing that, it just shows how hugely successful he has been.

The dragon's defeat

Verses 10-12 are thrilling for they give us the secret of victory over the devil! These are wonderful words of triumph! John says, *And I heard a loud voice in heaven, saying, 'Now the salvation and the power and the kingdom of our God and the authority of his Christ have come, for the accuser of our brothers has been thrown down, who accuses them day and night before our God. And they have conquered him by the blood of the Lamb and by the word of their testimony, for they loved not their lives even unto death. Therefore, rejoice, O heavens and you who dwell in them!'*

There is unsurpassed joy and sheer delight in heaven! There

is impromptu praise and glorious worship in the presence of God! There is a proclamation reverberating around the throne of the Most High that the great day has come! This note of victory is based on the prospect of the soon coming messianic kingdom. The saints populating heaven realise that it will not be too much longer until Jesus is seen ruling and reigning in his millennial kingdom.

The sense of total relief and spontaneous rejoicing which sweeps across the vast spaces of heaven is both real and understandable. For many a long year the devil has pointed his accusing finger at the people of God. That cannot happen any more! It can never occur again for he has been ousted, he has gone, there is no way in for him, the door has been barred and bolted; it is shut tight for God has slammed it in his face!

The documentation of the saints

Do you see what is happening in heaven? They are telling each other of *the cleansing of the saints*, how they overcame the devil by the power of the Lamb. Satan is not overcome by holy water from the Jordan or a heavenly gem dangling from a rearview mirror! The victory of the believer is not in binding Satan with some incantation or rebuking him with some magic prayer. It is only through the tremendous power in the blood of Jesus (cf. I Peter 1:18-19). We are forgiven because the battle was decisively won at the cross. Charles Spurgeon said: 'Nothing provokes the devil as much as the cross.'

They tell of *their confession*, how they overcame Satan by the word of their testimony. That is, because of who we are related to and because of what he has revealed to us in his Word. That shows us how vitally important it is to walk intimately with the Lord even though the environment is not user-friendly. It reminds us of the continuing need to speak up and speak out for the Lord Jesus. Satan will try to silence us, but we cannot be silent!

They tell of *their courage*, how they loved not their lives unto death. That shows us the desirability of living a life which is entirely surrendered and consecrated to Jesus. To quote the words of missionary Karen Watson, martyred in Iraq: 'To obey was my objective, to suffer was expected, his glory is my reward.' It is no wonder there is praise in heaven! If you cannot praise God for his salvation and deliverance, what can you praise him for?

The desecration of the earth

There may be deafening shouts of exuberant joy in heaven but it is an altogether different emotion which is felt on earth. We read in verse 12 the spine-chilling words, *'But woe to you, O earth and sea, for the devil has come down to you in great wrath, because he knows that his time is short!'*

This is a stark warning to the inhabitants of the earth that the devil is now on the same level as they are! He is angry, furious, full of wrath, and bent on causing enormous trouble in what amounts to his final fling. It appears he will explode in a volcanic eruption of unbridled fury in the last half of the Tribulation. Those who are followers of the Lamb will suffer intense persecution and many will experience martyrdom.

The devil wants to maximise his closing hours. He wants to go out with a bang, not a whimper. He is no fool, he is not stupid; he is an intelligent angel who knows his days are numbered. He adopts an air of realism for he is very much aware of the fact that time is rapidly running out. He is battling against all the divine odds heavily stacked against him. He is fighting back against the clock ticking away on God's wrist for time is short.

12:13-17

The persecution of the Jews

Anti-Semitism has been around for a long time, it is not just a phenomenon which emerged in the middle of the 20th century with the horrors of the Holocaust. From the beginning, Satan has been the driving force behind it. He is the promoter, prime suspect, and instigator of it. Verse 13 introduces us to what is probably the last wave of anti-Semitism that will roll over the world. The devil, portrayed here as the dragon, is bent on destroying the nation of Israel and, from his perspective, it cannot happen quick enough!

We should not really be surprised or taken aback by his fiendish attitude for it is a logical outworking of the prediction outlined in Genesis 3:15. It is an integral part of the constant enmity and hostility between the devil and the seed of the woman. He has ill blood flowing through his veins for his animosity and antagonism beggars description. That is why John makes it clear and plain: *And when the dragon saw that he had been thrown down to the earth, he pursued the woman who had given birth to the male child.*

We have seen that *the woman* mentioned here can be easily identified as the nation of Israel. Satan cannot stand the sons and daughters of Abraham. He has no time for them. He has always detested them because they are God's chosen people, the vehicle through which salvation came into the world. They gave us the Bible, and the Lord Jesus Christ.

That surely explains the reference to the *male child* in verse 13. That is why they are top of his hit list! That is why they are sure to receive his hate mail. He wants to obliterate, exterminate, and eradicate them. And he is spurred on with fresh impetus for he knows the time is drawing near for the Messiah to return to earth to set up his millennial kingdom.

Let us not fool ourselves, the devil knows the Bible. The chances are he knows it better than most other folk, and he knows a Jewish remnant must be ready to receive the coming King and form the nucleus for his promised earthly kingdom. If you want to dig deeper, this exciting truth is developed further in the closing three chapters of Zechariah.

On eagles wings

Persecution is only one side of the coin. In verses 14-16 we also read about protection! John says, *But the woman was given the two wings of the great eagle so that she might fly from the serpent into the wilderness, to the place where she is to be nourished for a time, and times, and half a time.* The serpent poured water like a river out of his mouth after the woman, to sweep her away with a flood. But the earth came to the help of the woman, and the earth opened its mouth and swallowed the river that the dragon had poured from his mouth.

One commentator has said about these amazing verses that they show how Israel 'will be hated and hidden and hunted and helped during the coming trial.' The glorious truth woven into the fabric clearly intimates that the Lord will look after his people, he will care for them, watch over them, and protect them. He will prepare a special place where the Jewish remnant can find a haven of rest and security, a place of welcome relief and respite.

It is interesting that her escape is likened to a flying eagle for this is an oft-repeated image in the Old Testament with reference to Israel. *Wings* symbolise strength (cf. Isaiah 40:31) and speed (cf. 2 Samuel 22:11; Psalms 18:10; 104:3) but, more often than not, they speak of protection (cf. Psalms 17:8; 57:1). Remember, God delivered Israel from Egypt 'on eagles wings' (Exodus 19:4). He cared for the people in the wilderness as an eagle would tenderly and faithfully provide for her young (cf. Deuteronomy 32:11-12). We also read that their return from captivity in Babylon was like 'mounting up with wings like eagles' (Isaiah 40:31).

God looks after his people

It is impossible for us to say with hand on heart that we know the location of this safe place. The Bible describes it as *the place where she is to be nourished in the wilderness.* The Lord knows where it is and that is what really matters. They will find out time enough! Having said that, some scholars have speculated on it being connected with the region of ancient Edom, Moab, and Ammon. This is based on the words of Daniel 11:41 where it seems these three areas will be immune from the invading forces of the enemy and remain untouched and unscathed.

Other folk, as I indicated earlier, have narrowed it down to Petra, a natural ancient fortress in the southern desert of Jordan. What matters most is that God will protect them in a specially designated area where they are beyond the strike capability of the enemy, and well beyond the reach of the serpent. And the God of their fathers will do it for a period of three and a half years (that is the meaning of the phrase, *time, and times, and half a time)*. The same period of time is mentioned further up the chapter in verse 6 where it specifically refers to 1,260 days.

The phrase, *water like a river,* which is mentioned in verse 15 is highly unusual. It is not explained but we find something of a parallel to it in the language deployed in Psalm 124, one of David's songs of ascent. A key to understanding this turn of phrase is found in Daniel 9:26 where we read that 'its end shall come with a flood.'

One writer suggests and I concur with him that '… this flood is an extermination policy directed against the nation of Israel to put to death every member of that nation. Previous anti-Semitic massacres and even the Nazi holocaust will have been but harbingers of the massive extermination programme against Israel. Centuries of anti-Semitism reach a terrible climax at this point.'

The devil does not like it

Again, with a single master stroke, God thwarts the enemy. The devil is not too happy for we read in verse 17 that *the dragon became furious with the woman and went off to make war on the rest of her offspring, on those who keep the commandments of God and hold to the testimony of Jesus.*

True to form, the devil mounts a massive counter-offensive. He is infuriated to such an extent that he unleashes one of his bloodiest attacks on remaining believers. He is acting like a wild cat; the more he is backed into a corner, the more deadly and ferocious he becomes. These are the ones who were not carried to the hidden place of safety and are easy meat for him. The term could refer to both Jewish and Gentile believers. Jews are part of her offspring by birth, Gentiles are part of her offspring by faith. The devil will go well for a wee while and will appear to gain the upper hand, but it is only lent to him. His doom is certain, his defeat is guaranteed, as in 13:7. The bottom line, there is nothing much the devil can do to gain the upper hand with the people of God.

If he locks them up in prison, they convert their warders! If he tortures them, they become partakers of the sufferings of Christ and heirs to a great reward! If he kills them, they become instant heroes in heaven! If he turns them loose, they evangelise the world! Surely, a powerful reminder that those who belong to Jesus are on the winning side. As one writer says: 'We have won because of the blood of Jesus, our hero and champion, and we have a big story to tell.'

And so the pace of events in Revelation is quickening. God's plan in human history is like a graph that has gone off the top of the page. It is moving toward its climax and culmination.

CHAPTER 13

An unholy trinity from hell

A 1979 article in *Time* magazine carried the headline, 'Inflation: Who is hurt the worst?' A worried blue-collar worker named Arthur Garcia said, 'I keep waiting for a miracle, some guy who isn't born yet, and when he comes, we'll follow him like he's John the Baptist.' The fact is, one day, Garcia's lament will become the cry of the world!

Revelation 13 is an important chapter for it introduces us to two men who will have a global impact in the final months of the last days. They are the Antichrist and his right-hand man, the false prophet. John was not in the business of handing out compliments or floral bouquets to these roguish individuals. Our initial introduction indicates they have one thing in common when he portrays them as beasts!

His identity

In verses 1 to 3a John says, *And I saw a beast rising out of the sea, with ten horns and seven heads, with ten diadems on its horns and a blasphemous name on its heads. And the beast that I saw was like a leopard; its feet were like a bear's, and its mouth was like a lion's mouth. And to it the dragon gave its power and his throne and great authority. One of its heads seemed to have a mortal wound, but its mortal wound was healed.* When we speak of Antichrist, we are thinking of the second person in this satanic trinity:

The Devil:	*he imitates God the Father.*
The Antichrist:	*he imitates our Lord and Saviour.*
The False Prophet:	*he imitates the Holy Spirit.*

The Antichrist is also known as the 'man of sin' and the 'son of perdition.' He is called 'the mystery of iniquity' and is sometimes labelled as 'the lie.' What a glaring contrast to Jesus! In him, we see 'the mystery of godliness' (1 Timothy 3:16) and, at the same time, he is truth personified! The Antichrist is the visible expression of the invisible devil. This is Satan's superman. He is the devil's Messiah, the devil incarnate, Satan manifest in flesh. Here is someone whose power base initially is Europe. He heads up a consortium which resembles a revived and expanded Roman Empire; he is the supremo of a United States of Europe, a ten-nation confederacy. In the second half of the Tribulation, he becomes the president of the planet, the world's last dictator.

This is what the people in today's world are looking for, someone to lead them—someone up front with imagination, flair, and personality—a colourful, charismatic figurehead. They are looking for a man with a sense of mission, destiny, and purpose; a man who knows where he is going and who knows what he wants.

13:1-3a

His association

We read, he comes *out of the sea.* That is an interesting turn of phrase. When you fast forward to 17:15 we come across the same term. It refers to the sea of humanity, the peoples of the world. Some Bible teachers feel this gives a measure of credibility to the notion that the Antichrist is of Gentile origin rather than someone who comes from Jewish descent. Actually, the locale can be narrowed down even further. When you turn back to Daniel 7 there is a parallel passage where the sea referred to is the Mediterranean. So it makes a lot of sense, when you put all the pieces together, to suggest that this person is of European extraction.

His ancestry

He is called a Beast. God does not see him as a man made

in the divine image; he sees him as a wild animal under the control of Satan. He is the kind of person you feel you have come across before, there is something familiar about him. It is the classic case of once seen, never forgotten. And the way John describes him says as much. If you look at 12:3 and read what John says about the devil, you can see the link straightaway. There is a family likeness—like father, like son! Both of them have seven heads and ten horns! The only areas in which they differ are in the number and position of crowns they have: the dragon has seven and they are on his head, the Antichrist has ten and they are on his horns!

The seven heads represent seven mountains (17:9) and, since Rome was built on seven hills, this must be a veiled reference to that powerful city. Back in John's day this would be a most meaningful allusion. The ten horns represent ten kingdoms. We have come across that before in Daniel 2, Daniel 7 and, again, in 17:12. It is a reference to a United States of Europe, the kind of scenario we see foreshadowed today in the European Union.

His appearance

Verse 2 reveals similarities to what we read in Daniel 7:1-6. John saw these animals or kingdoms in reverse order since he was looking back, while Daniel was looking ahead.

The leopard was symbolic of the Grecian Empire.
The bear represented the kingdom of the Medes and Persians.
The lion portrayed Babylon as the first great world power.

Antichrist picks up the best and worst of every world. He is the heir of the ages. He has the speed of the leopard as he conquers all in sight. It is a spotted animal. God has his spotless Lamb in the person of Jesus! What a contrast! He has the feet of the Persian empire; he is strong, well-organised, and fairly stable. He boasted of great things like Babylon, the lion. Antichrist is a man who will communicate arrogantly, he will control extensively, and conquer swiftly. He is the last person to claim the throne of the world prior to the second advent of Jesus.

His authority

Here is a man controlled by the devil. He is the one who calls the tune, who pulls the strings; Satan is the paymaster. Satan gives him his power and that implies he energises him. Satan gives him his throne and that means he enthrones him. Satan gives him great authority and that suggests he empowers him.

There is a fascinating cross-reference in Daniel 8:24 where we are told that 'his power shall be great—but not by his own power.' In other words, the devil is behind the emergence of this powerful, prestigious individual; he will have power to do everything he wishes and power to do anything he wants.

The third verse is really quite incredible for sometimes truth is stranger than fiction. He has some kind of accident. The implication is that there will come a day when he will appear to be assassinated, fatally wounded, and then in a remarkable turnaround, his wound is healed. He is brought back from the edge as the comeback kid! What we have here is an imitation of the death and resurrection of the Lord Jesus Christ. That proves the point I have already made that Satan is the greatest conman ever!

13:3b-10

His influence

The net result is recorded for us at the end of verse 3 where we read, *the whole earth marvelled as they followed the beast.* The impact is instant and quite incredible. The story is beamed around the world, he has them eating out of his hand, he has successfully pulled the wool over their eyes. He has done it his way and people have fallen head over heels for it. This is his trump card and he played it at just the right time. Joe Public is spellbound, people are captivated by his personality. Men and women go delirious with delight at the sudden unexpected change in his fortunes.

His adoration

This man is hailed as a hero, a superman, a genius, a Prince Charming. Ordinary people from every corner of the planet will idolise him and see him as some kind of cult figure. He is adored by millions and sways the masses. His rise to international fame and stardom is meteoric; one day he is just another face on the stage of world affairs, the next he has leapfrogged over everyone else and is seen as the man everybody who is anybody wants to know. His leadership will be established without question. Men will feel he is incomparable for they reckon there is no one else like him. They believe he is invincible for he has a proven track record.

They do not worship only Antichrist as a man, they also worship his backer, the devil himself! John tells us in verse 4, *They worshipped the dragon, for he had given his authority to the beast, and they worshipped the beast, saying, 'Who is like the beast, and who can fight against it?'* That is the recognition the devil has always wanted, the acclaim he has longed for, the adulation he craved from Day One. He wants to be worshipped. You find echoes of this in Matthew 4:8-10 where we read of his encounter with the Lord Jesus, and even further back in Exodus 15:1 in relation to the gods of Egypt.

Right here, he gets what he wants and he receives it through the Beast, the Antichrist! They worship him because of who he is and what he has done. He has won the hearts and minds of the people. The fact of the matter is, when men start to put the devil as Number One in their lives, they are embarking on a journey of no hope which leads to a place of total despair for eternity. They have only themselves to blame. They rejected the truth as it is in Jesus and now they are happy to toe the party line of the dragon. They fail to realise that God sends them a powerful delusion and that is the reason why they are the way they are! There is no other explanation. If you tango with Antichrist, you may as well dance in the dark with the devil. He will make the world believe that evil is good, that black is white, that down is up!

His arrogance

Antichrist will be given power to control the world but he is like a dog on a leash and God is holding the lead. The unassailable fact is that he can go so far and no further, he can do so much and no more. He can operate only within the parameters God sets down; he has to stay within the remit of his own orbit. This important truth emerges a few times in verses 5, 7 and 8 where it is made perfectly clear that he is delegated certain abilities. For example, we read he was given a mouth, he was given power to make war, and he was given authority over the peoples of the world. Global defiance leads to global dominance.

When you read about his mouth in verses 5 and 6 it is obvious by any standards that his is a big one, spewing out torrents of vulgar blasphemy! It flows like sulphurous lava from his lips. John tells us, *The beast was given a mouth uttering haughty and blasphemous words, and it was allowed to exercise authority for forty-two months. It opened its mouth to utter blasphemies against God, blaspheming his name and his dwelling, that is, those who dwell in heaven.*

He is the epitome of downright, brazen arrogance. He cannot lay a single finger on God, nor on the heavenly sanctuary, nor on the glorified saints, but he does the only thing he can do, and he does it well when he resorts to reviling them with his filthy tongue (cf. Daniel 7:8, 19-25). So far as the person of God is concerned, so far as the position of God is concerned, and so far as the glorified people of God are concerned, he is impotent. Helpless, and on a hiding to nothing. His strike capability is rendered useless. All he can do is call them names! The likes of Mussolini, Stalin, and Hitler are outclassed and outranked by him.

Blasphemy, in this context, is an echo of Paul's words

about Antichrist in 2 Thessalonians 2:4 where we read that he 'opposes and exalts himself against every so-called god or object of worship, so that he takes his seat in the temple of God, proclaiming himself to be God.' That means he will deify himself. He will set up a statue of himself in God's temple proclaiming himself to be God. Like Nebuchadnezzar before him and many a cult leader since, he will not be content until he has the swooning masses falling prostrate before him in worship.

His anger

In verse 7 John gives us a few more insights into what makes this man tick. He says, *It was allowed to make war on the saints and to conquer them. And authority was given it over every tribe and people and language and nation.* His aim is not only to defy the God of heaven, he is committed to destroying the saints of God. He cannot harm the deified saints in heaven but he can harm the believers on earth. These have not been specially sealed against him so that makes them vulnerable, easy targets. Many of these dear believers will be martyred for their solid allegiance to Jesus Christ. They will lay down their lives in an act of supreme sacrifice; they will do it with praise on their lips and love overflowing from their hearts.

There is a time limit of forty-two months, it is the second half of the Tribulation. It is long enough if you are the one going through the mill and on the receiving end but, thank God, at least it has a cut-off point. There is light at the end of the long dark tunnel.

His insatiable thirst for power is hinted at in the closing comments made by John in verse 7. To start off, his power base will be restricted to Europe, but that is not big enough! He wants more. He has the whole world in his sights. He wants to dominate the nations of the world, north, south, east, and west. He wants all people groups to acknowledge him as their leader, he wants every ethnic region to yield obedience to him. His influence will reach to the ends of the earth.

It is the old story, he will sneeze in Europe and they will catch a cold in America. This is a nudge in the direction of some kind of one world government, and he is the big chief. It will not last long, that is true, but for a season he will have universal acclaim. As James Allen points out: 'He is a world ruler, if not, indeed, the world ruler ... Satan has produced his own version of a man-ruled kingdom.'

His aim

This John sums up in verse 8 where he says, *All who dwell on the earth will worship it, everyone whose name has not been written before the foundation of the world in the book of life of the Lamb who was slain.* His long-term goal is to delude the masses of mankind and he will not be disappointed. He is guaranteed success from the word 'go.' The fact is, there are two types of people living in the world: there are those who are followers of the Lamb and those who are followers of Antichrist; there are those who follow Jesus and those who follow the devil.

It has always been like that and there is no reason to suggest it will be different then. You are either one or the other. You cannot have the best of both worlds with a foot in both camps. Every individual born on the face of the earth has his name recorded in the book of life but it is only those who have trusted Jesus as Lord and Saviour who have their names penned in the Lamb's book of life. The first is a record of our natural birth, the second is an eternal record of our spiritual birth! Thank God, once our name is recorded in the Lamb's book, it can never be erased! It can never be removed! It can never be deleted! It is permanent!

There is a beautiful reminder here of the redemptive work of Jesus on the cross at Calvary. His saving work is seen as eternal in its value and scheduled on heaven's agenda even before the world was made. Calvary was on God's mind and in his heart prior to anything which happened on earth. There is a timeless dimension to the cross of Christ.

All hail the Lamb!

A word of caution

The next verse, verse 9, is only a couple of phrases, but the first one sounds quite familiar. A similar phrase appears on numerous occasions in the Gospels (cf. Matthew 11:15; 13:9; Mark 4:9; 7:16; Luke 8:8; 14:35). We have come across it before in our studies in chapters 2 and 3 of Revelation. *If anyone has an ear, let him hear* is mentioned there seven times. That said, it is always followed by the phrase *what the Spirit says to the churches*. The omission of those words in verse 9 suggests that the church is not in view in this passage, having been raptured before the start of the Tribulation (cf. 3:10). John is more or less saying, 'Sit up, listen carefully! There is a vitally important message coming! Do not miss it!'

And we have the message right here in verse 10 where John tells us, *If anyone is to be taken captive, to captivity he goes; if anyone is to be slain with the sword, with the sword must he be slain. Here is a call for the endurance and faith of the saints.*

You could be forgiven for thinking that sounds rather strange, a bit obscure, a little unusual. What on earth is John talking about? When you stop and think about it, these words focus our mind on the law of sowing and reaping (cf. Jeremiah 15:2; 43:11; Zechariah 11:9; Galatians 6:7). They are words of great encouragement to the saints of the last days. All over the world, the screw is turning and faithful people are suffering for their faith in Jesus Christ and God does not want them to be discouraged or disheartened. He does not want them to cave in under the sustained pressure they are facing. He does not want them to wilt under the unrelenting sun of all kinds of trial and trouble.

The whole saga of suffering seems never-ending. The Lord is saying to his battle-weary soldiers, 'Look, judgment is coming soon and, do not forget, those who have persecuted you will receive the consequences of their sin. They will not get away with it. They will get their comeuppance. Do not let the seeming injustice and wholesale slaughter of these harrowing days hinder your faith. Hang in there! Hold on tight! Endure it for my sake! Keep the faith!'

The fact is the devil will have his say for a season, he will have his way for a time, he will have his day, but God says what he says in verse 10 as a challenge to each of us, even today. It speaks loud and clear of divine retribution and divine revenge. Judgment day is coming! God sees and knows all things, he has a good memory and a long arm. One day the culprits will be picked out from the crowd. God always has the last word! As someone said: 'This is the darkest hour before the dawn for a blood-stained earth and the endurance and faith of saints shines out clearly.'

13:11-18

Meet the spin doctor for the world's political leader

Now we are introduced to the third member of this satanic trinity. It is the *beast rising out of the earth.* He is the world's religious leader, the false prophet. He is the right-hand man of Antichrist, his personal *aide-de-camp.* He is a top PR man by profession; in modern parlance, a spin doctor. He is the propaganda chief or the spokesman for the man of sin. He knows how to handle the media so as to milk every situation for its maximum potential.

There is every chance that this person has a Jewish background. We read, he comes up *out of the earth* and that is often a symbol in the Bible for the Hebrew nation and God's earthly people.

At the end of the day, his main function is to glorify Antichrist. Nowhere does he put the spotlight on himself. He always turns the attention of the people towards Antichrist. He gives credibility and respectability to him. His key role in the Antichrist's administration is to keep his boss centre stage and make sure the main beam is always shining on him.

A helpful comparison can be made between his particular role in relation to Antichrist and the unique ministry undertaken by the Holy Spirit in relation to the Lord Jesus Christ. The implication is that the second Beast is a counterfeit of the Holy

Spirit of God. Now that he has arrived on the scene, the unholy trinity from hell is complete.

13:11-12

His description

John briefly describes him in verse 11 where he says, *It had two horns like a lamb and it spoke like a dragon.* That says it all! The first Beast, Antichrist, had ten horns, this one has two. The image of the horns suggests this fella has authority, but the absence of a crown indicates his authority is not political. We have discovered that the ten horns speak of territory and has to do with political clout and influence; the two horns are different in that they speak of testimony. His is a false testimony.

Yes, he looks like a lamb, but you cannot judge a book by its cover, nor a man by his mantle. He is not the kind of individual you can afford to take at face value, the stakes are much too high. You could not trust him as far as you could throw him. So far as he is concerned, what you see is not necessarily what you get! The great giveaway is when he opens his mouth for he *spoke like a dragon.* The minute he talks he lets the cat out of the bag. It is the voice of Satan! He is the mouthpiece of the devil via Antichrist!

I have never yet met anyone who is afraid of a lamb; it is a gentle creature, as innocent as they come, a fairly harmless animal. And when this guy first appears a few feet away from Antichrist, he will be seen to be all of these things. The danger is he will be seriously underrated by man but that is all part of Satan's diversionary tactics. It is a strategy ploy to lull men into a false sense of security, the devil wants the general public to feel relaxed and comfortable with him around. Professor Bruce called him, the 'minister of propaganda.'

'The symbolism portrays a man who comes into political prominence in Israel, very possibly through normal democratic political channels, whose apparent innocence and gentleness lead the people from all sections of the nation to trust him. His origins will be so well known that no mystery can surround him and this assists his rise to influence and power in Israel. Winning over the diverse elements in the regathered nation of Israel so that they accept him as the Prime Minister or President will be no small matter and call for consummate political skill. It is only when he has reached this place of prominence and power that the dulcet tones will carry a message straight from the dragon ... however the substance of his proclamations make it clear that he is not only the spokesman for the dragon but the associate of the [Antichrist],' writes James Allen.

John throws a lot more light on his deception when he informs us in verse 12 that, *It exercises all the authority of the first beast in its presence, and makes the earth and its inhabitants worship the first beast, whose mortal wound was healed.* The two of them work hand in glove, they are in it together, both of them are marching to the beat of the same drum, they are holding hands under one umbrella! The false prophet works as the chief executive officer of the new regime with Antichrist free to operate in a presidential capacity. He is the organiser and propagator of a new religion focused on Antichrist. It is the mindset which says, he deserves to be revered and acclaimed for he is like one who has come back from the dead!

He elevates Antichrist. It is a role in which he is eminently successful. All credit goes to him for ensuring Antichrist features as the main story on the top of every news bulletin! His antics are splashed on the front page of every newspaper and magazine around the world. It is like a syndicated news release. This guy is exceptionally good at his job.

He promotes religion. It is not in the least surprising that he uses religion as a means of unifying the peoples of earth. Something similar has happened down the years, it has been the pattern adopted throughout history by the good and great. He will use all types of religious props and gimmicks to pull the wool over people's eyes. When it comes to truth, he bends it, twists it, and distorts it; he is economical with it. He has no personal inhibitions as he plays on people's emotions, he takes advantage of man's basic need for some kind of religious experience. He makes it all look so plausible, it feels good, it sounds right, it makes a lot of sense to the unsuspecting man on the street. The fact remains, it does not go away, it is a religion without Jesus. The classic case of the blind leading the blind.

13:13

His deception

A miracle worker!

In verse 13 we read that, *It performs great signs, even making fire come down from heaven to earth in front of people.* This guy is a miracle worker. There will be all kinds of healings, many inexplicable happenings, and a wide range of significant events occurring; he can even bring fire down from heaven. If Elijah can do it, so can he! He sets the sky ablaze! This is no hocus-pocus of a well-paid magician, this is no mere sleight of hand. It is for real. He will blind mankind with his bag of spiritual tricks, there will be signs from heaven and hell; he will pull them like rabbits out of a hat.

God is not the only one who can perform miracles, the devil can do them as well. And that is why, even today, we need to be ultra-cautious when we attribute a miracle to someone. It may be the real thing; on the other hand, it may be a counterfeit spun in the deceptive web of Satan's thinking. He has men eating out of his hand to such a degree that they are bowled over with his legendary feats. The ordinary folk are impressed, they believe everything he tells them and shows them. They are taking it all on board.

13:14-18

His demands

To worship his idol

John's assessment of the situation is alarming for he informs us in verse 14, *And by the signs that it is allowed to work in the presence of the beast it deceives those who dwell on earth.* In fact, so skilful and successful has he been that John goes on to say that he told them *to make an image for the beast that was wounded by the sword and yet lived.*

That is bad enough but even that is not the end of the story. John continues in verse 15, *And it was allowed to give breath to the image of the beast, so that the image of the beast might even speak and might cause those who would not worship the image of the beast to be slain.* This is what Jesus spoke of in his major Olivet Discourse recorded in Matthew 24:15. It is what Daniel referred to in his writings (cf. 9:27; 11:31-32). It is called 'the abomination of desolation.'

Here is a lookalike statue of Antichrist erected in the newly-constructed temple in Jerusalem. It is not there just to make him feel good and to appeal to his seriously inflated ego, it is there as a focal point of his desire to promote himself as a god worthy to be worshipped. There is a twofold thought behind the word *image*: one, it represents a person in the sense of likeness and, two, it reveals a person in the sense of manifestation (see Colossians 1:15 and the reality that is Christ). He craves the affection and adulation of an adoring public and this is one way he is sure to get it.

Should there be any lingering doubts in the minds of the more sceptical inhabitants of earth, believe it or not, the wily devil is one step ahead. He breathes power into the statue and it begins to speak! It is a talking monument! In some ways, this is the crowning act of rebellion perpetrated by this less than illustrious duo. This is the height of blasphemy.

Since Satan could not command worship in heaven, he goes to the next best place, the Jewish temple in the Holy City. It is a shambolic mixture of politics and religion. We need to realise that if men fail to toe the party line and refuse to bow down to the image of Antichrist, they will incur the wrath of the Beast. They are dicing with death, they will pay an awful price for they will be immediately executed.

To bear his mark

John gives us another chilling reminder of what life will be like when Antichrist is in power. We read in verses 16 and 17, *Also it causes all, both small and great, both rich and poor, both free and slave, to be marked on the right hand or the forehead, so that no one can buy or sell unless he has the mark, that is, the name of the beast or the number of its name.* The pressure is piling on! It is his way and his way alone.

The political agenda of his government is to introduce a common faith policy, a common foreign policy, and a common financial policy. Every member of society from the highest to the lowest will be required to receive the mark of the Beast. There will be no exceptions to the rule, none will be exempt, it is all-inclusive. It is a global decision. If you have it, all will be well; if you do not have it, you will face massive, insurmountable problems. If you go with it, life will go on as before; if you rebel against it and oppose it, you will be economically sidelined. No seal, no sale!

That policy decision applies to the big-time industrialist trying to close a multi-billion dollar investment package as well as to the kids at the bottom of the street wanting to buy a packet of sweets in the corner shop. The boycott is total. The mark of the Beast is a token of allegiance, a show of solidarity, a mark of loyalty and identification. It is a passport to the future.

The only choice given to Joe Public is where he receives the brand of the Beast. The alternatives are spelled out for they can get it either on the right hand or on the forehead. Surely this is a strong allusion to Caesar worship in the Roman Empire, but this same policy has been used by political leaders throughout history. The cult of Cybele, for example, forced worshippers to have an image or mark put on their bodies. Solomon is right when he tells us, 'There is nothing new under the sun' (Ecclesiastes 1:9).

The technology to accomplish this is already in place. It is called a credit or debit card. A person's entire credit profile (and much more) can be encoded on that little magnetic strip on the back of the plastic card. Thanks to the credit/debit card, we are rapidly becoming a cashless society. The next step is obvious and logical; you can put whatever information you want on the card or on some other miniature device like a computer microchip which could then be implanted on a person's skin. It is happening in the animal and bird world where a number of conservation agencies are employing this particular strategy. They are even doing it in Europe for an aptly named 'pets passport.' What we have here in chapter 13 is not in the least absurd, it is not far-fetched, it is not John living in a fantasy world, he is not in cloud-cuckoo land, far from it! We need to realise this whole process could be implemented tomorrow if the powers that be wanted to go down that particular road.

It is no wonder John begins the final verse in the chapter with the statement, *This calls for wisdom.* He goes on to say, *Let the one who has understanding calculate the number of the beast, for it is the number of a man, and his number is 666.* That is a number we are familiar with, we hear it bandied about all over the place. It is the kind of catch question you expect to be asked on an evening of trivial pursuits, a hyped-up religious guessing game. Gallons of ink have been spilled as men have tried to crack the code of this biblical Sudoku; ream after ream of paper has been churned out by well-meaning writers trying to decipher its meaning. People have read all sorts of things into it. They have even come up with potential candidates to fit the bill. Some of the proposed names have ranged from sublime to ridiculous. The list is as long as your arm.

The theory goes, if you substitute numbers for letters you arrive at a numerical value that adds up to 666 thereby giving you the name of Antichrist. They base this on the fact that many ancient languages used letters for numbers; the Romans did it and the Greeks went along with it. The obvious fallacy so many seem to ignore is that they are trying to solve this riddle using the English alphabet! It makes as much sense as a first-century Greek trying to do the crossword in today's edition of *The Times*.

Some of the people blacklisted include the likes of Caligula, the mad despot of Rome; he was quickly followed by the ruthless Nero, and after him, with a little manipulation, the name of Domitian was added. Oliver Cromwell, John Knox, and Martin Luther have been included. A varied assortment of Roman Catholic popes made the list. In the last century, the infamous list included names as diverse as Adolf Hitler, John F Kennedy, Henry Kissinger, Pope John Paul II, and Mikhail Gorbachev.

We need to take on board what John says in verse 18 that *this calls for wisdom.* We are talking here about insight and perception (cf. Daniel 12:10). It says nothing about pocket calculators and an alphanumerical dictionary. One writer makes a wise comment, when he says: 'On this subject we seem to have a shortage of insight but no shortage of imagination.'

In the Bible, the number 6 is used on different occasions. Goliath, the giant from Gath, was 6 cubits in height, the head of his spear weighed 6 shekels, and he had 6 pieces of armour; Nebuchadnezzar's image was 60 cubits tall and 6 cubits wide; man was created on the 6th day and is expected to work 6 days out of 7; a Hebrew slave could not be a slave for more than 6 years; the fields of the Jews could not be sown for more than 6 years running. The most logical explanation for the mark is that 6 is the number assigned to man. And that is precisely what John is at pains to emphasise when he tells us it is the *number of a man.* Antichrist represents the ultimate in human ingenuity and cleverness. He is no fool!

The children of the great composer, Bach, found the easiest way to rouse their father from a siesta was to play a few lines of music and leave off the last note. Apparently, Bach would get up immediately, make a beeline for the piano, and strike the final chord. A similar story is told of the great preacher, Donald Grey Barnhouse. He awoke one morning during the Christmas season, went straight to the piano and played *Silent Night*, purposely stopping before striking the last note! He then walked into the hallway of his home and listened to the sounds coming from the children's rooms upstairs. His eight-year-old son was trying to find the final note on his harmonica. Another of the children was singing the last note with great volume and enthusiasm. His wife called, 'Donald, did you do that on purpose?' Wives seem to have that intuition!

The lesson is, human nature demands the completion of the last note! The number 666 powerfully reminds us that something is definitely missing. That missing 'something' is Someone! He is a 7 and that, as we know from earlier chapters, is the complete number, the number of perfection. Satan has his 6, but God is 7! The devil comes up as the triple six. The fact is, he works hard, he tries hard, but he always comes up short. The old masquerader will never be able to fool all of the people all of the time, he will only fool some of them some of the time.

CHAPTER 14

The Lamb who shepherds his people

As the world moves into the second half of the Tribulation, heaven is not silent. The voice of God is heard for what we have here is a preview of coming attractions on the movie screen of history. In verse 1 John says, *Then I looked, and behold, on Mount Zion stood the Lamb, and with him 144,000 who had his name and his Father's name written on their foreheads.*

We have met these good folk before in chapter 7. These are the 144,000 endtime Jewish missionaries, 12,000 from each of the twelve tribes who are the sealed servants of God. The last time we saw them they were on earth going into the Tribulation, here they are exiting the Tribulation and entering the millennial kingdom. Previously, they were anticipating the Great Tribulation, now they are looking forward with bated breath to the glorious triumph of Jesus the King. And, of huge importance, in spite of the chaos, cruelty, and confusion of the Tribulation, not one of them is lost!

14:1-5

Look at the special company

They are exalted!

The presence of the Lamb. This is truly marvellous when you appreciate all that is entailed in the compass of this single verse. The focus here is very much on the protection of God. God looks after his people! It is all about the presence of the Lamb. He is seen to be with them. That statement should not surprise us. He said he would in Matthew 28:20 and we have the same promise reiterated in Hebrews 13:5. How reassuring that must have been for them!

The place where they are standing. Did you see where they are? They are on Mount Zion! The key question is, Which one? Is it in heaven or on earth? It is probably a reference to the earthly one in Jerusalem which, from the days of King David, was the centre point of kingdom rule in Israel (cf. 2 Samuel 5:7). We have here a monumental moment that anticipates the coronation of Christ and the establishment of his kingdom when he returns to Planet Earth (cf. Psalm 48:1; Isaiah 24:23; Joel 2:32; Obadiah 17, 21; Micah 4:1; Zechariah 14:4). One writer says: 'The very mention of Mount Zion shows that the Lamb is about to assert his royal prerogative and take his place on the throne of David.'

As an aside, we discover from Psalm 2:6 that Christ is presently enthroned in the heavenly Zion and, according to the Apostle Paul in Ephesians 2:6 we, as redeemed saints, are seated alongside. We have grandstand seats in heaven. The thought encapsulated here is one of glowing assurance to God's people that he cares for us and that, finally, he will take us home to Glory. All his plans will be achieved and all his purposes and promises will be fulfilled (cf. Zephaniah 3:17).

The print of God's name. It involves the print of God's name on their foreheads. This seal is a reminder that they belong to God and the Lamb. It is in sharp contrast to the mark of the Beast we read about in chapter 13. The challenge facing each of us in the twenty-first century is this, What marks our lives? Is it the brand of a secular society? Or is it the imprint of the kingdom of God? Do we embrace the present world system or do we honour his great name?

They are euphoric!

John sets the scene in a way that captivates the imagination. He says, *And I heard a voice from heaven like the roar of many waters and like the sound of loud thunder. The voice I heard was like the sound of harpists playing on their harps, and they were singing a new song before the throne and before the four living creatures and before the elders.* This is colourful, expressive language. What a beautiful sound it must have been when the harpists were strumming away and how delicious the harmony to the ear when they began to sing their brand new song. It is strong, majestic, sweet, and sensitive as it is performed with idyllic tones of tenderness.

It is *new* because their experiences in the Tribulation are unique to them. Let us face it, not many have walked through the flood and flame as God's untouchables! We come across a select handful in Hebrews 11. Some of them are childhood heroes, like the Daniel's of this world who lived to tell the tale when God gave the lions lockjaw; like the trio of Hebrew teenagers—Shadrach, Meshach, and Abednego—who would not bend or burn when thrown into the fiery furnace ... such characters are few because good folk are scarce.

It is *new* because the 'old' song goes back to the morn of creation 'when the morning stars sang together and all the sons of God shouted for joy' (Job 38:7), but this new song goes back to Calvary and a hymn of thanksgiving never heard before unites heaven and earth. In 5:9 the praise chorus celebrates the person of the Lamb, here (and in 15:3) it celebrates his power.

They are deliriously happy in their worship and ecstatic with praise. One day, in God's time, all our sorrows will be transformed into songs! Unique pain brings unique praise as they sing from the deepest depths of personal experience. It is amazing, the minute you bring the Lamb into the picture you hear the people singing! As someone has said: 'You may be a byword for tone-deafness now, but then you will sing better than Pavarotti or Charlotte Church!'

They are exclusive!

John informs us that *no one could learn that song except the 144,000 who had been redeemed from the earth* (14:3b). It is a praise item that no other group can share as it is something exclusive to them. The Lord has saved them, delivered them, given them the victory, and brought them through. Redemption is theirs, it is no wonder they break forth into song! It would be strange if they did not! This is God's choir who have marched to Zion. They celebrate their victory with a freshly composed medley before the throne of God in heaven.

They are exemplary!

John fills in all the details when he says, *It is these who have not defiled themselves with women, for they are virgins. It is these who follow the Lamb wherever he goes. These have been redeemed from mankind as firstfruits for God and the Lamb, and in their mouth no lie was found, for they are blameless* (14:4-5).

Their conduct. These men are morally pure. The phrase which John uses here implies they remained celibate and never married. These men are not chauvinists. It just so happens marriage was not on God's agenda for their lives. Their time, energy, and life is totally wrapped up in serving the Lord. There is nothing to sidetrack them, no one to distract them, they are God-focused and Christ-centred. They are beacons of purity.

Their consecration. These men will go wherever the Lord wants them to go, theirs is a no-strings attached commitment. They will go anywhere and do anything. Their dedication to Christ and his cause is total, it is 100% surrender for their all is on the altar. They are latter-day Calebs. It is a fitting comparison for it was said three times of Caleb in Joshua 14 that he 'wholly followed the Lord.' The same spirit is found in the hearts of these gentle giants. Henry Blackaby writes: 'The wise Christian finds out where God is at work and simply joins him there.'

Their calling. John pays eloquent tribute to the work of God's grace in their lives when he freely acknowledges that they were purchased from among men. He goes on to say that they were offered as *firstfruits* to the Lord. This means they were a token of the harvest yet to come and, in that sense, they represented the whole harvest. The feast of firstfruits was one of seven feasts in the Jewish calendar. It always falls on a Sunday and follows the week in which Passover occurs. What happened was this: the farmer went into his field of swiftly ripening grain and cut out one sheaf to be presented to the Lord, it was given to the priest who waved it before the Lord as a sign that the entire harvest belonged to him (cf. Leviticus 23:9-14). A similar analogy is found in the well-known resurrection chapter of 1 Corinthians 15:20-23.

Their conversation. John mentions this as something of special significance. These men were individuals without any trace of guile in their lips. There was nothing false in them. When they opened their mouths, they spoke the truth, the whole truth, and nothing but the truth.

Their character. Allied to this tremendous virtue is the fact that they are exemplary in their character for John says they are blameless. They are without blemish. No one could point a finger at them, no one could stand up and accuse them. Their lives were above and beyond reproach. They were glasshouse believers, you could see right through them. They had no hidden agenda and no skeletons hiding in the cupboard. These men were genuine through and through, they were transparent.

We have here a grand company of men who are saved, sealed, separated, sanctified, and spotless. What a wonderful group of people—men who will do anything for Jesus, men who are sold out to Christ! It is a mouth-watering picture of the redeemed of the Lord. Can the same be said of us?

14:6-13

Listen to the special commission

A favourite song of mine has as its first line, 'Great is the gospel of our glorious God.' It was written by a Welshman, Vernon Higham, when he was minister of a flourishing church in the capital city of Cardiff. The lyrics are so full of meaning and pregnant with truth. He makes every word count! The same can be said of John's breathtaking insights in chapter 14.

The proclamation of the gospel

John shares his uplifting experience when he says, *Then I saw another angel flying directly overhead, with an eternal gospel to proclaim to those who dwell on earth, to every nation and tribe and language and people. And he said with a loud voice, 'Fear God and give him glory, because the hour of his judgment has come, and worship him who made heaven and earth, the sea and the springs of water.'* What can we learn about this gospel?

It is an everlasting gospel. Here is a message that is eternal in its significance. It is timeless. It does not have a sell-by date stamped on the outside. It is truth unchanged, truth unchanging. It is consistently relevant. The gospel has always been an integral part of God's eternal plan. There is nothing new outlined in this verse. It is the old, old story of redeeming love; it is the same glad tidings but we are coming at it from a different perspective, it is the evangel with an added dimension.

The general thrust of the message is the creative power and love of God. We read many times in the Bible that the universe is a potent witness to the presence of God. David in Psalm 19:1 tells us that 'the heavens declare the glory of God, and the sky above proclaims his handiwork.' Paul goes down a similar track when he says in Romans 1:20, 'For his invisible attributes, namely, his eternal power and divine nature, have been clearly perceived, ever since the creation of the world, in the things that have been made. So they are without excuse.' Those are only a couple of examples but they provide an eloquent testimony to the skilful work of his hands. The praises of God's people in heaven reflect the same combination of his work in creation and redemption (the same twin truths are echoed in Revelation 4 and 5).

It is proclaimed by an angel. This is most unusual for in this present age angels are not privileged to preach the good news. That solemn responsibility rests on your shoulders and mine. We are his witnesses, but in the closing days of Tribulation, this heavenly messenger will be sounding out the message of God's salvation. His pulpit is the firmament of heaven, which is out of the reach of man. This angel flies in mid-heaven, which refers to the apex of the sun at noon, at its meridian, the time when the sun has its greatest visibility. John MacArthur makes the point that 'this preaching angel will be unreachable and his ministry unhindered' by Antichrist.

It reaches all nations. In that day the great commission of Matthew 28:19-20 will be fulfilled. Here we have a communiqué which is universal in its scope and global in its appeal. It is reaching out to the ends of the earth for the whole world is his parish. A similar thought is expressed by the Lord himself in Matthew 24:14 where we read, 'And this gospel of the kingdom will be proclaimed throughout the whole world as a testimony to all nations, and then the end will come.'

It results in salvation. The direct result of the dissemination of this powerful message is that it brings men into a dynamic relationship with God. This is the gospel as it really is, a life-changing, life-transforming message! Antichrist with his synthetic gospel is saying, 'Fear me, glorify me, worship me!' The true gospel of sovereign grace declares, 'Fear God, glorify God, worship God!'

It involves conviction. This is the gospel as it always has been for it brings men in from the cold into the warmth of the love of God. In a nutshell, it is a healthy fear of the Lord. The gospel of Christ sorts out the agenda of our lives like nothing else; it enables us to get our priorities right when we are down on bended knees before the cross of Jesus. When we fear God, it puts the terror of the Lord in a heart strangely awakened.

It involves conversion. Conviction is the first step down the road which leads to conversion. This is the first time the word *judgment* is used in Revelation; this is not merely a coming day of judgment at some distant date marked in God's calendar, it is narrowed down so that John refers to the *hour* of judgment. The sinner denies God the glory which is due to his holy name, while the Christian gives God the glory which is rightfully his. Surely that is God's great goal as expressed on the morn of creation, that is also his all-consuming passion in securing our redemption, to bring glory to himself. A gospel that falls short of bringing men to God to give him glory is insufficient, it is only a watered-down version; it is so diluted it is not the authentic gospel of Christ.

It involves consecration. Conviction and conversion are followed by consecration. Worship is the ultimate experience we can have this side of heaven. It is the overflow of a life filled with wonder, love, and praise. It is the natural outcome when we are enraptured by the beauty of Christ. It is inevitable when our hearts are beating in sync with his. Intelligent worship is when we pour out our lives as a drink offering to the Lord; it is when we lay our all upon the altar in an act of complete surrender. It is your life and mine responding to the overtures of his love and grace.

Babylon ... the writing is on the wall!

The mood changes in verse 8 with the arrival of the second angel. His message is conclusive, a fait accompli. He says, *'Fallen, fallen is Babylon the great, she who made all nations drink the wine of the passion of her sexual immorality.'* If the first proclamation was good news, this prediction is great news! This is the first mention of Babylon in the Apocalypse and it is by no means the last. Here is a single brief statement that is later expanded on with considerable flair in chapters 17 and 18. In those two chapters, John has an eye for detail; here we have it in anticipation. It is forward to the day when the political, economic, and religious system of Antichrist will suffer total collapse; it anticipates the day when the whole organisation will crash around his feet.

The angel stressed the seriousness of the situation when he repeated the word *fallen* twice. It is a double exclamation, a double whammy. The evangelical prophet Isaiah was on the same wavelength when he reported in 21:9 that, 'Fallen, fallen is Bayblon; and all the carved images of her gods he has shattered to the ground.' There is no beating about the bush, Babylon is doomed!

The reason for her spectacular downfall is elucidated with precision in the same verse and the point is underlined in bold capital letters in 17:2 and 17:5. John pulls no punches when he reveals that political leaders throughout history have committed fornication with this woman; they have done a tango with this false and corrupt religious system and the people of Planet Earth have accepted it willy-nilly.

The second angel throws the spanner in the works with his declaration that judgment will come. In fact, from his vantage point, it is as good as done. The future is ominously bleak. Judgment cannot be avoided or averted. The obituary of Babylon has already been written, her demise is guaranteed. For the second time, the writing is on the wall. To all intents and purposes, she has gone past the point of no return.

Beast worshippers ... your time is up!

The next three verses are startling words, a spine-chilling reminder of the awfully dreadful fate of those who choose to say 'no' to Jesus Christ. John leaves us in no doubt when he says, *And another angel, a third, followed them, saying with a loud voice, 'If anyone worships the beast and its image and receives a mark on his forehead or on his hand, he also will drink the wine of God's wrath, poured full strength into the cup of his anger, and he will be tormented with fire and sulphur in the presence of the holy angels and in the presence of the Lamb. And the smoke of their torment goes up forever and ever, and they have no rest, day or night, these worshippers of the beast and its image, and whoever receives the mark of its name.'*

The evidence. If anyone worships Antichrist and his image they are showing allegiance and loyalty to him. To receive his mark is a matter of economic survival, we came across that in chapter 13. The implication is that the state will be god in that day, it will wield total and absolute control over the lives of its citizens. The message is, therefore, urgent. It is short, blunt, and plain.

The explanation. Their agony is self-inflicted because they chose to reject God's way. They have only themselves to blame. Antichrist cries out, 'Worship me ... or be doomed!' The Lamb cries out, 'Worship me ... or be damned!' That is it in a nutshell. It is a straightforward choice facing the inhabitants of this world. If you worship the devil's messiah, you will drink the wine of God's fury. The cup out of which they drink is described as the wrath of God himself and it is full strength! A cup of no mercy and no compassion.

The extent. It is spelt out in the clearest terms. Here the horrors of hell are depicted in most vivid language. It is eternal retribution, undiluted torment, never ending, it just goes on and on and on! There is no hint of simple annihilation, let alone a state of limbo. There is no reprieve, no escape. How frighteningly terrifying! How awesome a thing it is to fall into the hands of the living God! No rest is afforded them in an eternity of uninterrupted restlessness. Their days are one long tale of anguish and their nights are black nightmares of unthinkable dread.

The patience of the saints

In one sense, there is a feeling of enormous relief when John changes gear in verse 12 and addresses the subject of the patience of the saints. The contrast is patently obvious, it is an abrupt transition. He says, *Here is a call for the endurance of the saints, those who keep the commandments of God and their faith in Jesus.* It is a clarion call for patience, an incentive for the people to show remarkable perseverance (cf. Matthew 24:13).

Their characteristics. The wonderful characteristics of these good folk are outlined for us. Basically, they are happy to obey God's Word and are intensely loyal to God's Son. Antichrist says to them, *'I'll make you suffer!'* They reply, *'You'll make us saints!'* Antichrist threatens them, *'I'll persecute you to the grave!'* They reply, *'You'll promote us to Glory!'* Antichrist tightens the screw, *'I'll blast you!'* They reply, *'God will bless us!'* Antichrist may roar and rage. He may blow a lot of hot air and let off a fair bit of steam. It will all be in vain for he will fail at the end of the day.

Their condition. In verse 13 John speaks with a tender touch as regards their condition. He says, *Write this: 'Blessed are the dead who die in the Lord from now on.' 'Blessed indeed,' says the Spirit, 'that they may rest from their labours, for their deeds follow them.'*

They are *blessed who die in the Lord.* This is the second of seven beatitudes mentioned in Revelation. In other words, they will be ushered into the near presence of the Lord to see the King in flawless beauty. Their rest is gloriously eternal; there are no more struggles, no more pain or suffering, no more exhaustion, it is rest forever. These folk will be recompensed for nothing anyone has done for the Lord is overlooked. Everything done in his name and for his glory will be amply rewarded. Paul says as much in 1 Corinthians 15:58 when he encourages us to recognise that 'in the Lord [our] labour is not in vain.'

14:14-20

Learn from the special command

The final section of chapter 14 is most intriguing.

A word of introduction

John says, *Then I looked, and behold, a white cloud, and seated on the cloud one like a son of man, with a golden crown on his head, and a sharp sickle in his hand.* We are introduced initially to one who is the reaper of the harvest. There is no doubt as to his identity for the sower in the parable of Matthew 13:1-23 is now the reaper in Revelation 14. There are four things about him worth considering.

His human personality. He is called *the Son of man.* This was the title he used for himself; it reminds us that he knows what we are like. This is the last time we read of him using this particular name. The first was in Matthew 8:20 where we are told, 'Foxes have holes, and birds of the air have nests, but the Son of Man has nowhere to lay his head.' That familiar reference had to do with his first advent, this one refers to his second coming. Then, his poverty was in view; now, it is his power which is in sight.

His moral purity. He is seated on a white cloud and the cloud, as we have seen elsewhere, is a symbol of the presence of God. The white underlines the righteousness of God.

His great power. The golden crown is the mark of a king who is also a conqueror. If you fast forward to 19:12 you will notice he has many crowns adorning his brow. In the next breath, he is hailed as, *King of kings and Lord of lords.*

His awesome purpose. He has a sharp sickle in his hand. That can only speak of a harvest being reaped. Here we see the Lord acting in judgment (cf. Matthew 13:37-43).

A word of instruction

And another angel came out of the temple, calling with a loud voice to him who sat on the cloud, 'Put in your sickle and reap, for the hour to reap has come, for the harvest of the earth is fully ripe.' So he who sat on the cloud swung his sickle across the earth, and the earth was reaped. Then another angel came out of the temple in heaven, and he too had a sharp sickle. And another angel came out from the altar, the angel who has authority over the fire, and he called with a loud voice to the one who had the sharp sickle, 'Put in your sickle and gather the clusters from the vine of the earth, for its grapes are ripe' (14:15-18).

It is fairly clear from John's comments that the judgment of God will come according to his time schedule. Some people wonder why God has not acted sooner. They question why God does not stop all the trouble in today's world. Well, he will act when the time is right. The fact it has not happened yet does not mean it is on the back burner! The day will soon dawn when judgment will be felt to the uttermost ends of earth. It will all be brought to a grand climax.

Ripe and rotten. The picture is of a harvest that is ripe. The Greek word suggests it is 'ripe to the point of being rotten or withered.' So, when God does move in judgment, it will be long overdue but it will not be a minute too soon. Not even the extreme cynic can accuse God of acting on the spur of the moment. When his hand is lifted in such a manner, it will not be in haste for this is no rash decision of an ill-tempered God. His judgment is a reflection of his justice. And the apparent delay says more about the patience and longsuffering of God than anything else.

You have another picture of it unfolding in Joel 3:12-16. The Old Testament prophet draws back the curtain and shows us what will transpire when God acts in judgment on the nations who have come against Jerusalem and the people of Israel. They will meet their Waterloo in the environs of the Holy City; it is there that their blood will flow like a fast-flowing stream. For them, it is the valley of decision.

Grain and grapes. John talks about grain in verses 14-16 and then changes the metaphor in verses 17-20 to talk about grapes. The picture may change but the event remains the same; it is the judgment of the nations brought into sharp focus. If you want to find out more, you can read the appropriate section in Matthew 25:31-46. The grain harvest symbolises the seven bowl judgments and the grape harvest symbolises the judgment of Armageddon.

Timely and terrible. That is what this vision of Armageddon is, timely and terrible. The closing couple of verses are graphic as John reminds us of the incredible impact of this hour of judgment.

When Mary, daughter of King Henry VIII, ruled England, she was nicknamed Bloody Mary. She terrorised Protestant Christians, murdering as many as she could. Her soldiers would spill the blood of those who would not renounce their faith, then take their own Bible and dip it into the pool of blood, thus staining its pages with the actual blood of the martyred Christian. A few of these Bibles have been preserved and are known as Martyrs' Bibles. The reign of Bloody Mary is child's play compared to the events John outlines for us at the end of Revelation 14 ...

A word on its impact

John says, *So the angel swung his sickle across the earth and gathered the grape harvest of the earth and threw it into the great winepress of the wrath of God. And the winepress was trodden outside the city, and blood flowed from the winepress, as high as a horse's bridle, for 1,600 stadia* (14:19-20).

A winepress in ancient Israel was hewn out of solid stone. Grapes were cast into the press and crushed underfoot in the upper vat, until all the juice was squeezed out and flowed into the lower vat. That is the analogy John gives when he says they are like mulch in a winepress in the sense that they have been walked over! What an appalling scene! This is the winepress described by Jeremiah (25:30-31), Isaiah (63:1-4), and Joel (3:13-16).

It is all destined to happen *outside the city*, that is, outside the city of Jerusalem. Isaiah has pointed to Bozrah in Edom, just to the east of the Jordan (63:1-4). Joel reckons it will happen in the valley of Jehoshaphat (3:2) which is linked to the valley of Berachah (cf. 2 Chronicles 20:26) beyond Bethlehem, about fifteen miles south of Jerusalem. John later identifies it in Revelation as Armageddon (16:16) which is part of the plain of Esdraelon (cf. 2 Chronicles 35:24-25; Zechariah 12:11), about forty miles north of Jerusalem. (More about the precise location of this battlefield when we reach chapter 16.)

The distance from Dan to Beersheba is about 200 miles and that is how long the river of blood will be! The carnage will reach up to the horses' bridles, a height of four or five feet! It does not bear thinking about. Horrific scenes of slaughter. Men and women in that day would do well to heed the Psalmist when he writes, 'Kiss the Son, lest he be angry, and you perish in the way, for his wrath is quickly kindled. Blessed are all who take refuge in him' (Psalm 2:12).

CHAPTER 15

Then sings my soul, how great
thou art!

Length is not everything! Brevity means nothing! This is the shortest chapter in the book but that is no reflection of its significance and importance. Compacted into an octet of verses is a little chapter with a lot to say.

15:1-2

The sign

It is interesting to note that the sign depicted in the opening verse as *great and amazing* and the first few words of the song recorded for us in verse 3 are exactly the same. There is nothing tenuous or coincidental about such a link. The connection is valid because they both relate to the God of glory, the awe-inspiring God. He is the focus of attention. The spotlight is shining solely on him. So what can we learn about him?

A final nightmare for earth

We read all about the sign in verse 1 where John says, *Then I saw another sign in heaven, great and amazing, seven angels with seven plagues, which are the last, for with them the wrath of God is finished.* This third sign is of mega importance and one we dare not underestimate. It is called *another* sign meaning it is like the others that have preceded it, namely, the sign of the sun-clothed woman (12:1) and the sign of the red dragon (12:3). Here we are introduced to phase three on the agenda of God's judgment programme. These seven filled-to-the-brim bowls are poised to tip over, ready to spill out a torrent of white-hot wrath upon a fallen humanity. We have already come across the seven seals in phase one and the seven trumpets in phase two. Now we have seven bowls or vials scheduled to be poured out on Planet Earth.

There is no Plan B

Here is the final judgment of God. When these bowls are emptied, the wrath of God on this world will be complete. This final set of judgments is the turning point, the historical pivot upon which God's plan now turns. God is exceedingly angry with an increasingly rebellious world. His wrath will not continue forever; once he has exercised the divine prerogative and done what he has said he will do, that is it. There is no plague number eight, no plan B. We glean that much from Psalm 103:9 where David says, the Lord 'will not always chide, nor will he keep his anger forever.'

The word *finished* speaks of a plan being carried out, a goal being fully accomplished. It is inextricably linked to the phrase at the end of 16:17 where the voice from the throne says, *'It is done.'* It is a tad ironic that when this drama is unfolding on earth, at precisely the same time something extraordinary is happening in heaven!

Harps and heroes in heaven!

John fills in the details when he tells us in verse 2, *And I saw what appeared to be a sea of glass mingled with fire—and also those who had conquered the beast and its image and the number of its name, standing beside the sea of glass with harps of God in their hands.* The apostle sees a huge number of people in his vision standing beside the sea of glass. That is a phrase we first came across in 4:6 where we noted it functioned like a mirror reflecting God's glory and majesty (cf. Ezekiel 1:22). The sea is also symbolic of God's purity and holiness, and his separation from creation. The significant difference is that here it is *mingled with fire* typifying the divine judgment about to be manifested from a holy God.

I was intrigued with another interpretation of this particular picture which John paints for us so vividly in verse 2. It favours the view that the sea of glass represents the Word of God. So when you think of the sea of glass, do not picture an ocean or a lake; think of a laver or a basin similar to that found in the tabernacle in the wilderness or the temple in Jerusalem (cf. Exodus 30:17-21; 1 Kings 7:23). It stood adjacent to the holy place and those who ministered in the things of the Lord would first of all wash in the laver before entering the sanctuary.

The implication is, there is cleansing from our sin when we allow the Word of God to purify our hearts and that God is looking for clean vessels to engage in his service. Paul said as much in his moving letter to the believers in Ephesus (cf. Ephesians 5:26) and Jesus hinted at something similar in John 15:3 when he said, 'Already you are clean because of the word that I have spoken to you.' It is fascinating that the *sea* John describes here in verse 2 has no one washing in it. Instead, they are standing on it! The fact is, there is no further need for them to wash, they are in heaven! They have been promoted to Glory!

Some through the fire ...

The *sea* John writes of is *mingled with fire* and this particular view supports the idea that this speaks of the troubles the saints have experienced. They have come through the fire and, because of that, their troubles are beneath their feet. They have overcome! Fear no longer grips their heart and panic no longer dogs their every step for they are standing foursquare on the Word of God. There is stability on the Word of God.

Can we identify these people? They are the martyrs of the Tribulation. These are the ones who laid down their lives for the sake of Jesus, who paid the supreme sacrifice. These are the brave folk who refused to worship Antichrist. They gallantly swam against the tide of anarchy and lawlessness, they defiantly stood their ground and would not participate in any semblance of Satan-inspired religion.

They have been victorious in the day of severe trial. They have not succumbed to the fierce onslaught from the enemy when the battle was raging all around. In the hour of conquest, they did not cave in under enormous pressure. They said a firm 'no' to being branded with the mark of the Beast and, there they are, standing with their heads held high in heaven itself. They have been well rewarded. They may have died on earth but they are very much alive in heaven where they are treated and honoured as heroes.

That offers immense encouragement to all of us, and even more so, when we realise the Lord has designated a special ministry for them. They form a marvellous orchestra with their harps (apart from the twenty-four elders in 5:8 this is the only company in the book having harps). Harps—a ten-stringed instrument—are frequently associated with inspirational praise in the Old Testament (cf. 2 Samuel 6:5; 1 Chronicles 13:8; Psalms 33:2; 71:22; 144:9; 150:3). There is the sweet sound of beautiful music permeating the atmosphere. There is inspired singing, worshipful praise, emanating from their cultured voices. It is a delightful symphony and these folk are intimately involved in every part of the proceedings. They rejoice in the ultimate victory of God.

15:3-4

The song

John tells us they *sing the song of Moses, the servant of God, and the song of the Lamb, saying, 'Great and amazing are your deeds, O Lord God the Almighty! Just and true are your ways, O King of the nations! Who will not fear, O Lord, and glorify your name? For you alone are holy. All nations will come and worship you, for your righteous acts have been revealed.'* What a wonderful song of praise to our God!

The martyr's song

We can learn a lot from these words. It is the music of heaven and it is sung by those who have tasted deeply of the grace of God. They have known his forgiveness and cleansing (7:14), they also know what it is to suffer and give their lives for the Lord (20:4). This is a song of martyrs! A song of winners!

The title of the song is most informative, the *Song of Moses* and the *Song of the Lamb.* We are presently exploring Revelation 15 and you can find out more about the song of Moses in Exodus 15:1-18 and Deuteronomy 32:1-43 which, actually, is stamped upon the memory of every Jewish person. It was sung at the Sabbath evening service in the synagogue and, to this day, one of two prayers at every orthodox Jewish service refers to this song of Moses. Let me give you some remarkable comparisons between the two:

The song of Moses was sung at the Red Sea, the song of the Lamb is sung at the crystal sea; the song of Moses was one of triumph over Egypt, the song of the Lamb is one of triumph over Babylon; the song of Moses told how God brought his people out, the song of the Lamb tells how God brings his people in; the song of Moses was the first song in Scripture, the song of the Lamb is the last recorded on the sacred page; the song of Moses had a triple commemoration, the song of the Lamb deals with the same three themes – the execution of the enemy, the expectation of the saints, and the exaltation of the Lord; the song of Moses was sung by a redeemed people, the song of the Lamb is sung by a raptured people.

Basically, it is a song in two parts. The first tells us what the ransomed will sing. It is a threefold stanza for it says, 'How great thou art! how good thou art! how glorious thou art!' The second tells us why the remnant will sing and you find that alluded to in verse 4. It is because of the majestic virtue of God, the magnificent victory of God, and the manifest vengeance of God.

This stunning song in chapter 15 is pure, unadulterated praise! It is praise at its finest and best. It is praise as God intended it should be. The more you look into it, the more you listen to the words being sung, the more you recognise the sheer quality of each carefully chosen word and the more you appreciate and value the harmony of heaven. The Scottish-born evangelist, John Linton, said: 'There are as many commands in the Bible to sing as there are to pray.'

They are praising the marvellous works of God ... they emphasise his power

These varied judgments demonstrate the mighty power of God for he is omnipotent. They tell us what he can do. You find an echo of this in Psalm 145:10-13 where we read, 'All your works shall give thanks to you, O Lord, and all your saints shall bless you! They shall speak of the glory of your kingdom and tell of your power, to make known to the children of man your mighty deeds, and the glorious splendour of your kingdom. Your kingdom is an everlasting kingdom, and your dominion endures throughout all generations. The Lord is faithful in all his words and kind in all his works.'

They are praising the mysterious ways of God ... they emphasise his plan

The psalmist picks up the same thread when he reminds us that the Lord is right and just in all that he does. You find that in Psalm 145:17 where we read, 'The Lord is righteous in all his ways and kind in all his works.' He is faithful to all his promises. God is totally reliable. We may not always understand the plan of God especially as it relates to justice and the future, but we can be assured, there is a plan which is correct and on schedule. We affirm with a high degree of confidence, there is no panic in heaven over events on earth.

They are praising the manifold worth of God ... they emphasise his perfection

Here is one who is holy and transcendent. Our God is completely separate from all that he has created, a distinction unique to him. Only he deserves the glory and praise. It is something quite exclusive.

They are praising the majestic worship of God ... they emphasise his purpose

God's ultimate purpose is for all nations to praise him. His eventual goal is for all creation to praise him. You find that outlined in Psalm 66:4 where we read, 'All the earth worships you and sings praise to you; they sing praises to your name.' We have a similar note in Psalm 72:11 where Solomon says, 'May all kings fall down before him, all nations serve him.' And when we take a look at Isaiah 66:23, we see an amazing prophecy which anticipates a day when 'from new moon to new moon, and from Sabbath to Sabbath, all flesh shall come to worship before me.' Paul declared in Philippians 2:10-11 that one day all men will bow the knee before him and every tongue will confess that Jesus Christ is Lord! Yes, all nations, all of creation will worship him!

15:5-8

The scene

John shares a profound experience in verses 5-8 by informing us, *After this I looked, and the sanctuary of the tent of witness in heaven was opened, and out of the sanctuary came the seven angels with the seven plagues, clothed in pure, bright linen, with golden sashes around their chests. And one of the four living creatures gave to the seven angels seven golden bowls full of the wrath of God who lives forever and ever, and the sanctuary was filled with smoke from the glory of God and from his power, and no one could enter the sanctuary until the seven plagues of the seven angels were finished.*
We are taken into the holy of holies in heaven, and what

do we notice? We have the appearance of seven angels. These are the same ones you read about elsewhere in the Apocalypse. They are specifically chosen by God to execute his purposes upon the world and that teaches us a couple of important lessons:

Their coming out of the temple reminds us of the faithfulness of God

The temple is called *the sanctuary of the tent* and the *witness* refers to the Law of God. These were the ten commandments that were written on two tablets of stone and placed within the ark of the covenant (cf. Exodus 25:16). It reminds us that God's covenant with his people will be kept for it has never been annulled or set aside. God will honour his high and holy standards for it is his name which is at stake. His severe judgment will fall upon those who reject him and his principles. In other words, God will be rigidly faithful to what he has said.

Their clothing reminds us of the righteousness and majesty of God

What they will do in pouring out God's wrath upon the inhabitants of earth is a powerful demonstration of God's holiness and righteousness. This is terrible but, at the same time, it is right! They also have *golden sashes around their chests* and that could be seen as symbolic of the priests who ministered in the temple but, more than likely, it is a picture of the majesty and greatness of our kingly God. You can compare their clothing with that worn by our exalted Lord in 1:13 and, when you do that, it is apparent that this is the apparel of a sovereign ruler.

Their assignment is spelled out clearly in verse 7 when one of the worship leaders gives the seven golden bowls to the seven angels. The Greek word for *bowls* refers to shallow saucers (cf. 1 Kings 7:50; Zechariah 14:20), not unlike those into which you might pour milk for your cat. As John MacArthur notes:

'The imagery is not that of a stream being poured gradually out of a pitcher, but of the whole contents of the shallow saucers being hurled down in an instant flood of judgment.' Each of these saucers is filled and running over the edge with the undiluted anger of God. God's anger is at boiling point as the seven last plagues are emptied out upon this world in a most comprehensive manner.

We see him as the eternal one and that is a token reminder of the nature of his punishment. There is nothing cuddly or cosy about our God for he will not turn a blind eye to sin. As Steve Wilmshurst points out: 'Still less does he resemble the dying, decrepit figure of the Philip Pullman novels. No, this is our God: all-knowing, all-seeing, glorious, and holy.'

The atmosphere in the temple is easily detected in verse 8. What an awesome display of God's presence and power! Two facets of this noble attribute are emphasised in this verse:

the intensity of God's power ... when the evangelical prophet Isaiah had his spectacular vision of the Lord of hosts, we read in 6:4 that 'the foundations of the thresholds shook at the voice of him who called, and the house was filled with smoke.' Remember the incident detailed in Exodus 40:34 where again we observe that God's presence was often pictured by a cloud or smoke. There we read, 'Then the cloud covered the tent of meeting, and the glory of the Lord filled the tabernacle.' Something similar occurred at the dedication of the temple in 1 Kings 8:10-12.

the importance of God's plan ... God's wrath is part of his unerring plan and it will be completed. His mission will not be aborted. Until it is effectively and efficiently carried out, no one can enter the temple in heaven. The words of Lamentations 3:44 in the days when God judged rebellious Jerusalem are relevant, 'You have wrapped yourself with a cloud so that no prayer can pass through.' Now, in this later day, when God judges the earth, he rules out any intercession. Even a righteous Abraham would be wasting his time and energy at this critical point (cf. Genesis 18:16-33). One commentator teases out this truth when he writes: 'When the smouldering fires of God's wrath arising from his glory and his power are about to erupt in volcanic fashion God is absolutely unapproachable.'

One evening a dad went on a walk on the Canadian prairie with his little daughter. They had gone a long way when they saw in the distance a roaring prairie fire rushing in their direction. The father knew they had but one chance to escape the onrushing inferno, and that was to burn the ground around them. He quickly took out some matches, burned an area of ground, and then stood in the middle of that area, tightly holding his frightened daughter. As the flames of the prairie fire got closer and closer, his little girl's screams became louder and louder. Soon the flames surrounded them, but he comforted her with these words: 'Don't worry, honey, the flames can't get to us because we're standing where the fire has already been.'

When you and I are 'in' Christ, we are standing where the fire has already been. We have nothing to fear, at all. Jesus took the flames upon himself so that we will never have to face God's wrath. But, for those who are not yet 'in' Christ, they need to watch out. The fire is fast approaching.

That is quite dramatic but it reminds us of the importance of these seven last plagues in the maturing purpose of God. The Tribulation is a demonstration of the wrath of an angry God against all those who flatly refuse to trust in the Lord Jesus. So far as the sinner is concerned, the worst is yet to come.

CHAPTER 16

Post-Armageddon: tremors and trembling

Revelation 16 is one of those chapters in the Bible that makes the hair stand on the back of your neck. You can feel the shivers going down your spine. It makes your legs turn to jelly and the butterflies work overtime in your tummy. It is a chapter where you can almost feel a tremor in each line as the scale of the disaster facing the world becomes increasingly apparent. One respected Bible commentator describes this chilling chapter as the 'Saturday evening of the age.'

Judgment and justice

The storm is about to break. What follows is, undoubtedly, the darkest chapter in the history of mankind. John informs us, *Then I heard a loud voice from the temple telling the seven angels, 'Go and pour out on the earth the seven bowls of the wrath of God.'* There is no mistaking that message! It is precise and straight to the point as God is going for the jugular. As we shall see, the consequences do not make for pleasant reading. The scale of this series of salvo-like judgments is lifted to a new level with the repeated use of the word *loud* in the chapter, it appears no fewer than six times (cf. Joel 2:31). The *voice* is coming from the temple (16:1) and the throne (16:17).

A helpful analogy is seen in the outpouring of the drink offering (cf. Genesis 35:14; Exodus 29:40; Leviticus 23:13) over the sacrificial victim on the altar in that it was carried out in a single movement. One writer notes that '… earth is pictured as the victim ready for the sacrifice and swiftly bowl after bowl is emptied over it.'

The world has been ruined by the Fall, the world has flatly rejected the Lord Jesus Christ, the world has been ruled by Satan and now, in an hour of swift, decisive judgment, God initiates a rescue mission. The ways of God are strange. They are often shrouded in an air of mystery. There is a certain mystique about the mind of God but, in the midst of all the chaos and confusion, we must never forget the final chapter insofar as God is concerned, those closing lines have already been penned. That is the supreme goal our God is tirelessly working towards. But before it can be fully achieved, man must be taught a salient lesson on the unchanging character of God—God is holy, God is angry, God is sovereign, and God is a God of justice!

And so, one after another, with speed, the seven angels empty their bowls and, as they pour out the wrath of the Lord, indescribable things happen. Charles Swindoll makes the point that the angels 'did not simply crowd at the edge of heaven and empty their saucers like a mob of kindergartners slinging mud.' There is nothing drip-drip-drip envisaged here! It was one at a time, in preset order. God makes short work of it. It is over and done with in a matter of days or, at the most, weeks. Much of what is recorded here is reminiscent of the plagues called down by Moses on the land of Egypt.

16:2

Plague number one!

In verse 2 John says, *So the first angel went and poured out his bowl on the earth, and harmful and painful sores came upon the people who bore the mark of the beast and worshipped its image.*

The hit list

The principal target of this plague are the committed followers of Antichrist. These are the people who have the mark of the Beast on their right hand or forehead, who are happy to worship the image of the Beast set up in the rebuilt temple in Jerusalem. Their past catches up with them with breathtaking speed. Their crazy decision to opt for the easy alternative and go with the crowd returns to haunt them. Remember, Antichrist thinks he is God Mark 2. By this time, he is well established as a world leader and highly respected as a major player on the stage of global affairs. Here is the final government credited to modern man, these are the last of the last days. When Antichrist is at his peak, God strikes with impunity!

The game plan

God's strategy is to attack the health of men and women. He hits them where it hurts most and it is not a pretty sight. We are told that *harmful and painful sores* break out on their bodies (cf. Luke 16:21 where the only other occurrence of the word *sore* appears in the NT). These are ugly, ulcerous, contagious, putrefying sores which infect the body like a malignant cancer. It is some kind of incurable skin disease. If you have ever experienced an outbreak of boils on your body, you will know they are extremely painful, they are inflamed and pus-filled; that gives you a tiny inkling of what it will be like in a coming day, only then it will be so much worse.

The scientist Henry Morris suggests that '… since it is confined to those having the mark of the Beast, it may well be that God allows the laser beam or radioactive ray used in their branding to become a tool of judgment.'

The upshot

What an awful affliction that must be and it is made a million times worse because these folk are used to pampering themselves. How much worse it is when inflicted on a people obsessed with their personal appearance! Pain affects a person's disposition, they are hard to live with and they find it difficult to get along with other people. Emotionally, it will be a radical upheaval; psychologically, it will be a disaster!

16:3

Plague number two!

Plague number two is outlined for us in considerable detail in verse 3 where we read, *The second angel poured out his bowl into the sea, and it became like the blood of a corpse, and every living thing died that was in the sea.*

The hit list

That is grim, it really is. It does not bear thinking about. Away back in the days of Moses it was the River Nile that was turned to blood, here it is the sea itself. Since two-thirds of the world is covered by ocean, this underlines the global nature of this outpouring of divine anger.

The game plan

What an incredible sight for the naked eye! The sea becomes an ocean which is foul, offensive, and poisonous. It turns into a thick coagulated mass of fluid which stinks like a badly decomposed corpse. A disgusting smell for an aroma conscious generation to inhale! The reek is stifling and oppressive. One commentator writes: 'If you have ever been to an ocean beach when jellyfish have washed ashore and died, you have an idea of the kind of stench involved. Yet this vision in Revelation is millions of times worse.'

The upshot

Every living creature in the sea dies and that is nothing short of a major catastrophe for it hits the food supply of the world and adversely affects the global economy. It will be as though the bruised world is lying in its own gore. Everything to do with the sea grinds to a sudden halt, it comes to a standstill with a jerk. What a tremendously awesome display of the power of a God who can do anything! Man is left reeling from the impact of this lethal blow of the wrath of God which, according to eminent scientist Henry Morris, caused 'the sea to become a turgid pool of death.'

Can you even begin to imagine the fetid stench that will rise from such terribly polluted waters? And the characteristic burning sensation of the eyes and nose, and a dry, choking cough to human beings?

I do not know if John means the sea will literally turn to blood for he says it will be *like that of a corpse*. There is a condition known as the 'red tide' which is caused by micro organisms—dinoflagellates—that multiply incredibly fast and cause everything in one area to die. Scientists cannot put their finger on the reasons behind this condition; they do not know what causes it but they presume it is due to cobalt from nuclear waste.

16:4-7

Plague number three!

John continues in verses 4-7 to provide us with vital information relevant to plague number three.

The hit list

He says, *The third angel poured out his bowl into the rivers and the springs of water, and they became blood. And I heard the angel in charge of the waters say: 'Just are you, O Holy One, who is and who was, for you brought these judgments. For they have shed the blood of saints and prophets, and you have given them blood to drink. It is what they deserve!' And I heard the altar saying, 'Yes, Lord God the Almighty, true and just are your judgments.'* The sheer magnitude of this is unimaginable, it is inconceivable!

The game plan

The Lord's first miracle in Cana of Galilee was to turn water into wine; now he turns water into blood. All of the world's springs and rivers are now affected. That means the drinking water supply is polluted and corrupted to such an extent that global panic is unavoidable. If the world is so bloodthirsty, God will give it to them – fountains of blood, springs of blood, rivers of blood, oceans of blood! As John MacArthur notes: 'Fittingly, those who have spilled so much innocent blood will be given blood to drink.' And, to quote the angel, *it is what they deserve* (cf. Romans 12:19; Hebrews 10:30). The divine rationale is summarised in the familiar saying of 'an eye for an eye and a tooth for a tooth' (Deuteronomy 19:21; Galatians 6:7).

The upshot

That which is essential for the maintenance of life is now rendered useless. You cannot quench your thirst if you cannot drink the water! There is a limit to the stockpiles of bottled mineral water and canned soft drinks. There will be health problems as a direct result of what has happened and this will serve to increase the agony of daily life.

James Allen says: 'With all the technology of earth at his disposal the Beast will find it hard to find potable water for his kingdom just as King Ahab did in the time of Elijah (cf. 1 Kings 18:5-6). Perhaps this is the very time when the cup of cold water becomes very precious indeed (cf. Matthew 10:42).'

All the comforts and necessities of life are being taken away gradually, bit by bit, and then finally! It will slowly dawn on the minds of people that the end of the world is just around the corner. This is not man messing around with the environment. This is supernatural, this is divine, this is God! Down through history, we discover an age-old principle which dictates that the punishment fits the crime.

Pharaoh tried to drown the Jewish male babies, but it was his own army that drowned in the warm sparkling waters of the Red Sea. Haman planned to hang Mordecai on the gallows and exterminate the Jews, but the tables were turned when he himself perished and his family was wiped out entirely. Saul refused to obey the Lord and slay the Amalekites; his foolish scheme tragically backfired when he was slain by one of them.

The response of the angels to this intervention by God in the affairs of man indicates a recognition of the righteousness of God; they also make much of the holiness of God and are happy to elucidate so clearly the eternal nature of God. Here we have volumes of praise dedicated to one who acts. It is an eloquent tribute to a God who is unafraid to move when he senses the time is right. The God we meet here sets the record straight. This incident reminds us that God answers the prayers of those martyred saints which are recorded for us in 6:9-11. They asked, *'How long?'* God says, 'Their time has come, their number is up!'

16:8-9

Plague number four!

In verses 8 and 9 we are introduced to plague number four which, in all likelihood, links in with Luke 21:25 where the Lord spoke of 'signs in the sun.'

The hit list

The verse begins in the same way as all the others have when John says, *The fourth angel poured out his bowl on the sun, and it was allowed to scorch people with fire. They were scorched by the fierce heat, and they cursed the name of God who had power over these plagues. They did not repent and give him glory.*

The game plan

The light from the sun is not reduced but its capacity to bring heat to the earth is massively increased. It will get hotter and hotter. It will seem that the atmosphere is on fire. What is normally seen as a blessing to man quickly becomes a curse as men are scorched by the sun's burning rays. Global warming.

The upshot

Anyone who has been exposed to the sun for any length of time knows it can be a merciless foe rather than a warm friend. Ask anyone who has suffered sunstroke for their opinion and you will discover it is not something they would like to experience again. This plague strikes right at the heart of man's personal security and his quest for survival. This is no Indian summer or freak heatwave. The earth will be scorched and the heat so intense it will have a searing effect upon man (cf. Malachi 4:1; Isaiah 24:6). The extreme heat will boil the oceans dry and melt the polar ice-caps as well as affect the global community of Beast worshippers. One commentator puts it succinctly: 'The earth turning on its axis begins to resemble a pig roasting on a spit.'

What is man's initial response to this crisis in his personal life? He cursed the name of God; fairly typical, isn't it! Par for the course, methinks! To put it mildly, they blame God! They blaspheme the precious name of the Lord of heaven. You can detect something of the dogged determination of ordinary people when they dig in their heels and actively pursue their wilful rebellion against God. They refuse to repent.

The same sun that melts the ice hardens the clay. Their granite hearts are so hardened that they cannot even be melted by the torch of a solar flare. They are as stupid and stubborn as that. That is what sin does for you and to you. Like the sun, it blinds you and, at the same time, it leaves you in the dark, sweating it out!

16:10-11

Plague number five!

The hit list

Plague number five is spoken about in verses 10 and 11 where John tells us, *The fifth angel poured out his bowl on the throne of the beast, and its kingdom was plunged into darkness. People gnawed their tongues in anguish and cursed the God of heaven for their pain and sores. They did not repent of their deeds.*

The game plan

So far Antichrist has been immune but now his throne is shaken and, like Pharaoh of old, he is powerless to defend himself (cf. Exodus 10:21-29). His kingdom is plunged into tar-like darkness. James Allen offers this insightful comment: 'Now in the darkened cabinet room of the mightiest empire the world has ever seen, the mightiest emperor and his prime minister, the false prophet, face the fact that their satanic master is not almighty.'

We are not talking here about a dark night. It is not when the clouds cover the moon and the stars cannot be seen. It is worse! It is so inky-black that men cannot see each other when they pass by on the Main Street. This means no one dares move! It is a veritable blackout! In some ways, this darkness is a preview of hell itself. Jesus described that as a place of 'outer darkness' where men will 'weep and gnash their teeth.'

The upshot

The darkness is so intense and the pain so bad that macho men express their anguish by gnawing their tongues. Darkness makes their pain unbearable. And things always get worse at night time! There is no ease, no let-up, no relief. And what happens? Man just goes on cursing the God of heaven, refusing to get right with God. It is worth noting that this is the last reference to their unwillingness to repent as they defiantly ignore God's final call. Even though it is tough, they want to continue with their sinful lifestyle.

This crescendo of hurt brings in its wake a crescendo of hate. Even when men experience the fury of God and their circumstances are so appallingly awful, they still go on heedless and careless. They are happy to live their lives without the Lord. In their darkest hour, they maintain the status-quo so far as their relationship with God is concerned. They have a victim's mentality!

16:12-16

Plague number six!

The next paragraph in chapter 16 leads us to consider plague number six. It is the penultimate one and is probably the one most people are familiar with for it is all about the Armageddon campaign.

The hit list

The details are spelled out with remarkable insight in verses 12 to 16 where John tells us, *The sixth angel poured out his bowl on the great river Euphrates, and its water was dried up, to prepare the way for the kings from the east. And I saw, coming out of the mouth of the dragon and out of the mouth of the beast and out of the mouth of the false prophet, three unclean spirits like frogs. For they are demonic spirits, performing signs, who go abroad to the kings of the whole world, to assemble them for battle on the great day of God the Almighty. 'Behold, I am coming like a thief! Blessed is the one who stays awake, keeping his garments on, that he may not go about naked and be seen exposed.' And they assembled them at the place that in Hebrew is called Armageddon.*

The game plan

This is mind-blowing stuff! It is fascinating! The river Euphrates, one of the great rivers of the world, dries up! It is interesting to note that it appears twice in the first book of the Bible (Genesis 2:14; 15:18) and twice in the last book (Revelation 9:13-15; 16:12). The Euphrates is called *great* because of its significant location. It is the longest river in western Asia, flowing almost 1,800 miles from its source in the snowfields and ice-cap high on the slopes of Mount Ararat (located in modern Turkey) before emptying into the Persian Gulf. It formed a natural and formidable eastern boundary for the Roman Empire and was often spoken of as the dividing line between the Near East and the Far East.

In ancient times the garden of Eden was located in the vicinity of the Euphrates (cf. Genesis 2:10-14). The Euphrates also formed the eastern boundary of the land God gave to Israel (cf. Genesis 15:18; Deuteronomy 1:7; 11:24; Joshua 1:4). One writer makes the point that 'along with the nearby Tigris, the Euphrates is still the lifeblood of the Fertile Crescent.' In fact, in 1993, Turkey diverted half the waters of the Euphrates to fill a new dam and the world's media gave it a casual nod before moving on to another news story. When it dries up in a day soon to dawn, it will be an entirely different matter! The God who opened a path through the Red Sea and dried the Jordan river with a word has put his hand on this mighty river. The impact is colossal and immediate as irrigation pumps seize up, power generators fall silent (note the candle in 18:23), and the great distilling plants are closed down. This is evidence, if it were needed, that God is running the entire show.

The upshot

John informs us it dries up to prepare the way for *the kings from the east*. If that were to happen, and it will, it then makes it possible for a huge army of 200,000,000 from different nations (many of them Islamic) to come across from the Orient into the

Middle East (cf. Revelation 9:16). The winding depths of the dry, cracked riverbed will be the pavement for their march to the final battlefield. In that day, the yellow peril will become a reality!

On the face of it, that may seem like an outrageously high number of soldiers but, according to the UN, the population of China in 2014 is close to 1.4 billion souls. On top of that, add another 1.3 billion from India, the world's second most populous nation, and the burgeoning numbers from the likes of Malaysia, Indonesia, and Japan, and the figure is easily attainable. What is envisaged here, therefore, is the gathering of the armies from the lands of the rising sun to participate, unwittingly and unknowingly, in the bloodbath at Armageddon.

It is all about a coming invasion and John leaves no stone unturned when he says they, along with *the kings of the whole world*, will be present at the final conflict of the ages. For the sake of clarity, it is important to realise that these are two different armies which start out with different agendas but actually end up fighting together against the coming King! Some have gathered to destroy the Beast, mainly from the east; others have gathered to defend the Beast, mainly from the west. As one writer says: 'They little realise they are all, in some degree, but puppets in a terrible deception. When that deception is unmasked and it is far too late, they will find they are all enrolled under the banner of Satan in opposition to God and his Christ.' The reality is, they are nothing but pawns on a satanic chessboard!

Many folk refer to this military confrontation as World War III. I have often heard people quoting the famous line from Rudyard Kipling which says, 'East is east and west is west and never the twain shall meet.' Well, that is not strictly true, for one day they will meet, right here at Armageddon.

The name Armageddon comes from two Hebrew words, *har Megiddo*, which mean 'the hill of Megiddo.' The word 'Megiddo' means 'the place of troops' or 'the place of slaughter.' It is also called in today's map-speak the Plain of Esdraelon and the Valley of Jezreel. The area is about fourteen miles wide and twenty miles long and forms what Napoleon called, 'the most natural battlefield of the whole earth.' You can stand on Mount Carmel and see for yourself exactly what Bonaparte meant when he said what he did.

It was here that Deborah and Barak defeated the armies of Canaan (cf. Judges 5). It was on this plain that Gideon met the Midianites (cf. Judges 7). It was here that David defeated the giant Goliath of Gath (cf. 1 Samuel 17). It was here that King Saul lost his life in a tragic manner (cf. 1 Samuel 31). It was here that an Egyptian king killed Josiah (cf. 2 Kings 23). Titus and the Roman army used this natural corridor, as did the Crusaders. The British General, Allenby, used it when he defeated the Turkish army in 1917.

On 2 September 1945 when General Douglas MacArthur supervised the signing of the peace treaty with Japan, this is what he said: 'We have had our last chance. If we will not devise something greater and more equitable than war, Armageddon will be at our door.' Those words have come back to haunt us, they are prophetic in the best sense of that word. He was absolutely right!

Today, Planet Earth is like a powder keg. The fuse is lit and very soon the explosion will be heard. U Thant, a former secretary to the United Nations, said: 'I'm afraid that what we are witnessing today is the setting of the stage for World War III.' The prophet Amos said the nations are like 'a basket of summer fruit' (8:1-2). If that is the case, it means Planet Earth is rotting, it smells and is ripe and ready for judgment. Armageddon is no figment of the imagination. One day, it will be a fait accompli and, on the morning after, it will be history.

The strategy deployed at Armageddon. John draws attention to three evil spirits that looked like frogs coming out of the mouths of this trinity of evil. Frogs have long been associated with the occult world and are an abomination to Israel (cf. Leviticus 11:10-11, 41). In days of yore, the Egyptians worshiped Heka, a frog-headed goddess. In fact, she was one of the oldest goddesses who was said to have demonic power.

Basically, they are there to wage a concerted propaganda

campaign. It is an exercise in PR as they rally people together in a racist spirit of anti-Semitism. They are there to sow seeds of hate, to inflame the passions of men, to stir things up, and to ensure Armageddon becomes a certainty *on the great day of God the Almighty.*

Already, there are evil men causing all sorts of trouble in the Middle East, but when these demons go to work there will be a final push to unite the Arab world against Israel – that is reflected in the military presence of those from the east. Satan, the author of death, looks forward with a measure of glee to the harvest of souls he will reap at Armageddon. Great hordes of people from every point of the compass will march in gathering for the final battle. You can read some of the grim and gory statistics in the closing verses of chapter 19.

These demons are extremely capable of *performing* miraculous *signs* and wonders. In some ways, this will be the final delusion before the millennial reign of Jesus Christ. Men and women are hoodwinked as they are led further down a dark alley of spiritual blindness. They will lull men into a false sense of security and incite them to war; men will believe what they see with their own two eyes.

Their single devil-inspired objective will be realised when all hell breaks loose on the plains of Megiddo and in the environs of Jerusalem. As I intimated earlier, these hyperactive demons are pulling the strings and manipulating world leaders, setting up situations and manoeuvring nations from behind the scenes. Their ultimate goal is the same throughout for their evil mission will not be accomplished until the final war of human history is launched.

In the middle of all this, in verse 15 we have the Lord reminding his people of his coming. He says, he is *coming like a thief* and that suggests the idea of surprise. Those who are passing through times of severe suffering in the dark days of Tribulation can hold on a little while longer for they know his advent is no longer imminent, it is immediate! There is the promise of blessing to those who remain on red alert and avoid contamination from the world around them. It is a challenge for them to walk with their heads held high for they know the Lord is returning for them, and them alone. They have something to look forward to when the pressure may seem unbearable. This truth keeps them going!

One of the key purposes of the Lord's coming is to strip off the garments of hypocrisy with which the human race has clothed itself. And that is explicitly stated at the end of verse 15 where Jesus coined a rather unusual phrase. It is always God's work to remove the facade, to expose the sham, to strip away any highly polished veneer, to tear off the mask. He cannot tolerate anything which smacks of a cover-up, he detests that which is not authentic and real. He will do whatever he needs to do to bring the truth out into the open.

Armageddon may be a lot closer than people care to think, the drums of war can be heard in the distance. World War I was given the optimistic title of 'the war to end all wars.' It is a name that could not stick, it was not earthed to reality. But the war effort that takes place on the vast plain of Esdraelon in the beautiful, fertile valley of Jezreel will undoubtedly be 'the war to end all wars.' No one is disputing that fact! The man who argues with this assessment is not living in the real world, he is in cloud-cuckoo land. His pie-in-the-sky views do not tally with the teaching of the Bible. Armageddon will precipitate the final bowl of judgment. It will bring down the final curtain on the human drama and signal the end.

16:17-21

Plague number seven!

The hit list

John continues to inform us of what is destined to happen to earth when he says that *the seventh angel poured out his bowl into the air, and a loud voice came out of the temple, from the throne, saying, 'It is done!' And there were flashes of lightning, rumblings, peals of thunder, and a great earthquake such as there had never been since man was on the earth, so great was the earthquake. The great city was split into three parts, and the cities of the nations fell, and God remembered Babylon the great, to make her drain the cup of the wine of the fury of his wrath. And every island fled away, and no mountains were to be found. And great hailstones, about one hundred pounds each, fell from heaven upon people; and they cursed God for the plague of the hail, because the plague was so severe.*

This is the last of the seven bowls of judgment which will finish God's wrath upon the earth. It will be the most terrible and awful judgment to hit this world, and hit it, it certainly will. Like the seventh seal (8:5) and the seventh trumpet (11:19), the seventh bowl is introduced with the imagery of a violent thunderstorm.

The game plan

It comes hard on the heels of Armageddon and describes the effects of nuclear warfare which would release vast clouds of poisonous radiation upon earth. The disastrous accident at Chernobyl (Ukraine) on 26 April 1986 gives us some idea of what would happen to the air we breathe in the event of a nuclear fallout. So it may well be, as one commentator remarks, that 'the final bowl of God's judgment is tipped by the finger of man himself – a finger that is even at this moment poised over the nuclear button. In our hi-speed, hi-tech, ballistic age, humankind is never more than a few minutes away from potential doom.'

God's answer to the pollution of the atmosphere is to shake the earth with the greatest quake the world has ever known. There has never before been anything like this recorded on the Richter scale. This is the 'big' one the punters talk about.

The upshot

The earthquake causes phenomenal damage to property and an enormous loss of life. The lives of ordinary people are shattered, countless millions of hearts are broken, there is blind panic on a massive scale as the magnitude of the earthquake finally sinks in. Men are scared stiff. They are frozen with fear. Every tremor causes them to tremble in their shoes.

This convulsion is unprecedented in terms of world history! It brings, in its wake, a tale of jumbo destruction to the major cities of the world. The infrastructure is reduced to rubble, to a state of total collapse. All the metropolitan centres of population—for example, London, New York, Moscow, Beijing, Tokyo, Paris, Rome, and others—are razed to the ground, important capital cities are virtually wiped out, the world is rocked in a global disaster of mega proportion.

The *great city* which John mentions in verse 19 is probably a reference to Jerusalem (cf. 11:8). Echoes of the earthquake are found back in the Old Testament, especially in the writings of Zechariah where he describes the aftermath in detail (14:4-10; cf. Haggai 2:6-7). The Mount of Olives will split in two, and a new valley running east and west will be created (cf. Zechariah 14:4). A spring of water will flow year-round from Jerusalem to the Mediterranean and Dead Sea (cf. Zechariah 14:8), causing the desert to blossom like a rose (cf. Isaiah 35:1). That means Jerusalem will be elevated and the surrounding region flattened into a plain (cf. Zechariah 14:10). Thus, to quote John MacArthur: 'The purpose of the earthquake as it relates to Jerusalem is not to judge the city, but to enhance it ... the physical changes will prepare Jerusalem for the central role it will play during the millennial kingdom, when Christ will reign there as king (cf. Psalm 110:2; Isaiah 2:3; 24:23; Micah 4:7).'

There is not only chaos and confusion so far as the cities of the world are concerned, the aftershocks reach out to the mountains and islands. You could not see them, you cannot find them. This implies there will be considerable changes in the topography of the planet (cf. Isaiah 40:4). Nothing will ever be the same again. The once easily recognised features of earth will be radically altered. John MacArthur makes the point that 'the shaking will be so severe that it will renovate and reconfigure the earth in preparation for the millennial kingdom, restoring it to something like its pre-Flood condition (16:20).'

John also talks about huge hailstones falling at random from the sky. They will pepper the earth at great velocity. Man will be bombarded and blitzed with solid missiles of ice hurtling down on him. These are estimated to weigh about one hundred pounds or a little over 45 kilos each and that is nothing to laugh at! The heaviest hailstones ever recorded weighed a little over two pounds each and that was in Bangladesh on 14 April 1986. These will be fifty times heavier, give or take a few ounces. That is mega heavy! Can you imagine it? Great chunks of ice, like billiard balls, falling from the sky, landing all around you with indiscriminate force. And, because of the earthquake, there is little place for adequate shelter. Unthinkable! It is horrific! This is global cooling.

Just as Pharaoh and the Egyptian leaders did not repent, so the earth dwellers will not repent. It is the last thing on their mind. Actually, if the truth be told, it is not on their mind at all! In fact, they curse God! They blaspheme his great and holy name. In one sense, it is no wonder the hail comes for blasphemers are supposed to be stoned to death (cf. Leviticus 24:16). These folk are getting their just desserts and have brought it on themselves.

When you go back up the chapter to verse 17, it is good to remind ourselves of the message coming from the throne of God. It is short, sweet, and straight to the point. It indicates that God's work of judgment is complete. He says, *It is done.* A similar cry echoed from the lips of the Lord Jesus when he was crucified on the cross at Calvary. He shouted in a loud voice in John 19:30, 'It is finished!' That was a declaration of victory, a note resounding with glorious triumph, a celebration of his conquest over sin and Satan. On that first Good Friday he bore the punishment for our sin. On a future day, men will bear the judgment of God for their sin. They will pay an awful price for rejecting the Lord Jesus Christ. And they will do it in time and eternity.

CHAPTER 17

The world's greatest flirt – Satan's Megachurch

In Revelation 17 and 18 the spotlight is on the classic tale of two Babylons—one is mystical, the other is material; one is religious, the other is economic. One grows out of the other: Antichrist controls the first and creates the second; the religious system paves the way for the political system. In the early days, the religious system supports the political system but, as time marches on and things begin to change, the political system supplants the religious one. The religious system is represented in chapter 17 as the Babylonian mother, the political system is graphically portrayed as the Babylonian monster.

Babylon is mentioned more times in the Bible than any other city with the notable exception of Jerusalem (about 277 times in the OT and 12 times in the NT). It brings to mind a host of images of a nefarious city-state enmeshed in an abominable religious system. The tentacles of this highly-organised, well-blended mixture of religion and politics reach out to the far flung corners of the earth. True to form, it will corrupt and taint everything it touches! This is the kingdom of the Beast, also known as the Antichrist, the Man of Sin. It is the last world empire where man is centre stage.

John draws back the curtain with an extensive insight into the far-reaching implications of God's statement of intent in 16:19 where in an almost throwaway line we read, *God remembered Babylon the great, to make her drain the cup of the wine of the fury of his wrath.* This duo of chapters fills in the blanks.

We are left in no doubt as to what God thinks of this final kingdom of man. It is the worst kept secret in the entire book!

God is not in the least impressed nor is he amused with her antics either! In the laser eye of God, Babylon does herself no lasting favours with all her shenanigans. These eventful chapters spell desolation and destruction! From God's perspective, it is as good as done. You will remember the words of the high flying angel in 14:8 where he called out, *'Fallen, fallen is Babylon the great.'*

These two chapters are, therefore, a running commentary on the couple of verses just referred to. And that is good. It makes life a lot easier for all of us. You may recognise the name of A W Pink, a highly respected and much-loved Bible commentator who passed away in 1952. As he lay dying at his home in Stornoway on the Isle of Lewis in the Outer Hebrides, some of his last recorded words were: 'The Scriptures explain themselves.' He could not have said a truer word. That is certainly the case with chapters 17 and 18.

17:1-6

The scarlet woman

The Bible says, *Then one of the seven angels who had the seven bowls came and said to me, 'Come, I will show you the judgment of the great prostitute who is seated on many waters.'* The scene outlined is one of high drama. The seven bowls have been poured out on earth resulting in unimaginable pandemonium and havoc. The world is littered with the scars of an invasion from another platform, the dust and debris of a devastated world is everywhere.

And then, out of the blue, one of the seven angels comes over to John and has a word in his ear. He explains the ins and outs of all that has happened. He exposes the power structure of the empire of Antichrist. He shows it for what it is and we see it in its true colours. When the angel invites John to see this great harlot or prostitute, he is told quite candidly that he will be viewing her punishment.

Her apostasy

A prostitute engages in a promiscuous sexual relationship offering a momentary thrill of sexual gratification at a price and with no commitment or love attached. The analogy is clear! The woman depicted here is guilty of a serious breach of faithfulness to God. She is two-timing the God of glory and is, therefore, guilty of infidelity. She says one thing and does the exact opposite. (A similar image is presented in Scripture in relation to Israel in the bad old days when she jumped into one relationship after another with other nations and their gods—basically, she betrayed Jehovah—read all about it in Isaiah 1:21; Ezekiel 16:28-29; Jeremiah 3:6).

Her ability

She is also heralded as something which is *great*. That underlines her all-pervasive influence throughout history and highlights the seriousness of that seduction in the eyes of God. It is not to be taken lightly. She stands out above all others. It cannot be glossed over and it certainly cannot be swept under the carpet. The sequel to this forecast of doom and gloom is found in 19:2 where we read, *he has judged the great prostitute who corrupted the earth with her immorality, and has avenged on her the blood of his servants.*

Her address

We are told she is *seated on many waters* (cf. Jeremiah 51:13). This phrase is explained further down the chapter in verse 15 where John says, *The waters that you saw, where the prostitute is seated, are people and multitudes and nations and languages.* People all over the world are swayed by her to one degree or another. She has a fair bit of clout and, as far as public opinion goes, she can muster an incredibly high level of support. Her influence is widespread. She has reached out to the ends of the earth and successfully permeated every people group and infiltrated every ethnic minority. She has embraced all the nations of the world with her ideology.

Her associations

John goes on to make some incisive remarks about her when he says in verse 2 that *with whom the kings of the earth have committed sexual immorality, and with the wine of whose sexual immorality the dwellers on earth have become drunk.* Simply put, *sexual immorality* is adultery. She has used sex and alcohol to entice and seduce world leaders; she has pursued the same course of action with the rest of the population as well. This is graphic and vivid language which John is employing (cf. Jeremiah 51:7) as he paints a picture of unrestrained deception and wholesale manipulation. That is her way of doing things and she has been eminently effective. From Day One she has sought to influence the governments of this world and history confirms how competent she has been. She has flirted with world leaders. By fair means or foul, she has been happy to further her own interests by jumping into bed with anyone.

Call it what you will, it boils down to illicit intercourse with the political systems of the world. People are intoxicated with her. They think she is wonderful. The fact is, people can be so gullible. They can be easily led astray, and fooled. She has dulled their powers of perception and deadened their critical faculties. She has all but removed their ability to assess situations correctly. She has tampered with the truth. She will do everything in her power to make people happy and everything possible within her remit to bring a false sense of elation to men and women.

She knows how vitally important the feel-good factor is to the man in the street. That is what John says quite categorically in verse 2. All that he says here fits perfectly into the jigsaw of the end times. Having said that, even though the prostitute will have her day of prominence, her downfall is guaranteed. We must never forget that God is on the throne. He knows what is going on!

Her ascendancy

Before John continues with a fairly comprehensive picture of what is happening, he throws in a single sentence which says more than we possibly realise. The apostle refers to his transit experience by saying that the angel *carried me away in the Spirit into a wilderness.* This is where John sees the great whore and he is taken there by the Spirit of God. She is in a desert, a place of desolation, waste, and barrenness. It reminds us that death, not life, is the environment in which she thrives best.

There is more than just a touch of irony here. Genesis 2 speaks of a pure bride in a lovely garden in the idyllic setting of Eden; but, by the time you come to the end of the Bible, civilisation has degenerated to such an extent that the picture changes to an impure harlot stuck in a wilderness. A case of beauty and the Beast. That is what sin does to the world!

When John reaches his destination in the desert he is confronted with a most unusual sight. He tells us in verse 3 what he saw with his own two eyes: *I saw a woman sitting on a scarlet beast that was full of blasphemous names, and it had seven heads and ten horns.* The fact that the woman is sitting on the Beast indicates that she is in control. She is asserting authority over it and directing its movements. At this point in time, she is the dominant one in that relationship.

We have come across the Beast before in 13:1 where John was speaking at great length about Antichrist; it is a classic case of once seen, never forgotten! The two descriptions are exactly the same, they match each other in every important detail so there is no possibility of mistaken identity. The one we are talking about here is the leader of the western bloc of world powers, the president of the United States of Europe, the top dog in a federation of states which resembles a revived Roman empire. (We will talk about the seven heads and ten horns when we progress down the chapter.)

Her alliance

Her shameless depravity is seen in her unholy alliance with such a despicable political leader. It is almost a case of church and state being wedded together as the woman rides the Beast. She will milk the system for as long as she can, and she will do everything she can to achieve her goals. She has her own agenda.

At this point the religious system will have the upper hand over the political system, but that will not last. It will all change. Politics and religion commit themselves to each other for a relatively short time. It is like many other marriages of convenience; one member of the team wants to buy out the other and sometimes push gives way to shove in such a fragile partnership. She is on a precarious perch but seems oblivious to that fact.

Her apparel

The stunning appearance of the woman in verse 4 leads many folk to equate her with the religious system we know as Roman Catholicism. That was certainly the opinion of the Reformers and it was the solid conviction of many of the early Church fathers. That may be the case but I do not think we can narrow it down to just one religion. We should widen the net for this is a mixed bag, a pot pourri of many cults and isms in a worldwide ecumenical movement.

One commentator said: 'The scarlet woman represents an apostate religious system that will combine weak Protestantism with Catholicism, spiritualism, humanism and the occult into one great satanic connection.' It is a bag of religious allsorts! Satan's megachurch. At the end of the day, it is a false religious grouping which is acutely riddled with apostasy.

She is seen as a harlot in stark contrast to the true church for she is portrayed as the bride of Christ. The apparel of this woman catches John's eye for he says *she was arrayed in purple and scarlet*. The fabric she wears was the most expensive cloth available in the ancient world and typifies one who enjoys the glamour of ecclesiastical pomp and pageantry (cf. 2 Samuel 1:24). In terms of colour, the lady in 'red' is unmissable!

The clothing we wear is usually a reflection of our character—what I wear gives an indication of what and who I am. When Israel adopted Babylonish practices the daughters of Zion began to dress like those around them (cf. Isaiah 3:18-26). The simplicity of a godly lifestyle as outlined in 1 Timothy 2:9-10 is far removed from the upmarket style we have promoted here. These are the garments of royalty and prosperity and are often seen as the colours associated with the papacy.

Her adornment

We read in verse 4 that she was *adorned with gold and jewels and pearls.* It is a look of ostentatious extravagance (cf. Proverbs 7:10). One writer notes: 'The flaunting of wealth in this way has always been a sign of voluptuous and licentious debauchery.' Down the years, think of the phenomenal wealth accumulated by organised religion. All the facts indicate that the staggering riches acquired in the name of religion throughout human history is awesome. The coffers are bulging. The cynics are right when they tell us that religion is big business!

Her abominations

At the end of verse 4 we are given an inkling of her abominations. John says she is *holding in her hand a golden cup full of abominations and the impurities of her sexual immorality.* A golden cup in anyone's hand is an item of beauty. It is an object to be admired, something most pleasing to the eye.

Gold in the Bible is a symbol of divine activity, so this golden cup gives every appearance of being a utensil used in the service of God. That is fine until you look inside, and then we are horrified to find it is filled to the brim with her unholy passions. Her idolatry, spiritual adultery, immoral liaisons, and flirtatious behaviour with all and sundry, all these are in the cup!

Yes, it looks attractive on the outside but inside it is repulsively vile and nauseating. Her cup is full and the reference in Jeremiah 51:7 to this analogy spells it out with precise clarity that her days are numbered. God looks on false religion as an abomination which he detests and cannot tolerate. This is what happens when biblical truth is abandoned.

Her appellations

In verse 5 we discover she has a name or a title written on her forehead. This is what God calls her and how he refers to her. The common prostitute in John's day wore her name on a headband upon her brow; in a similar way, the great whore of chapter 17 is recognised by the names on her forehead. Steve Wilmshurst says: 'Tattooed across her face are the words, World's Biggest Slut. She is the original vampire!' John advises us in bold capital letters that her title, *a name of mystery,* is *Babylon the great, mother of prostitutes and of earth's abominations.* There are two things which are perfectly clear from this appellation.

She is a mystery. This would suggest that neither ancient Babylon nor its site is intended. It teaches us to look a little deeper and explore beneath the surface. She is representing something in a figurative manner rather than in a literal sense. A mystery is not something mysterious but something previously hidden that has now been revealed to those given understanding. To grasp one of God's mysteries requires a combination of spiritual intelligence and discernment.

She is a mother. She represents that which began with Babylon and has continued throughout history. She is the mother of prostitutes which means she is not alone in her adulteries. She has spiritual offspring who also practice her idolatries and spread her false teachings. She has been instrumental in seducing multitudes and using other harlots to accomplish her objectives. The Babylonian system has in one way or another given birth to all false religions. The finger of blame points in her direction, it is aimed at her and her alone!

Babylon means different things to different people. As mentioned earlier, it is a word which appears almost 300 times in the Bible. So when we talk about it, it helps if we know what we mean when we speak of it. When Babylon is mentioned in the context of chapter 17 there are generally three main positions embraced by conservative Bible teachers:

Number one, the word 'Babylon' represents an ecclesiastical and political organisation. Ecclesiastical Babylon refers to apostate Christendom with its headquarters in Rome, it speaks of a one world church (verses 1-6). On the other hand, political Babylon is a revival of something like the old Roman empire. It is the last form of Gentile world domination headed up by Antichrist (verses 7-18).

Number two, the word 'Babylon' refers to the religious and political systems which I have just mentioned and then it goes on to say that it also anticipates a rebuilt city of Babylon located near the Euphrates river.

Number three, it refers to the rebuilt city of Babylon whose endtime existence and subsequent annihilation were predicted by Isaiah, Jeremiah, and Ezekiel. According to this interpretation, Babylon is a literal city of religious and political significance yet to be constructed. Proponents of this theory base their argument on the teaching enshrined in verse 18.

It seems fairly clear from this chapter that *a name of mystery: Babylon the great* is linked to Rome in two ways. Firstly, in a religious sense and, secondly, in a political sense. At the same time, it would appear from reading between the lines in chapter 18 that Babylon may be rebuilt!

When we speak about Babylon as a religious entity, it is good to look back in the annals of history and trace her roots. They stretch right away back to the early chapters of Genesis where we come across a man called Nimrod. He is credited with the establishment of the city of Babel in Genesis 10:8-10 and is recognised as the world's first dictator. It was through him that a false, diabolical, religious system was born on the plains of Shinar in ancient Babylon.

In an act of total defiance and because the people wanted to make a name for themselves, he built a huge tower that would reach to the heavens. It was known as a *ziggurat* and was made of sun-dried bricks. It was like a pyramid except that the successive levels were recessed so that you could walk to the top on steps. At the top was a special shrine dedicated to a god or goddess. In building this imposing edifice the people were not trying to climb up to heaven to dethrone God; rather, they hoped that the god or goddess they worshipped would come down from heaven to meet them.

The structure and city were called Babel which means 'the gate of the gods' (Genesis 11:4). The tower was recognised as a temple or rallying point and it stood as a pugnacious symbol of man's pride and open rebellion against God. It was not long before other nations jumped on the bandwagon and constructed similar towers in honour of their heathen deities. This infamous tower of Babel was also used for studying the stars and it established the basis and foundation for astrology. So, from the very beginning, Babylon was linked with sorcery and a wide range of extra-terrestrial activities.

You will recall from Genesis 11 that this was more than God was prepared to take, so he poured out his judgment on the people by scattering them across the face of the earth. At the same time, they were thrown into a state of total disarray for seeds of confusion were sown in their language. Before their dispersal, they were one people and one language; now, they are all over the place and cannot communicate with one another.

That did not mean the demise of the Babylonian religious system. The bell may have tolled but it was not the death knell. History records that Nimrod's wife, Semiramis, became the first high priestess of a system of secret religious rites known as the Babylonian Mysteries. This was user-friendly idolatry easily accessible to the ordinary people.

According to legend she had a son, Tammuz. The story

goes that he was miraculously conceived by a sunbeam. He was presented to the people as a saviour in fulfilment of the promise made to Eve concerning her seed in Genesis 3:15. Tradition says that Tammuz was killed by a wild boar but, after the people fasted for forty days, he was resurrected from the dead on the feast of Ishtar. Part of the celebration of Ishtar was the exchanging of Ishtar eggs, symbolising new life. Believe it or not, the term Easter is derived from Ishtar!

It was in this story of Semiramis and Tammuz that the cultic worship of 'mother and child' began to spread to the four corners of the earth. Such folklore was rapidly absorbed into many religious practices and it developed to such an extent that it was headed by a priesthood that promoted salvation by means of sprinkling holy water, ceremonial cleansing, and purgatorial cleansing after death. Semiramis went on to establish an order of virgins dedicated exclusively to religious prostitution. The liturgy of worship was clearly defined as the mother was identified as the 'queen of heaven' in Jeremiah 44:15-19.

On one occasion the prophet Ezekiel was called by the Lord to go to the temple and see this cultic practice in process. The prophet watched the women of Israel observing the forty days of Lent for the slaying of the pagan Tammuz. The Lord called this an abomination in Ezekiel 8:13-14. Jeremiah condemned Judah for offering cakes and burning incense to the 'queen of heaven' in 7:18 and 44:17-19, 25.

After the Medo Persian empire took over from Babylon the city and temples were eventually destroyed. You can read all about that transfer of power when Daniel prophesied concerning it in his interpretation of Nebuchadnezzar's dream in Daniel 2.

Having said that, the Babylonian cult survived and found a new home in Pergamum of Asia Minor. We came across that in an earlier study in Revelation 2:12-17. Apparently, it was repackaged and it thrived under the new name of Etruscan Mysteries and, eventually, it was based in Rome. The chief priests wore mitres shaped like the head of a fish in honour of Dagon, the fish god, the lord of life; this was another form of the Tammuz mystery.

In Rome, the chief priest assumed the title of Pontifex Maximus, which means the greatest high priest. When Julius Caesar became head of the Roman Empire, he had no personal inhibitions so he took this name for himself. From that day down to Constantine, the title was held by all the Roman emperors. Constantine was head of church and state; he mixed religion with politics and made Christianity popular when he adopted it as a state religion.

The title of Pontifex Maximus was later adopted by the Bishop of Rome and, today, this person is recognised as the Pope. It is a well-documented fact that over an extended period of time the church in Rome took on board many of the Babylonian practices and idolatrous teachings, the obvious one being the worship and elevation of the Virgin Mary. There is no such thing in the Bible as the worship of a female deity and Mary was never presented as anyone other than a humble servant of God who was chosen as the vessel to bear the Lord Jesus Christ.

'All roads lead to Rome' is what the familiar proverb tells us, but they began in Babylon. In the last days, Rome as a religious system is inextricably linked with Babylon, and vice-versa, Babylon is intertwined with Rome. The link between the past and present so far as global religion is concerned is more than just a coincidence, much more than a casual acquaintance, and a lot more than a nod and a wink. In fact, part of the problem we have discovered already is that this false, counterfeit religion is amazingly like the true Christian faith in so many facets.

Evangelical unity which has a high view of Scripture and is based on the doctrines of grace is one thing, an ecclesiastical unity which is all things to all men is quite a different matter. And the picture we have emerging here in Revelation 17 is a cameo of the latter. It is highly likely that readers in John's day would have no problem identifying the harlot with the Roman empire. The chances are that readers in the Middle Ages would identify her as Roman Catholicism. Many of us see a close link between the harlot and the Babylonian system in an apostate world church; a church where doctrinal truth is minimised, where the authority of the Word of God is rejected, where attempts are made to unite professing believers on some basis other than faith in the Lord Jesus Christ. In a nutshell, it is Satan's superchurch!

It rises as the consummate manifestation of religion without reality. It is a religion, as John says in verse 6, which is *drunk with the blood of the saints, the blood of the martyrs of Jesus.* John's reaction to all that he saw and heard left him dumbfounded, for he *marvelled greatly.* He could not quite work out all that was happening as a lot of it did not make sense.

Her atrocities

He could understand why pagan Rome would torture and kill believers because he had seen this with his own eyes, he had witnessed it himself. At the time John recorded his vision, the believing church in Rome was the church of the catacombs. It was a persecuted, suffering community of Jesus-followers which had no earthly power and no worldly influence. But John was mesmerised to think that religious Rome could be so malevolent. That really took the wind out of his sails, it left him shocked and surprised. When we look at the 'benevolent' church of Rome today, we find it hard to believe that it could ever be classified in this way.

However, if we study the annals of history, it all fits together like pieces in a jigsaw puzzle. It is a fact that down the years apostate Christianity has always persecuted true Christianity. In the name of religious zeal and with a spirit of unbridled fanaticism, many people have been butchered and cruelly slaughtered. The atrocities wreaked upon God's people by Rome fill whole volumes of church history. In the Middle Ages, she ravaged like a tiger for we have the horrors of the infamous Inquisition. It was the main agency in the papacy's effort to crush the Reformation. For example, it is stated that in the thirty years between 1540 and 1570 almost one million Protestants were put to death. Untold numbers have been burned at the stake, more have gone missing and never been found, millions have spent days in the gruelling confines of a torture chamber. We are told that when the massacre of Saint Bartholomew took place and Christians throughout France were murdered, Rome appointed services of thanksgiving as church and cathedral bells pealed out in victory. Sir Robert Anderson estimates that she is guilty of the death of 50 million Christians.

Her activity

The harlot is depicted in verse 6 as one who is *drunk* indicating that it is continual carnage which is envisaged. It is not just a one-off moment in history when believers were martyred. The imagery is quite repulsive. We have a woman who becomes intoxicated, and euphorically so, by drinking the blood of the righteous! The bottom line is, it has happened before, it will happen again. During the Tribulation, the proponents of this false church will hunt down and kill anyone who makes a brave and bold decision to follow Jesus Christ.

John talks here about *saints* and *martyrs of Jesus.* It is an interesting dual description for it may be referring to the same group of people; on the other hand, it may apply to those before the time of Jesus and those after the time of Jesus. If that were the case, it means this woman would then picture a religious system both before and after the time of Christ.

17:7-14

The angel's explanation

When we move to verse 7 we find the angel's immediate response to John's stunned reaction to the vision of verses 1-6. John is obviously out of his depth, he is lost for words and struggling to cope with what has just been revealed to him. So the angel says to him, *Why do you marvel? I will tell you the mystery of the woman, and of the beast with seven heads and ten horns that carries her.* That must have come as an enormous relief to John. At least someone was going to explain the entire picture to him making him feel immeasurably better.

The angel elaborates a little more in verse 8 when he says, *The beast that you saw was, and is not, and is about to rise from the bottomless pit and go to destruction. And the dwellers on earth whose names have not been written in the book of life from the foundation of the world will marvel to see the beast, because it was and is not and is to come.*

The resurrection of the Beast

This is a rather strange verse, to say the least. If we are going to understand it, we need to remember that the emphasis is not so much on the Beast as an empire but on the Beast as an emperor. It is his personal history that is chronicled for us. The Roman empire will be revived in some form, but the language employed here goes far beyond that! An empire cannot emerge out of the abyss and later be consigned into perdition. The terms and phrases used here best describe the history of an individual, not a nation. This individual comes up out of the abyss for the narrative concentrates specifically on that part of his chequered history which is plainly supernatural.

It begins with a satanic miracle of the highest calibre for the Beast is seen to be a resurrected man. It appears that Satan will duplicate as far as possible the miracle of Christ's resurrection. You can imagine the global sensation caused by such a high-powered miracle. (We thought about the impact of that in our study which focused on chapter 13.)

At first, the Beast will be a fairly normal human being. He will be a world figure in his own right by virtue of his charismatic personality, his genius, and his political acumen. He will appear to be assassinated and then before the eyes of the world he will come back to life. After that incredible feat his authority on earth will be absolute, at least for a short time. He is Satan's man and his second coming will take the world by storm.

The reason for his appearance

He is coming to deceive the Christ-rejecting masses of mankind. It is inevitable, when you read verse 8 in conjunction with Paul's insightful comments in 2 Thessalonians 2 that when a person deliberately turns his back on truth, he automatically embraces a lie. In his superhuman appearing the Beast emerging triumphant from the abyss, still bearing in his body the marks of his deadly wound, will fire the imagination of men and lead them captive at his will.

Ordinary people will be eating out of his hand and they will hail him as the greatest thing since sliced bread. They will worship him with outlandish doses of adoration and devotion. They will be spellbound by his magical charm and they will be won over with his big-hearted, liberal generosity. They will stand in awe of him. The sad fact is their names are not written in the book of life, and they are ready for the lie of all lies. They will follow their leader, all the way to hell itself!

The angel's caution

Verse 9 begins with the words, *This calls for a mind with wisdom.* In one sense, the angel is putting all his cards on the table and reminding us of the need for spiritual insight if we are going to successfully unravel the mysteries of this section. We need to prayerfully think it through and look to the Lord for clarity of mind and openness of heart as we approach it together. We need illumination from above. Having said that, such a principle holds true for any portion of Scripture which we seek to interpret. It is just that sometimes we need more wisdom than others!

Seven heads

The Beast has seven heads and ten horns. Here, in verse 9, we note the seven heads represent seven mountains and, in verse 10, they symbolise seven kings or kingdoms. That means they can be interpreted in one of two ways: first, they can be viewed geographically as the seven hills of Rome or, second, they can be seen in their historical context as seven kingdoms.

We read in verses 9-11 that *the seven heads are seven mountains on which the woman is seated; they are also seven kings, five of whom have fallen, one is, the other has not yet come, and when he does come he must remain only a little while. As for the beast that was and is not, it is an eighth but it belongs to the seven, and it goes to destruction.*

The seven hills of Rome are the Aventine, the Caelian, the Capitoline, the Esquiline, the Palatine, the Quirinal, and the Viminal. Having named the hills, we cannot ignore the clear implication of verse 10 that they typify seven kings for mountains are sometimes used in the Old Testament to represent rule or power (cf. Psalm 30:7; Isaiah 2:2; Jeremiah 51:25; Daniel 2:35). The seven kings, therefore, represent political empires or kingdoms as well as individual rulers. We are told that five of these have passed off the scene, one was present in John's day, and one was yet to come.

That means the five kingdoms are Egypt personified in a Pharaoh, Assyria represented by a Sennacherib, Babylon symbolised in a Nebuchadnezzar, Medo Persia identified in a Cyrus, and Greece personified in an Alexander. The present kingdom, so far as John is concerned, is Rome personified in a Caesar; and the future kingdom anticipated is a federation of ten European states in and around the Mediterranean seaboard. Out of this seventh empire of ten nations will arise a world leader, whom we identify with no problem as Antichrist or the Beast, who will in himself become the eighth empire of the world. You find that alluded to in verse 11.

Ten horns

If we want to appreciate in a fuller measure the teaching enshrined in verses 10 and 11, we must consider them in light of what John reveals to us in verses 12 and 13. There we read, *And the ten horns that you saw are ten kings who have not yet received royal power, but they are to receive authority as kings for one hour, together with the beast. These are of one mind, and they hand over their power and authority to the beast.*

The Beast not only has seven heads, he also has ten horns which represent ten kings. These are very special kings as they enable the Beast to rise to a place of ultimate power. They are even willing to relinquish their own authority and hand it all over on a plate to him. If you want a fuller discussion on these kings, flick back in your Bible to Daniel 7.

When we looked at Revelation 6, when the first of the seven seals was opened, that was when Antichrist began his peaceful conquest of the nations. He organised a United States of Europe, he brought a measure of peace and calm to the cauldron of the Middle East, he appeared to be the great leader a troubled world was seeking, he was the answer to every man's prayers. Then, in the middle of the seven-year period of Tribulation, he broke his covenant with the nation of Israel and began to ruthlessly persecute the people of God as well as the nation of Israel. Then in chapter 13 we noted he was energised by Satan, he was ably assisted by his right-hand man, the False Prophet and, at the end of the day, he became the world's dictator and its god. In that sense, the Beast was both one of the seven kings or kingdoms but he was also the eighth. His kingdom was designated as one of the seven but, at the same time, it was a new kingdom, hence it was labelled number eight! It is the final form of Gentile world rule.

His personal destiny is destruction, you find that in verse 11. His global enterprise will be obliterated by Christ at his second advent in power and great glory (you find that later in the book in chapter 19). His crowning achievement rises with him, it also falls with him! He does not have a particularly bright future! The same can also be said for his partners, even though their time spent in his service will be relatively brief. It appears their role will be to head up the kingdom of Antichrist. It will be divided up into ten administrative districts, each one managed by one of these ten officials.

There is no way these kings can be literally or symbolically applied to any nation in the past because they will not receive a kingdom until Daniel's Seventieth Week. They will not reign successively but they will govern simultaneously during the Tribulation. Their power will be allocated to them by Antichrist and their allegiance to him will be total.

The influence of the kings will extend to the end of the Tribulation for we read in verse 14 that *they will make war on the Lamb, and the Lamb will conquer them, for he is Lord of lords and King of kings, and those with him are called and chosen and faithful.* They will do everything in their power to defy the Lamb, they will harness all their resources, pull out all the stops, and leave no stone unturned. The truth of the matter is, they are fighting a battle they cannot possibly win, they are on a hiding to nothing, they are losers all the way. The Lamb is victorious! The Lamb is triumphant! The King of kings is coming and nothing will impede or hinder his progress! The Lord of lords is on the march and no one will stand in his way!

The Lord is accompanied by a vast company of those who are devoted to him and dedicated to his cause. These godly believers who are *called and chosen and faithful* will share in Christ's victorious conquest and in his moment of glory. What a thrilling statement of intent for the people of God! We are on the winning team! And by the same token, what a glaring contrast between the bride of Christ and the prostitute of world religion! The same truth is echoed in the words of Psalm 2 and it pays eloquent testimony to the ability of God to turn every situation around for his praise and glory.

17:15-18

The shoe is on the other foot!

The final paragraph of chapter 17 is breathtaking in its scope as it is a powerful reminder that the tables can turn very quickly! We read in verses 15-18, *And the angel said to me, 'The waters that you saw, where the prostitute is seated, are peoples and multitudes and nations and languages. And the ten horns that you saw, they and the beast will hate the prostitute. They will make her desolate and naked, and devour her flesh and burn her up with fire, for God has put it into their hearts to carry out his purpose by being of one mind and handing over their royal power to the beast, until the words of God are fulfilled. And the woman that you saw is the great city that has dominion over the kings of the earth.'*

These words are unbelievable! They predict a day when Antichrist and his European empire will do an about-turn. Up to this point, halfway through the Tribulation, they have been going along with every whim of the scarlet woman who represents the global false church of the last days. She has been riding the Beast and he tolerates it! Now the tables turn, the shoe is on the other foot, and Antichrist assumes control. It all ends in bitter tears with recriminations against one another. The whole saga ends in divorce! Her charm and seduction will have lost their lure and their openly professed love for all things religious will turn to hate and contempt. The harlot will be made desolate by the very system that carried her.

It is vitally important for us to note that the Beast carries the harlot. The fact is, Satan and Antichrist will use the apostate religious system to accomplish his own ends and that for him means attaining world power. When he has arrived at the pinnacle of his career, he will do away with the harlot and establish his own religious system and that fulfils the Word of God as detailed for us by John in verse 17. The emphasis weighs heavily in favour of the truth of the sovereignty of God in the affairs of man. They do not know it but they are pawns in the divine game of chess! God is behind the scenes directing the scenes he is behind!

Since the Beast sets up his image in the temple in Jerusalem about the middle of the Tribulation, we can safely assume that the harlot and the Beast work together during the first three and a half years. You find a hint of that in verse 16 for the ten satellite kings who initiate and bring about her downfall are the same ones who set him up in power. There is nothing strange about that; political systems have often used religion as a tool to further their own ends and advance their own cause, and when they have achieved their goal, they ditch them! A parallel in history is the moment when Henry VIII, with political and military power in his hands, decided he no longer needed the support of the Roman Catholic church in England and proceeded with the dissolution and destruction of the monasteries and the seizure of their wealth.

The entire incident can be summarised: at first, the harlot will team up with Antichrist; at the end, she will be torn apart by Antichrist. This is the great reversal. It is poetic justice! It is God making the wrath of man praise him! We read, she is detested for there is no love lost between them. She is put out of business for they are determined to bring her to her knees. She will be divested of all the extraordinary wealth she has amassed over the years, her goods confiscated, and her properties seized. She is disgraced for they will not rest until they have stripped her of every vestige of respectability as the news media expose one scandal after another. She will be seen for what she really is and her corruption will be exposed for all to see. In that sense, she will be left *naked*. She is devoured for they will consume her like a pack of wild dogs for the media will 'make a meal' of this once-so-reclusive harlot; and, finally, she is destroyed by the Beast for she will be left smouldering in a pile of ashes.

To all intents and purposes, there will be nothing left for she will be totally eliminated and wiped out. She will be yesterday's church! She will be the has-been religious movement of the end times. If you believe that all roads lead to Rome and you are happy to be a member of the church that Satan builds, your future is bleak! Even worse, your destiny is guaranteed.

CHAPTER 18
A double whammy for Babylon

A quick glance at chapter 18 reveals that we are still talking about Babylon, but from a different angle and a new perspective. The Babylon presented here is effectively portrayed by John as a political and economic force, representing the world system of Antichrist.

Do you recall the story of Nebuchadnezzar when he was at his peak? In a few moments of arrogant pride he looked out over the magnificent city of Babylon with its massive walls, its hanging gardens, its broad boulevards, its stunning beauty, its unequalled strength, and he cried out in Daniel 4:30, 'Is not this great Babylon which I have built?' In a coming day, the last of the great Gentile rulers will boast over a rebuilt Babylon. It seems in Bible prophecy that Babylon should rise again from the dust in order to meet its final doom.

It was foretold of Babylon that it would be a place of perpetual desolations (cf. Isaiah 13:9-12), where no man would dwell any more (cf. Jeremiah 50:1-4, 40-46), where the Arabian would be afraid to pitch his tent; it would be the abode of dragons, empty, and without inhabitants, a place whose destruction would be exceptionally violent (cf. Isaiah 13, 25, 50, 51). None of these prophecies have been completely fulfilled yet. One day in God's perfect time they will come to pass.

Babylon, founded by Nimrod, became the first centre of population we read of in the Bible which was ruled by violence; she was once the capital of the then-known world; in a day soon to dawn she will again rise to prominence and become the central city of the world. She will again be known as the home of idolatry and a place where the occult is encouraged; a city renowned for its interest in demonism and recognised as a centre of false religion.

The clear indications are that Babylon will be rebuilt with a commercial system that will function on a global scale. What better site than ancient Babylon on the banks of a river that dominates east and west! Computer studies have shown that Babylon is very near the geographical centre of all the earth's land masses. It is within navigable distance to the Persian Gulf and is at the crossroads of the three great continents of Europe, Asia, and Africa.

One commentator makes the valid point: 'It seems reasonable that the Beast will see the necessity of having a compact, centralised, computerised control centre for the commerce on earth. Disdaining the discredited capitals of earth there seems to be no reason why he should not find it useful to return to an ancient site in a strategic location in his empire for a new Babylon to emerge suddenly on the world scene.'

There is no more ideal location anywhere for a world trade centre, a world communications centre, a world banking centre, a world educational centre, and a world capital. The British economic historian, Arnold Toynbee (1852-1883), wrote that Babylon would be 'the best place in the world to build a future cultural metropolis.' In fact, this movement of world capital and commerce back to Babylon is in fulfilment of Zechariah's prophecy of the ephah (cf. Zechariah 5:5-11).

Revelation is virtually silent on how and when it will be built, since it is concerned primarily with her fall! Having said that, there is a lot happening in the region at present and it is a well-established fact that the former Saddam Hussein of Iraq was committed to rebuilding the city to the specifications of Nebuchadnezzar. He poured millions of petro-chemical dollars into the project and an amazing amount of manpower and resources were channelled in that direction. Apparently, he even used some of the stones from old Babylon.

18:1-3

The prediction ... a voice of condemnation

John introduces the subject of Babylon when he addresses the matter surrounding her fall. We read in verse 1, *After this I saw another angel coming down from heaven, having great authority, and the earth was made bright with his glory.* John is very impressed with what he sees in verse 1. The angel is described as one who has *great authority*.

At the same time, John is startled and amazed at his sudden appearance and the immediate impact it has when he lights up the earth with his resplendent glory (cf. 1 Timothy 6:16; Psalm 104:2). H B Swete sums it up like this: 'So recently has he come from the [divine] Presence that in passing he flings a broad belt of light across the dark earth.' It happens when you walk into a darkened room and switch on the light! This angelic being is one of God's shining ones, and that explains why his presence caused such a stir in John's heart and mind. The identity of the angel is not revealed but the chances are he is the *mighty angel* mentioned back in chapter 10.

It is against this backdrop of glory that the double-barrelled message is heard resounding throughout the earth in a moment of high drama. The angelic shout is a sign of cataclysmic destruction. He said in the opening phrase in verse 2, *Fallen, fallen is Babylon the great!* It is a double exclamation and is an echo of the cry of Isaiah 21:9. In other words, if you did not get the message first time, you would be sure to get it second time around. It is clear and unmistakable.

The repetition of the word *fallen* adds considerable fuel to the fire for it suggests a dual judgment. We can look at it like this: we have one fall, but in two separate stages. We have phase one which zooms in on the downfall of ecclesiastical Babylon, depicted as the prostitute in Revelation 17; and we have phase two which anticipates the demise of political and economic Babylon, demonstrated here in chapter 18.

A double whammy!

This line of argument is amplified in verse 6 when God announces that Babylon will receive *double* for her many sins. Without question, this is a momentous event, a significant milestone in the ripening of the eternal purposes of God. From God's vantage point, Babylon is as good as gone! So far as God is concerned, she has fallen already! Her destruction is earmarked for a future date but from God's perspective it is a classic case of mission accomplished! This confirms that prophecy is history written in advance.

The reasons for her eventual extermination are spelled out very clearly in verses 2 and 3, *She has become a dwelling place for demons, a haunt for every unclean spirit, a haunt for every unclean bird, a haunt for every unclean and detestable beast. For all nations have drunk the wine of the passion of her sexual immorality, and the kings of the earth have committed immorality with her, and the merchants of the earth have grown rich from the power of her luxurious living.*

Why is Babylon snuffed out?

Because of the sheer magnitude of her sins. Her character is despicable as the city is given over to demonism and depravity on a massive scale. It is the home of demons and the headquarters of depravity. The thought is that of imprisoned evil spirits hovering over the entire area like scavenger birds over their prey (cf. Jeremiah 5:27; Isaiah 34:11-15; Matthew 13:4). It is a repugnant description of the occultist system of the president of the planet, the Antichrist; it speaks of the foul spirits that will control the minds of men. It refers to Satanism, witchcraft, and astrology.

Because of her evil and decadent relationship with other nations and people groups. She is the centre of social, political, cultural, and commercial life on this planet. And because of her privileged position, she has seized the initiative, taken advantage of the prevailing situation, and polluted the whole world; her influence has reached out to the ends of the earth. The tentacles of her pernicious ways have spanned the universe. Her impact is global.

Because she used her powers of seduction to ensnare others in her tangled web of deceit. The fundamental sin which has driven her every action is that of wooing in order to win. The system intoxicated the people of the world with all the riches and pleasures it had to offer and, human nature being what it is, they were very glad to be on the receiving end. When you stop and analyse the situation from an unbiased perspective, it all boils down to greed; the bottom line is money, everyone wants to line their own pockets, everyone is in it for what they can get out of it, everyone wants to milk the system for their own ulterior motives. The financial rewards are uncountable.

It is ironic but the trap set by this system will lead to its eventual downfall. The Bible warns about rich oppressors (cf. James 5:1-5). The chances are if you dig a hole big enough, you will fall into it yourself one day! And that is what happens right here!

18:4-8

The plea ... a voice of separation

In verses 4 and 5 we have an impassioned plea to the people of God, transmitted by another voice from heaven which said, *Come out of her, my people, lest you take part in her sins, lest you share in her plagues; for her sins are heaped high as heaven, and God has remembered her iniquities.* This is a clarion call to biblical separation, a challenge to God's people to adopt a position of holiness. As a serious admonition, it parallels the stern warnings in Jeremiah 50:8 and 51:6 and echoes the challenge of Isaiah 52:11.

God says in rather terse and brusque language, *Come out of her.* That simply means, have nothing to do with her! Do not touch her with a disinfected barge pole! You cannot run with the foxes and, at the same time, hunt with the hounds. You cannot two-time the Lord. There is to be a disassociation from this diabolical system and from the purveyors of such appalling evil who are operating within the system.

There is nothing unusual about such a call. This is not the first time it has happened: When God called Abraham, he ordered him to get out of his country; God separated the Jewish nation from Egypt and warned them not to go back; even believers are commanded to steer well clear from all that is ungodly and from anything which has the potential to seriously damage our testimony or impede our service for the Lord (cf. Romans 16:17-18; 2 Corinthians 6:14-7:1). From Day One the Lord has been looking for a purified people, who will walk only with him and be 'in the world' but not 'of the world.' Kiddle writes that 'the saints are called to a spiritual withdrawal from Vanity Fair.'

It is fairly clear from the text that God has two vitally important matters written on his agenda. Number one, he wants to protect his people and, number two, he wants to punish Babylon where it will hurt most for her trade and traffic is accursed by God. The message is that believers are to withdraw from her embrace. The umbilical cord must be cut. Every enticement and allurement offered should be resisted at all times and at any cost. The assumption is that some true believers will be entangled within her web otherwise the appeal would not be necessary.

Separation from apostate Christendom is something God demands with this unambiguous and clear-cut injunction. There are no bargaining chips on the table when this matter is handled in Scripture. It is one of those major issues which are non-negotiable. The man is a fool who thinks he can do a tango in the dark with the devil. The people of God need to come clean and stand clear. He says, do not become tainted by her in any way, do not give in to her enticing ways and words.

The charge levelled against Babylon is that she has filled her cup of sin to the brim. Or to change the metaphor to the one John employed in verse 5, *her sins are heaped high as heaven and God has remembered her iniquities.* Remember Genesis 11 and the infamous tower of Babel? That is the analogy we have here for her sins are stacked one on top of another like bricks in the old tower; it is a situation where each stone is an indictment about its sick condition. God says, you are at it again! You are up to your old tricks!

We can put it like this, God sees, God knows, and when the time is right, God will deal with her effectively and efficiently. That is the way it was in the days of Noah and that is why he sent the Flood. It was true of the twin cities of Sodom and Gomorrah, they were blitzed from above and, within an hour, reduced to a pile of rubble. It was equally true of the city of Nineveh after God intimated in Nahum 1:5 that he was standing against her.

There comes a time when the repugnant stench from the sins of a city or a nation reaches up to heaven and cries aloud for God to act. Heaven may seem to be silent but God is not indifferent to such corruption and crime. He does not turn a blind eye to what is going on down here on Planet Earth. One day, in his sovereignty, he will act in judgment and, when he does, it will be swift and decisive.

18:6-8

The payment ... a voice of justice

That is why verses 6-8 send a quiver down the spine, you feel a chill when you read them. They are an awesome reminder that no one gets off or gets away with anything; it is payday, someday! The baseline is that you cannot sidestep the Lord, hide from the Lord, or outwit the Lord. That is what makes the extent of her payment all the more pertinent for we read in verse 6, *Pay her back as she herself has paid back others, and repay her double for her deeds; mix a double portion for her in the cup she mixed.*

There is a timeless principle woven into the fabric of this verse: what we sow, we reap. God would treat her just as she treated his people. The Babylonians visited upon Jerusalem all the awful, unthinkable horrors of war; the sons and daughters of Abraham experienced her unbelievable cruelty, they encountered her violent lusts as she ravaged the people and the community and they came face to face with her horrendously horrible excesses. The Jewish people cried out, 'Lord, pay her back in kind!'

The law of Moses, a just and righteous law, demanded an eye for an eye and a tooth for a tooth (cf. Leviticus 24:17-22). Many a Jewish mother picked up the broken lifeless form of her little one and called out to heaven, 'A life for a life, O God of our fathers; a life for a life!' You find tender echoes of that sad prayer in Psalm 137.

It is the law of retribution which is applied in this particular context and it is fitting and proper that it should be. It is not just an eye for an eye or a tooth for a tooth, it is double! Three times in one short verse it is written; for all the hard times inflicted on others, double! It is doubled to emphasise the colossal enormity of her sin. No mercy shown, no grace extended. She is handed down a double portion of the undiluted anger of God and, with more than a hint of irony, she drinks it from her own cup! That is a cue to what we saw earlier in 14:10 and 16:19. God will get her, and for her, there will be no hiding place.

We read in verse 7, *Give her a like measure of torment and mourning, since in her heart she says, 'I sit as a queen; I am no widow, and mourning I shall never see.'*

The fact is, she is not living in the real world and is downright naive! She reasons that the kings of the earth are her lovers; the truth is, she is a widow in that God has forsaken her. These words are gleaned from Isaiah 47:5-9 and, even though they applied in the first instance to the fall of ancient Babylon, they were surely a shadow of things to come.

There are two prominent traits in her character: she glorifies self and indulges in a sensuous lifestyle. When the day of judgment comes, it is not unexpected or undeserved; she gets her comeuppance. She has brought it on herself because of her rampant infidelity. She has only herself to blame! You cannot sin and win!

We read some sober words in verse 8 where the angel

declares in a very matter-of-fact kind of way, *For this reason her plagues will come in a single day, death and mourning and famine, and she will be burned up with fire; for mighty is the Lord God who has judged her.* When judgment eventually comes, it will be swift, sudden, and sure. In a single day she is gone. Actually, verse 10 intimates it will all be over in 60 minutes! As quick as that!

Remember the scenario at the end of Daniel 5 where the writing was on the wall and Belshazzar was so petrified he was riveted to the spot in a state of blind panic. Before the dawn broke on a new day, he was a dead man and Babylon had fallen to the Medes and Persians (cf. Daniel 5:30). The head of gold had given way to the chest and arms of silver as predicted in Nebuchadnezzar's metallic statue vision of Daniel 2:31-32, 38-39.

There is no pussy-footing when God strikes in judgment. There is no messing around when God moves to execute justice. He makes no idle threats for he means what he says and he says what he means. If he makes a promise, he will carry it out. He does not back off and he never backs down! A combination of divine anger and divine aggression ensure that the entire operation is carried out smoothly and without a hitch. Such divine intervention pays eloquent tribute to a God who is mighty and sovereign. Her total collapse is such that only God could be responsible for it!

It was the last thing on Babylon's mind. She exudes confidence, is the epitome of defiance, and never even entertained the thought that judgment was a possibility. She lulled herself into a false sense of security and found herself living in a false paradise. But come it will. God will bring Babylon to the dust in ruin beyond repair. The much-vaunted global economic system will plummet to such a degree that it makes any fall on Wall Street look like a temporary blip on a computer screen. In fact, this will be the greatest economic crash in the history of the world's financial markets.

Sometimes God's judgments work silently like a moth eating away at a garment hanging in a closet, other times they are compared to a lion and spring suddenly. Whatever angle you choose to view it from, there is no escape route. Those fascinating allusions culled from the world of nature are in Hosea 5:12-14.

From a prophetic standpoint, all is going according to the divine schedule, all is on track for God never goes off the rails. In every sphere of life the principle enshrined in the law of cause and effect comes into force. That is most definitely the case when it comes to the spectacular fall of Babylon. The repercussions from her downfall are staggering, the ripples emanating from the disaster are felt in many different areas. The reactions to her collapse are understandable and fall broadly into two camps. On one side, there are those who are genuinely grieved and, on the other, there are those who are jumping up and down for joy!

18:9-19

The people ... a voice of lamentation

The long tale of woe told by all kinds of people and the grief shared by many individuals makes most impressive reading in this section. Not only do the merchants lament the fall of Babylon, the kings of the earth go down the same road. Business and government are so intertwined that what affects one seriously impinges on the other. It is a solemn lament based as it is on the dirge for the city of Tyre, the commercial capital of the Phoenician empire in Ezekiel 27. It is a situation where the air is heavy, where the atmosphere is sullen and people are brooding in the pits of abject depression. The bottom has fallen out of their lives and, in one sense, it has! They have every reason to beat their breasts and mourn.

The effect on government

The response of the high and mighty, the movers and shakers, the royalty of this world, is outlined for us in verses 9 and 10 where we read, *And the kings of the earth, who committed sexual immorality and lived in luxury with her, will weep and wail over her when they see the smoke of her burning. They will stand far off, in fear of her torment, and say, 'Alas! Alas! You great city, Babylon! For in a single hour your judgment has come.'*

These folk have shared her bed and, because of the intimacy and closeness of their relationship, enjoyed tremendous prosperity. There was a high level of stability in the markets so that a downturn seemed light years away. And so, when the unthinkable happened, theirs is a profound sense of loss; there is a depth to their personal feelings of anguish and bereavement and a fearful apprehension surrounding the future. They are terrified. Scared stiff. Maintaining a stiff upper lip is out of the question. They are really struggling to come to terms with all that has happened. They are finding it immensely difficult to cope with the massive losses sustained. Their gilt-edged security has nosedived into tarnished oblivion.

Alarm bells are ringing in their ears. They are increasingly edgy and nerves are frayed. They are living on tenterhooks. They probably sense that their own days are numbered and that time is rapidly running out. They are sitting on a potential time bomb. It is a scenario which is not that uncommon but it is one they can well do without. The political pundits often refer to it as the years of boom and bust! The fact is, it is a high risk policy when you put all your eggs in one basket. That is what they have discovered. The problem is it is too late to do anything about it for they will never recoup their losses!

The effect on commerce

There is more to it than meets the eye for we read in verse 11 that those involved in the commercial sector are seriously affected. The voice from heaven says, *And the merchants of the earth weep and mourn for her, since no one buys their cargo any more.* These folk are in a bit of a quandary because they have lost their customers. If you have no customers you have no source of regular income. It is as simple as that! The net result is their standard of living will fall. It means luxury items will be hard to come by, unless you want to pay an inflated price on the black market.

Babylon's collapse has come as a bolt from the blue, it has left the business community reeling. It is something they did not plan for, it is something they never seriously anticipated, it is something they never made provision for. To make matters a million times worse, it all happened so quickly, there was little or nothing they could do about it. From cash to crash!

John gives us an inventory of some of the commodities that brought enormous wealth to the traders of Babylon. The list is amazing! We can do a stock-take ourselves in verses 12 and 13 and this is what we find, *cargo of gold, silver, jewels, pearls, fine linen, purple cloth, silk, scarlet cloth, all kinds of scented wood, all kinds of articles of ivory, all kinds of articles of costly wood, bronze, iron and marble, cinnamon, spice, incense, myrrh, frankincense, wine, oil, fine flour, wheat, cattle and sheep, horses and chariots, and slaves, that is human souls.*

That is an impressive list of stuff from every part of the known world: incense from as far away as Arabia and Somalia, precious stones from India, pearls from the Red Sea and the Persian Gulf, gold from Spain, and so on. It is nothing but the best for anything else is not good enough! You name it, you can have it; you want it, you can get it! It does not matter what the item is, anything from a needle to an anchor, if you are willing to pay the price, it is yours! Such was the opulent lifestyle of those resident in Babylon!

However, when the system went down and took everything with it, it was a classic case of your best dream turning overnight into your worst nightmare. It is a level playing field for everyone and the environment is one of rust and dust! There is no point in them praying to the secular god of materialism in that day, for he has gone. The profit motive, the 'get all you can as quick as you can' syndrome, the self-help, rags to riches philosophy, all of these are fine in a textbook on business management, but in the real world in which these folk now find themselves, it is cold comfort!

The last entry on the list and probably the one which is most disturbing is the mention of *human souls.* In that day, life will be cheap and people will be exploited by ruthless, unscrupulous individuals in a kind of sweatshop environment. They will be treated as if they were merchandise sitting on a shelf. No hint of fair trade? No mention of human rights? Is John making a veiled comment on the way people are handled by senior management in the workplace? An employee's freedom is gradually eroded to such an extent that he feels he has no option but to cave in to the pressures of those in the board room. It is either toe the party line and do what is demanded of you or you are out of a job!

On the other hand, it could be a reference to pornography and prostitution where men and women barter their bodies for some insignificant trifle. One thing is absolutely clear, the world system championed by Antichrist will dehumanise mankind as any system without God will do.

The effect on the people

When we turn to verses 14 and 15 we are reminded that Babylon deceived the people of the world about wealth. The Bible says, *'The fruit for which your soul longed has gone from you, and all your delicacies and your splendours are lost to you, never to be found again!' The merchants of these wares, who gained wealth from her, will stand far off, in fear of her torment, weeping and mourning aloud.* It is sad to say it but religion has been guilty of materialistic goals. It has often conned people into believing that prosperity was a token sign of God's approval and blessing. In many instances it has created a hunger for wealth so that people are never satisfied with what they have, they are always wanting more! This is borne out very clearly in verses 16 and 17a when we hear the cry of broken hearts and shattered dreams.

The devastated people say, *'Alas, alas, for the great city that was clothed in fine linen, in purple and scarlet, adorned with gold, with jewels, and with pearls! For in a single hour all this wealth has been laid waste.'* It is the old story, riches are temporal, they do not last. These folk may have been born into the lap of luxury with a golden spoon in their mouth; the truth is, they brought nothing into this world and they will discover before long that there are no pockets in a shroud! All that they worked for, all that they accumulated, all that they made by fair means or foul, has all gone up in a plume of smoke. One minute they had it and they were not afraid to flaunt it; the next minute, all their stocks and shares and everything else they had in their personal portfolio had slipped through their buttery fingers and they have nothing to show for it. It was reduced to heaps of rubble and they were reduced to tears!

The effect at sea

The spin-offs of this awful calamity do not affect only the monarchy, the merchants, and the masses, they also encroach on the livelihood of those in the maritime industry. We read in the second half of verse 17 through to the end of verse 19, *And all shipmasters and seafaring men, sailors, and all whose trade is on the sea, stood far off and cried out as they saw the smoke of her burning, 'What city was like the great city?' And they threw dust on their heads as they wept and mourned, crying out, 'Alas, alas, for the great city where all who had ships at sea grew rich by her wealth! For in a single hour she has been laid waste.'*

Mariners will be seriously affected by the consequences of Babylon's fall. It is interesting to note that the prophet Ezekiel spoke graphically of God's coming judgment on the seaport city of Tyre in chapter 27 of his prophecy. His pronouncement of doom focuses on the reaction of the shipping magnates to the fall of ancient Tyre and it is remarkably similar to John's description of the fall of Babylon.

What will happen is this: the need for freight to be transported on the busy sea lanes of this world will grind to a halt, the fishing industry will suffer astronomical losses, the luxury cruise liner holiday market will experience a massive downturn in profits. This means that a lot of ordinary people will be out of a job. They will have to depend on handouts from relatives and friends and whatever social security they can muster from the government of Antichrist.

When you sit down and piece the entire jigsaw together, you can see the complete picture; it makes the teaching in chapter 13 on the mark of the Beast easy to believe. The response of these folk as they bemoan their fate is to reminisce of better times. They are thinking about the good old days when order books were full and bank accounts were in the black. Their sore lament is peppered with meaningful reflections on halcyon days. One writer notes: 'Like the Nazis in Berlin on the eve of the Allied victory, the reality of the Antichrist's followers defeat will be obvious as their satanic Reich disintegrates before their eyes.'

No matter which of these groups you look at, they have a trio of common features: they all extol the wonderful virtues of Babylon as a city for they acknowledge something of her greatness; their doleful lament on the once great city begins with a double woe; and they all draw attention to the rapid speed with which she fell – the most decadent metropolis the world has ever known was reduced to ashes in sixty minutes and that has left all of them gasping for breath.

18:20-24

Praise and pronouncement ... a voice of celebration

The reaction in verse 20 to the fall of Babylon is markedly different from anything we have witnessed so far. The people of God see the whole episode from a loftier perspective. We read, *'Rejoice over her, O heaven, and you saints and apostles and prophets, for God has given judgment for you against her!'*

Vindication!

Heaven rejoices! Heaven resounds with praise! Heaven is vitally interested in what happens on earth. All those who wrote about it, foretold it, and preached it, they will know it has happened. They are called upon to look down on the world they left behind and see the vile figure of Babylon has come to her final doom, and they know she will never recover! She has been counted out cold on the canvas! For her, there is no way back.

The prayers of God's people have been answered. They are thrilled with what God has done. They cannot contain their excitement so they break forth into spontaneous praise and in a song of unison and rapturous worship they shout, 'Glory!' For them, it is a good enough reason to throw a party. It is a cause for joyous celebration. They give to their God a round of applause and they hail him as one who always vindicates his people. And he does it in his own good time.

Violence and vengeance!

The narrative continues in verse 21 where an angel informs us that her fall is violent. We read, *Then a mighty angel took up a stone like a great millstone and threw it into the sea, saying, 'So will Babylon the great city be thrown down with violence, and will be found no more ...'* That is fighting talk! The analogy speaks for itself and it underlines the indisputable fact that for Babylon there is no way back. A similar picture is found in Jeremiah 51:59-64 where a man heading for Babylon is told to take a scroll carrying words of judgment, read it out loud, then tie it to a stone and throw it into the Euphrates as a sign that Babylon will fall, never to rise again (cf. Nehemiah 9:11). This angel goes one better!

Instead of picking up a pebble by the river bank, he grabs a boulder the size of a millstone—usually four to five feet in diameter, one foot thick, and weighing at least one thousand pounds—and hurls it far out to sea. Like the boulder in the ocean, Babylon has gone down and under, she will never reappear in any shape or form. That is it! She is finished! End of story! The fullstop has been placed at the end of the sentence and nothing more will be written about her. She has come, and gone!

The curtain falls!

The vastness of her fall is indicated in verses 22 and 23 where the words *no more* are repeated like a haunting note from a funeral march. We read, *The sound of harpists and musicians, of flute players and trumpeters, will be heard in you no more, and a craftsman of any craft will be found in you no more, and the sound of the mill will be heard in you no more, and the light of a lamp will shine in you no more, and the voice of a bridegroom and bride will be heard in you no more, for your merchants were the great ones of the earth.*

There is an awesome finality to what has happened for an eerie stillness permeates the atmosphere in fulfilment of Jeremiah 51:62. The curtain falls. There is no music for the orchestra has played the last waltz. There is no marriage for romance and love will be a thing of the past. There is no manufacturing for the bottom has fallen out of the economy. Darkness envelops the streets. God flicks the switch and puts out the lights of Babylon.

The language used in these verses is similar to that used in a legal document as though God were covering the pronouncement from every possible angle so as to leave no loophole. Pardon the pun, but in the light of verse 21 he leaves no stone unturned.

God makes no apology!

The final thoughts, the closing epitaph, on the fall of Babylon are left to the angel who is convinced of the rightness of what has happened. We read, *And all nations were deceived by your sorcery. And in her was found the blood of prophets and of saints, and of all who have been slain on earth.* God never has to justify his actions; he does what he does because he is who he is! God offers no apology for his attitude to Babylon. He pulled the plug. Her pride, presumption, perversity, and persecution of God's people – all these sins, and scores more that have not been catalogued, contributed to her ultimate downfall. What happened to her is perfectly valid.

In one sense, she brought it on herself; on the other, it was an event waiting to happen. And happen, it certainly did! She went out with a bang, God lit the fuse!

CHAPTER 19

Hallelujah! the King returns!

On 23 March 1743, in the Covent Garden theatre, George Frideric Handel's *Messiah* was performed for the first time in London. In attendance was King George II of England. He was deeply moved as the Hallelujah Chorus was sung and at the words, 'For the Lord God omnipotent reigneth,' the king spontaneously rose to his feet and stood until the end of the premiere performance of this major oratorio. From that time to this, people all around the world have stood when the Hallelujah Chorus is performed.

When Handel at the age of 56 composed this, his best-known work, he was so immersed in what he was doing for the twenty-four days he took to write it that he hardly ate or slept. At times he would run to the harpsichord, waving his arms and singing, 'Hallelujah! Hallelujah!' Handel apparently said in the presence of one of his servants: 'I think I did see all heaven before me, and the great God himself.'

19:1-6

The praise of God is proclaimed

In these opening verses John did not see the Lord but he recorded a strangely similar experience. We read his moving testimony in verse 1, *After this I heard what seemed to be the loud voice of a great multitude in heaven, crying out, 'Hallelujah! Salvation and glory and power belong to our God.'* The phrase *after this* refers back to the dark, ominous scenes recorded in chapters 17 and 18 where the focus was on the demise and ultimate doom of Babylon as an apostate religious system operating alongside and in cahoots with the Satan-inspired economic-political system.

The scene then shifts with dramatic emphasis from earth to heaven. The inky blackness has gone, now the sun is shining brightly! John's description of the scene flashing before him is vivid and graphic. It is so real you would know that he is writing firsthand from his own experience. The sound he hears is compared to the roar of a great multitude in heaven shouting. Louder than the fans in a thousand football stadia! That is powerful stuff. It is loud and clear. There is nothing muffled about the noise, it is thunderously deafening! For an old man, there is nothing defective with John's hearing. He missed nothing, hearing every word.

This vast innumerable company are extolling the virtues of the one seated upon the throne. The voices of this heavenly congregation are blending together in harmony as they praise the Lord for battles fought and victories won. Can we identify those in God's celebration choir? It is the church triumphant, all those redeemed by precious blood, saints at home with the Lord!

The chances are it includes those martyred in the killing fields of the Tribulation. There they are, beholding the King in his impeccable beauty! There they are, gazing on the lovely face of Jesus! There they are, worshipping the glorified Lord in his unrivalled holiness! And what do they do? They break forth into song, rising to their feet in a standing ovation of praise.

Hallelujah!

This is the only time this word is mentioned in the entire New Testament, yet in the space of six verses, it is heard four times. The first is sung for what God offers (1), the second is for what God settles (3), the third is for what God fulfils (4), and the fourth is for what God occupies (5-6).

However, it is an expression that is used frequently in the Old Testament, where it is a transliteration of the Hebrew words *hallel* ('praise') and *Jah* ('Jehovah') meaning 'praise the Lord.'

Its first use in the OT also expresses praise for God's judgment on the wicked oppressors of his people (cf. Psalm 104:35).

In this chapter, they are praising the Lord for all that he has done. They are praising the Lord for who he is: the one who inhabits eternity, God blessed forever. They are praising the Lord for where he is: the Lamb exalted on high, the King seated upon the throne.

Redemption ... he is the Saviour!

Their paean of praise is a recognition of the salvation of God in their lives. The one who plucked them as brands from the burning, who kept them daily by his power, has now taken them home to Immanuel's land! As in Romans 8:30, they have been called, justified, and glorified; and together they acclaim the marvellous truth that salvation is of the Lord.

They are quick to point out the intrinsic wonders of his glory. Here is the *shekinah* of God, the brightness of his person, the excellence of his wonderful name. Here is glory personified in one who is all glorious within! They make much of his strength for they acknowledge his power. Here is one who is omnipotent, who can do anything, who is abundantly able, who is limitless in his might ... with him, all things can become reality.

Retribution ... he is the Judge!

The second stanza in the hallelujah chorus puts the main beam on the severity of God. Paul makes mention in one of his epistles of the 'kindness and sternness' of God (cf. Romans 11:22 NIV). That is what we have here in cameo. In the first verse of the chorus, we saw the goodness of God; now we fix our eyes on the other side of God's nature, his ability to act in judgment. The scene so vividly portrayed for us is one of total destruction and complete devastation. We read in verses 2-3, *'For his judgments are true and just; for he has judged the great prostitute who corrupted the earth with her immorality, and has avenged on her the blood of his servants.'* Once more they *cried out, 'Hallelujah! The smoke from her goes up forever and ever.'*

Satan's superchurch has been erased. From the onset it was obvious the devil was the captain of a sinking ship. This global ecumenical shrine of the last days lies smouldering in the dust of earth. The language used is similar to that used of God's destruction of Sodom and Gomorrah (cf. Genesis 19:28) and Edom (cf. Isaiah 34:8-10). This great harlot and mother of harlots has met her doom, wiped out in one fell swoop. The one who corrupted the minds and hearts of men with her spiritual fornication is now in ruins.

The empire of evil has at last been eclipsed by the inrushing kingdom of love and light. And the singing has begun! The Bible bluntly states that her smoke goes up forever and ever. There is an undercurrent of permanence with what has happened. It is irreversible! Over! God has the final say (cf. Romans 12:19; Deuteronomy 32:35); the last word is exclusively his!

The emphasis here is not primarily focused on the titanic struggle between God and Satan, epic and momentous as that is, it is centred on the fact that God is true and righteous. The proper way to honour him is not only to rejoice at the greatness of Babylon's fall as if this were the be-all and end-all, the best way to magnify him is to elevate his attributes to a high place in our praise and worship. We discovered in chapter 8 that God's throne and altar are always related to his judgments. There is never a contradiction between his attributes and the wide range of his activities for they actually complement one another.

Realisation ... he is the Greatest!

The third praise item is found in verses 4 and 5 where the focus is on the sovereignty of God as they affirm his greatness. John informs us, *And the twenty-four elders and the four living creatures fell down and worshipped God who was seated on the throne, saying, 'Amen. Hallelujah!' And from the throne came a voice saying, 'Praise our God, all you his servants, you who fear him, small and great.'*

This is the last time the elders and living creatures are mentioned in the book. They appear first when the throne of God is introduced and they appear now at the climax of all things to say a hearty *amen* as a ringing endorsement of the purpose and plan of God (cf. Psalm 106:48). They are prostrate before the throne of God in heaven for they realise the stunning magnitude of the greatness of God. As my friend Woodrow Kroll says: 'God is not just filled with some awe; he is awesome!'

The fact that they bow before him is a meaningful tribute to the sovereignty of one who is King of kings and Lord of lords. Every being in the universe is encouraged to give praise to the Lord as an act of solidarity with the one who has been guiding events on earth. It does not matter who they are or where they see themselves on the ladder, the invitation is an open one to the small and great; the only criteria stipulated is the need to fear him. Each one is exhorted to bless the name of Jesus in a tidal wave of enthusiastic, ecstatic celebration.

Ruling and reigning ... he is the King!

All the host of the redeemed shout a final hallelujah in verse 6 which emphasises the supremacy of our God. John gives us a remarkable insight into what happens when he says, *Then I heard what seemed to be the voice of a great multitude, like the roar of many waters and like the sound of mighty peals of thunder, crying out, 'Hallelujah! For the Lord our God the Almighty reigns.'* What a tremendous finale to the hallelujah chorus! It is a rousing crescendo of praise, an unambiguous acknowledgment that our God reigns. It is marvellous for it echoes throughout the hills of heaven and it is majestic for it resounds around the valleys of earth.

The comparisons John makes are quite stunning in their own right. The voices of this choir will sound like a waterfall cascading down the side of a mountain and the booming of thunder reverberating throughout the sky. This magnificent burst of praise is an echo of Psalm 97:1 where we read, 'The

Lord reigns, let the earth rejoice; let the many coastlands be glad.' The literal translation is, 'The Lord God Almighty has begun to reign.' This does not suggest that heaven's throne has been empty or inactive, for the omnipotent God has been accomplishing his purposes on Planet Earth, all day, every day, from the very first day!

In his sovereignty, he has permitted evil men and fallen angels to do their worst; but now, in his providence, the time has come for God's will to be done on earth as it is in heaven. And nothing, absolutely nothing, will circumvent the plan of God! It will not be hijacked, he will not be sidelined!

19:7-8

The preparation of the bride is announced

The great hallelujah chorus is an introduction to the most magnificent wedding festivities of the ages. There is a word of instruction to all in verse 7 where the words, *'Let us rejoice and exult and give him the glory'* are really an encouragement to keep on praising the Lord (it is interesting to note that these verbs are found together again only in Matthew 5:12). We are urged to get enthused and excited about the marriage of the Lamb and his bride. There is a celebration and it is all a prelude to the ceremony. James Allen makes the point that 'the blood of the Lamb (7:14; 12:11) has pointed back to Calvary, the wrath of the Lamb (6:16) has pointed upward to the throne, now the marriage of the Lamb points forward to days of gladness and joy.'

Today, in most western cultures, when we think of a wedding, all eyes are on the bride. Even before the special day we have bridal showers, she can visit bridal shops, and there is a host of other events which the bride can attend so that her big day can be suitably enhanced. She is the centre of attention, and rightly so. It is ironic, you have all of this and so much more, and the man standing beside her, who is not even called the 'best man' is dressed in a hired suit! This elegant wedding is significantly different. It is unique. This is the wedding of time and eternity where the focus is on the bridegroom, he makes the difference, he alone is the centre of attention.

The marriage of the Lamb is patterned after the Jewish marriage custom of Bible times. If we look at this it will clarify the distinctive teaching we have in these wonderful verses and we will be in a position to better understand what John is saying.

The arrangement

After the fathers of the bride and groom negotiated a marriage contract, the bride's father was given the 'bride-price' as a dowry. The bride-price for God the Father was the blood of his Son (cf. Ephesians 5:25). This usually happened when the couple were quite young but the question of age depended more on local custom. The engagement was binding and could be broken only by a form of divorce (cf. Matthew 1:18-19). Any unfaithfulness during the engagement was considered adultery. To all intents and purposes, the couple were legally married but they were not allowed to have sexual relations during this particular period.

The betrothal

Phase two is generally spoken of as 'the preparation' or 'betrothal.' It normally lasted for a year or sometimes longer and during this time the bride was closely observed to display her purity. During the year the bridegroom would work long hours to prepare a home for his bride; more often than not, this was attached to his father's house. In like manner, Christ is in heaven preparing a place for his bride, the church (cf. John 14:1-3). On the wedding day, the groom would leave his father's home to claim his bride. After taking her from her home, the groom would then lead the bridal procession back to his own home. This typifies the rapture of the church which Paul talks about in 1 Thessalonians 4:13-18.

The marriage ceremony

Before the marriage there was the writing of a legal wedding document called the *Ketubah,* which was signed by two witnesses not related to the wedding couple. This important document was a marriage covenant, a willing agreement between the bride and groom that included specific obligations in relation to the husband and it also outlined many of the rights of the wife.

On this occasion the bride was beautifully dressed, she looked like a queen. She had precious jewels plaited in her hair and clothing and a long veil covering her face. In Bible times the ceremony was conducted at the home of the groom. It was attended by the immediate family, two witnesses, and a few close friends. Today, the ritual and customs vary from country to country, a lot depends on local tradition.

The ceremony is normally held under a *huppah*, a marriage canopy. It begins with the benediction of betrothal, recited over a cup of wine, taken by the groom and his bride. A ring is placed on the bride's finger, the *Ketubah* is read, and Seven Blessings are recited by a rabbi over a second cup of wine. The ceremony concludes with the groom breaking a glass in memory of the destruction of the temple.

Back in Bible times it was the done thing for the couple to leave their guests at an appropriate point to actually consummate the marriage. This is a wonderful picture of the church as the bride of Christ consummating the marriage of the Lamb.

The marriage feast

The fourth and final phase is known as the marriage feast. The friends of the bride and groom were invited to this so they could share in the joys of this happy occasion. It was a good excuse for a long party. Sometimes it lasted a few days, other times it went on for a week; it depended how rich the host was! After the feast, the couple would settle into their new home and get on with the rest of their lives together.

The bride's apparel

The second half of verse 7, into verse 8, serves to remind us of the importance of the bride's apparel. We read, *'For the marriage of the Lamb has come, and his Bride has made herself ready; it was granted her to clothe herself with fine linen, bright and pure'*—for the fine linen is the righteous deeds of the saints.

The status of this is seen from the parables of our Lord. One classic example is Matthew 22:1-4. There, the kingdom of heaven is likened to a marriage supper which a certain king gave for his son. Those who did not have a wedding garment were cast out into an eternity of loss and separation from God. The implication is, if you have not got a wedding garment, you cannot get into the wedding banquet.

In these two verses the bride is ready and robed. I have been to many weddings and I have conducted quite a number as well and I cannot remember a single occasion when the bride was not beautiful! She has planned and prepared for this moment and comes out looking her best. Her clothing, her wedding dress, is described in detail and a fascinating explanation is appended to it. We know from reading elsewhere in Scripture that we are clothed from head to toe in the garment of his righteousness—an imputed and imparted righteousness, it is one given to us at the moment of our salvation, a gift of sovereign grace (cf. Philippians 3:9). The garment we read about here in verse 8 is different. The only similarity is that it is given to us.

The *fine linen* represents the righteous deeds of godliness and goodness produced in us and through us by the Holy Spirit. These are the 'good works' Paul refers to in Ephesians 2:10 which bear witness to our personal relationship with Jesus Christ.

The timing of the event

The key event addressed here will be immediately after the

judgment seat of Christ which Paul writes about at length in 1 Corinthians 3 and 2 Corinthians 5. It is payday for the people of God, our moment of evaluation and appraisal, the place of accountability for the servants of God. All our foibles and mistakes will burn up before our eyes for they are symbolised as wood, hay, and straw; the gold, silver, and costly stones of our service and devotion will stand the test of his scrutiny and he will amply reward us for these. The reference here points us in the direction of the Bema for it speaks of our ability to magnify him and the greater our reward, the greater is our capacity to glorify Jesus.

When the church arrives in heaven for her hour of grand review, she is not the most attractive or beautiful; in fact, she is covered in spots, wrinkles, and blemishes, according to Paul in Ephesians 5:27. But now! What a difference! She is radiant in her glory! How true, we weave on earth what we wear in heaven. As Walter Scott writes: 'The light of the throne had done its work, bringing into bold relief the whole story of her history on earth.' Sometimes the reality of that has not sunk in, that how we use the gifts God gave us on earth will determine the way we are presented to the bridegroom when he comes. Will we be dressed shabbily or lavishly? That is a challenging thought. It reminds me of the familiar lines: 'Only one life, it will soon be past; only what's done, for Christ will last.'

19:9-10

The marriage feast

Have you ever done something on the spur of the moment and lived to regret it? Have you ever responded in an emotion-charged atmosphere only to discover minutes later that you got it all wrong? If we are honest, most of us would have to answer 'yes' to each of these questions! John certainly would. Right here, as a mature man and a well-seasoned observer of all things spiritual, he got it disastrously wrong.

It all happened after the praise party in heaven to celebrate the intervention of God in the affairs of men; it came about after the rousing angelic invitation to the wedding feast of the Lamb which we read about in verse 9, *And the angel said to me, 'Write this: Blessed are those who are invited to the marriage supper of the Lamb!' And he said to me, 'These are the true words of God.'*

It was after this that John made a serious error of judgment, a rare gaffe on his part that shows he is just as human as the rest of us, and that is good! We will have more to say about John's blunder in a moment but let us backtrack and open the envelope which has heaven's postmark stamped on it. It would be good if we examined this invitation in a bit more detail.

Who is on the guest list?

It is an extremely positive invitation! It indicates clearly that all those whose names appear on the guest list are truly blessed. This is the fourth of seven beatitudes found in the book. Who receives an invitation to this legendary banquet? It is not the church for the bride is never invited to her own wedding! She is there already for you cannot have a wedding without a bride! The invitation is extended to those who fit into the category of Old Testament saints, to those saints martyred during the Tribulation, and to those believers who emerged from the seven years of Satan's rule and reign of terror.

The time and the place!

There is a difference between the 'marriage of the Lamb' and the 'marriage supper of the Lamb' and there is no real reason for us to be confused by them. They are different events, at different times, and in different places. The 'marriage of the Lamb' takes place in the Father's house in heaven. This wedding banquet will take place on earth and it could even take place during the forty-five days mentioned in Daniel 12:11-12. That means, it could happen during the interregnum between the end of the Tribulation and the beginning of the millennial kingdom of Christ. In that sense, the kingdom would then be seen as a one-thousand year honeymoon to be enjoyed by the church as she shares in the glorious rule and reign of Jesus as King.

His banner over us is love, and the whole experience will be a feast for the eyes for we will see the Lord, a feast for the ears for we will hear his voice, and a feast for the heart for we will be enthralled with him. He says, 'Come and dine!' and most of us will be happy to do just that!

The host

Then in a bold attempt to allay our fears as to the source of the invitation, the angel appended to it the cast-iron assurance that it came direct from the Father. It is genuine! Authentic! It bears his signature, the handwriting of God! This is no fairytale, this is for real!

A breach of etiquette!

John's immediate response to all of this is what I was referring to above. It is a serious breach of etiquette! Poor John, he got it badly wrong! The problem was he did not only do it once, he slipped up a second time; that faux pas is mentioned in 22:8-9. We read about the initial incident in verse 10: *Then I fell down at his feet to worship him, but he said to me, 'You must not do that! I am a fellow servant with you and your brothers who hold to the testimony of Jesus. Worship God.' For the testimony of Jesus is the spirit of prophecy.*

In all fairness, John is big enough to admit his mistake and it is there for the rest of us to learn from! He was so carried away by the wonder of all that he saw and heard that he instinctively fell down and worshipped the angel. The angel was having none of it; he rebuked John and told him in no uncertain terms that God is the only one who deserves to be worshipped! The angel had no airs or graces for he saw himself as a bondslave; there was nothing pretentious about him for he was only a servant; this was no ambience of false humility. He and John were standing on a level playing field.

Prophecy is a person!

Another fascinating thought in this verse surrounds the explanation given to the phrase, *the testimony of Jesus.* We are told it is *the spirit of prophecy.* That means prophecy is not a fortune teller who reads the palm of your hand or the leaves in a tea cup; it is not an astrologer who consults the stars nor a good guesser or date fixer; prophecy is a person! And that person is Jesus!

Some folk think that the purpose of prophecy is to open a window on the future. Nothing could be further from the truth. The pure essence of prophecy is to bear witness to Jesus. He is the central figure of all Scripture and history. Our focus is the Lord for all prophecy is wrapped up in him. On one hand, he is the revealer; on the other, he is the revelation! That is what the Apocalypse is all about ... it is a full-blown revelation of Jesus Christ!

19:11-14

The rider on the white horse

We are moving now into the second half of chapter 19. In many ways, this is the climax of Bible prophecy, the hour when the King will come, the second advent of Jesus Christ in power and great glory (cf. Matthew 24:29-30). This has to be the most extraordinary event in history. It is certainly the most dramatic moment in prophecy. This is a major doctrine woven into the fabric of Scripture.

Did you know that ... one-fifth of the Bible is prophecy? one-third of those prophecies relate to the second coming of Christ? there are at least 333 prophecies concerning Christ in the Old Testament? only 109 of these were fulfilled at his first advent, that leaves 224 (more than twice as many) to be fulfilled at his second appearing!

Did you know that ... of the 46 Old Testament prophets, fewer than ten speak of events related to Christ's first coming, while 36 speak of events linked with his second coming? there are 7,959 verses in the New Testament, 330 of which refer directly to the second coming of Christ? the Lord Jesus speaks about his return to earth no fewer than 25 times? throughout the New Testament there are more than 50 exhortations for people to be ready for the coming of Christ?

Those are interesting facts, but they are more than fodder for an enthusiastic statistician for they drive home the truth that Jesus is coming again! That was the message in 1:7 where we read, *Behold, he is coming with the clouds, and every eye will see him.* Here it is at long last! The impassioned cry of 'How long?' (Habakkuk 1:2) that echoed from many a faithful heart down the ages is now answered—the day has finally dawned!

He is reliable!

John informs us in verse 11, *Then I saw heaven opened, and behold, a white horse! The one sitting on it is called Faithful and True, and in righteousness he judges and makes war.* It is a helpful exercise to make a comparison of John's experience on this occasion with what happened to him earlier (cf. 4:1; 11:19). Then, he saw only a door opened and the temple of God opened, but here he sees all of heaven open. This is a grander, fuller view than he had before. This is the great unveiling. The scene is awe-inspiring. John sees a rider on a white horse. This one is called *Faithful and True* in direct contrast to the pseudo ruler of the world we met in chapter 6.

At his first advent, Christ rode into the city of Jerusalem on the back of a donkey on that first Palm Sunday (cf. Zechariah 9:9); he was given no throne, only a cross; his crown was one of thorns, his sceptre a reed. At his second advent, the Lord of heaven is seated on a white stallion, ready to depart heaven as a warrior king, poised for battle! When he comes, he will deal effectively and summarily with his enemies.

We saw him earlier sat on a white cloud (14:14), later he will sit upon a white throne (20:11), that he is returning on a white horse is highly significant. In Bible times, Roman generals always returned from victorious campaigns riding white horses. It is well known that the Roman Senate granted Julius Caesar permission to drive a chariot drawn by white horses through Rome to celebrate his victory in North Africa. During victory celebrations like these, Rome would decorate everything they could with white fabric and white flowers. Juvenal, the Roman poet who lived during the time of John the Apostle, referred to such times when Rome would become 'a city in white.' They, and their legions, would parade up the Via Sacra, the main street of Rome, that led from the Forum to the Temple of Jupiter on the Capitoline Hill. They would be hailed as heroes as the cheers of a jubilant people would greet them all along the route. So the white horse is a symbol of triumph!

The rider is called *Faithful and True* and that emphasises the reliability of his name. Back in 1:5 he is described as *the faithful witness* and then in 3:14 he is seen as *the faithful and true witness.* This name is, therefore, a fitting description of his character; it is also a pointer to a couple of his attributes for he is a God of faithfulness and truth. He is trustworthy for he can always be relied upon and he is dependable for he always keeps his promises.

To say he is true is to affirm that he is genuine, he is real. He is not a counterfeit. There is nothing fake or false about him. He is authentic. Because he is eternally faithful and true, it means many wonderful blessings are ours to enjoy right now. For example, he makes good on his promises (cf. Deuteronomy 7:9; Hebrews 10:23), he helps us in our temptations (cf. 1 Corinthians 10:13), he protects us from Satan (cf. 2 Thessalonians 3:3), he will never forsake us (cf. 2 Timothy 2:13), and he will forgive our sin (cf. 1 John 1:9).

He said he would bring peace and social and political justice to mankind, and he will; he will deliver the goods in his own good time. The rider on the same colour of horse in 6:2 is the exact opposite. He is dangerously deceptive and dishonest. One writer highlights the contrast when he says: 'During his sojourn on earth he was faithful to God and true to his own nature; now this same one returns to earth to confront the Beast who is the personification of faithlessness and falseness.' Without doubt, there is all the difference in the world between Antichrist and the Lord Jesus Christ.

He is right!

This verse makes it abundantly clear that what he does, when he comes again, is done justly. There will be no charge of injustice levelled against him when he makes war (cf. Isaiah 11:3-5; Psalm 110:6). In heaven's Cabinet, he is the Minister for War. The nations have been depicted already as an overripe harvest, rotting and smelling like a basket of summer fruit; when he touches down on earth, his will be a swift execution of justice. He is the grim reaper. Here is the one who, through the millennia, made peace through the blood of the cross; now he makes war over that blood. Human sin has reached the high-water mark and global rebellion has gone over the top. It must be put down once and for all, and when it is, it will all be over in a flash!

He relates!

John does not stop there. He tells us more in verse 12 for we read, *His eyes are like a flame of fire, and on his head are many diadems, and he has a name written that no one knows but himself.* The reference to the eyes of Christ indicate a penetrating gaze that flash with intelligence and righteousness. It is the incandescent blaze of divine wrath upon sinful man. His eyes pierce through every human shield. His is an all-searching eye that discerns, roves, and scans. Nothing can be hidden from his all-seeing eye, no one can hide from his sight. In that day all will be exposed and come under his scrutiny. All will be laid bare before him. The coming King is one who sees all and knows all!

He rules!

The many *diadems* or crowns speak of his magnificent rule and sovereignty so here is one who is omnipotent. It draws attention to his royalty and majesty and is a token reminder of the title given to him in the Psalms where we often read that 'the Lord is King!'

John was able to see the name written on him but for some reason it was incomprehensible to him; it is a name shrouded in mystery. There is so much about our Lord we simply do not know, but he knows! It is a secret name; maybe it is the same as the *new name* we read about in 3:12.

The knowledge of the Lord is described in the same way in Psalm 139:1-6 where David honestly concludes, 'Such knowledge is too wonderful for me; it is high; I cannot attain it.' We read elsewhere in Psalm 145:3 that 'his greatness is unsearchable' – that is, it cannot be fathomed. That is what makes eternity an exciting enterprise, it will be an educational experience for in heaven we will learn new things about the Lord Jesus!

He routs!

John continues in verse 13 by sharing with us, *He is clothed in a robe dipped in blood, and the name by which he is called is The Word of God.* At a quick glance it seems a strange comment for John to make, but the question is, Where did the blood come from? One thing we do know for sure, it was not his own blood shed on the cross at Calvary for the work of redemption is complete, that event has long since passed. Rather, it is the blood of his enemies (cf. Isaiah 63:1-4). The evangelical prophet gives us a breathtaking description of the approach of a great warrior with crimson-stained garments. It is a prophecy about the coming of the Lord and his robes are stained with the blood of those he destroyed. This is the same bloodbath described in vivid detail in 14:20. He is a God of vengeance and anger!

He reveals!

He is called *The Word of God.* The same ascription is given to him back in John 1:1. It is the same person in view for he is the embodiment of God's truth, he is God on display. He is the Father's revelation of himself. When you look at him, you see God. When you listen to what he says, you hear the voice of God. James Allen writes: 'God was revealed in Christ in the days of his flesh acting in grace; now that same God is revealed in Christ acting in truth (cf. John 1:17).' Anne Graham Lotz comments: 'The Bible that people even today deny, distort, dilute, defy, doubt, and disobey is the same as his name!'

He is royalty!

Then we read in verse 14, *And the armies of heaven, arrayed in fine linen, white and pure, were following him on white horses.* This is tremendous! He is not just bringing a choir with him, he is bringing an army! It is a powerful reminder that when our Lord returns he will not be alone for the armies of heaven accompany him; they follow in his train. Who is he talking about? Well, first of all, the angels have a vital role to play in this military-style operation. We know from the Olivet Discourse in Matthew 25:31 that they will be present and Paul says as much in 2 Thessalonians 1:7. But we also know from 1 Thessalonians 3:13 and 2 Thessalonians 1:10 that the saints will also participate in this venture. You and me! We will be there as part of his entourage. After all, it is a royal visit and we just happen to be the wife of the Lamb!

Jude is batting from the same crease when he alludes to the ministry of Enoch, seven generations from Adam (cf. Jude 14-15), as is the prophet Zechariah in 14:5. The 'holy ones' in both cases have a dual meaning in that they can refer to believers and angels. We are there beside him, and behind him.

This is the moment Paul talks about in 2 Thessalonians 1:10 when he says, 'He comes on that day to be glorified in his saints, and to be marvelled at among all who have believed.' We are not there to fight, ours is purely a supportive role, for Christ himself will defeat the enemy through a trio of great victories. It is an awesome display of glory, a regal demonstration of splendour, a stunning sight of unbelievable grandeur. It is a magic moment for this is the hour when every eye will see him, every knee will bend before him, and every tongue will confess that Jesus Christ is Lord!

> *All hail the Lamb enthroned on high,*
> *His praise shall be our battle cry!*
> *He reigns victorious, forever glorious,*
> *His name is Jesus! He is the Lord!*

19:15-21

The Lamb wins!

In verse 15 John tells us, *From his mouth comes a sharp sword with which to strike down the nations, and he will rule them with a rod of iron. He will tread the winepress of the fury of the wrath of God the Almighty.* This is an amazing, action-packed verse.

He strikes the nations

The *sharp sword* refers to the long, heavy, tongue-shaped sword commonly used by the Thracians. Having said that, it can also describe a sword long and light enough to throw as a spear or javelin. We are all aware that the Word of God is represented by a sword in Ephesians 6:17 even though the phrase used there refers to the two-edged hand weapon popularised by the Romans.

It is the word of the warrior-king that strikes the nations. He speaks and his judgments are executed swiftly. This lethal blow is outlined in Psalm 2:9 and Isaiah 11:4. Not a shot will be fired! The last battle in the conflict of the ages will be won by the word of God! The opposition will crumble before him; the enemy will bite the bullet and melt in the sunlight of his glorious appearing. Christ will be victorious! One word, and that is that!

He shepherds the nations

That is the thought behind ruling them with an iron sceptre or, as some translations put it, a rod of iron. Either way, it employs the Greek word for 'shepherd.' The shepherd's rod is frequently used for correction. Paul hints at this in 1 Corinthians 4:21 when he poses the question, 'Shall I come to you with a rod, or with love in a spirit of gentleness?' The Lord Jesus is called the 'great shepherd' in Hebrews 13:20, the 'good shepherd' in John 10:11, and the 'chief shepherd' in 1 Peter 5:4. All of these express warm encouragement to the people of God. Because of the unique relationship we have with him, even the shepherd's rod can be a measure of comfort to the believer (cf. Psalm 23:4).

However, the rod or sceptre the shepherd of the nations will use is made of iron. This is not to be taken lightly. It is a rod that will bring order and justice to a world riddled with chaos, confusion, and corruption. The nations will be shepherded with sovereign, kingly authority. This is no softly-softly approach to global government. This is Jesus Christ putting his foot down, exercising his right to universal domination. He and his followers will rule the nations of the world when his kingdom is established on earth, it will be one thousand years of Jesus rule. Men will have no option but to conform to the righteous standards of God. They will have no say in the matter, there is no alternative, no other way! As someone has said: 'A chicken won't peep, a rooster won't crow, and a man won't move without his permission.'

He stomps the nations

This is echoed in the last phrase of verse 15 where it describes the trampling of the peoples of the world in the winepress of God's wrath. This imagery portrays grapes being trampled underfoot until all the juice is squeezed out of them. The chilling fact is, it is blood, not grape juice, that will spurt from the winepress of God's anger! This is the great and terrible Day of the Lord, the day of vengeance of our God, the awful day of his wrath when his unbridled fury is poured out upon unbelieving nations.

These same terrifying truths are reiterated by the prophets in Isaiah 63:3 and Joel 3:13-14. No matter where you look, all these drive us to the sad conclusion that in the day of judgment it is too late for men to expect mercy from God. Nothing is more inflexible than divine judgment where the grace of God has been spurned.

His identity

His title

In verse 16 John says, *On his robe and on his thigh he has a name written: King of kings and Lord of lords.* What a splendid title! King of kings! Lord of lords! Daniel 8:25 throws in another for good measure when he says, he is the Prince of princes! Truly, the Lord is sovereign, exalted, and enthroned on high. He is unique as the unrivalled Son of God and peerless as the incomparable Christ!

This is Christ's most important name. It brings to mind such glowing references as Daniel 2:47 and Deuteronomy 10:17 where his transcendence is underlined (cf. Psalm 45:3). Paul jumped on the bandwagon when he used the same title in 1 Timothy 6:15. So far as Paul was concerned it did not matter one iota what Caesar was on the throne, Jesus Christ was his Lord and King. He is God, and before him, all must bow the knee (cf. Philippians 2:10-11).

His robe and thigh

The thigh on which this title is emblazoned is symbolic of power; the robe on which this title is conspicuously portrayed has to do with his position.

The impact of his return

The closing verses remind us of the terrible destruction to come. Armageddon has arrived, that feared day when the final war of humanity takes place. Human history, as we know it, will come to a close. God's day will explode upon the world scene in a spectacular display of his power and glory. The whole world will know that Jesus Christ is King of kings and Lord of lords! We see Satan's rickety empire collapsing like a pack of cards when the Lord appears from heaven.

The essential information is provided by John in verses 17 and 18 where we read, *Then I saw an angel standing in the sun, and with a loud voice he called to all the birds that fly directly overhead, 'Come, gather for the great supper of God, to eat the flesh of kings, the flesh of captains, the flesh of mighty men, the flesh of horses and their riders, and the flesh of all men, both free and slave, both small and great.'*

The angel

The unusual position of the angel is a moment of high drama. He is *standing in the sun.* Some folk have taken this to be a one-off phenomenon but the most natural explanation is that the angel is standing in the light of the sun which means he is shining with even greater brilliance than normal. The image is one of white-hot light speaking of the glory of God. The prophet Joel intimates that the sun will be turned into darkness (2:10). Perhaps the position of the angel initiates that process by which people on earth will know that judgment day has arrived.

His voice. The sound of a loud voice is an activity we have come across six times previously in Revelation. It always introduces some event of mega importance relative to the vengeance and victory of God.

His message. The omens are dreadful. The message directed explicitly to the birds is akin to the Olivet discourse of Matthew 24:27-28 where both speak of carnage at the coming of Christ. One writer says that 'a macabre table is spread, gruesome even to contemplate.'

In that portion in Matthew 24 the 'corpse' depicts the nations of the world gathered against the Lord and his people in the Armageddon campaign, whereas the 'vultures' represent all the birds of heaven who will feed on the flesh of those armies vanquished by the advent of the King. A vulture is a voracious eater, descending swiftly upon carrion and devouring it in minutes. In that hour, they will have a field day, millions of men from every strata of society will be consumed within a 200-mile radius of Jerusalem. It will be a shocking spectacle, enough to make your blood run cold; it is beyond human imagination.

It is ironic that the great supper of God anticipated here in verse 17 is in direct contrast to the supper of festive joy envisaged at the marriage of the Lamb in verse 9. No prizes for guessing which one I would rather be at! The choice is, attend his supper, or be the supper!

The Beast and his army

John reflects in a solemn mood in verse 19 when he testifies, *And I saw the beast and the kings of the earth with their armies gathered together to make war against him who was sitting on the horse and against his army.* The world is mobilised, they have come from every corner of earth and converged on the vast plains of Megiddo for World War III. For a while they fight one another in the conflict of the ages; the killing is mindless, senseless, and relentless.

Then, suddenly, something happens. There is a change in their attitude as old animosities are quickly forgotten and past grudges are rapidly buried, and they are united by the challenge from on high. They join hearts and hands in their rebellion against the coming King. The Beast and the kings of the earth marshal the armies of the world, they line up their tanks, aim their missiles, poise their nuclear warheads, and position their battleships, all to make war against the Lord! Against one who is their Creator!

It is the same old story. The nations stood shoulder to shoulder against the Lord Jesus at his first coming and it is not in the least surprising that history will repeat itself at his second advent. The man leading his troops from the front is none other than Antichrist. It is the final cataclysmic punch-up between good and evil.

The outcome

It is an ill-fated assault on the advancing army of the King of kings. It is doomed from the moment they get out of the trenches! They are on a collision course with the Lord of the universe and we know who comes off worst! John says as much in verses 20 and 21, *And the beast was captured, and with it the false prophet who in its presence had done the signs by which he deceived those who had received the mark of the beast and those who worshipped its image. These two were thrown alive into the lake of fire that burns with sulphur. And the rest were slain by the sword that came from the mouth of him who was sitting on the horse, and all the birds were gorged with their flesh.*

Hyped-up though Armageddon was, at the end of the day it boiled down to a rather one-sided contest. The assembled armies with all their hi-tech weapons of war do not present any real threat to the Lord Jesus Christ. He is invincible! He speaks a word and it is all over! O the power in the spoken word by the living Word! As the great reformer Martin Luther put it: 'One little word shall fell him.'

He has done it before. Once, he spoke a word to a fig tree, and it withered away (cf. Mark 11:20-26). Once, he spoke a word to the wind and the waves, and all was peace and calm as a millpond (cf. Luke 8:22-25). Once, he spoke a word to a legion of demons, and instantly they fled (cf. Mark 5:1-20). Now, he speaks a word, and the war is over! For these armies, he is death in a word (cf. Isaiah 11:4).

The loud-mouthed Antichrist is riveted to the spot. He is captured and taken away by the scruff of his brazen neck. The miracle-working false prophet who is a PR windbag from the pit is punctured and suffers a similar fate to his supremo. The pair of them are rounded up and unceremoniously bundled into the lake of fire. Their time is up. They have had their say, their way, and their day. Now they get their just desserts. They have the rare honour of being the first two who are cast into the lake of fire for even the devil is not there yet!

In that day 777 will take care of 666 when the Antichrist, probably the greatest intellectual, the greatest politician, the greatest statesman, the greatest economist who ever lived, becomes the greatest fool when he tries to mastermind a quick one over the Lord Jesus Christ.

Another word and the massed troops from around the world fall down dead. Not one person escapes. It all happens so quickly, no one can jump ship or change sides; there is no time to hoist the white flag of surrender. The sombre fact is that no one is left standing. It is a total wipeout! An old Southern preacher once said: 'Your arms are too short to box with God!'

The birds can hardly believe their luck. One writer summarises it with this statement: 'The birds of prey swoop down upon this terrible battlefield; they rest gorged to repletion in the eerie twilight of the darkest day in human history.' It is a blanket victory for the King of kings and Lord of lords. It is no wonder that Martin Luther once said that there were only two days in his calendar—'today' and 'that day.'

CHAPTER 20

Sinners in the dock

Revelation 20 is one of the great chapters of Scripture because it shows what happens immediately after the second coming of Jesus Christ. We have clear indication of this because one phrase is repeated no fewer than six times in the first seven verses where it talks about *a thousand* years—we call it, the millennium. It comes from two Latin words, *mille* and *annum*, meaning a thousand years. Six times he says it, surely that means God is serious about this time period.

From the year of dot, theologians have differed in their views of the millennium and, for many godly believers, the subject has been rated so highly controversial that honest, open discussion has frequently generated more heat than light!

Approaches to the millennium

Amillennialists believe there will be no earthly reign of Christ before or after his second coming. To them, the kingdom is not something political or visible, it is principally spiritual in nature and is experienced in the life of believers now. Many embrace replacement theology whereby the promises and blessings of the kingdom, originally given to Israel, have now been inherited by the Church.

Postmillennialists believe the world will continue to get better and better and Satan's power grow weaker and weaker as Christians spread the gospel and the church goes from strength to strength. A sense of optimism they may have, a sense of realism they do not have! The present gospel age turns into the millennium, and *then* Christ returns.

Premillennialists believe that Christ will return before the millennium to reign on earth for a literal one thousand years.

On a personal level, I will interpret this passage from a premillennial standpoint. From that angle, the teaching of John makes a lot of sense. The ultimate over-riding purpose of human history is the glory of God. God was not created for man, man was created for God. We are brought into the family of God so that God's glory will shine through us forever.

God's glory was manifested in creation. God's glory was manifested in redemptive history. God's glory was manifested in the tabernacle and temple. God's glory was manifested at Calvary in the death of Jesus. God's glory was manifested in the church. God's glory was manifested, above all else, in the person of the Son of God. And, in an amazing way, God's glory is manifested through the nation of Israel.

If men want to see and know what God is like, they should watch how he deals with Israel! When Jacob was about to leave the land of promise, God spoke to him in Genesis 28:15. He told him, 'I am with you and will keep you wherever you go, and will bring you back to this land. For I will not leave you until I have done what I have promised you.' In those five promises the entire history of the nation of Israel was kaleidoscoped.

If God does not keep his word to Israel, then he is not true. If God does not have power to fulfil his purposes, then he is not omnipotent. If God does not know certain things are going to occur, and gets caught off-guard, then he is not omniscient. If God has wearied of Israel, then he is not long-suffering. If God has changed his mind, then he is not immutable. In this we must be absolutely clear: if God has changed his mind in relation to his purpose for Israel, perhaps then he could change his mind concerning his purposes for the church.

A reflection of God's character

In the first instance the millennial issue is not prophetical, it is theological. It is not so much a consideration of what will happen tomorrow, it deals with what God's character is like today and he is a faithful God! He will keep his promises to Israel and that requires a literal kingdom on earth over which Jesus Christ will preside. He will keep his promises to the believer and that requires a home in Glory in his presence forever.

When you draw the strands together and, at the risk of sounding simplistic, that is where amillennialism infringes on God's glory by calling into question his attributes when they say there will be no literal kingdom. Postmillennialism detracts from God's glory by attributing to the church a purpose God never intended. It was never God's idea and it was never written on his agenda that man through the proclamation of the gospel will bring in the kingdom.

Premillennialism acknowledges God's glory by taking God at his word; this is implicit in the recognition that Jesus will rule on the earth for one thousand years. It is a special time when the kingdom of God is here upon earth—days of peace, prosperity, and untold spiritual blessing. These are days when he will be king over all the earth and sit on the throne of his father David in the city of the great king; these are days when the kingdoms of this world will become the kingdom of his dear Son and when the glory of the Lord will cover the earth as the waters cover the sea; these are days of heaven on earth with times of refreshing because Jehovah Shammah will be in the midst. It is a golden age! Above all, these are days when Satan is under the feet of Jesus as outlined here in the opening verses of chapter 20.

20:1-3

The devil on death row!

We are advised in verses 1 and 2 of the period when Satan is bound; in the first half of verse 3 we are informed of the place where Satan is bound and in the second half of the same verse we are shown the purpose for which Satan is bound. It is to keep him from deceiving the nations any more!

John says in these verses, *Then I saw an angel coming down from heaven, holding in his hand the key to the bottomless pit and a great chain. And he seized the dragon, that ancient serpent, who is the devil and Satan, and bound him for a thousand years, and threw him into the pit, and shut it and sealed it over him, so that he might not deceive the nations any longer, until the thousand years were ended. After that he must be released for a little while.*

Satan is under detention, held in secure custody, and there is no escape (cf. Daniel 6:17; Matthew 27:60-66). He finds himself on death row! God has sidelined the devil for a very long time. His influence is nil, his power zero, he has been completely disarmed. So long as he is in the pit, he is a spent force. In 12:9 he was cast out of heaven, now he is cast out of earth! He is out of the way and, because he is under lock and key, life on Planet Earth is a million times better. It is always like that when Jesus is in control!

20:4-6

Spotlight on the saints!

John tells us, *Then I saw thrones, and seated on them were those to whom the authority to judge was committed. Also I saw the souls of those who had been beheaded for the testimony of Jesus and for the word of God, and those who had not worshipped the beast or its image and had not received its mark on their foreheads or their hands. They came to life and reigned with Christ for a thousand years. The rest of the dead did not come to life until the thousand years were ended. This is the first resurrection. Blessed and holy is the one who shares in the first resurrection! Over such the second death has no power, but they will be priests of God and of Christ, and they will reign with him for a thousand years.*

This is great stuff! Wonderful news! The devil is well out of harm's way, confined for ten centuries in the abyss (cf. Luke 8:31). He is chained under lock and key and going nowhere during the millennium. That explains why in these few verses John gives us a further trio of reasons to justify his incarceration.

Do you remember what Paul promised the Christians in Rome? He said in Romans 16:20 that 'the God of peace will soon crush Satan under your feet.' Well, this is it! Here it is!

They are crowned!

Those on the thrones are the people of God in the church and the saints who have walked close with the Lord through the ages. John sees those who are loyal to the Lord during the dark days of Tribulation and who gave their lives in an act of supreme sacrifice. It is fascinating to read elsewhere in 1 Peter 2:9 that we are 'a royal priesthood' and away back in 1:6 that we are kings and priests unto God. The kingly aspect of it comes out in our role with him during the millennial kingdom (cf. Matthew 19:28). What a tremendous privilege to be ruling and reigning with him!

He makes it very clear that this is all part of the first resurrection. It is also called in Scripture the 'resurrection of the righteous' (Luke 14:14; Acts 24:15), the 'resurrection of life' (John 5:29), the resurrection of 'those who are Christ's at his coming' (1 Corinthians 15:23), and the 'better resurrection' (Hebrews 11:35).

If this is the first one, and it is for those who are saved, what happens at the second and when is it? It happens at the end of the millennium and is for the lost sinner, but more about that when we reach verses 11-15. Try as you might, you will be hard pushed to find a reference in the Bible to sustain the argument for a so-called 'general resurrection.' In fact, the opposite is the case. The reality is there are two resurrections, one before the millennium and one at the end of the millennium.

The first resurrection is in three distinct stages and what makes the whole subject much more interesting is the way it is compared to a harvest.

Stage one is when Christ arose on that first Easter Sunday morning as the firstfruits (cf. 1 Corinthians 15:20). When they had a harvest in the Old Testament, the high priest would go out into the field, take a handful of grain and bring it into the temple as a sacrifice to the Lord (cf. Leviticus 23:9-14). It was a guarantee of that which was yet to come. That is what happened when Jesus rose from the grave. He is the firstfruits of the promises of God. It is the assurance that what happened to him will one day happen to us!

Stage two is what Paul refers to in 1 Thessalonians 4:13-18 when the saints of God are gathered into the immediate presence of the Lord. If you like, this is the harvest proper. All of us who are in the Lord will meet him in the air, that will be the greatest harvest of souls ever; this is the fruit of his death at Calvary.

Stage three is at the end of the Tribulation when the Old Testament saints, along with the Tribulation saints, will rise to new heights of glory. These are the gleanings, the leftovers, which are picked up after the main harvest has been gathered home.

We can put it like this: it is one resurrection in three different phases which sometimes is called the 'resurrection unto life' (Daniel 12:2). The key phrase, if we want to understand the resurrection aright, is found at the end of verse 4 where John says, *they came to life*. It actually means 'to stand up!' Apparently, the Dutch have a word for it in their vocabulary when they call it 'oopstanding!' That is what the resurrection does for it enables us to stand up!

The story is told of the famous American evangelist, D L Moody, who one day was addressing a company of people. 'One of these fine mornings,' he is reported as saying, 'you will read in your newspaper that D L Moody is dead. Don't you believe it! On that day, I'll be more alive than I've ever been!' That is the resurrection spirit!

Their character

Again, at the beginning of verse 6 we have one of those familiar beatitudes (this is number five; the last two, numbers six and seven, are in 22:7 and 22:14.) *Our state*. We are what we are because we are active participants in the first resurrection. To be blessed is to be happy. It hints at joy and satisfaction. *Our standing* is one of holiness. We cannot be anything else for we are in the presence of the Lord. How true, happiness and holiness always go hand in hand for God has set such saints apart in their blessedness.

Their confidence

At the end of verse 6 we discover that the saints have confidence because the second death has no power over them. I recall a true saying of a friend, the late Pastor James Armstrong: 'To be born once is to die twice, but to be born twice is to die only once!' Because we have taken part in this great resurrection programme, we are not only kings who will share in his rule, we are also confirmed as priests. That means we will enjoy unlimited access into the presence of the Lord and benefit from unbroken intimate fellowship with our God and Father.

Ministry will take on a whole new meaning in that day with an added dimension to it. We are exalted in Christ and entrusted with diverse roles in the kingdom of God, there is great dignity and responsibility attached to all that we are doing. Our pride and pleasure in that day will be found in our association with Jesus Christ as his vice-regents on earth (cf. the sons of David in his kingdom in 2 Samuel 8:18). It will last for one thousand years, and then something incredible happens!

20:7-10

The devil plays Russian roulette!

We read in verses 7-10, *And when the thousand years are ended, Satan will be released from his prison and will come out to deceive the nations that are at the four corners of the earth, Gog and Magog, to gather them for battle; their number is like the sand of the sea. And they marched up over the broad plain of the earth and surrounded the camp of the saints and the beloved city, but fire came down from heaven and consumed them, and the devil who had deceived them was thrown into the lake of fire and sulphur where the beast and the false prophet were, and they will be tormented day and night forever and ever.*

At the end of the millennium the devil will be released from prison for a short season. It is his final fling for the clock is ticking away. You cannot teach an old dog new tricks, so what does the devil do? True to form, he is at it again! He has lost none of his cunning. He does not know anything else or know any better. Deception is the name of the game! He has had a thousand years to plot his revenge.

After his dramatic reappearance—his re-entry into the real world—he makes a dynamic appeal to man. He gathers dissidents from around the world, he rounds up all the rebels from the four corners of earth (cf. Isaiah 11:12) and together they launch a concerted attack on the city of Jerusalem. He is hyped-up, the adrenaline is flowing, it is high risk. He is playing a dangerous game of Russian roulette. It is an insurrection but the devil meets his Waterloo. They perish to a man, zapped by a tornado of fire from heaven. It is mass cremation. The only evidence that something has happened is the ashes on the ground.

At the same time, the devil is thrown into the lake of fire forever. He will not be alone for the first people he meets are the Antichrist and the false prophet. This is not annihilation for they have already been there for one thousand years. This is felt, this is real! This torment is something they actually experience. They know all about it and it never ends, it just goes on and on and on for as long as God lives. That is, eternally!

We can summarise these few verses like this: in verse 8, we have the deception of the nations; in verse 9, we note the destruction of the rebellious nations; and, in verse 10, we see the final destiny of Satan.

The reference to *Gog and Magog* in verse 8 has nothing to do with the major battle referred to in Ezekiel 38-39. The same names are used but this battle is different in time and detail. The Ezekiel battle will take place during the first half of the Tribulation. The Revelation battle will take place after the millennium. In Ezekiel 38-39 the nations will not come from the four quarters of the earth as they will in Revelation 20. After the Ezekiel battle, the dead will be buried; in Revelation, they will be devoured from heaven. Satan will lead the army mentioned in Revelation 20 but he is conspicuous by his absence in the Ezekiel battle.

The term is used here symbolically for the unsaved people who will rally to Satan's cause in a foiled attempt to overthrow the Lord's rule on earth. It is amazing but these folk have spent their days in an ideal environment (cf. Psalm 72), in near-perfect living conditions, in an era when the Sermon on the Mount is the norm, and still they want to go their own way and do their own thing. It says a lot about the heart of man!

20:11-15

Sinners in the dock!

Before God wraps up human history, one great event remains – the day when sinners are in the dock, when 'movers and shakers' stand alongside dropouts and drunks. This is the greatest trial in history, the great judgment morning, the moment when men will meet their Maker and when they will wish they could turn back the clock and rewrite their personal history!

John says, *Then I saw a great white throne and him who was seated on it. From his presence earth and sky fled away, and no place was found for them. And I saw the dead, great and small, standing before the throne, and books were opened. Then another book was opened, which is the book of life. And the dead were judged by what was written in the books, according to what they had done. And the sea gave up the dead who were in it, Death and Hades gave up the dead who were in them, and they were judged, each one of them, according to what they had done. Then Death and Hades were thrown into the lake of fire. This is the second death, the lake of fire. And if anyone's name was not found written in the book of life, he was thrown into the lake of fire.*

These are solemn words indeed! I have preached on this passage many times over the years and, every time I come to it, my heart aches for those who do not know Jesus as Lord and Saviour. When I think of their awful fate when they stand before God, the tears flow and my heart melts with compassion on their behalf. The problem for them is by now it is too late! They are beyond the help of man and beyond the reach of prayer.

My blood chills to read in Winston Churchill's biography that when he was once asked if he was ready to meet God, he responded: 'I am ready to meet my Maker. Whether my Maker is prepared for the ordeal of meeting me is another matter.' There is no human bravado before this almighty Judge. Jesus Christ has been seen on the white horse (19:11), and now he is seen on the white throne. Read on ...

The bar

It is great. This is true because of its unique position, the precise location known only to the one who knows all things. There is no earth beneath or heaven above and no sight of planets, constellations, or galaxies. Its greatness is also reflected in the millions of people who stand before it. Famous trials, conducted in court rooms around the world, pale into insignificance in light of this one. All eyes are turned upon it, all paths converge there.

The maximum penalty handed down each time pays silent tribute to the momentous nature of this occasion. This is no petty sessions, this is no high court, this is no supreme court, this is no European court; this is the only court convened by one whose jurisdiction is universal! It is great because of the majesty and mystery which surround it. This is the greatest assize ever held. Try to envisage the sheer vastness of the scene.

It is white. In Bible-speak this is the symbol of purity, justice, and holiness. After all, the one sitting there is the righteous Judge, one who cannot be bribed; those in the dock receive their due rewards, they get exactly what they deserve. Men will stand there in the terrible ugliness of their sin and against the white backdrop everything will be shown up in bold contrast. In Isaiah 6 the throne has an altar of sacrifice beside it; the throne in the holy of holies had blood sprinkled on it (cf. Leviticus 16:15-18); the throne in chapter 4 had a rainbow encircling it, reminding us of the covenant promises of God; but here in chapter 20, there is no blood, no sacrifice, and no rainbow!

It is a throne. In Hebrews 4:14 we read about the throne of grace, a place of supplication for the saints; in Hebrews 12:1-2 we read about the throne of God, a place of exaltation for the Saviour; in Matthew 25:31 we read about the throne of glory, a place of glorification for the Sovereign Lord; and here in Revelation 20:11 we read about a throne of gloom, a place of condemnation for the sinner!

The Judge

We read in the Gospels that all judgment has been committed unto him (cf. John 5:22; 5:26-27). Richard Bewes writes: 'How amazed Jesus' listeners must have been! Before them was a man in working clothes – the son of a carpenter. Was he really to be the judge of all humanity? Only a few at that time recognised in him the pivotal figure of all history, the focal point when the balances are weighed at the last.' On the cross of Calvary, it was God in Christ reconciling a lost world unto himself; at the great white throne, it is God in Christ judging a world which rejected his offer of love and mercy in the gospel.

We read that before his face the heavens and earth flee away as they dissolve and melt with fervent heat; as it were, they are loosed from their moorings and undergo a massive change. It is renovation time for the old gives way to the new. The same truth is outlined in greater detail in 2 Peter 3:12 and in the following two chapters in Revelation. Anticipated here in every sense is a new world order.

As James Allen notes: 'Earth that had no place for Christ in his first coming as Saviour (cf. Luke 2:7) now flees from before him as Judge. There is nothing but a throne and limitless space. The very face that men spat upon (cf. Matthew 26:67), that in cruel mockery they covered (cf. Mark 14:65), that they struck with the rod (cf. Luke 22:64) now strikes terror to the cosmos. This is the one before whom the dead must stand.'

The prisoners

These are men and women of all shapes and sizes, classes and colour, ordinary folk from every corner of the world, and they find themselves in the dock, before a God with whom there is no respect of persons! Among that number are out-and-out sinners who hate God and his people, are self-righteous men and women who think they are too good to be sent down to the penitentiary of a burning lake of fire, are nice people with nice manners, nice families, nice homes, nice cars, nice jobs, and nice friends.

Also, among that number are procrastinators who intended to get right with God but just couldn't find the time in their busy schedule to do it, are unsaved church members who have been baptised, who take communion a few times every year, who pay into the church, who are happy to sit on the board and get involved in various church activities—people who are devoutly religious but who do not know Jesus personally. Tragically, men and women go to hell from the pew as well as the gutter.

They are fetched here on the morning of their trial from the prisons of death and Hades. As someone has said: 'Those who were buried at sea or on land, those who were eaten by cannibals or who died peacefully in their sleep, those who were burned on some fiery pyre or embalmed in some Egyptian tomb, those who were laid to rest in satin-lined caskets or in primitive pine boxes, those who were buried in vaults, surrounded by treasure, and those whose bodies were left for the vultures – all will be raised to stand before the Judge! God knows every speck of human dust, and he calls it forth from deserts, caves, jungles, seas, tombs, ghettos, and palaces.' Death holds their bodies and Hades holds their souls. The two are united and marshalled before the Judge.

The prisoners are standing before the throne. They are not kneeling for this is not the time to pray nor plead for clemency. The day of opportunity has long since flown. Those who are present on this final day of reckoning are labelled as the *great and small*. It does not matter how insignificant these people may be; in that day, they have nothing and no one to hide behind. They may be great intellectually, financially, politically, and religiously, but that holds no water. All will be there, irrespective of who they are, what they are, or where they are from.

The books

Augustine explained these books as symbolic of what he called 'the divine memory' (cf. Daniel 7:10). These are the records of your life available to the Judge – the deeds, words, thoughts, and motives that are packed into your life have not gone unrecorded. All is noted in God's book and nothing is missing!

Think of all the wrongs that have been perpetrated during the seventy or eighty years of our human story! All the egotistical designs that came off; every evil coup that succeeded; the tricks, lies, conspiracies, and takeovers that have passed into history. Many of them have stayed undiscovered and to this day remain a secret. But not forever! He knows all there is to know about you! And you cannot fool him! Because of the evidence available to him, each person is guaranteed a fair trial. As Steve Wilmshurst notes: 'It is *damning* stuff: for once that word is literally true ...'

The sentence

The proceedings reach a climax when the triple-impact sentence is handed down: one, it is an eternal death sentence, as mentioned in verse 14. It is the maximum penalty to be separated from God eternally. What would it be like to never know the voice of God, to never feel the touch of God, to never sense the love of God, to never receive any blessing from God – to be totally without God forever, and ever, and ever!

Two, it is a life sentence for this will go on forever, it will never end, it just keeps on going, it is everlasting (cf. the words of Jesus in Matthew 7:22-23). And, three, it is a fire sentence as John indicates in verse 15. The pain and hurt do not bear thinking about for it is excruciating agony in a place of total darkness. The agony and feeling of being abandoned will play havoc with the mind and, to make matters infinitely worse, the sinner is conscious throughout these aeons of eternal punishment.

One writer makes the stark comment: 'To pass to the lake of fire means that there takes place a separation from which there is no recovery and a death called the second death from which there is no resurrection.' There is no parole, no possibility of an early release, no special privileges granted for good behaviour, no escape, no higher court of appeal, and no advocate to represent you at the bar of God! The harsh reality is that you are on your own! Here is a judge with no jury, a prosecutor with no defence, and a sentence with no appeal!

The nagging question in my mind is, Will you be there? You do not have to be! You can trust in Jesus today and know the joy and peace of sins forgiven! If you know him and love him as Saviour, you will never have to face him as Judge. That makes a lot of very good sense!

CHAPTER 21
A new world order

We have spent a lot of quality time together as we have travelled with John on a prophetic time machine. We have met a lot of people, seen a lot of faces, and been to many places. After the devastation and destruction of previous chapters, here we are taken forward into a fabulous future where we enjoy the presence of God in the midst of his people. As Dorothy said in *The Wizard of Oz*, 'There is no place like home!'

Scripture refers to heaven more than five hundred times. Revelation alone mentions heaven about fifty times. The Bible actually talks about three heavens (cf. 2 Corinthians 12:2). The first heaven is the earth's atmosphere – home of the sparrows (cf. Genesis 1:20; Job 12:7; Ezekiel 38:20); the second heaven refers to the planets and space – home of the stars (cf. Genesis 15:5; 22:17; Deuteronomy 1:10; 4:19; Psalm 8:3; Isaiah 13:10); the third heaven is the place where God dwells – home of the saints (cf. Deuteronomy 4:39; 1 Kings 8:30; Job 22:12; Psalm 14:2; Daniel 2:28; Matthew 5:34; Acts 7:55).

John gives us a breathtaking, exhilarating preview of eternity in the future when he speaks of a day when a new heaven and a new earth will be created. It is immensely difficult for you and me to imagine what it is going to be like; it is genuinely hard to comprehend what lies before us. We need a lot of creative thinking to try to visualise in our mind's eye what awaits us on the other side of death.

In God's eternal day the crowning jewel will be the Holy City, the new Jerusalem. You will not find this city on a road map or even on Google Earth! However, this is the future, this is what it is all about. This is what contributes to make our salvation by grace eminently worthwhile. Warren Wiersbe writes: 'Human history begins in a garden and ends in a city that is like a garden paradise.' Fair comment, we have gone full circle! We could say, here is paradise regained for what began in Genesis is brought to completion in Revelation.

There is something new anticipated here. We read about a *new heaven* and a *new earth* and a *new Jerusalem*. In verse 5 we hear a voice declaring, *'I am making all things new!'* To me, that is thrilling. It will not only look fresh and new, it will feel fresh and new! Here is a God who is timeless and unchanging and one who delights in doing new things. He is not stereotyped in any way, he is not typecast, you never find him in a self-imposed straitjacket. So come with me on the last stage of our voyage of discovery into a bright new world!

21:1-8

A new creation

It is distinctive!

All that God has in mind for us is planned as a new creation. John says, *Then I saw a new heaven and a new earth, for the first heaven and the first earth had passed away, and the sea was no more.* This should not surprise us for this is what God has consistently promised to his people. We read along similar lines in Isaiah 65:17 where God says, 'For behold, I create new heavens and a new earth' (cf. Isaiah 66:22). The bottom line, the old creation must make way for the new creation if God is to be glorified. The world as we know it today will be phased out in God's time and a new world will come into being.

It will disappear!

Our present physical environment will pass away. Jesus called this great event, 'the new world' or, as the NIV portrays it, 'the renewal of all things' (Matthew 19:28). It was part of his answer to an earlier question posed by the disciples which showed they were not a little confused about his mission and message. The picture portrayed by Christ in his response is that of rejuvenation. Peter explained it in much more detail when he envisaged it as a cleansing and regeneration by fire (cf. 2 Peter 3:10).

Someone has said: 'Our world has a core of molten fire and one day God will light the fuse that will explode this seething mass. Every stain of sin and every evidence of evil will be taken away, and we will have a new heaven and a new earth that will abide forever.'

There is no thought of the world being totally annihilated. That would be a serious misreading of the text if we took that idea on board; the thought is they will be remade or rebirthed in a sovereign act of cosmic renewal. The word *new* actually means 'freshness' or 'renovation.' It is like taking an old building and remodelling it, refashioning it, redesigning it. In that sense, it is new in character!

It is different!

Our future environment will be radically different. The Bible is essentially silent concerning the earth's atmosphere as well as the structure of planets in the universe. All it does say in verse 23 is that there is no need for the sun or moon. Very little is said on the new earth's form, colour, or vegetation; we are only told what God feels is best for us to know at this point in time! We are in for a pleasant surprise when we get there and we will not be disappointed.

Having said that, John does share a fascinating insight when he comments on the absence of any sea. This does not mean that there will be no more water for we read about the river of life in 22:1. It simply indicates that the new earth will have a different arrangement so far as water is concerned. Two-thirds of the globe is under water but things will be fundamentally different in the eternal state. The earth will take on a very different look. In John's day, the sea threw up all sorts of unpleasant images in the minds of the people for it meant danger, storms, and separation. John is giving us more than just a geography lesson in this phrase!

A new city

We are told several wonderful things in verse 2 where John is thrilled with the provision of a new capital city. It is essential to realise that this city has no connection with any city of that name which has gone before—the new Jerusalem does not belong to the first creation. He says, *And I saw the holy city, new Jerusalem, coming down out of heaven from God, prepared as a bride adorned for her husband.*

People friendly!

Its intrinsic character is the first factor which grips John's understanding. And for the ninth time in the Apocalypse he personally affirms, *I saw*. What did he see? A city that is cleaned up! There is no more sin, or crime, or pollution, and it is a place where not a single sinner will be found walking the streets. It is holy, in the best sense of that word.

Out of this world!

John also makes a meritorious contrast for the new Jerusalem is unlike the earthly one. It was spoken of as 'the holy city' seven times in Scripture, five times in the OT (cf. Nehemiah 11:1; 11:18; Isaiah 48:2; 52:1; Daniel 9:24), and two times in the NT (cf. Matthew 4:5; 27:53). The fact is, it lost the plot on more than one occasion—so much so, in Revelation 11:8, the earthly city where our Lord was crucified and rose again was referred to as Sodom and Egypt, less than complimentary terms! But this one—*new Jerusalem*—is significantly different!

An architect's dream!

He was quite impressed with its coming down from heaven to

settle upon earth and this reminds us that the source is divine. God is the designer, builder, and maker; this glorious city is the place the patriarch Abraham was looking forward to with bated breath and itchy feet (cf. Hebrews 11:10; 12:22).

A 'big day' experience!

The apostle makes an absorbing comparison when he likens it to a bride on her wedding day, for this city will be renowned for its unsurpassed loveliness, a special place of incredible charm and idyllic splendour. John Walvoord writes: 'What we have here is ... a city or dwelling place having the freshness and beauty of a bride adorned for marriage to her husband.' The God who painted the butterfly, who sculpted the rose, who designed the sunset, is the brains behind this eternal city. It is the kind of place that will make your head turn with a sense of awe at its stunning beauty. A knockout! A winner! A gem!

A new community!

Perhaps the most important thing about the city is that God dwells there with his people as the heavenly Immanuel. We read in verses 3 and 4 that it is a place specially prepared for a new community. John tells us, *And I heard a loud voice from the throne saying, 'Behold, the dwelling place of God is with man. He will dwell with them, and they will be his people, and God himself will be with them as their God. He will wipe away every tear from their eyes, and death shall be no more, neither shall there be mourning, nor crying, nor pain anymore, for the former things have passed away.'*

This is terrifically good news for the people of God! This is the last of twenty-one times that *a great voice* or *a loud voice* is mentioned in Revelation. The fact that the voice is loud implies that the subsequent information is important and authoritative. And so it is!

There are two main points: in verse 3 the purpose of God will be fulfilled, his eternal dream will become a reality; and in verse 4 the past will be erased for John tells us what God will do with a string of *no mores.* The inhabitants—the saints of all ages—of this fine city are blessed with the presence of God among them for he is Immanuel (cf. Psalm 73:25; Isaiah 7:14; Matthew 1:23). Because the Lord is with them they experience a fulness of joy and a sense of boundless delight.

Remember the garden of Eden before the Fall when God came and walked with Adam in the cool of the day? In eternity, God will stay with men forever and they will delight in his nearness and close company. We will be taken up with him and in with him. We will be captivated by him to such an extent that our affections will be drawn out after him with every passing moment. Thank God, we will be there, and best of all, he will be there!

Some things will not be there! The past is firmly behind us; it will vanish and, according to the prophet Isaiah, it will be blotted out from our memory (25:8). These missing elements have been deliberately omitted. They are all familiar aspects of earthly life that we can identify with. Death will be a thing of the past, there will be no more funerals, no more open graves, no more fond farewells, no more hospitals or medical centres, no more Alzheimer's, no more broken homes, no more arguments, no more hurt feelings, no more injured egos, no more shattered dreams, no more fractured relationships, no more pain, and no more tears!

There is a time soon coming when God will turn every tear to a telescope, every hurt to a hallelujah, every Calvary to an Easter. What a day of rejoicing that will be! Robert Lee reminds us that 'our best music here on earth will sound like a bumble bee in a bottle compared to the music that will be there.' This is sublime. This is ineffable blessedness, uninterrupted bliss.

In the first century these words must have been a source of tremendous uplift and encouragement to a suffering church. In our day, the hope of heaven retains its huge appeal. It has lost none of its built-in power to keep us going even when the going is incredibly tough! John more or less tells us to hang in there, the future is bright, the best is yet to be!

A new constitution!

Verse 5 is one that has richly blessed the hearts of God's people down the years. It puts into sharp focus the truth that the one seated on the throne is not just an interested spectator standing on the terraces of heaven! He is down there on the field of play, actively engaged in a transforming ministry so that all he creates will ultimately radiate the rich diversity of his attributes.

He is able to do it because of what he is!

John says, *And he who was seated on the throne said, 'Behold, I am making all things new.' Also he said, 'Write this down, for these words are trustworthy and true.'* This confirms our growing awareness that the promises of God will all be realised. The one who brings the whole package together is none other than the Creator God. His ability is beyond question. After all, he made the heavens and the earth in the beginning so it should not be too much of a problem for him to change it all and get it into better shape for eternity. He knows what he is doing.

He is able to do it because of what he says!

He reinforces his argument by affirming to John the authentic nature of his word. We can rely on it. Everything he proposes rests upon the veracity of God. It is a million times more than a verbal promise, it is a written guarantee, a divine undertaking. It is God signing his name on the dotted line! He writes the cheque and it will not bounce! It can be trusted and so can he!

He is able to do it because of who he is!

The entire concept is taken a major step further in verses 6 and 7 when John reveals a little more of the conversation the Father had with him. He says, *And he said to me, 'It is done! I am the Alpha and the Omega, the beginning and the end. To the thirsty I will give from the spring of the water of life without payment. The one who conquers will have this heritage, and I will be his God and he will be my son.'*

It all happens in an instant. As quick as that! He snaps his finger and it comes to pass. The God who is the First and the Last does not need any lapse of time for this whole project to come together (cf. Isaiah 44:6; 48:12). There is nothing revolutionary about it, neither is it a long drawn-out exercise. The God who begins is the one who ends, the God who initiates is the one who consummates. That was true of his finished work of redemption at Calvary. It is equally appropriate that we apply the same criteria to his provision of an eternal home for us in Glory. The cross was the foundation, the new creation is the fulfillment. It is complete! It is done!

Has there ever been anything which he commenced and failed to finish? The answer is a resounding 'no!' Here is a God who controls everything in such a way that all his counsel is accomplished, all his designs are fulfilled, all his promises are performed, and all his ends are reached. The God who inspired Paul to pen Philippians 1:6 is the God who can bring it to fruition.

A great place to live ... because of what is there!

It is a satisfying place to put down your roots. The resources are infinite. The saints who thirst after God will be refreshed in him and by him (cf. Psalm 42:1; Isaiah 55:1-2). Our souls will be totally satisfied in eternity for the springs of living water never dry up. We also receive a special inheritance when we enter into the good of the Lord's last will and testament. It will be a privilege and a responsibility for us to administer that to the glory of God. We are acclaimed as *conquerors or overcomers!*

A glorious place to live ... because of who is there!

Probably one of the most rewarding aspects of eternity is the relationships we will enjoy. How wonderful is our God! In the compass of a few words, John transferred to the glorified saints the messianic formula of intimate relationship which God the Father has with Christ. Look at it like this: he gave us his Son, as in John 3:16. Then he gave us his Holy Spirit, as in Luke 11:13. And, finally, he gives us himself!

A grand place to live ... because of what is not there!

John makes it abundantly clear in verse 8 that it will be an extremely safe place to live for certain categories of people will not be present among the population. We have a long list of those who are barred and banned from God's new world. Their eternal destiny is the lake of fire (cf. 20:11-15). There is, for them, only the grim prospect and harsh reality of the second death staring them in the eye. They face a life of separation from God. Such is the fate of those who do not know Jesus. It reminds me of Mark Twain who, in his proud unbelief, once said: 'I'll take heaven for its climate, but hell for its company.'

In your mind's eye, can you visualise a holy city? A community where no one lied, no shady business deals would ever be discussed, no unclean movies or pictures would be seen. The sole reason why these influences are eliminated is because, as we read in verse 8, *But as for the cowardly, the faithless, the detestable, as for murderers, the sexually immoral, sorcerers, idolaters, and all liars, their portion will be in the lake that burns with fire and sulphur, which is the second death.*

In all honesty, you would not expect these folk to be present in God's heaven. They had their chance to turn to God and they blew it. They messed around with their own lives and with other people's lives. The sin that has ruined this present world will not be allowed to ruin the world to come. The new earth will be pure and the people in it will be pure. Nothing and no one will be allowed to jeopardise the perfect environment of God's eternal abode. It is immune from any and every outside influence; they will never gatecrash into Glory!

21:9-27

The character of the Holy City

John places an important emphasis on the character of the Holy City, the new Jerusalem. He begins that theme at this point and it remains the main thread of his argument through to 22:5.

It is exclusive

What a place! This is what sells houses in our day and generation. Any estate agent worth his salt will tell you there are three factors which go a long way to boosting the sale of a property: location, location, location. Well, you cannot get a better location than this. It is a new city in a brand new world for the people of God! It is the exclusive residence of those who know Jesus as Lord and Saviour.

Its mystique

In verses 9 and 10 John says, *Then came one of the seven angels who had the seven bowls full of the seven last plagues and spoke to me, saying, 'Come, I will show you the Bride, the wife of the Lamb.' And he carried me away in the Spirit to a great, high mountain, and showed me the holy city Jerusalem coming down out of heaven from God.* This is truly amazing for the city is identified with the Bride. There is nothing unusual about that! Babylon was set forth in a dual way, as a woman and a city. The same is true of the Holy City, the new Jerusalem. In other words, the city and its inhabitants are closely linked. The eternal city is not only the home of the Bride, it is the Bride!

Its sanctity

A city is not buildings, it is people. The city John saw in his vision was beautiful, holy, and heavenly; it descended to earth from heaven where it was prepared. That vital piece of information is an echo of the promise of Jesus in John 14:3. This means it is a sanctified city.

Its beauty

The vista John saw staggers the imagination even accepting the fact that a great deal of symbolism is involved. His first impressions are mouthwatering. John saw it and he wrote about it in terms meaningful to him. That in no way detracts from the fact that this is a real place for real people.

We read in verse 11 that *having the glory of God, its radiance [was] like a most rare jewel, like a jasper, clear as crystal.* It is lofty and dignified; there was something regal and majestic about it. At the same time, it felt strange for it gleams with a light all its own. It has an inherent lustre and this is unique. It shines with the resplendent glory of God. It is not unlike the *shekinah* glory that filled the tabernacle in the wilderness and the temple in Jerusalem because of God's divine presence (cf. Exodus 40:34-35). John MacArthur says: 'To John, the heavenly city appeared like a giant light bulb, with the brilliant light of God's glory streaming out of it.' It will be illuminated by the light of Jesus as we read further down in verse 23.

The jasper stone is like transparent crystal, it is opaque. This city is very similar to a diamond as it sparkles in the sky, and its facets scintillate with every colour found in the rainbow. It is a stone which is brilliant in its brightness and surely that is a poignant reminder that the city reflects all that God is. It is a spectacle which glistens with his renown and eminence. The place glows with the dazzling glory of God. It is incandescent with his splendour.

Its security

We read in verses 12 and 13, *It had a great, high wall, with twelve gates, and at the gates twelve angels, and on the gates the names of the twelve tribes of the sons of Israel were inscribed—on the east three gates, on the north three gates, on the south three gates, and on the west three gates.*

This is tremendously impressive. And what is even more remarkable is that God has deployed a highly reputable security firm to look after the place! His angels—honour guards—are on patrol at each point of entry. So much for all the jokes we hear about Peter standing at the pearly gates! A sentinel from heaven's security service is always on guard duty at the four points of the compass. There will be no intruders, no one can break in and no one can break through. Security is top priority and it is guaranteed.

These walls are a highly visible reminder of God's protection of his people. The many gates symbolise freedom to enter the city from all sides. The citizens of eternity will be able to travel elsewhere on the new earth and possibly also in the new heaven. Maybe an echo of John 10:9 where we read, 'He ... will go in and out and find pasture.' And the gates are all open because the cross of Jesus has unlocked them.

We are not told the precise order in which the names of the twelve tribes will be placed on the gates but the chances are they will correspond to the pattern presented in the millennial Jerusalem which we read about in Ezekiel 48. If that is the case: on the north side, going east to west, will be Levi, Judah, and Reuben; on the east side, going north to south, will be Joseph, Benjamin, and Dan; on the west side, going north to south, will be Naphtali, Asher, and Gad; and, on the south side, going east to west, will be Simeon, Issachar, and Zebulun.

This is what father Abraham looked forward to all his days according to Hebrews 11:10, and the fascinating truth is the city will have the names of his descendants engraved on its gates to show Israel's direct role in God's programme in eternity.

Its strength

John also informs us in verse 14 that *the wall of the city had twelve foundations, and on them were the names of the twelve apostles of the Lamb.* This suggests that the walls are firmly embedded in twelve foundations and the names of the apostles are inscribed there. In other words, when you think of Paul's comments in his letter to the church at Ephesus, the city is rooted and grounded in truth (cf. Ephesians 2:20-22). Again, John MacArthur writes: 'The layout of the city's gates pictures God's favour on all his redeemed people, both those under the old and new covenants.'

Its permanence

It also conveys the idea of permanence in contrast to the tents in which pilgrims and strangers lived (cf. Hebrews 11:8-10). Although the twelve apostles came out of Israel, the mention of one of the twelve apostles on each foundation links the church to a major role in the new Jerusalem. Even though Israel and the church are brought together in the new Jerusalem they will continue to retain their distinctive identities in eternity and they should not be lumped together in one group. Saints of the old covenant and saints of the new covenant are united in a way that pays a moving tribute to the grace of God.

Its dimensions

John provides us with some incredible detail on the finer points of the city plan and at the same time he gives us a vast amount of information relative to the whole city of God. He starts the ball rolling by focusing on the dimensions of the place and these are outlined in verses 15 and 16, *The one who spoke with me had a measuring rod of gold to measure the city and its gates and walls. The city lies foursquare, its length the same as its width. And he measured the city with his rod, 12,000 stadia. Its length and width and height are equal.*

There are no cutbacks or half-measures in the architectural department of God's government. It is a golden rod which the angel has in his hand to measure the place and the result is truly staggering. A reed of measurement was generally assumed to be about ten feet long but, sometimes, it could be longer. One stadia is considered to be around 600 feet. The city is a perfect cube in shape, about 1,500 miles square and high. In terms of distance, that is roughly the distance from Britain to Greece! One writer notes: 'Such a city would reach from Rome in the west to Jerusalem on the east and from the Baltic Sea in the north to the southern boundary of the Sahara desert.' It is hard to comprehend the size of this city but, it seems to me, in light of this, all cities in today's world are mere villages compared to the new Jerusalem.

Where big is beautiful!

One engineer calculated the total base area of the city to be 2.25 million square miles and this is not counting the height which reaches far above the atmosphere into the regions of space! This is the ultimate high-rise! It is amazing! It is immense! It is colossal! One writer says: 'To grasp something of the enormity of the city, consider that this figure is 40 times the area of England, 20 times that of New Zealand, and 10 times that of Germany or France. The ground floor alone would provide enough living space for far more people than have ever lived in the history of the world. And this is just the first floor ... there are around 1,500 miles of additional floors above it.'

You have a similar analogy in the Old Testament when you think of the shape of the holy of holies in the tabernacle and temple. This one, however, is 240,000 times as big! And even more exciting, this time there are no partitions, no curtains, no walls, and no restrictions barring the people of God from enjoying moments of intimacy with the Almighty.

Design and build!

It has often been referred to as 'the city foursquare' and that indicates the perfection of God's eternal city. Nothing is out of shape or balance. It is known for its symmetry. It is a place where everything is in harmony and proportion. This golden city of God will be perfect in its measurements, materials, and majesty. It is really quite ridiculous to suggest it could be anything else for God himself combines a dual role as architect and builder.

It is awesome

John talks about the wall and he describes it with superb imagery in verses 17 and 18 where he says, *He also measured its wall, 144 cubits by human measurement, which is also an angel's measurement. The wall was built of jasper, while the city was pure gold, like clear glass.* Here is a wall approaching 216 feet in thickness (based on a cubit being eighteen inches in length). It is made of jasper, the clear, unblemished crystal mentioned earlier. No city has ever had such a magnificent enclosure! This will be one of the many wonders of the new world!

To add to the glistening impact of the jasper, the city itself is comprised of pure gold. Its see-through effect makes it a joy to behold. The whole place resembles a huge holy of holies! There will be no hindrance to the glory of God being transmitted from top to bottom, from the inside out; no matter where you are in the city, you will be consciously aware of the blaze of God's glory. The sheer effulgence of God's radiant glory will be manifest all over.

Its foundations

John says in verses 19 and 20, *The foundations of the wall of the city were adorned with every kind of jewel. The first was jasper, the second sapphire, the third agate, the fourth emerald, the fifth onyx, the sixth carnelian, the seventh chrysolite, the eighth beryl, the ninth topaz, the tenth chrysoprase, the eleventh jacinth, the twelfth amethyst.*

Twelve foundations, twelve precious stones! The foundation of a building is generally underground, out of sight, but these foundation stones are visible and beautifully garnished with all kinds of precious gems. These stones represent the glory of God in a dozen different ways. Whatever angle you view it from, the lasting impression is one of unsurpassed wealth on a grand scale. It is so magnificent, it is well beyond anything ever seen on earth. It is, in essence, out of this world ... these are, without doubt, the palaces of God.

Think of all the colours blending beautifully together! Our God will lavish his beauty on the city he calls 'home' for his redeemed people! The colour palette of the stones is such that they may be classified into the four basic colours that every artist uses in variation on his palette. It is different this time for here we have the master designer who has drawn the blueprint and he has specified the most exquisite colours. He has chosen a fireworks of splendour! It is an inspiring sight!

The jasper stone is clear crystal and reflects all the colours of the spectrum in wondrous brilliance; the sapphire is blue in colour and possibly flecked with gold; the agate is a translucent milky or greyish quartz with coloured stripes running through it; the emerald is a brilliant grass-green transparent variety of beryl; the onyx is a stone with alternating brown and white bands running through it; the carnelian is a red limpid stone like a ruby; the chrysolite is gold in colour resembling a yellow beryl or a golden jasper stone; the beryl is a diaphanous bluish or sea-green coloured stone; the topaz is a pellucid yellow or yellow-green stone; the chrysoprase is a see-through apple-green stone; the jacinth is a pure-glassy bluish-smoke, violet-coloured stone; and the amethyst is a brilliant purple or violet transparent stone. The foundations of the city will be an extremely pretty sight. It simply underlines the point that our God is a God of beauty and, in the words of Ecclesiastes 3:11, 'He has made everything beautiful in its time.'

It would not surprise me if the Apostle Peter had the holy city in mind when he wrote about the 'manifold graces of God' in his first epistle (1 Peter 4:10 NIV). The word translated 'manifold' means 'many coloured, variegated.' Paul goes down the same track in Ephesians 3:10 where he makes much of the 'manifold wisdom of God.' Our God is a God of infinite variety who is multicoloured in the display of his attributes. There is nothing drab or boring about him! Indescribably beautiful.

Its gates

In the opening sentence of verse 21 John talks about the gates of the city. We read, *And the twelve gates were twelve pearls, each of the gates made of a single pearl.* Isn't that wonderful! The old gospel songs says, 'He the pearly gates will open.' Back in John's day the pearl was reckoned to be a royal gem (cf. 1 Timothy 2:9). A pearl is formed within the oyster, it speaks of beauty born out of pain. The oyster receives an irritation or a wound when a tiny grain of sand gets inside its shell and around the offending article that has penetrated and hurt it, the oyster builds a glowing pearl.

That means the pearl is the answer of the oyster to that which injured it; we can say the Gloryland is God's answer in Christ to wicked men who crucified his beloved Son. Every time we look at the gates, we will remember we are only there because of Calvary!

Its street

The remainder of verse 21 introduces us to the street of the city where John informs us, *The street of the city was pure gold, like transparent glass.* The word *street* is in the singular but that is intended to be a generic expression to refer to all the streets of the city. It is hard to visualise what it will be like to walk on a street of gold in God's eternal city. It will be so clear, you can see right through it. All the walks and ways of that city will reflect the glory of God; every step we take will bring glory to Jesus!

What the city does not have

This city is some place, it is the city of the future. It is extra special, not only for the things that are there but also for the things that are not there. There are certain elements missing, for example:

No sanctuary. We read in verse 22, *I saw no temple in*

the city, for its temple is the Lord God the Almighty and the Lamb. One is not needed! The entire city will be indwelt by the presence of God; people will be aware of him no matter where they are. This eliminates the dichotomy we often make between the secular and the sacred. Over there it will be impossible to distinguish between the two for whatever we do will be seen as an act of worship.

We need to remember that our God is not localised, restricted to a few metres in the same sacred corner; he is not confined to one particular spot. He will be all and in all! That means we will not go to church, as it were, in the new Jerusalem; there will not be a special place or day set aside for times of worship. Buildings and structures will be redundant in that eternal day, prayer books and hymn books will be a thing of the past. We will not need them for the Lord will be with us. Our worship of him will be spontaneous and, thank God, it will be unaided by any emblem or liturgy for faith will have given way to sight.

No substitutes. In verse 23 we read, *And the city has no need of sun or moon to shine on it, for the glory of God gives it light, and its lamp is the Lamb.* That means exactly what it says. There will be no need for the sun or moon; the city will be well lit with the glory of God. There will be no created light for the light which he diffuses throughout eternity is the unclouded, undimmed glory of his own holy presence. God's light will permeate every nook and cranny and illuminate every corner of the new Jerusalem (cf. Isaiah 60:19). The Lamb of God will be its eternal lamp and over there we will walk in the light of his countenance. There will be no dark days, no cloudy days, and no night, for this is God's eternal day.

These are the most ideal conditions imaginable! It is a land of no shadows! Today, in this gospel dispensation, Jesus is the light of the world; in a day to come, he will light up a whole new world for eternity and in a wonderful way he will brighten up all our lives!

No secrets. We glean this from the information John shares with us in verses 24 to 26. He says, *By its light will the nations walk, and the kings of the earth will bring their glory into it, and its gates will never be shut by day—and there will be no night there. They will bring into it the glory and the honour of the nations.*

The gates stand open all the time, there will never be a single moment of darkness, everything is out in the open, and there is no hidden agenda. In other words, there will be no secrets. The mystery of God will be over and all things will be made plain. In that day the promise of Paul in Romans 8:18 will be a glorious reality for the ups and downs of this life will fade into oblivion in light of the glory of God. This is the hour the old song refers to when it says about life's hassles and hurts, 'we'll understand it better bye and bye.'

People will come and go, they will bring honour to the Lord and God will abundantly bless them and enrich them in return. John appears to be saying that heaven and earth will be accessible to all the redeemed of the Lord. Freedom of movement is the name of the game and wherever we go we will still be conscious of the closeness of the Lord.

No sinners. The last thought on John's mind in this section is recorded for us in verse 27 where he reminds us, *Nothing unclean will ever enter it, nor anyone who does what is detestable or false, but only those who are written in the Lamb's book of life.* Name a city, any city, in today's world, and what do you find? They are centres of sin! Why? Because they are populated by sinners and where you have one you invariably have the other. That is probably stating the obvious but it needs to be said nonetheless. However, in the new Jerusalem, they will not be there, not one! This is an exclusive haunt for those whose names are recorded in the Lamb's book of life. It is only those who know the joy of sins forgiven who are eligible for entrance into God's eternal city. The sad fact is, if your name is not there, you will not be there.

CHAPTER 22

God's last word to man

We are in the final chapter now and, in many ways, it follows on neatly from the previous one as John continues to place an important emphasis on the character of the Holy City, the new Jerusalem. When we consider the opening paragraph, we move inside the city precincts and it is like walking into a beautiful garden. John gives us a guided tour, a kind of walkabout. It is reminiscent of the idyllic garden in the east, apart from the fact that there were four rivers in Eden and there is only one river in the heavenly city (you find that comparison mentioned in Genesis 2:10).

22:1-5

The life of the city

In verse 1 John says, *Then the angel showed me the river of the water of life, clear as crystal, flowing from the throne of God and of the Lamb through the middle of the street of the city.* Every time I read this verse I recall the words of the well-known song in Psalm 46:4 where we read, 'There is a river whose streams make glad the city of God, the holy habitation of the Most High.'

Down by the riverside!

Jerusalem is one of the few major cities in the world not built on the banks of a river. Many of the great Egyptian cities were located on the banks of the Nile, Babylon was built on the Euphrates, Rome is built by the Tiber, London by the Thames,

Glasgow by the Clyde, Edinburgh by the Forth, Belfast by the Lagan, Dublin by the Liffey, and so we could go on! It was not until Hezekiah dug his famous tunnel that Jerusalem had a water source within the city walls.

Although the new Jerusalem is not situated beside a river, it has one! And it comes from the holy place, the throne of God, indicating that he is the fountainhead. A similar truth is echoed in John 7:37 where we are reminded that the rivers of living water, rivers of joy, flow out from his presence. In the Bible, water for washing is a picture of the Word of God, but water for drinking is a picture of the Spirit of God. We may drink by faith from this heavenly stream and, when we do, we will have the joy, refreshment, and empowerment of the Lord.

The river we are talking about here is a pure river, pollution free; it is clear and clean, and it flows from the throne of majesty. This river contains the very essence of life itself. And coming from where it does it reminds us of the blessings and benefits which are ours when we drink from him. There is pleasure and prosperity associated with this stretch of water. We find that alluded to in Psalm 1:3 and Psalm 36:8 where he says, 'You give them drink from the river of your delights!' Life in God's city is renowned for purity, pleasure, and prosperity, and each of these rich qualities is inextricably linked to a right relationship with the throne of the Lamb.

Fruit of the month!

This is the theme of verses 2 and 3 where John says, *On either side of the river, the tree of life with its twelve kinds of fruit, yielding its fruit each month. The leaves of the tree were for the healing of the nations. No longer will there be anything accursed, but the throne of God and of the Lamb will be in it, and his servants will worship him.*

We have uninhibited access to the magnificent tree of life. It flourishes in Glory, it graces the celestial city, it lines both sides of the bank of the river, it runs in splendour down the central boulevard. It is not there just to be admired for we can enjoy the fruit of the tree and the nations of earth benefit from the healing properties of its leaves. When you put all of this together we are reminded of the abundant life which is ours in such a beautiful, delightful environment. It is picturesque. It is paradise! This tree is different from anything we know of in today's world. It will produce an annual harvest of twelve different fruits. Someone has said, tongue in cheek: 'This is the ultimate fruit of the month package!'

The thought behind the word *healing* conveys the idea that there is something therapeutic or health-giving about its leaves (cf. Luke 9:11; 12:42). The fact remains, there will be no disease in the new Jerusalem for the curse will be removed and eradicated forever. That takes us back to Genesis 3:14-19 where the curse began but, thank God, it will be lifted! The leaves will probably be used in some way known only to the divine horticulturist to enhance the sheer joy of life in eternity. Someone has written: 'No longer will leaves fall, plants die, grass wither, flowers fade, and birds sing in minor key!'

The loyalty of the city

In verse 3 we are told we will *worship him* ('serve him' NIV). We are not going to heaven for a perpetual holiday, we are there to engage in joyful service and true spiritual worship (cf. Matthew 4:10; Deuteronomy 6:13). We are not there to serve one another, important as that is. We are not even there to serve ourselves and look after Number One; first and foremost, we are there to serve the Lord Jesus. There will be nothing to hinder us and nothing to hamper or frustrate our efforts; it will be the thing to do and we will simply get on and do it! And, believe it or not, we will relish and enjoy every minute! It is perfect service in a perfect environment.

The Lord of the city

In some ways verse 4 is the climax of everything. It is all we have ever dreamed of, the moment of supreme pleasure and satisfaction, the icing on the proverbial cake. John says, *They will see his face, and his name will be on their foreheads.* What a blissful moment that promises to be! What a noble, eternal occupation, to gaze on the lovely face of Jesus (cf. Moses in Exodus 33:18-23). To see him will make all the hassles, hurts and hiccups of this life worthwhile! To see him will put everything encountered down here into perspective! To see him will be the crowning joy in our salvation experience! To see him ushers in the dawn of God's eternal day!

This is what Paul talks about in his great chapter on love in 1 Corinthians 13:12, this is the rapturous moment he anticipates when we see him 'face to face.' John tells us in his epistle that when we see him we will not see him as he was but 'as he is' (1 John 3:1-3). He is the Lamb, exalted far above all, enthroned on high. He is the Lord, crowned with glory and clothed with honour. The more I think about it, the more excited I become! I can hardly wait to walk through the gates of heaven and get my first glimpse of Jesus (cf. Matthew 5:8).

The inscription of his name on our forehead indicates that we belong exclusively to him. He is the one who bought us with his precious blood at Calvary. Now, in eternity, he is the one claiming us for his own! We are his prized and purchased possession.

The light of the city

The final insight in this intriguing section is found in verse 5 where John homes in on the light of the city. He says, *And night will be no more. They will need no light of lamp or sun, for the Lord God will be their light, and they will reign forever and ever.* Heaven will be incredibly bright because of the light of the face of Jesus. He will shine eternally and we will shine as the stars of the morning reflecting his glory. The citizens of the Holy City will experience life in the illumination of God's *shekinah* glory.

We also have the distinct honour of sharing in his rule and reign. From God's vantage point we are not only recognised as servants in heaven, we are also reckoned as kings! That means we will gladly share in Christ's royalty and we will live like kings in the palaces of God! What a fantastic reward awaits us on the other side! What an inestimable privilege is ours!

We have no idea what this particular role and responsibility entails and there is no point in wasting our time on idle speculation. Suffice to say, when we get there we will find out soon enough! There are so many questions which remain unanswered but, one day, we will come out of the dark into God's eternal light and then all the problems will be solved and all the mysteries revealed. 'We shall know as we are known' (1 Corinthians 13:12).

Heaven is more than a destination, it is a motivation. Knowing that we shall dwell there eternally should make a huge difference in our lives at this moment. The exhilarating prospect of the *there and then* should spur us on in the *here and now*; it should motivate us to live today in light of tomorrow! It was the prospect of a brighter, better tomorrow that enabled the patriarchs to walk with God in an alien society. That explains why they served God to the best of their ability (cf. Hebrews 11:10, 13-16). The same can be said of the Lord Jesus Christ. The fact that heaven was just around the corner encouraged him as he faced the agonies of the cross (cf. Hebrews 12:2). It makes all the difference in the world if we keep heaven to the front of our minds; it makes a world of difference to our mindset in relation to all that is happening around us.

22:6-10

The Word of God

This final section is an epilogue to the entire book. It is John reminding us that what God starts, he always finishes! There are no loose ends in his plans for the planet. In the prologue, in chapter one, we were told that prophecy is from God. We also know that he sent an angel to bring this message to John. And when we read the message from cover to cover we are promised a blessing. We were also informed that the end is near. When you turn to the last chapter, the same promises are repeated in verses 6-8! The vital lesson we learn is this: God does not change his mind part-way through a manuscript and decide to end the story with a question mark. No, what he begins, he completes! So let us see what we can learn from these last words of God to his people.

Some folk have suggested that all we have in these closing verses is an untidy collection of random thoughts from an aged apostle. They feel he has finished saying what he had to say, but he just cannot get stopped! Nothing could be further from the truth. In verses 6-10, for example, John has a lot to say about this. I cannot think of a better way to end a book than to affirm your convictions about the word of the Lord.

The Bible is accurate

In verse 6 he highlights the accuracy of Scripture when he says, *And he said to me, 'These words are trustworthy and true. And the Lord, the God of the spirits of the prophets, has sent his angel to show his servants what must soon take place.'* Obviously, the immediate reference here is to the great truths enshrined in the Apocalypse. Sooner or later they will come to pass! The same God who spoke through the prophets also spoke through John. But the statement is much wider than that; there is no need to narrow it down to the Revelation, it embraces the whole Bible.

The truths it contains have been transmitted, recorded, arranged, and preserved, exactly as God intended. In the original manuscript, every word, every letter, every jot and tittle, was God-breathed. When we hold the Word of God in our hands we can say with heartfelt conviction that it is divinely inspired, inerrant, and infallible. The Bible is the living Word of the living God. Because of that, it is trustworthy and true. It is credible, dependable, and reliable; it is something on which we can stake our life! There are no doubts about the veracity of God's Word, it is renowned for its integrity. In legal speak, the Word of God is the truth, the whole truth, and nothing but the truth! John addresses this subject in verses 7 to 9 and he has three things to say about it.

The Bible has authority

In verse 7 he shows us how the truth is declared. We read, *'And behold, I am coming soon. Blessed is the one who keeps the words of the prophecy of this book.'* In the previous verse we heard the distinctive tones of the angel; in this verse we detect the voice of the Lord himself. What he had to say was far too good to be passed along merely by an angel! The Lord says, *'I am coming soon, I am coming quickly!'* That means, his coming is personal for his word is his bond. And his coming is near; in fact, it has never been nearer than it is right now!

Then he throws in a stirring challenge when he says, *'Keep my word!'* In other words, the spur to holy living is the imminent appearing of the Lord from heaven and the steps to holy living are given in his Word. A special blessing is guaranteed to the followers of Jesus, not only when they assimilate the truth of his Word into their hearts and minds but when they live in light of it day by day. It is not just a matter of taking his truth on board, it is a matter of working it out in the rough and tumble of everyday life. That is where the blessing is found! (This is the sixth beatitude in Revelation.) The driving force, the motivational influence, the get-up-and-go factor, is the realisation that the advent of Jesus is getting so much closer every passing hour. We need to keep the advent hope burning bright in our hearts. It is a positive experience!

In verse 8 John shares a word of personal testimony when he takes the lid off his response to the angel's message. It is a candid confession. He is open and honest. This is what he says, *I, John, am the one who heard and saw these things. And when I had heard and saw them, I fell down to worship at the feet of the angel who showed them to me.* John did not learn the lesson first time, he makes the same mistake a second time. It happened before and now it happens again. He falls down in worship before the angelic messenger! John is so overwhelmed with the wonder of it all that he just keels over. One minute he is standing up and the next he is prostrate on the ground.

This thrilling book is all about the exaltation of Jesus Christ and yet, here is John, in the frailty of the flesh, attempting to worship an angel. The Lord has broken in with some fantastic earth-moving news, and what does John do? He worships an angel! I think it reinforces the idea that we need to be ultra-careful lest we fall into the same trap. It is so easy to be enthralled with the message and in a moment of madness to give all the credit to the messenger. The best of men are only men at best. Sure, they should be appreciated and acknowledged but, when it comes to homage and reverence, it is God who deserves the glory. He alone, and no other, is the focal point of worship.

The angel did not beat about the bush in his immediate response to John. He did not mince his words for he told him in no uncertain terms in verse 9, *'You must not do that! I am a fellow servant with you and your brothers the prophets, and with those who keep the words of this book. Worship God.'* After the angel sternly rebuked John it is interesting to see with whom he aligns himself. He took his place with all those who govern their lives by the revealed Word of God. He says, in effect, all authority is in this book; it speaks of God, it brings you to his feet! It is excellent counsel and advice to pass on to anyone who hijacks the glory of God. The way the angel did it was to lead John back again to the authority of Scripture. He did it courteously, conscientiously, and completely. The Word of God is our first and final court of appeal for all matters of faith and practice.

The Bible is accessible

John says in verse 10, *And he said to me, 'Do not seal up the words of the prophecy of this book, for the time is near.'* What an unusual message! Remember Daniel 12:4 where he was told to do the exact opposite? He was instructed to seal up the vision that God had given him. Why? Well, another dispensation was to intervene before the vision would be fulfilled. But that is not the case with the great truths revealed in the Apocalypse. They are written in an open book for all to read. We have the Word in our hearts and minds; we hold the Word in our hands, it is accessible to each of us.

A lot that is prophesied in Scripture is coming to pass before our eyes! The stage is set. It will not be long until the Lord returns and then Revelation will come online. The prophecies John wrote about will then be fulfilled, one by one. The challenge we all face in light of the near return of Christ is to live with the values of eternity in view! The future is now!

22:11-16

The work of Christ

John writes a seemingly strange and enigmatic comment in verse 11 where he says, *'Let the evildoer still do evil, and the filthy still be filthy, and the righteous still do right, and the holy still be holy.'* This verse is best understood in the context of the entire chapter where the emphasis is on the suddenness of the advent of Jesus Christ. It is a fast-moving event; in fact, it all happens so quickly that men will not have time to change their characters or adopt a different lifestyle. John is advocating the status quo for the believer and the non-believer. If the sinner does not respond positively to the message, then that is it! He may as well just keep on going the way he is going and keep on doing what he is doing. The same rule of thumb applies to the Christian. The message should impact our lives to such a degree that we will be led into a more fruitful and meaningful relationship with Jesus Christ. Having heard the prophetic Word of God we can never be the same again!

It settles what we are!

It all goes back to Calvary and how men have handled the finished work of Christ in their personal decision-making process. The cross of Christ is the great divide, the watershed between those who are saved and lost. Remember, on the cross the Lord Jesus separated two common criminals, two petty thieves. Times have not changed, he separates them still! One trusted in the dying Saviour and went on to paradise; the other turned his back on Jesus, rejected him, and is lost forever in hell (cf. Luke 23:32-43). The Bible tells us that all men are born in sin and everyone shaped in iniquity (cf. Psalm 51:5). It is only through the atoning death of Jesus that they can be fashioned anew and fitted for Glory.

There is a line of demarcation between the two and, at the second coming of Jesus, you cannot jump from one side to the next. It is an either/or proposition and no one can sit on the fence. Today's decision has eternal ramifications for the consequences will be felt for aeons to come! Charles H Spurgeon said at this point: 'There is no hope of change of character. Where death leaves us, judgment finds us, and eternity keeps us.' Did you cast your vote for Jesus? Time will tell and so too will eternity!

It settles where we are!

In verses 12-15 we are introduced to a couple of groups of people. In verses 12-14 we meet those who will be with the Lord Jesus and, in verse 15, we come across those who will be without him. Those associated with Jesus Christ have two things in which to rejoice: there is the promise of his coming and the provision of his cross.

Those who will be with the Lord. The emphasis on this event is found in verses 12 and 13. Jesus Christ is returning and when he does he will reward his children. John passes on the message which the Lord spoke directly to him, *'Behold, I am coming soon, bringing my recompense with me, to repay each one for what he has done. I am the Alpha and the Omega, the first and the last, the beginning and the end.'*

What a tremendous incentive to walk with Jesus today and in all our tomorrows! What a fine stimulus to serve the Lord now and to keep at it for the rest of our lives! The King is coming! That is wonderful news! The verb is in the present tense and that means even though it is futuristic, the action is impending! His reward is with him. Our God is ever mindful and aware of all our sufferings and service and nothing we do down here will ever be done in vain if it is done for him and his glory! That is the ethos and heartbeat of 1 Corinthians 15:58. At the Judgment Seat of Christ, or the *Bema* which it is sometimes called, believers will be fairly judged according to their works (cf. Romans 14:9-12; 1 Corinthians 3:10-15; 2 Corinthians 5:10). Generous rewards will be given to those who have been loyal and faithful to him.

After telling us what he is going to do, the Lord now shows us the reason why he is able to do it. It is because of who he is! He identifies himself in three ways and this is enormously uplifting and encouraging. Each of the three double-barrelled titles refer to this aspect of his character. Because he is *the Alpha and the Omega*, there is nothing before him or beyond him; because he is *the First and the Last*, he was before creation in eternity past and he will be present in eternity future for he is the author and finisher of all things; because he is *the beginning and the end*, he created all things, controls all things, and will consummate all things. Impeccable credentials!

In verse 14 John harks back to his provision of the cross to sustain his people. We read, *Blessed are those who wash their robes, so that they may have the right to the tree of life and that they may enter the city by the gates.* It is clear from this verse that cleansing is found only in the blood of the Lamb of God. It is because the blood of Jesus has been effectively applied to our hearts that we have access into the heavenly city. We are there only because of God's amazing grace. And John tells us that we are *blessed* because of the redemptive aspect of his work in our lives. (This is the last of the seven beatitudes in Revelation and it is a really good one to finish with!)

Those who are without the Lord. The next verse in the chapter is quite disconcerting and even the opening word sends a cold shiver down the spine. We read a long list of those who are denied access to the presence of the Lord. John spells out who they are in verse 15 where we read, *Outside are the dogs and sorcerers and the sexually immoral and murderers and idolaters, and everyone who loves and practises falsehood.*

They are outside! What a powerful phrase! It is bad enough for them to be lost throughout eternity but it will be even worse to know that they are on the 'outside' with no prospect of ever coming inside. In hell, such people will have full knowledge of all that might have been theirs in heaven, but it is lost forever to them. The agonies of the rich man in Luke 16:19-31 must have been greatly intensified by the sight of the bliss of Lazarus. The damned, wealthy individual in the parable told by Jesus was not only conscious of where he was but he was very much aware of what he had missed!

Those who are lost are in eternal exile and the shame and scandal of their sin will haunt them forever. They will be cut off and isolated from all that is good, beautiful, and lovely. They will easily recall neglected opportunities, they will remember friends of old who were saved and who are now walking the golden street of heaven. These folk are shut out to face the remorse, awful despair, misery, and pain of a Christless eternity. The tragic fact is they brought it on themselves!

It settles whose we are!

Verse 16 says, *'I, Jesus, have sent my angel to testify to you about these things for the churches. I am the root and the descendant of David, the bright morning star.'* This is a mind-blowing verse for it provides us with a strong personal testimony from Jesus that leaves us in no doubt that he authored the book of Revelation. He attests to that fact and he says it is indisputable. He affirms and authenticates that the content of this book was inspired and revealed by him. Here is a title of Jesus to make the most pessimistic heart thud with expectation!

The titles Jesus assumes here when speaking about himself are most interesting and instructive. The *root* is buried in the ground where no one can see it but the *star* is in the heavens where everyone can see it (cf. Isaiah 11:1; Numbers 24:17). In the *root and descendant of David* we have the Jewish national name of Jesus but in the *bright morning star* we have his universal name, a global name. One speaks of humility, the other of majesty and glory. As the *root of David,* Jesus Christ brought David into existence; as the *descendant of David,* Jesus came into this world born a Jew from David's line. Both the deity and humanity of Jesus are evident (cf. Mark 12:35-37; 2 Samuel 7:12-16; Psalm 132:11-12). A suitable parallel is drawn in Matthew 22:41-46.

The *morning star* announces the soon arrival of the dawn. It is the brightest star in the heavens prior to the new day breaking. Jesus Christ will come for his church as *the morning star.* When he returns to earth with his saints to judge it will be as the 'sun of righteousness' in burning fury (Malachi 4:1-3).

22:17-21

The witness of the Holy Spirit

It is fitting and appropriate that the sacred canon of Scripture should finish with a reference to the chief executive of the Godhead. After all, it was through his inspirational influence that the book was birthed. He is the omniscient genius behind this miracle which we call the Bible. He holds a fair bit of clout when it comes to the ripening of the purposes of God as outlined in the masterpiece of Revelation.

The last welcome

In verse 17 John says, *The Spirit and the Bride say, 'Come.' And let the one who hears say, 'Come.' And let the one who is thirsty come; let the one who desires take the water of life without price.* Here we have the grandest word in the gospel, the four-letter word, *come.* It was first heard in the days of Noah (cf. Genesis 8:15) and down through the centuries it has often been heard. Now, before closing the book for the last time, we hear it again. It is a triple invitation, for the Holy Spirit says *come,* and the Bride says *come,* and even those men who have responded to the message join in by saying, *come.*

We can understand the Holy Spirit extending an invitation to sinful men to come to faith in Christ for that is his unique role and specialist ministry. But the fact that the Bride is also involved in a similar exercise is something which should challenge all of us. It is a clarion call for the people of God to be totally involved and heavily committed in a ministry of evangelism. We need to reach out to people where they are and offer them an alternative in Jesus to their present lifestyle. We have an obligation to share our faith openly with others. We owe it to them to tell them of one mighty and strong to save. We have a solemn responsibility to the unconverted man down our street to tell him at least once that Jesus is a wonderful Saviour.

It is an open invitation to all who are thirsty, to those who are parched, to those whose lives are dry and arid, that they can come and drink freely from the water of life; their thirst can be fully quenched in the Lord Jesus. The classic example is the Samaritan woman of John 4.

The last warning

John challenges us in verses 18 and 19, *I warn everyone who hears the words of the prophecy of this book: If anyone adds to them, God will add to him the plagues described in this book, and if anyone takes away from the words of the book of this prophecy, God will take away his share in the tree of life and in the holy city, which are described in this book.*

That is a fairly stern warning, straight from the shoulder stuff. He says, do not tamper with the truth of the Word of God by adding anything to it or taking anything from it. Do not make it say anything other than God intended it should say! Do not twist the truth of Scripture! Failure to toe God's three-line whip on this leads to the imposition of a severe penalty. Either way, on both counts, it is a fait accompli (cf. Deuteronomy 4:2; 12:32; Proverbs 30:6).

People cannot take what they want, the bits they like, the portions that do not squeeze their comfort zone, and leave the chunks they find unacceptable or unpalatable! It is all or nothing! We are not to add to God's Word as though it is insufficient in itself and we are not to take one word away from it as though it is irrelevant, unreliable, unimportant, or untrue! There is nothing new! There is nothing less! There is nothing else but the Word of God, as it is!

We need to remember that with the giving of this book the canon of Scripture is complete. All that God wants to say he has said to this generation. Anyone who claims to receive direct communication from God today is deceiving himself. He is disobeying the clear teaching of the Bible. It just does not happen for God never contradicts himself. He never backtracks on his Word. He never goes against anything he has said. The last word has been written. The fullstop has been added. God has drawn a line at the bottom of the page and, from his perspective, that is it! There will be no further disclosure from heaven; there will be no appendix to the Word of God.

The last word

In the closing two verses of the Bible we read, *He who testifies to these things says, 'Surely I am coming soon.' Amen. Come, Lord Jesus! The grace of the Lord Jesus be with all. Amen.* This is the third time in this chapter we have heard him say that he is coming soon. The reason for the apparent delay in his return is explained well by Peter in 2 Peter 3:9 as an ideal opportunity for men to repent of their sin and enter into a dynamic, personal relationship with Jesus Christ.

Two thousand years have come and gone. We are nearer today than we were yesterday. We are a lot closer now in the twenty-first century than they were in the first. At any moment he may choose to break through the clouds. It is no wonder the people of God respond with a heartfelt, spontaneous cry, *'Even so, come, Lord Jesus!'*

This all-consuming passion for the advent of Jesus is the last prayer recorded in the Word of God and it is one that we would all do well to pray on a daily basis. *Maranatha!* Perhaps today! That is what living with a sense of expectancy is all about. That is what it means to have a keen spirit of anticipation in your heart and mind. Our hearts should be beating faster, our pulse should be racing ahead, the excitement should reach fever pitch as time marches on.

The invitation in verse 17 and the invitation in verse 20 are two sides of the same coin. The first is an invitation for the world to come back to Jesus Christ, so we preach it. The other is for Christ to come back to the world, so we make it a matter of urgent, fervent prayer.

The benediction focuses exclusively on the grace of our God. Isn't that just like him to end the book in this way! John's closing comment is akin to one of Paul's salutations. Both pay compelling tribute to the grace of God in the lives of his people. From start to finish, it is all of grace! Grace chose us, saved us, and keeps us. Grace will present us faultless in Glory.

No more fitting conclusion can be given to this volume which puts the spotlight on the God of eternity who has a vested interest in the things of time. And that is only because he is a God oozing and overflowing with grace.

Like John Newton, we join hands with the people of God down the ages, and together we celebrate the grace of God in our lives as that which is truly amazing! It is grace abounding to sinful men. It is grace which is adequate and available for all the saints of God. There is a superb sufficiency to the grace of God. And you know:

> *When we've been there ten thousand years*
> *bright shining as the sun,*
> *we've no less days to sing God's praise*
> *than when we've first begun!*

To quote one of my favourite songs, penned by Keith and Kristyn Getty:

> *Hear heaven's voices sing;*
> *Their thunderous anthem rings*
> *Through emerald courts and sapphire skies.*
> *Their praises rise.*
> *All glory, wisdom, power,*
> *Strength, thanks, and honour are*
> *To God our King, who reigns on high*
> *Forevermore.*

And that song of praise is ...

'Worthy is the Lamb who was slain, to receive power and wealth and wisdom and might and honour and glory and blessing!'

God's last word to man

All hail the Lamb!